Netnography Unlimited

Netnography has become an essential tool for qualitative research in the dynamic, complex, and conflicted worlds of contemporary technoculture. Shaped by academic fields, industries, national contexts, technologies and platforms, and languages and cultures for over two decades, netnography has impacted the research practices of scholars around the world.

In this volume, 34 researchers present 19 chapters that examine how they have adapted netnography and what those changes can teach us. Positioned for students and researchers in academic and professional fields, this book examines how we can better use netnographic research to understand the many ways networked technologies affect every element of contemporary business life and consumer existence.

Netnography Unlimited provides an unprecedented new look at netnography. From COVID-19 to influencer empathy, gambling and the Dark Web to public relations and the military, AI and more-than-human netnography to video-streaming and auto-netnography, there has never been a wider or deeper treatment of technocultural netnographic research in one volume. Readers will learn what kind of work they can do with netnography and gain an up-to-date understanding of the most pressing issues and opportunities. This book is a must-read for those interested in technology, research methods, and contemporary culture.

Robert V. Kozinets is Professor and the Jayne and Hans Hufschmid Chair of Strategic Public Relations and Business Communication at the Annenberg School for Communication and Journalism and Marshall School of Business, University of Southern California, Los Angeles, CA, USA.

Rossella Gambetti is Associate Professor of Business Communication at Labcom (Research Lab on Business Communication) in the Department of Business Administration and Management Sciences, Università Cattolica del Sacro Cuore, Milan, Italy.

Netnography Unlimited

Understanding Technoculture Using Qualitative Social Media Research

Edited by
Robert V. Kozinets and Rossella Gambetti

Routledge
Taylor & Francis Group

NEW YORK AND LONDON

First published 2021
by Routledge
52 Vanderbilt Avenue, New York, NY 10017

and by Routledge
2 Park Square, Milton Park, Abingdon, Oxon OX14 4RN

Routledge is an imprint of the Taylor & Francis Group, an informa business

© 2021 Taylor & Francis

Library of Congress Cataloging-in-Publication Data
Names: Kozinets, Robert V., 1964– editor. | Gambetti, Rossella, editor.
Title: Netnography unlimited : understanding technoculture using qualitative social media research / edited by Robert V. Kozinets and Rossella Gambetti.
Description: New York, NY : Routledge, 2021. |
Includes bibliographical references and index.
Identifiers: LCCN 2020035768 (print) | LCCN 2020035769 (ebook) |
ISBN 9780367431426 (hbk) | ISBN 9780367425654 (pbk) |
ISBN 9781003001430 (ebk)
Subjects: LCSH: Social sciences–Computer network resources. |
Social media. | Qualitative research.
Classification: LCC H61.95 .N38 2021 (print) |
LCC H61.95 (ebook) | DDC 300.285/46–dc23
LC record available at https://lccn.loc.gov/2020035768
LC ebook record available at https://lccn.loc.gov/2020035769

ISBN: 978-0-367-43142-6 (hbk)
ISBN: 978-0-367-42565-4 (pbk)
ISBN: 978-1-003-00143-0 (ebk)

Typeset in Minion Pro
by Newgen Publishing UK

"It appears less as a solution, then,
than as a program for more work,
and more particularly as an indication
of the ways in which existing realities
may be CHANGED."

William James (1907)

Contents

Figures

Tables

Contributors

Pierfranco Accardo is Managing Director at Artcosmetics Srl. With more than 20 years' experience as a Senior Executive in FMCG, cosmetics and luxury industries, he supported the key cosmetics market players in launching game changer products.

Rachel Ashman is a Lecturer in Marketing at University of Liverpool, England. She enjoys researching manifold aspects of digital consumption.

Michael Bartl is CEO of HYVE. He is a member of the Senate of Economy and editor of the E-Journal *The Making-of Innovation*.

Stefan Biel is currently Innovation Director at Beiersdorf AG developing new approaches for innovation efforts at OSCAR&PAUL, the corporate indie brand unit within Beiersdorf.

Volker Bilgram is Managing Director at HYVE, an innovation and design company, and Associated Research at RWTH Aachen University.

Luisella Bovera is Marketing Director at Artcosmetics Srl. With more than 20 years' experience in the cosmetics industry, she managed marketing departments of consumer brands and B2B make-up contract manufacturers.

Constance Casper is a Senior Innovation Researcher at HYVE. During her career she has led many projects with a focus on open innovation methods in Germany as well as in international markets.

Roberto Cervelló Royo is an Associate Professor of Economics at Universitat Politècnica de València (Spain). Dr. Cervelló-Royo's current research interests include financial and regional economics.

José Clemente-Ricolfe is an Associate Professor of Economics at Universitat Politècnica de València (Spain). Dr. Clemente-Ricolfe's current research interests include consumer behavior and marketing.

Henrik Eriksson (RNT, PhD) is Professor in Nursing Science at The Swedish Red Cross University College and Visiting Professor at University West, located in Sweden.

Rossella Gambetti is Associate Professor of Business Communication at the Università Cattolica del Sacro Cuore in Milan, Research Fellow of the Jayne and Hans Hufschmid

Chair of Strategic Public Relations and Business Communication at the University of Southern California, and Business Development Director at Netnografica.

Ulrike Gretzel is a Senior Research Fellow at the University of Southern California and Director of Research at Netnografica.

Lyz Howard is Faculty of Wellbeing at the University College of the Isle of Man. She is passionate about making sense of the world around us through exploring the interaction between practice and theory.

Signe Worning Løgstrup Jensen has a Joint M.Sc. in Global Innovation Management at the University of Strathclyde and Hamburg University of Technology, and a B.Sc. in Global Business Engineering at Aalborg University.

Amy Johnson is a Lecturer in Journalism and Public Relations at Central Queensland University, Australia. Her research interests include military families and social media.

Robert V. Kozinets is the founder of Netnografica and the Jayne and Hans Hufschmid Professor and Chair of Strategic Public Relations and Business Communication at the University of Southern California in Los Angeles, California.

Alexia Maddox (PhD) is a Lecturer in Communications at Deakin University, Australia. Her research interests include online communities, research methods and digital frontiers.

Anna Marchuk is a Service Design Practice Lead at HYVE, she has a M.Sc. in Consumer Science & Innovation, and a M.Sc. in Finance & Business.

Paolo Mura is an Associate Professor in Tourism at Zayed University, UAE. His research interests focus on ethnography, gender and qualitative approaches to research.

Birgit Muskat is a Senior Lecturer at the Australian National University in Canberra. Her research interests include service experience management, knowledge transfer and entrepreneurship with a focus on international aspects of tourism and hospitality management.

Killian O'Leary is an interpretive consumer researcher at Lancaster University. His research explores the existential and social effects of gambling online and offline.

Anthony Patterson is a Professor of Marketing at Lancaster University, England. He most enjoys taking a literary perspective on consumption matters.

Natalie Pope, PhD, LCSW, is an Associate Professor in the College of Social Work at the University of Kentucky.

Sarah Quinton is Reader in Digital Society at Oxford Brookes University, UK. Sarah's focus is interdisciplinary digital and social media projects as both phenomena and method, and digital research ethics.

Caroline Renzulli is an Associate Director at the Campaign for Tobacco-Free Kids. She has over a decade of experience in international media relations and advocacy.

Nina Reynolds is Professor of Marketing at Woollongong University, Australia. Nina employs her quantitative skills to investigate consumer transformative services.

Martin Salzmann-Erikson is a registered nurse specialized in psychiatric care. He holds a Ph.D. in medicine with the specialty in health and caring science. He also serves as Associate Professor in Nursing Science at the University of Gävle, Sweden.

Donald L. Schuman is an Assistant Professor of Practice at the University of Texas at Arlington School of Social Work. He has 30+ years of combined service, both active duty and with the U.S. Army Civilian Corps.

Donna L. Schuman, PhD, is an Assistant Professor at the University of Texas at Arlington School of Social Work. Her research focuses on military-connected populations.

Maribel Suarez is Associate Professor at Federal University of Rio de Janeiro and editor-in-chief of the *Latin American Business Review*.

Rokhshad Tavakoli is a Senior Lecturer in Tourism at Taylor's University, Malaysia. Her research interests focus on netnography, gender, Iranian women and qualitative approaches to research.

Margalit Toledano, APR, Fellow PRSA, PRINZ, is a Senior Lecturer in Management Communication and Public Relations at the University of Waikato, New Zealand.

Dino Villegas is Marketing Associate Professor of Practice, Rawls College of Business, VP of the Ibero-American Communication Strategies Forum. Over a decade as a consultant including political campaigns.

Yi-Sheng Wang is Associate Professor in the Department of Marketing and Distribution Management at the Oriental Institute of Technology (Taiwan).

Section 1
Netnography Mobilized

1

Netnography Today

A Call to Evolve, Embrace, Energize, and Electrify

Robert V. Kozinets

It is May 2020 and I am writing this introductory chapter from my home office in Los Angeles, California. Hollywood and the film industry have shut down. Shopping malls are shuttered. The view from my screen when I access the local Los Angeles county public health website is captured in an impressionistic painting that I include here as Figure 1.1. According to the city of LA's public health website and its running counter, there are 1,843 new cases of COVID-19 in the city today, and today 27 people lost their lives because of the virus. The vulnerable and fleshy colors of Figure 1.1 replace the cold blue color scheme of the original site because the figure comes from an immersion journal noting. It represents an artistic and emotional capture of the screen that encapsulates my sense of being in a particular place caught in a specific moment of time.

Adaptation is top of mind. COVID-19 is a force we feel each day, and its representation in traditional and social media pervade our collective thought and discourse to a very high degree. On-screen, influential social media content creators are treated as "essential workers," their partnership is sought to help governments disseminate accurate information about public health (Heikkilä 2020, Solis 2020). In my life, the days are filled with work at my desktop and lots of Zoom meetings. These are punctuated by daily long walks, taken with protective masks worn over our faces, during which I notice the beauty of blooming plants and flowers, the calls of birds and shapes of clouds as I never have before. My school's commencement was just broadcast online. Will Ferrell Zoombombed our school president's speech to congratulate graduates and inform them that the school would be buying them each a new car. Deans, alumni, and school faculty were joined by celebrities and politicians. All of them were situated in their living rooms and offices, with bookcases, fireplaces, mantles, and art works in the background, expressing different sides of themselves than the ones we usually see. With camera connections, we open our homes and private sides to our screens. Media evolves and represents this new reality, such as in the *Wired* magazine cover in Figure 1.2.

THESE ARE THE TIMES

It is a time of openness. Every day, seeing and hearing the unavoidable and unfathomable, the crisis breaks our hearts. It feels uncomfortable and homey, both familiar to me and strange, this collision of our public and private spaces and selves. As we are drawn into the spidering webworks of viral visualization, the predictive statistics of epidemiology, the numbers and

Figure 1.1 My Impression of the LA County Public Health Screen, May 2020.

Figure 1.2 Cover of *Wired* Magazine, May 2020, Representing Our New Technological Adaptations to Coronavirus Sheltering In Place.

charts with each tick a person taken ill, each number a soul departed, our minds struggle to grasp and hearts struggle to open against the quantification and objectification of so much fear, pain, and misery, whose sharing breeds more fear, and outrage.

In this midst of pandemic and technology are human voices, so many of them. We open also to them as they humanize the times by making jokes, sing from balconies, rage at the idiocy of the government, show their pets, talk openly about their loneliness and isolation, speak to us, and connect to us as we struggle to reach out to them. A young ballerina did a dance in her driveway with a garbage bin. Maybe people watched it this week, but we don't say it went viral any more. I'm heartened and awed every day by the presence of so much shared creativity, so many original people online. The humor is hilarious and never-ending as humanity uses social media to amuse and soothe itself. As I click, talk, and scroll through another day, I hear, recognize, and save the following woman's voice, saying:

> I've become more and more aware of a rather embarrassing truth about myself in all this. I'm much more content in this scaled down shelter in place lifestyle. I didn't realize how much of my spending was related to my fear of missing out or not living as full a life as others seems to be. My husband and I are sheltering with our son, daughter-in-law and 2 granddaughters. Our days are spent playing with our 2-year-old grand-daughter, taking walks in the park, watching movies and taking an occasional trip to the grocery store. I actually feel more fulfilled and happier with my life than I think I ever have. I will be fascinated to see the lasting effect this "back to the basics" period has on me and on our country.
>
> ("Allison Garvey," posted in a leading American newspaper's comment section, April 10, 2020)

Allison Garvey expresses the new reflectivity of the age. Like her, my life now seems more grounded and emplaced, more stable. We have more time to think, to read and reflect. That time was liberated by the constraint of our mobility, as major parts of the social and physical worlds we used to inhabit migrate online. Online life is much of our life now. Connective media have become a major part of how we experience society and perhaps how we want to experience it. The embodied world slows down as the electric world speeds up. Whereas netnography used to offer a window into some people's behavior some of the time, all human experience today is opening to its grasp. Right now, in the age of coronavirus, and moving forward, netnography is more expansive, relevant, and necessary than ever.

ADAPTATION IS EVOLUTION

This chapter is obviously not about the coronavirus, but about netnography. But it begins with this overview of the current historical moment for three important reasons. First, because netnographies, like all ethnographies, have evolved within their contexts. Does this contextualizing mean that a historical study of an expired online site is worthless to our understanding of events today? This morning I received a rejection email from the organizers of the 2020 Association of Internet Research conference for a presentation that was based on the social media regulation work related in Chapter 4. It was my first submission, and the conference had gone virtual. The reviewer comment justifying the rejection appeared to be concerned that we quoted Ribisl (2011, 43), who wrote about how "the internet is fast becoming a new battleground" that provides tobacco companies with "a venue that may stimulate demand for them through advertising and promotional messages." The reviewer emphatically notes that this was "a wholly different 'internet' than the one we're experiencing now. The literature review needs to be brought up to date." But does it make sense to reject out of hand "internet" research that is more than a few years old, based on the notion that the context is completely different now?

To answer, perhaps we might look back at what that research actually says, rather than judging it by some silly conception of a research stale dates. The first online ethnographies I read were by researchers like Henry Jenkins, Shelley Correll, and Howard Rheingold. They were obvious acts of bricolage, inspired by Malinowski's notions of participant-observation, and although they are situated in what is now a historical technological context, the technocultural world they captured is remarkably relevant today. Writing about the practices of online fandom, Jenkins' (1995) study of a Twin Peaks Usenet group (which expanded work he had initially presented in 1990), details the same fascinations with authorial vision, admiration for complex world-building, debates over canon, splits between experts and amateurs, and crowdsourced problem solving that we would find in any online fan group today. Correll's (1995) work using the BBS system reveals a very familiar online setting featuring its users' desire for a sense of family and community, tensions between conformity and individualism, a predominance of lurkers, the use of nonverbal symbols (emoticons rather than emojis), and the annoyance of incendiary and insulting trolling ("bashers," she called them). I have written many paeans to Howard Rheingold's foresight and his work's continuing relevance (e.g., Kozinets 2010, 8–9; Kozinets 2020, 51–2). Rheingold (1993), situated in The WELL of the early '90s, offers deep insights into the same politics and power struggles that vex contemporary social media. As a final example, consider the social media discussion of the Ebola outbreak I write about in Kozinets (2015, 208–218). At the time, I noted the tensions around forced quarantines, the blaming of foreign governments, the conspiracy theories about its creation in secret laboratories, the debates around various medical issues and the hopefulness for vaccines. All of these insights are directly applicable to the COVID-19 context today. That tells us something about the persistence of these patterns.

This is not to say that the world of connective technoculture is the same now as it was in the time of BBS, Usenets, and The WELL. Changed contexts often create substantial change and novel adaptations. But it is to say that people are similar, and that technocultures have lineages. Technologies and the names for things may change, and platforms may come and go. But there are many principles, practices, identities, values, and meanings that persist. And for this, capturing our context and providing a thick description of the present confer lasting value. The way we think about related topics, the ways we use technoculture to relate to one another about them, these are part of a historical trajectory that includes, recapitulates, and extends our past. Thus, the netnographies of those times contains valuable lessons for our time and for all times.

TECHNOCULTURE IS OUR EVOLUTIONARY CONTEXT

The second reason I start with the coronavirus crisis is because, as a tool, netnography is subject to the same kinds of contextualizing adaptations as other tools. Cultural and technological contexts have been changing since our ancient ancestors climbed down from the trees and took to the savannahs. Our species, homo sapiens, adapted to a range of environments, both harsh and hospitable. We turned plants and animals into crops and livestock, rocks and trees into tools and buildings, ideas into engineering, sand into computer chips. Our tool-building and techniques have been our adaptations. And then we became adapted to the tools we built, evolving bodies and minds that were better at making and using them. We evolved technologies and culture that transformed together, "the various identities, practices, values, rituals, hierarchies, and other sources and structures of meaning that are influenced, created by, or expressed through technology consumption" (Kozinets 2019, 621)—and we adapted research tools to study them. We can think of technocultural contexts as places where technology consumption and culture meet. Phenomena such as selfies, social media protests, bitmojis, memes, ransomware, and Instafame are examples of technocultural contexts amenable to study by netnography. Individually and collectively, we are, inevitably, both co-creating and being influenced by technoculture today.

Netnography is an adaptation of ancient methods of understanding what it means to be human, methods that were already ancient when Herodotus applied them to his tales of foreign conquest in the Greco-Persian wars. Netnography partakes in the ongoing evolution of the human sciences over thousands of years as they migrate, are altered, and must endlessly transform to take advantage of new environments and the novel tools and techniques we develop and to which we must adjust. Heraclitus wrote that you never step into the same river twice, because it is not the same river and you are not the same person who stepped into it before. Every netnographer is like Heraclitus, a keyboard jockey stepping into a different field behind their screen, an ever-new social media data stream. Because of this, every netnographer must accommodate their research to new devices, new rules, new platforms, and new types of data.

AN ELECTRIFIED SOCIALITY

And the third and final reason I begin with the coronavirus is because the current crisis has electrified sociality, making the topics and methods of netnography more important than they have ever previously been. Almost as soon as I began developing the method, netnography shapeshifted into its next form like an agentic being whose transformations I was fated to chronicle. Each netnographic investigation of a new site—from Quake video games to soda pop fans blogs, Second Life embodiments to Facebook virus information, Instagram foodporn, and YouTube utopias in the wild—each study became an opportunity for me to rethink what a netnographic site was—and what a netnography currently must be. Rapidly blowing winds of change created vast openings for innovation in the way media connected us and the means by which we study it. This volume, with most of its chapters written just before the virus hit, reveals that pace of change.

Today, as I sit here writing, most of the concerns in the news and on connective media are coronavirus crisis related. Tomorrow, there will be something else. Endless change. Endless struggles to adapt, and each of those evolutions creates new situations requiring their own adaptations, novel puzzles for researchers to solve. Every day we wake up, like Heraclitus, to a new world, a new set of challenges, and the stream keeps rushing faster and faster. Overflowing the banks, the river is flooding, threatening to engulf us all.

THE NETNOGRAPHIC NUCLEUS

It is through a lens on this overflowing technocultural world that this chapter introduces you to the world of netnography today. Adjusted and adapted to their times and contexts, the specific ways netnographies are conducted can be slippery and flexible and there is no real point in trying to stabilize them too much. But the core of netnography is constant. Despite the surface transformations, "the essence" or sine qua non regarding what a netnography is and is not remain crystal clear to me.

Netnographies *always* focus on social media and technoculture. They usually rely on data from social media, and often extend them. And netnographies *always* feature researcher immersion: an ethnographic—nay, a *netnographic*—sensibility. They draw from human impressions, from the central conception of the netnographic-researcher-as-instrument, to form cultural understandings about language, power, identity, and desire in the worlds where technology and the social intersect. Netnographies apply a technocultural lens to explain and conceptualize the things that make us human and draw us together. And there are common texts, common concepts, tools, and techniques we share as netnographers, ethics operations and data collection procedures we agree are good for achieving the goal of technocultural insight. What a netnography is *not* is a simple content analysis, a coded or automatically processed data scrape. Big data type analyses by themselves are not netnographies. And the callousness of unreflective or go-it-alone approaches to research ethics shame the good reputation of netnography and must also be excluded. At its nucleus, this is what netnography is: social media-related, immersed, technocultural, using common texts, concepts, and procedures. Beyond that, the possibilities are unlimited.

EVOLVING BEYOND LIMITS

Unlimited? What does that mean? Well, when we create netnography, we are not simply categorizing various posts on social media or printing up word clouds, but describing and decoding the socialities of life online. We are seeking in the connective media of Tweets and TikToks what the British philosopher Gilbert Ryle (1968) called "thick description." Thick description is not mere depiction, but a translation of social actions from the perspective of the actors themselves.

When something is posted on social media, netnography is there to tell us not merely what it says, but what it means. If we take Lugosi and Quinton's (2018) idea of "more-than-human netnography" seriously, netnography also includes other acts and actors beyond posts and those who post them, expanding to explain, for instance, the meaning of a platform or a site's buttons or forms, to interpret the hidden exclusions of algorithms or decipher the chattering of bots (see Chapter 16). Where the algorithm goes, the astute netnographer will follow, chasing down what it allows, what it removes, what it randomizes, whose interests it exalts, whose it exploits, and whose are excluded altogether.

Netnography unlimited means that these thick descriptions are not only of human cultures, but technocultures, technologies, interfaces, buttons, platforms: the dimensions normally inhabited by human-computer interaction, technology design, and other computer science scholars.

TRANSCRIPTION AND INSCRIPTION UNLIMITED

But wait, there is more. Excellent netnographies, like excellent ethnographies, can provide us with a sense of vicarious—virtual!—travel: an impression that we have been "there" (where, in fact, there is no there, there). The act of "polyphonic" curation, of "complication and juxtaposition" is termed "thick transcription" by Arnould and Wallendorf (1994, 500). In netnography, thick transcription takes the form of curations of deep data, presentations of scrapbooks of technocultural mementos such as those presented in Figures 1.1 and 1.2. In *Netnography Unlimited*, there are no constraints on the type of field we can explore, the data we can present, and the ways we can present it

On the other hand, "thick inscription" is the result of the immersion of the ethnographer/netnographer, the relating of their research experience as an intimate technocultural insider. In ethnography, these are presented as fieldnote excerpts. They are immersion journal notes in netnography, and we see depictions of them in Chapters 14 and 15. They often blend together deep data collection with reflection, chronicling, introspection, and theorization.

Unlimited, netnographers should feel liberated to combine thick description, transcription, and inscription. As the netnographer—with or without the help of natural language processing programs (see Chapter 11, this volume)—pursues the more automated routines of data collection, he is faced with the same "multiplicity of complex conceptual structures, many of them superimposed upon or knotted into one another, which are at once strange, irregular, and inexplicit, and which he must contrive somehow first to grasp and then to render" as the ethnographer of old (Geertz 1973, 10). And, just like that old ethnographer, the keyboard jockey will hack her or his way through "jungle field work levels" of ethnographic activity: searching Google, scouting Facebook, following Instagram influencers, tracking hashtags, watching YouTubes, "interviewing informants, observing rituals, eliciting kin terms, tracing property lines," and writing in an immersion journal. Making sense of it all requires care, technical skill, attention to detail, and understanding. It also requires compassion, reflection, humility, and humanity.

Doing netnography is like trying to interpret meaning from "a vast manuscript" one that is written in a strange tongue and "faded, full of ellipses, incoherencies, suspicious emendations, and tendentious commentaries"—as well as trolling, extremism, click-bait, porn links, and heaps of advertising and branded content. This "manuscript" or "artwork" (Heffernan 2016) is painted not on paper or canvas but in transient examples of social media posts and replies. This endless Google doc, this videoconference with four and a half billion tiny faces that is the online world, is shaped and rendered by conventions and infrastructures that now extend to the very ends of our Earth, cables rattling deep beneath the sea, antennas beaming far into orbit. This is our playground for netnography: the culturally experienced entirety of the ICT noosphere (Gorbachev 1999). Tracking its elements, connecting and explaining them, understanding who is excluded: this requires careful contextualization. Adaptation through contextualization is a vital part of the idea of netnography unlimited: netnography loosened from tight methodological strictures.

TOWARDS TECHNOCULTURAL STUDIES

This book is not only about what netnography is, and has been, but what it is becoming. This is a book and a chapter about the challenges, the struggles, and the adaptations of social scientists who need to understand the world of technoculture. So, in a way, this book is also about our wider collective struggles to adapt to technologies and all that they bring. This struggle needs people like you to activate it, and our collective goal in putting our ideas into writing has been to inspire other thinkers to want to contribute and build on them.

With this volume, it is time to take stock not only of past accomplishments, prior adjustments, and accommodations, but of missed opportunities. One of my chief roles throughout the proposing and editing of this book and the writing of this chapter has been to notice interconnections among the contributions and to bring them out. It has also been to pose some difficult questions about netnography's future and to offer fuzzy outlines of what I can only hope might one day become answers. I see this edited volume as a chance to offer ideas, to prescribe tools that one day you might use and develop to advance the evidence-based social scientific understanding of technoculture and social media.

I have previously imagined that netnography is the methodological arm of a new discipline, "social media studies," a branch of knowledge that cuts across communication and media studies, computer science, marketing and consumer research, media anthropology and sociology, and other related fields (Kozinets 2020, 12–13). But social media is often studied using the quantitative methods of big data analysis, and this not entirely what I meant. There is a missed opportunity to spotlight a particular kind of knowledge.

That focal point is the technocultural context. And if it is the cynosure of this new social media focused discipline, then perhaps we could call it *technocultural studies*. Technocultural studies would not be limited only to the application of netnography. Instead, I visualize it as a nexus of thought about social (or "connective"; van Dijck 2013) media, a sub-discipline of the wider areas of communication, media, and cultural studies. As a discipline, it would seek to develop technocultural understandings of social media, accumulate knowledge across wide swaths of human behavior in this area, utilize specialist theories, concepts, terminology, and apply the method of netnography.

This chapter opening, then, is dedicated to those who wish to dream about a field of technocultural studies. It is dedicated to portrayals of netnography that illustrate its potential to ground a new discipline. The history of online worlds lives on, captured moments pinned in past netnographies, and their lessons persist. But with the world altered so drastically now, brought together and divided so profoundly by information and communications technologies, what are we to do? Technocultural studies would inquire about the possibilities for investigation, critique, imagination, and inspiration that netnography might open up. In other words, our contemplation of a new discipline of technocultural studies would wonder not only about what netnography can say about what is, but what it can say about what might be.

ENERGIZED BY AXIOLOGY

Netnography's promise draws inextricably from its purpose. To energize, purpose must provide a moral praxis to understand and act in the world. Throughout this chapter, you will find boxes that contain provocations. The goal of these provocations is to inspire contemplation about the paradoxes of technoculture and social or connective media today. Inspired by Dickens' opening to *The Tale of Two Cities* ("It was the best of times, it was the worst of times, it was the age of wisdom, it was the age of foolishness, it was the epoch of belief, it was the epoch of incredulity, it was the season of Light, it was the season of Darkness, it was the spring of hope, it was the winter of despair …"), some of these boxes depict the shining promise and the realized benefits of technoculture and social media today alongside its perils and dark side, the paradoxical utopian and dystopian sides of the technocultural coin.

In Kozinets (2015, 115–116), I suggested that the axiology, the guiding motivational heart and soul of netnography should be "to shake our fists at dystopian threats and speak the truth to power," to consider the trade-offs and abuses of power in social media and technoculture, and to develop a research informed praxis designed to help change social conditions and create a better society. With a bit more specificity, we might shake our fists in the right direction and speak clearer truth to the correct powers. The boxes can direct us to particular problems and perhaps guide us to research topics. Power imbalances can be corrected first with understanding and then with action, and, for netnography, one of the most important forms this action will take is informing public action.

Across many of the chapters in this book, from the emphasis on relieving suffering in health care (Chapter 5, this volume) to a humanized look at crypto-markets (Chapter 2), we can see signs of this new axiology emerging. Chapter 4 presents a netnography that inspired a detailed public petition to a regulatory body in the United States (the FTC) requesting them to investigate corporate players who were abusing their power in social media on a global scale—and it became part of an effort that resulted in real changes being made to Facebook and Instagram. Chapter 7 contributes to the discussion by conceptualizing the political uses of netnography to investigate and expose issues around private and public exercises of power and their resource distribution decisions and mechanisms. In addition, Chapter 8 reveals how community groups are using social media to self-organize, act as their own public relations consultants, and successfully oppose private interests.

An axiology driven by technoculture's utopian and dystopian flipsides is one of the great missed opportunities of netnography. It remains vitally important to help businesses and industry (and, especially, I think, small and local businesses) to understand and serve consumers. It remains critical to understand people acting in their neoliberal capacities

---

Box 1 Technology brings out the best in us. It brings out the worst in us.

With today's technologies, we live in a wonder world of progress. The online universe is the greatest Gift Economy ever built, and it taps into a wellspring of kindness, creativity, generosity, emotional support, optimism, and altruism. We use telecommunications to reach out to the world and make strangers into friends and partners, breaking through ancient fears and barriers. We use social media to stay close to the ones we love and the people we care about. "A new generation of activists, entrepreneurs, and 'creatives' is taking the social Web to the next level" (van Dijck 2013, 176). And yet those same technologies are also creating a chaotic dystopia. The online world has been turned into a gated shopping mall, a billboard-ridden superhighway. We use social media to spread fear, disinformation, hatred, and extremism, fanning the flames of anger and violence. We use telecommunications to reach out into the world to glorify ourselves, feeding our egos, trying to gain social media followings in order to promote useless overconsumption and vapid brands for our own personal profit.

---

as "consumers" and "consumer-citizens." However, studying and addressing the power imbalances around technology and social media, and the lack of public action to address them, is an incredibly pressing matter. Netnography, applied, gives us a lens, a toolbox, and an axiology to begin addressing this opportunity as well. Social media and technology, structured and used appropriately for the common good, can clearly play a role in mitigating these changes. It is a time of great despair, right now, great fear and trepidation. And I think that this is a perfect time to ask of both ourselves and of netnography, "what now?"

NETNOGRAPHY MOBILIZED

This book is split into five discrete sections. The first section, "Netnography mobilized," begins with this chapter, which emphasizes the openness of netnography unlimited and calls on netnographers to evolve, embrace, energize, and electrify their approach. The "Netnography mobilized" section of the book is dedicated to four chapters that illustrate beautifully the disciplinary possibilities emerging from this application and adaptation of netnography.

Chapter 2, by Alexia Maddox, takes us on a personal, historical, and conceptual voyage down the Silk Road and into the unlit back alleys of crypto-markets, online locations where anonymized users utilize encryption technologies to buy and sell drugs. Aside from its illustrations of the crypto-market context, and the many challenges to research that it poses, Maddox's illuminating chapter provide numerous insights into how the researchers have had to customize and even "subvert" netnographic practices—and which have remained rock solid. Some of her most interesting adaptations are to netnography's ethical operations. How can researchers balance the need for researcher disclosure with its obvious dangers when dealing with illegal drug cultures? How does the anonymity of netnographic work favor research on illicit and illegal practices, and what ethical problems might this raise? How can netnographers operate effectively and with integrity in contexts "pervaded by scams and deceit," like this one? Chapter 2 explores and introduce two themes echoed throughout many of the chapters in the book. First, it conceptualizes the importance of learning and understanding "technical protocols," in this case encryption technologies. Next, it describes as a "theme of obsolescence," the "technical game of cat and mouse," and the rapid evolutions it requires of researchers and technique. Rapidly altering technologies, near-constant ruptures, and liquid identities form a flowing narrative that compellingly introduces us to the netnography unlimited perspective.

In Chapter 3, Killian O'Leary takes us into the world of online gambling, a twilight context on the borderlands of legitimacy, but one that partakes in a history of more illicit operations. Chapter 3 introduces online casinos, poker sites, and betting on e-sports and fantasy sports, and the many online collectives that engage in them. With deft skill and a keen eye, the author historicizes and contextualizes the many forms of online gambling and then provides rich examples and illustrations showing us how netnography has been mobilized within these burgeoning settings. Reflecting on the socio-material circumstances of digital gambling—from the platforms themselves to Artificial Intelligence (AI) algorithms, software "solvers," and bots—O'Leary provides a convincing demonstration not only of the value of netnography to understand online gaming consumption, but of the generalized benefits of its disciplinary use and adaptation.

The final chapter of this section, by Rossella Gambetti, Ulrike Gretzel, Maribel Suarez, Caroline Renzulli, and myself, relates how netnography has recently been used in the context of regulatory investigation and public policy advocacy. In this chapter, we see how netnography has been adjusted and applied to meet the needs of a non-profit advocacy group. The Washington, DC-based *Campaign for Tobacco-Free Kids*, where Caroline works, hired our group explicitly to conduct a multi-language, multi-platform netnographic investigation to reveal the use of social media content creators and strategies in tobacco promotion in a number of different countries around the world. As the chapter relates, the non-profit chose a netnography to become the research focal point around which were based attempts to alter public opinion and pressure social media companies, as well as a regulatory agency petition. The chapter illustrates how netnography was mobilized to impel public action and resulted in meaningful change to social media platforms. It reveals how netnography was adapted to provide the research participant anonymity necessary for the project to successfully connect influencer content with the commercial conditions of its creation. It demonstrates that netnography can be an important tool for a scientific and evidence-based approach to the government regulation of the use of social media by companies, and of the technology companies who run these platforms for profit, sometimes to the detriment of society.

NETNOGRAPHY TERRITORIALIZED

The second section of this book, "Netnography territorialized," presents netnography as it has been adapted by researchers across different disciplinary domains and research contexts. In many of these chapters, the nuancing of netnography is completed by the proposal of a new form, for example "military netnography" or "political netnography," in which research

---

Box 2 Technology allows breakthroughs in self-governance and institutional access. It also exacerbates inequality and confusion.

With today's technologies, we share vital health information instantly with anyone who needs it, with telehealth services that can help bring knowledge and advice to even the poorest and most remote locations. Meanwhile, the conspiracy theorists on social media question even the most basic public health information, spreading fear and misinformation that cause massive harm. On the educational front, technology is used to reduce the marginal cost of public education almost to zero. People deploy social media tools to teach one another and pursue all sorts of new learning in the wild that captures their imaginations and builds their skillsets. Yet that same technology is used to increasingly privatize and wall off education and its benefits from the underprivileged, becoming increasingly bent to the needs of powerful elites.

procedures and focus are subject to such specific adaptation to the needs of particular contexts that they might merit their own disciplinary sub-field. One of the things I find fascinating about these chapters, and indeed about the entire book, is how much these authors cite, adapt, and refer to the work of one another. In my view, this cross-pollination indicates that these are not (only) smaller sub-fields within a particular discipline, but (also) branches of something transdisciplinary and emergent, still indistinct and unnamed, but bearing down hard to finally be born.

The section kicks off with the work of two scholars who were early adopters of netnography in their field. Like many of the scholars who are introducing their specialized areas to the general audience of this book, Martin Salzmann-Erikson and Henrik Eriksson begin by introducing readers to their general disciplinary focus, the field of health care and nursing research. Then, they detail how social media technologies have altered the world of nursing and health care. In a world of burgeoning health-related online information and telehealth platforms, scholars need techniques that can bring technocultural forms of understanding to topics such as caring, support, and suffering. With a wealth of deep data, cogent analysis, and human compassion, Chapter 5 develops a typology of "cyber-nursing archetypes," and clears the ground for the use of netnographic techniques in the study of nursing robots. Paying it forward, Salzmann-Erikson and Eriksson offer helpful guidance to those considering netnographic inquiry in nursing and health care.

Writing from the disciplinary field of social work, Donna Schuman, Donald Schuman, Natalie Pope, and Amy Johnson provide an inside look at how netnography has been and can be applied to understand online military populations. Their chapter points out some of the important challenges surrounding research on military communities, including their need for secrecy and security, because, as they discuss "the use of social media networks by service members and families presents a threat to military organizations around the world." Ethical considerations are thus vital to research in this space, just as they were to the gambling and crypto-market contexts discussed in Chapters 2 and 3, and Chapter 6's excellent contribution is to develop greater sensitivity to the adaptations to ethical procedures that the military context requires. In particular, and aligned with some of the advice in Chapter 2, the chapter stresses some novel additions to the netnographic toolkit: the duty to warn and protect participants and the negotiation of researcher risk.

From disciplinary contexts of nursing and military studies, we then turn to the study of power and political science. Chapter 7 features Dino Villegas' conception of a novel sub-field of political netnography and his descriptions of how it might be used to better understand contemporary forms of power and ideology as they now transpire increasingly using the tools of social media. Proceeding from a definition of politics that sees it in situations where the distribution of social goods is at stake, the chapter charts the broader territory of netnography, which includes formal politics such as elections and candidacies, political encounters such as crises and debates, and lived political experiences such as protest, boycotts, and clicktivism. The chapter discusses incorporating other qualitative methods into political netnography projects. With its rich range of topics and examples, Chapter 7 provides a view of a more politically attuned netnography that convincingly demonstrates how broad and useful such a conception might be.

In Chapter 8, Margalit Toledano develops the use of netnography in public relations research and practice. Public relations research is focused on providing practitioners insights into the communicative processes and experiences of various different organizational stakeholders, such as customers, investors, donors, volunteers, activists, local communities, and government agencies. Critiquing much of the current evaluative practice in the field as designed mainly to enhance corporate profitability, Toledano advocates and then illustrates how netnographic methods can help to focus public relations towards a commitment to the public good, what she terms a "contemporary pro-social public relations." Continuing this rich and informative chapter, Toledano interviews an insights executive, overviews related research, and then presents two research studies. The first looks at how untrained "amateur PR users," such as Meetup group organizers, might be taking over traditional public relations work in facilitating community networks. The second presents the case of a crowdfunding campaign in which a community group organized using social media to protest private ownership of a local beach, and then to raise the funds necessary to ensure free public access to it. In all, the chapter demonstrates the broad purview and importance of public relations research. It situates social media studies and netnography as the core elements of a human-based research toolkit that should become featured in future industry toolkits and within public relations educational curricula.

The final chapter in the "Netnography territorialized" section examines how netnography has been adapted in the field of tourism. After marketing and consumer research, tourism and hospitality studies were one of the earliest, and have been one of the most prominent, adopters and adapters of netnography. In Chapter 9, Rokhshad Tavakoli and Paolo Mura begin with an outline of the development of the World Wide Web over the last two decades. Taking us from Web 1.0 to Web 5.0, they link the changes in online platforms to different levels of immersion, and discuss the requirements for researchers who want to rigorously investigate social phenomena while immersed within them. Interrelated with this is an insider's perspective on the tourism industry, seeing it from the viewpoint of stakeholders as various as tourists, tourism service providers, programmers, and tourism researchers. Tavakoli and Mura critique the reliance of most social media scholarship in tourism as overly focused on textual analysis, tourists, and Web 2.0 platforms, and call on tourism scholars to take a broader view. Suggesting multiple ways that netnographic researchers have adapted their techniques to study virtual and non-virtual touristic experiences, Chapter 9 highlights the important role that netnography can continue to play in tourism and hospitality research.

NETNOGRAPHY INDUSTRIALIZED

The third section of the book is called "Netnography industrialized," a self-explanatory title. The four chapters that constitute this section provide what I consider to be an unprecedentedly deep and contemporary look at how netnography has been adapted to serve the needs of business, and how it is being utilized in business practices today, particularly in

---

Box 3 Technology creates a golden age of opportunity for entrepreneurs, and small and local businesses. But, unchecked, its network-driven business models empower large corporations and their owners to harvest most of the benefits.

With cell phones, cameras, social media, and the Internet, the benefits of an information age and the ability to self-publish and make your voice heard create massive opportunities for everyday people to participate in democracy, harness their collective intelligence and build out their civic imagination. Because technology is not viewed as a public good, technology companies and their executives have become some of the richest and most powerful people on Earth, and their influence only grows with each crisis and each pandemic. Technology ushers in a revolution in small business allowing people to connect peer-to-peer, exchange, and build value directly and without encumbering bureaucratic institutions as never before. These benefits are harvested by large technology companies whose stock market prices skyrocket, driving them towards profit-seeking over public benefits, and leading to more and more jobs becoming automated.

the realm of innovation and consumer insight research. These four chapters are a microcosm of the book as a whole. As you will see, they do not completely cohere in terms of their view of netnography or their enactment of its practices. This lack of accord is a perfect illustration of one of this book's central tenets—that netnography is and has been adapted for different purposes and altered by different circumstances. I have written previously that no two netnographies are ever conducted in exactly the same way. And throughout the book, and especially in the "Netnography industrialized" section, we can see how different organizations and individuals manifest the idea of netnography unlimited using different and ever-changing, yet also clearly related, research philosophies and practices.

The section opens with a chapter that reflects on 16 years of adapting and applying netnography to client projects at HYVE, a Munich, Germany-based innovation and product development firm. HYVE was (to my knowledge) the first, and is still probably the largest user of netnographic research techniques in an industry setting. So, I think that it is a special treat for the readers of this book to be able to read a chapter written by the company's specialist team. The chapter, written by Michael Bartl and Constance Casper, highlights five key lessons learned from applying netnography to the needs of business clients. As the chapter shows, researchers at HYVE developed preferences for particular types and forms of social media. For example, they favor the rich discussions of forums and the deep data of written interactive textual narratives. Because they were looking for ideas that might have wide appeal, they also favor large amounts of data and the generalizable insights they might carry. They thus enthusiastically embrace data mining, machine learning, and other software tools for collecting and processing large amounts of social media data. And because of their workflows and the way they relate to clients, they prefer not to use interviews or formal immersion journals as a part of their netnography projects. As the chapter's superb illustrations reveal, HYVE is extremely strong in their use of visual designs to illustrate key cultural insights. Bartl and Casper's chapter provides an unprecedented and valuable look into the way netnography became an important business service offered by one very successful and extremely innovative company.

Chapter 11 provides another industry application, this one to the operation of retail banking loan operations. This chapter and the one following it provide the most deductive and quantitative examples of netnographic adaptation in the book. In this chapter, José-Serafín Clemente-Ricolfe and Roberto Cervelló Royo first describe the relevance of their approach to the banking sector. Then, they illustrate it by analyzing social media data in order to identify similarities in consumer narratives about mortgage loans. After they quantitatively analyze and visually model the data, the authors discern cultural meanings from the social media conversations. The results highlight not only a different approach, but also the usefulness of netnography for further research on other financial and banking sector customers.

Chapter 12 complements Chapter 10, presenting another invaluable look inside the way that HYVE conceptualizes, develops, and applies netnography. In this chapter, Anna Marchuk, Stefan Biel, Volker Bilgram, and Signe Worning Løgstrup Jensen (a mix of HYVE and Beiersdorf personnel) relate an experiment in which they sought to understand how artificial intelligence might be used to improve the way that they (and others) conduct netnography. The problem that HYVE faced was related to handling the massive amounts of social media data that threaten to engulf netnographers. The way that HYVE decided to address this problem was through a comparative scientific investigation. Chapter 12 presents the analysis of two HYVE innovation projects conducted with the German company Beiersdorf (which manufactures and markets Nivea products). Both projects shared the same briefing and the same objective. However, one project used mainly human labor, and the other relied heavily on the latest technologies in the domain of machine learning and

AI. The chapter presents a careful analysis that splits the netnographic process into sections and then, by the analogy of a competitive race, declares one project team a winner and the other a loser. The results are intriguing. The authors clearly demonstrate the advantages of AI in certain kinds of data processing functions, but also reveal their limitations. The authors are brutally honest in their assessments of the current limitations of the application of AI for certain vital functions of netnography, such as the telling of meaningful consumer stories. This chapter points an important way forward for other researchers seeking to generalize these results and develop the use of AI in netnography.

The final chapter in the section, Chapter 13, presents a recent commercial netnography project that Ross Gambetti, Ulrike Gretzel, and I conducted with Pierfranco Accardo and Luisella Bovera of ArtCosmetics in Milan along with eight other talented researchers. Our task was to inform the new product development efforts of a global B2B cosmetics manufacturer by helping them to understand contemporary Chinese female consumers' notions of beauty and the way that they affected their use of brands, products, social media, and beauty routines. The chapter provides some detail about the customizing work we did to develop an effective netnographic research design that had transnational and effective sampling, foreign language and foreign cultural data from new platforms, heterogenous data forms, vast cultural complexity, and the need for sophisticated ethnographic findings to be translated into pragmatic consumer, brand, and new product development insights. As we outline in the chapter, Chinese women's notions of beauty and identity are firmly rooted in historical ethnic and national identities but are also fluidly global. Transposing anthropologies and social media data revealed how the patterns of flows in what we termed "global beautyscapes" provide vital consumer insights for cosmetics new product development.

NETNOGRAPHY HUMANIZED

Section 4, "Netnography humanized," is the book's shortest section. But its length belies its importance, for in many ways its lessons lie at the heart of netnography today. Complementing and contrasting the quantification and AI focus of some of the chapters of Section 3, the two chapters in this section provide vital frameworks and overviews that deepen its connections to qualitative research practice and magnify its humanistic tendencies.

In the first chapter of this section, Elizabeth Howard leads us through her incorporation of human experience into netnographic engagement. With her research positioned at the nexus of education and social media, Howard develops the conceptualization of auto-netnography further and deeper than anyone had previously. Relying on critical reflexivity, and providing a wealth of directive advice to readers, Howard's goal in Chapter 14 is to broaden netnography's

---

Box 4 Technology is used to enhance the public good. It is also used to monitor, manipulate, and divide the peoples of the world.

Some government leaders wisely invest in new technologies that enhance the public good by providing them with access to vital information and resources and use advanced data processing to understand and manage the diverse needs of their citizens. Other governments use advanced data processing to undertake surveillance of us, to collaborate with businesses by demanding that they share our personal data, using it in sometimes nefarious ways to ensure compliance and increase their own power. Other government leaders use social media to divide us, distract us, and dominate our discourse and thought. The divides between nations, races, people, and classes grow more and more insurmountable.

intellectual and practical orientation, adapting it for novel circumstances and fine tuning its empathic apparatus. In particular, she seeks to advance the way that netnography can emotionally sensitize researchers to data about their own actions. Drawing on her own research experiences, she shows us how her netnography of online teacher and learner interaction enabled her to extend an extant distance education interaction model.

Howard's auto-netnography led her to develop a novel and viable framework for this type of research. Through it, she harmonizes emic and etic, presenting narratives that balance the self ("auto"), digital culture ("netno"), and the ethnographic research process ("graphy"). But most powerfully of all in this chapter are her many demonstrations of the explanatory power of her attunement to reflexivity. She states the matter succinctly in her chapter's closing summary: "Despite explaining the discomfort I felt as I deconstructed the emotional aspects of my findings, these feelings ultimately empowered me to reframe my emotions and direct my development as an online teacher." And, I would add, as a researcher. Her central argument here is a powerful one, and one that I embrace: that auto-netnography can be adapted into any field or inquiry in which digital mediation is present.

Chapter 15 closes out this section, and in it Anthony Patterson and Rachel Ashman use their experiences with social media content creators (aka "influencers") to discuss the sometimes intimate relationships that crop up between researchers and those they research. There is a long history of intimate ethnography in anthropology and sociology, where researcher and researched often forge bonds of closeness and solidarity. Patterson and Ashman's chapter partakes in the emotional and social connections that attend the concept of researcher-as-instrument. In the netnographies of influencers that Patterson and Ashman relate, these connections moved from more distanced styles of intimacy, the so-called "parasocial" relations of following them, to communicating with them and also to meeting and interviewing them in person at events.

Through a powerful immersion journal excerpt from one of their projects, the authors of Chapter 15 share details of their own inner research experiences: "I think from watching others I get a sense that I am not alone and that I am OK, other people are doing the same things as me." Confessions such as these are not only a way to communicate about empathy and intimacy, they also act to emotionally connect the reader to the researcher and the research. In addition to their contemplations of intimacy in netnography, they also offer some helpful practical advice about recruitment strategies as well as tactics suited to the tendency for social media data to "evaporate" unexpectedly. This latter condition seems related to Chapter 2's theme of obsolescence, pointing to the temporariness and fragility of social media data, and the need for historicity and contextualization in netnography. The methods we use in netnography must adapt to an ever-increasing pace of change, quicker, perhaps, than almost any other method because the environment we work within is profoundly dynamic.

NETNOGRAPHY THEORIZED

The fifth and final section of the book, "Netnography theorized," contains four chapters that interrogate and expand the conceptual foundations and empirical domains of netnography. Netnography will continue to adapt, expand, and grow through encountering the novel ideas in these final four chapter.

In Chapter 16, Sarah Quinton and Nina Reynolds extend some of the ideas in Lugosi and Quinton (2018), expanding the idea that netnographies include platforms, technologies, and other non-human and what they call "more-than-human" actors and agencies in its purview. In a way, Chapter 16 complements Chapter 12's emphasis on artificial intelligence. However, while Chapter 12 focuses on artificial intelligence as a practical tool and form of

---

Box 5 Technology promises humanity a new golden age. Technology also threatens us with a new dark age.

Utopian dreams persist, in Silicon Valley and elsewhere. There are communities of dreamers who realize that we are the caretakers of both human civilization and the God-given bounty of the natural environment. These groups of optimists plan for a future that uses the powers of technology for the common good, for systems of health, security, clean energy, environmental protection and preservation, and existential and spiritual self-actualization that we will hand down to our children and grandchildren and the many human generations that will follow them. For these people, the wise use of technology and our positive attitude towards it leave us filled with hope for the future. Technology is an unregulated technocapitalist experiment unleashed on human civilization. Today's technologies are a non-stop treadmill and a night-mare health and environmental resiliency experiment. We are bombarded by cancer-causing EMF radiation from our cellphones, 5G towers and, soon, orbiting satellites will rain down massive amounts of radiation on every surface of the Earth. Dictated ultimately by the whims and whimsy of the stock market, our leaders, governments, and technology companies pro-vide us with no direction except towards more and riskier technology. With no unifying plan for sharing the benefits of technology, little governance save restrictive terms of service, and scant wisdom in high places, most of the world's population is relegated to a spectator's role. Technology consumers with little say in how their data or its power is used, they are second- and third-class passengers on Spaceship Earth, distracting themselves as its limited resources dwindle with each passing year. The depletions of the natural environment and climate change combine with the technology-induced slides of our civilization. Together, they leave us fearing that we will bequeath little to future generation beyond a dark and ever more threatening future.

---

non-human labor that can help in data analysis, Quinton and Reynolds focus on it as an agentic force in the world, that, along with the internet of things, forms complex assemblages and enactments with which the mindful netnography of today must reckon. Their chapter highlights this "new landscape," raising questions about research ethics and data collection. Echoing concerns in Chapters 2 and 15, the authors emphasize the fluidity and temporality of netnography. Ultimately, Chapter 16 reminds us that netnography can be used to study more than social media content and the people who create them, but also the many other active and interdependent elements that form the current technocultural industrial complex of social media.

Chapter 17 continues the conceptual emphasis on temporality in netnography that the prior chapter, and other chapters, in the book introduce. But in Chapter 17, these tem-poral concepts are thickened by considering their positioning as mobile elements within netnography and mobile ethnography. In this chapter, Birgit Muskat considers the relation of netnography and mobile ethnography to the mobility and dynamic emplacement of social phenomena. Viewing social phenomena as liquid and longitudinal, Muskat sees time as an integral component of netnographic research design. Offering conceptual differentiations between processual immersion, focus on particular moments, and recurring actions, Muskat's chapter attunes readers to requisite shifts in research practice. Finally, to illustrate the multi-faceted and subjective nature of time, the chapter explores the possibility of conducting deci-sion journeys using netnography.

The conceptualization of netnographic adaptation to the technological affordances of new devices and social media platforms continues with Chapter 18's focus on live video streaming. In the book's penultimate chapter, Yi-Sheng Wang conceptualizes live video streaming as a relatively new type of consumer experience, providing an explanation of its key characteristics and user experiences. Wang describes a netnography of the Twitch platform that utilized online interviews and observations of live streaming content creators. The chapter provides an embedded illustration of netnography adapted to the live streaming context and emphasizing concepts that include naturalism, immersive research, and specific description. One of the chapter's most compelling contributions is the author's proposal of a new one-step framework for constructing theory using netnography.

The book's final chapter is written by my irrepressible volume co-editor Ross Gambetti. Chapter 19 provides the reader with a robust and unique reboot of Pierre Bourdieu's work on social fields, habitus, and cultural capital. With dexterity and insight, Gambetti weaves a social media focus and netnographic sensibility into these established sociological notions. In the process, she updates and revivifies them. For example, in one of my favorite moves in the chapter, Gambetti transforms cultural capital into "technocultural capital." We can think of traditional cultural capital as a stock of abilities, aptitudes, and externalized resources that reveal a particular cultural savoir faire. Think of Gambetti's technocultural capital as these skills, abilities, and resources applied to the universe of social media. People with high technocultural capital (and you know who you are) have that special social media influencer something extra, that *je ne sais quoi*. As Bourdieu would instantly recognize, technocultural capital can translate into and be derived from other forms of capital such as economic, cultural, and social.

Important sub-sections of Chapter 19 are also dedicated to four provocations (which I see also as opportunities) to which netnographers must adapt. The first of these four provocations is the technoculture of computation and algorithm and its challenges to netnographic relevance. The second is visual technoculture and its challenges to netnographic analysis and interpretation. The third is objectualized, anthropomorphized, and robotized technoculture, and its challenges to implicit netnographic notions of agency (see Chapter 16 as well). The final instigation relates to the technoculture of emotional and affective labor, and its challenges to netnographic depth and insight development. The chapter's various admonishments and conceptual developments are often usefully grounded in examples from Gambetti's current and recent netnographic projects, And, aside from these interesting notions, Chapter 19 also draws upon and explains an erudite treasure trove of research that may be of interest to many practicing netnographers and scholars of social media. These include descriptions of innovative new developments such as Brock's (2018) Critical Technocultural Discourse method. In all, Chapter 19 contains a wealth of insight and important new notions, and they fittingly close the fifth section and finish the book.

UNLIMITED FLOWS

These are 19 leading edge chapters by 34 leading edge netnographers. As I hope you perceive from my descriptions, *Netnography Unlimited* presents a view of netnography that you have never seen before. These 19 chapters present an approachable netnography, whose fluidity flows from a nucleus of technocultural focus. They offer various observations, patterns, and interpretations about how researchers adapted netnography to better fit their various contexts. Those contexts stretch across the world. As a number of the chapters related, netnographies may be one way to bring international researchers together for global projects. Academics and scholars should not wall up knowledge, reinforce borders or partake in petty nationalisms. Our science, and especially our unlimited netnography, can be an opportunity to bridge cultures, nations, peoples, and places. If those who sit in seats of power in the world's nation-states cannot build harmony into public discourse, if they cannot control the new feudal technology lords, then someone must try. If not us, then who?

As with online sociality itself, netnography today is stretching beyond what was previously possible. It is energized with purpose, electrified by access to new platforms, devices, and media. It shapes and is constantly being shaped by the various specific research contexts in which it is embedded. To do this, like Plastic Man, it must have a basic shape to which it reverts, a nucleus. But, when faced with the challenge of the new, it becomes free to adapt and evolve to the needs of divergent and dynamic contexts. The idea of being unlimited expresses the inner tension of netnography to self-perpetuate as "netnography" but also to be adaptively transformed by active researchers and their efforts across platforms, geographies, fields, industries, and times.

Rapid evolution requires that the code be open source and the effort be crowdsourced. More than 20 years ago, one of my MBA-law students at Northwestern told me that I should trademark the term netnography. It was an innovation, he said, and I should own it and the fruits of my efforts, like many of the business school professors did with their side hustle pet concepts. But if I did that, the term netnography^{TM} would become something that only I could use or license others to use. I wasn't interested in ownership, and declined his kind offer to file the requisite documentation for me at no charge. And I was happy a few years later, when some greedy little sneak tried to use the US Patent Office to appropriate it, to note that the term netnography had passed into the public domain. No one can trademark it now.

Netnography, like ethnography, like interview, is now a recognized word for a legitimate method. Legally, it has gone open source. It grows and changes through crowdsourcing projects like this one. Rightly, it belongs to us all. For, just as I could not have written this book without the insightful, tireless, and endlessly enthusiastic co-editorship of Ross Gambetti and the generous and provocative contributions of a global group of researchers and thought leaders, I could not have moved my initial ideas about netnography forward without the feedback, publications, and joined efforts of thousands of colleagues to whom I am indebted. This has always been a collective and, in some ways, even a utopian enterprise. The questions raised about technoculture and society by this chapter and this book are too large for any one of us, or any group of us, to consider single-handedly. We must, if we are to make a difference, break down the silos that separate us and consider how we can all work together for common purpose and good.

RIGOR WITHOUT METHODOLATRY

Evolving netnography means adapting it to new contexts. It also means that the netnographer must adjust and evolve. One of the ways we evolve is to embrace the humanity in what we do: to open our hearts, our minds, open our eyes, and truly listen. We are unlimited in our reach. Keeping netnography unlimited means keeping a little bit of our minds untrained, a bit of our learning in the wild, a small section of our hearts unrestrained and open. Consider your practice of netnography to be like your use of a technology, a piece of open source code that allows you to do something, rather than some sort of procedural doctrine to be followed.

Keeping things loose and moving is not only a way to keep things dynamic and adaptable, but also to avoid the methodological fetishism that was noticed in the history of experimental psychology research by Danziger (1990) and called "methodolatry." Janesick (1994, 215) defined methodolatry as a combination of method and idolatry that described "a preoccupation with selecting and defending methods to the exclusion of the actual substance of the [research] story being told." In many fields, methodolatry becomes a fixation and a substitute for the discussions of substantive research quality and the importance of research topics. Rejecting out of hand all references that are more than a few years old or seeing all past studies of social media as irrelevant are good examples of counterproductive fixations.

Methodolatry occurs in qualitative research as well as in quantitative (Chamberlain 2000). In qualitative research, methodolatry tends to present as a range of symptoms including: privileging description over interpretation, overly burdensome reviewer concerns with issues of generalizability, recency, relevance, and validity (and even sample sizes), researchers' avoidance of critical stances, a surprising lack of realism, and the invisibility of the researcher in the research. Perhaps because it is still considered new (even after over two decades in print), and because it tries to stay steady on the constantly shifting ground of technoculture, the drift to methodolatry has been relatively minor in netnography. Certainly, some of us guard the ethical standards of netnography, stand up for the importance of the role of immersion and the engaged researcher-as-instrument, and insist that prior work be cited and acknowledged. But with almost every publication, the theory and practice of netnography seems to be widening. The discipline of technocultural studies, perhaps, becomes a little bit clearer as it does.

As technologies increasingly encompass and affect our socialities, our cultures are electrified into technocultures. When we electrify our studies, they attune to the technocultural elements of our experience and interaction. I hope that this book furthers, even if in only some small ways, the momentum towards a more electrified social science. And along with an electrified social science, may netnographers of the future increasingly embrace diversity and openness, as well as deeper levels of interpretation and more critical viewpoints on social media governance, regulation, and technical structures.

OF TOOLS AND TRADEOFFS

Too much openness risks irreparable fragmentation and dissolution. In the field of netnography, one of the schisms concerns the role of automation and the desire to include large amount of data (so-called "big data," defined in wonderfully gendered terms as data sets that are too huge to handle). As you will see throughout this book, investigators of social media are more tempted than ever to combine big data scraping, automated data analysis, natural language processing, and other big data analysis tricks of the trade, and to graft them onto netnography. Done well, why would we not embrace them? Chapter 12 provides some fascinating insights into careful ways that we might parse the tasks of netnography but still try to maintain its potential for grasping larger insights.

However, while some are saying that AI is not *yet* ready to interpret cultural data in netnography, I expect that there are many aspects of the technoculture that software programs will never, *ever* grasp. Whether we can conceive of it as an agentic and object-oriented actor or not, AI will always be a tool. Once the tools take charge and start directing what the humans do, we may as well start building and worshipping moai like the denizens of Easter Island.

Yet there is no denying the diverse and beckoning calls of electrification. And I am optimistic that intelligent people will steer their way through some of their most important challenges. Number crunchers will hunger for the latest fix of more and more data. And understanding algorithms may require us to develop the calculative capacities of a computer scientist's steady grip on reality. But my fear is that something small and vitally important slips away when we reach for that mathematical and mechanical hand. Some kind of understanding moves beyond our grasp.

From Aladdin and Faust to the Monkey's Paw, in all stories of deals with conjured genies and other dark agents, there is always a tradeoff and always a cost. Why would our partnerships with allegedly thinking technologies be any different? In netnography, what do those tradeoffs look like? The current opportunity cost of crunching massive mounds of social media text using machine language processing is the lost possibility of deep contemplation on the sound of a human voice. It is the missed opportunity to read the body language and the expression of someone caught in the act by a camera's nosy eye. It is the chance to truly grasp—to embrace—in our embodied minds and hearts the humor and irony in what a post actually means to us and perhaps to others. Perhaps, if we are not very careful, we lose the opportunity to be morally energized by the outrage and fear of those we open to, the chance to assess who is excluded and who is empowered by these technologies, a possibility to feel the optimism and altruism in which so much of the original social media was based.

BECOMING A BIT MORE HUMAN

As you will see in the pages of this book, there is no shortage of existing topics for netnographers to explore. And there are many more. Where are the explanations of telepresence that draw people to sit for hours in gong bang live streams, watching other people study in recorded videos, or eat in mukbang live streams? Where are the studies of the truths and fiction, the conspiracies of lies and the geysers of confessions that fill so much of our social media experiences? How could social media fail us so terribly during the coronavirus crisis, and who benefited from that failure? (Here's a hint: as of today, Zoom is worth more than the world's top seven airlines combined.) What are the new technocultural experiences that are emerging right now, this very day, and what are their ongoing changes to individually lived experience, collective culture, and social power?

We don't need to interpret the dreams of droids just yet. There is no shortage of intelligent human life online for us to investigate. Indeed, it may be that most of our new life has already been uploaded: our relationships, our meetings, our travel, our finances, our politics, our health, our funerals. Toward these contexts, our science must evolve. It must embrace their stories. Its purpose must be energized by their dystopian and utopian possibilities. And its methods must become electrified.

This week I used an Airbnb virtual experience to take a cooking class. Although I was in lockdown, I toured the house of Ayu and Ngurah, a Balinese couple living in Denpasar. Zooming along interactively with ten other subscribers to the class on my iPad, Ayu and Ngurah guided my wife and me in cooking a feast that brought the scents and flavors of their traditional cooking into our kitchen and onto our tongues. Is this multi-sensory experience a genuine cultural connection, virtual post-colonialism, netnographic tourism, or some combination of the three? At some level, I wholeheartedly believe that these technologies make us all a bit more connected, a bit more interdependent, a bit more attuned to one another. A bit more human. These types of uses are the call of the wired: they bring us into one another's homes, into one another's worlds, perhaps into each other's hearts as we hear, as never before possible, one another's voices.

> Netnography unlimited is a winding electric road
> the netnographers follow to hear human voices,
> a road with evolving pathways and constraining tunnels
> that admit the sound of our own crying,
> a passageway that we alone
> traverse to gather with spirits,
> and let their energies open
> the blossoms of our own hearts.

> Netnography unlimited is a chance to be energized
> with the opportunity to empower,
> a quickly fading moment to answer
> the call to make those human voices
> to make your self
> to make us all free.

REFERENCES

Arnould, E. J., & Wallendorf, M. (1994). Market-oriented ethnography: Interpretation building and marketing strategy formulation. *Journal of Marketing Research*, 31 (4), 484–504.

Brock, A. (2018). Critical technocultural discourse analysis. *New Media & Society*, 20 (3), 1012–1030.

Chamberlain, K. (2000). Methodolatry and qualitative health research. *Journal of Health Psychology*, 5 (3), 285–296.

Correll, S. (1995). The ethnography of an electronic bar: The lesbian cafe. *Journal of Contemporary Ethnography*, 24 (3), 270–298.

Danziger, K. (1990). *Constructing the subject: Historical origins of psychological research.* Cambridge: Cambridge University Press.

Geertz, C. (1973). *The interpretation of cultures.* New York: Basic Books.

Gorbachev, M. S. (1999). *The biosphere and noosphere reader: Global environment, society, and change.* London: Routledge.

Heffernan, V. (2016). *Magic and loss: The Internet as art.* New York: Simon & Schuster.

Heikkilä, M. (2020). Finland taps social media influencers during coronavirus crisis, *Politico*, April 2, available online at www.politico.eu/article/finland-taps-influencers-as-critical-actors-amid-coronavirus-pandemic/, accessed May 17, 2020.

Janesick, V. J. (1994). 'The dance of qualitative research design: Metaphor, methodolatry, and meaning', in Denzin, N. K. & Lincoln, Y. S. (Eds.), *Handbook of qualitative research* (pp. 209–219). Thousand Oaks, CA: SAGE.

Jenkins, H. (1995). 'Do you enjoy making the rest of us feel stupid?': Alt. tv. twinpeaks, the trickster author, and viewer mastery', in Lavery, D. (Ed.), *Full of secrets: Critical approaches to Twin Peaks* (pp. 51–69). Detroit, MI: Wayne State University Press.

Kozinets, R. V. (2010). *Netnography: Doing ethnographic research online.* London: SAGE.

Kozinets, R. V. (2015). *Netnography: Redefined.* London: SAGE.

Kozinets, R. V. (2019). Consuming technocultures: An extended JCR curation. *Journal of Consumer Research*, 46 (October), 620–627.

Kozinets, R. V. (2020). *Netnography: The essential guide to qualitative social media research.* London: SAGE.

Lugosi, P. & Quinton, S. (2018). More-than-human netnography. *Journal of Marketing Management*, 34 (3–4), 287–313.

Meyer, K. E. (2014). What the fox says, how the fox works: Deep contextualization as a source of new research agendas and theoretical insights. *Management and Organization Review*, 10 (3), 373–380.

Rapaille, C. (2007). *The culture code: An ingenious way to understand why people around the world buy and live as they do.* New York: Broadway Business.

Rheingold, H. (1993). *The Virtual Community: Finding Connection in a Computerized World.* Boston (MA): Addison-Wensley Longman Publishing.

Ribisl, K. M. (2011). Research gaps related to tobacco product marketing and sales in the Family Smoking Prevention and Tobacco Control Act. *Nicotine & Tobacco Research*, 14 (1), 43–53.

Ryle, G. (1968). *The thinking of thoughts.* Saskatoon, SK: University of Saskatchewan Press.

Solis, J. (2020). Surgeon General Jerome Adams is begging for Kylie Jenner's help to stop the spread of coronavirus, *Newsweek*, March 12; available online at www.newsweek.com/kylie-jenner-1493259, accessed May 15, 2020.

Van Dijck, J. (2013). *The culture of connectivity: A critical history of social media.* Oxford: Oxford University Press.

2

Netnography to Uncover Cryptomarkets

Alexia Maddox

INTRODUCTION

In the early hours of 3 October 2013, I woke up groggy but happy, after the successful completion of the first interview the day before. I was excited to be finally doing what I had spent months preparing for. I could not have known that while I slept, Dread Pirate Roberts (DPR), the site administrator, was in handcuffs and the field site upon which my hopes for future research were firmly planted had been seized and shut down.

My interview participant had shown me ebullience and bravado in their belief that Silk Road was untouchable by law enforcement, giving the middle finger to 'the man', they said. I felt the immediate loss of this rich microcosm, built through coded acts of refusal and resistance. As its insouciance was snuffed out, the study skidded to a sudden halt.

In response, this study was reframed to investigate the drug use trajectories of people who had bought drugs on Silk Road, the most well-known and archetypal cryptomarket in the Dark Web, retrospectively. I was the active researcher in the field with the lead researcher, Monica Barratt, holding an external view of the field research during and after maternity leave. Together, we had designed an online study of the community surrounding the Silk Road marketplace. Data collection involved monitoring the Silk Road marketplace and forums, conducting interviews and engaging in the online discussion associated with the cryptomarket, a socially and technically anonymous e-commerce platform where people bought and sold illicit drugs. In this chapter, I consider the hallmarks of the netnographic method in the cryptomarket environment and highlight the elements in this and four other studies that illustrate the dynamism of its techniques. The chapter will demonstrate how the use of netnography to investigate this cultural realm has altered and has been at the same time transformed and subverted by the context.

The Five Studies

Cryptomarkets on the Dark Web are online drug markets engendered by a constantly evolving set of platform technologies, privacy practices, market forces and a politics of resistance. There is an emerging body of work in which researchers deploy ethnographically sensitised methods, such as netnography, to engage with online populations surrounding and using drug cryptomarkets. This chapter traces the learnings and adaptations of research practices used within five qualitative studies of cryptomarkets and their online populations.

In the initial three-phase project conducted by Van Hout and Bingham (2013a, 2013b, 2014), the qualitative approach was deployed as there was little pre-existing knowledge about Silk Road and its member experiences. As argued by Martin, Cunliffe and Munksgaard (2019, 83), qualitative approaches can provide insight into what is occurring and help to develop knowledge, particularly in the novel socio-technical contexts within which cryptomarkets are situated. The study by Van Hout and Bingham was the first to engage with drug users on cryptomarket forums, with data collection running for 12 months during 2012 to 2013. The study involved monitoring Silk Road in three phases: the first phase was a holistic single case study with a Silk Road member. The first phase focused on multiple aspects of the user's experience including their motives for online drug purchasing, experiences of accessing and using the website, drug information sourcing practices, decision-making and purchasing practices, outcomes and settings for use, and perspectives around security (Van Hout & Bingham, 2013a). The second phase systematically integrated site monitoring of forum activity and online interviewing of a cohort of Silk Road customers to describe user motives and the realities of accessing, navigating and purchasing on the Silk Road marketplace (Van Hout & Bingham, 2013b). The third phase drew on insights from the previous phases into purchaser–vendor relationships and incorporated interviews on vendor experiences of retailing on the site (Van Hout & Bingham, 2014). This research took a public health approach from a harm reduction angle and conceptualised the activity as drug consumerism. Together, these three phases of the study provided initial insights into why people use cryptomarkets, how they engage, and the variety of experiences and practices encountered by those who are buying and those who are selling drugs on the Silk Road cryptomarket.

The second study under review was also contextualised through a public health and harm reduction approach, and incorporated the lenses of internet studies and sociology focusing on online activism. This study was led by Monica Barratt, with data collection conducted by myself from 2013 to 2014, and covered a six-month period during which the Silk Road cryptomarket was seized (Barratt et al., 2016; Barratt & Maddox, 2016; Maddox, Barratt, Lenton, & Allen, 2016). The aim of this research was to examine the impacts of access to drugs via cryptomarkets on participants' drug-use trajectory. Our entry to the field was facilitated by the public outreach work Monica had conducted for years on the Bluelight forums, which are online forums in the clearnet dedicated to drug use discussion (but not purchasing). We also drew on the experiences and positive reputation for research that Tim Bingham had laid down as the active researcher in the field during the initial three-phase study.

The final three studies were more closely connected through an anthropological framing, and demonstrating continuity in the ways they engaged with the previous two studies and then doing things differently. The third study was conducted by Ferguson (2017) and looked at online drug dealing through cryptomarkets and smartphone apps, starting with Silk Road in 2012 and continuing for over four years. Ferguson (2017) situated her research within existing ethnographic work on traditional drug markets and the cryptomarket element of the study sought to investigate the performance of a pseudonymous identity in high-risk transactions and how this relates to reputation, authenticity and trust. Her entry into the field was facilitated by her previous experience researching offline drug markets and represents a different pathway in to the field site from the previous two studies. The fourth study by Masson and Bancroft (2018) was also an extended study combining interviews and passive observation between 2014 to 2017. The authors sought to explore the embedded values around drug distribution and consumption within the drug-centred cryptomarket community. Masson and Bancroft (2018) also draw upon anthropological framing, while situating their research within the anthropology of markets and exchange. In the final study by Kowalski et al. (2019), the lead author conducted active research for seven months during 2016 and sought to identify whether cryptomarkets held the capacity to scale up through widespread acceptance of the technology. They highlight that acceptance is a combination of ease of use with perceived usefulness and observe that accessing and navigating the cryptomarket environment requires complex networks of understanding and pre-existing knowledge. Consequently, the rationale for this study – to examine these complex networks of user understanding and knowledge – is inherently linked to the netnographic method and, of all the studies, bears most of its hallmarks.

The studies selected do not all overtly identify as applying the netnographic method; however, they all implement a structured, ethical and robustly transparent methodology that allows us to examine the netnographic principles that they do exemplify. In line with Kozinets' most recent definitional work (2020, 16–18), the studies under analysis all collect, reflect and interact with online traces and extend these online explorations with other forms of data collection. Within all five studies, ethnographically sensitised data collection involved a spectrum of engagement including passive observation, downloading and saving their data, online engagement and online interviewing, with two studies also reporting in-person interviews (Kowalski et al., 2019; Masson & Bancroft, 2018). All researchers practised immersion within the cryptomarket spaces online, while Kowalski et al. (2019) reported the use of an immersion journal (referred to as field notes). In overview, these studies cover a very active period within the cryptomarket environment, and their research trajectories and encounters provide a grounded example of the dynamism of the netnographic approach.

Extending Netnographic Principles

Netnography is a constantly evolving set of research practices that has the capacity to transform alongside the fluid cultural conditions characterising the dynamic social and technological contexts of the online environment. Kozinets (2020) frames netnography both in terms of its distinction from other forms of qualitative online research methods and the structured and systematic approach it facilitates in methodological and operational choices by the researcher. The application of netnography to cultural investigation in the online environment is first articulated in the way its name is derived – a portmanteau combining network, internet and ethnography. This frame signifies that the researcher is taking a relational approach to the study of cultural meaning-making in digital contexts that are centred upon the study of online traces. It also acknowledges the diverse fields of study that may intersect through the application of this method. We have seen this multidisciplinary nature in the diverse origins and academic foci that the researchers bring to the five studies selected.

In this chapter, we first consider the question of why the netnographic approach has utility to the study of cryptomarkets and the communities surrounding them, specifically by examining its structured approach to ethical considerations in online research. Subsequent to this, the chapter begins to unpack how the dynamic context of the field site prompts researchers to adapt netnographic techniques and, at times, subvert their principles. I refer to this as the thematic interplay or resonance between the characteristics of the cryptomarket environment and the development and refinement of methods and techniques used by researchers to investigate them.

These themes build upon previous work where I explored the anthropological literature on piracy to characterise cryptomarket environments and actors and generate an in-depth consideration of my own ethnographic practice (Maddox, 2020). The themes that emerged through that reflexive practice included opportunism, replication, obsolescence, regeneration, iteration, adaptation and proliferation. In this chapter, I focus on methodological matters and the nature of building netnographic practices and producing knowledge across the five studies. Through the process of extrapolating the thematic insights from my own practice to those of others, I have further refined them to construction, disruption/rupture, contention, redirection, obsolescence and iteration. By considering these context-specific themes, this chapter provides comparative case examples drawn from the five studies to illustrate how the characteristics of cryptomarkets and their communities both articulate and push against the principles of netnographic research practice.

WHY NETNOGRAPHY?

The most significant question of this chapter is why netnography would provide a meaningful framework through which to evaluate and articulate the knowledge production practices across the five studies. Kozinets (2020) argues that while all other types of online ethnography incorporate aspects of netnography, the distinction is in its systematic approach. For Kozinets, this systematic approach involves the specificity of stages through which the researcher designs, immerses, engages, reflects and communicates their practice and findings. Specific distinctions include the field site as data site, how the researcher approaches user engagements and the ethical stance of the researcher towards practices of disclosure. Across all the studies, a sophisticated and nuanced dialogue is held with regards to the ethical considerations raised by conducting research into the communities and cultures surrounding cryptomarkets. The researchers followed, and developed, best practice for cryptomarket research; however, the five studies also demonstrate the dynamic and context-specific nature of ethical practice over time. Netnography reduces the risk for participants by ensuring that appropriate and ethical methodological choices are taken by the researcher within this environment. Kozinets (2002, 2010) outlines the ethical principles for netnographic practice as covering five domains with elements of these domains relating to researcher disclosure and positionality, participant anonymity, member-checks and the slippery lines between public–private behaviours in the online environment. This section will focus on these distinguishing ethical considerations associated with the netnographic technique and examine how they were articulated within the studies.

Researcher Disclosure

The first ethical domain relates to researcher disclosure to the community of their presence, affiliations and intentions (overt research practice). In the online environment, this usually occurs within the curated community space, such as the Silk Road forums. The site admin and moderators oversee and curate the space in relation to the values and governance architectures of the site and active community members, which Martin (2014, 11) refers to as nodal governance. In the studies examined, clear but differing protocols were reported in terms of following processes of researcher identity disclosure while conducting online monitoring and engagement in forum spaces. For the third phase of their study, Bingham had been active on the Silk Road site for 12 months prior to data collection, and had used this time to establish rapport and build trust with potential study participants, in this case vendors. Permission to undertake the study phase was sought from the site administrator, as it had been for the previous phases, and recruitment threads were published on site forums (which were a separate. onion domain to the marketplace). The researcher was requested by site members to provide access to previous publications in order for the community to establish the researcher's motives and intended approaches. This practice indicates that the researcher's identity within Silk Road's public context was consistent with their real-world identity, at least for those who wanted to know.

In contrast, Ferguson (2017) navigated disclosure differently, preferring to remain anonymous as a researcher in the public space of the community through the use of an online pseudonym. From her account, she spent six months in preparation before discussing directly with participants via private messaging features on the marketplaces, encrypted emails and later the Signal messenger app. While not approaching the site admin for permission to conduct her research on Silk Road, she did report informing the population and the moderators of the Hub that she was there for research purposes. Upon private messaging contact, she reported directing members to a website describing her past and ongoing research projects. Consequently, she provided her participants the opportunity to learn her real-world researcher identity through the private context of direct correspondence with potential research participants. Masson and Bancroft (2018) do not report on their disclosure practices; however, they do share that one participant showed an interest in the wider research of the second author and during the interview 'disclosed' pirating their publications. Thus, disclosure in cryptomarkets has a distinct nuance to it, where the agency is not always on the side of the researcher.

Within the socio-cultural context of cryptomarkets, users do not connect the identities they construct within cryptomarkets to their real-world identities. Consequently, it can be a stark contrast to site convention for the researcher to use their real-world identity, as Monica and I did. As I have previously discussed (Maddox et al., 2016), early Silk Road members subscribed to the cyber-libertarian ethos of personal privacy/online anonymity accompanied by radical transparency. Consequently, online anonymity went hand-in-hand with the free-market ethos upon which Silk Road was founded, rather than being only related to the illicit practices occurring there. In an online study of a Dark Web Social Network, Gehl (2016, 2018) discussed offering the participants the choice to know who he was, with some opting to not know. Following the work of Cromie and Ewing (2008, 637), I argue that the utility of the netnographic method is its capacity to align the researcher with the cultural norms of the environment. Thus, the netnographic distinction on the ethical approach to researcher disclosure must be balanced with its capacity for cultural sensitisation to the community under study. As with the study examples discussed, researcher identity disclosure may be navigated through choices by the researcher in terms of whether this is published (contained in a forum post or ascribed in their online avatar), nodal (through a discussion with site admin and moderators) and direct (where the researcher offers to reveal their identity to participants in direct communications). Naturally, members of online forums and communities talk with each other and know how to find information, as their doxxing practices demonstrate, so if the researcher chooses to reveal their real-world identity through any of these means, one can assume that they will become widely known.

Insider–Outsider Dynamics

To gain insight into the world view of people who purchase and use illicit drugs, and who experience social stigma for these practices, ethnographic approaches have long been an effective technique (Bourgois, 1995; Feldman & Aldrich, 1990; Moore, 1993; Weppner, 1977). Given ethnography's edict for participation and empathy, disclosure also involves the researcher positioning themselves transparently in relation to the community. Traditionally, this distinction is found in whether the ethnographer considers themselves a member of the community (holding an emic perspective) or an outsider (holding an etic perspective) (Southgate, Shying, & Grandy, 2014). Within the contemporary context of the ethnographic field lacking the exoticism of being 'somewhere else', I would argue that this dichotomy is somewhat false, with the researcher usually occupying a space in between (Dwyer & Buckle, 2009). In their study, Masson and Bancroft (2018) observe that cryptomarkets are communities composed of multiple layers, suggesting that this could be conceptualised according to the degree that users are 'inside' them, and the multiple positions they occupy in them. This observation further suggests a deeper nuance and lack of distinction of who 'us' is within cryptomarket communities. Drawing on the work of Becker (1973), Southgate et al. (2014) argue that in some cases it may be more useful to blur the boundaries between categories such as insiders and outsiders rather than adhere to strict dichotomies. They also highlight that researchers may experience courtesy stigma, or stigma that rubs off from merely associating with marginalised groups. For the Silk Road community, defining the researcher as insider or outsider may not be as direct as the researcher disclosing whether they have experience using recreational drugs. None of the studies selected discuss this aspect of how the researcher is positioned towards the community. In previous drug user studies, researchers have reported taking drugs with participants, or conducted an autoethnography on their personal experience of taking drugs, enhancing their subjective knowledge of the practices and experiences of others and themselves (Ettorre, 2017; Race, 2017). I would argue that such disclosures must serve a methodological purpose that speaks directly to the aim and approach of the study.

Similar to Ferguson who had previously studied offline drug markets, I have previously conducted immersive research with a marginalised community both online and offline (Maddox, 2016). Through this work I became familiar with navigating the boundaries between legal, grey zone and illegal practices within social contexts and digital communities. In the case of this study, I was able to draw upon my professional practice and prior exposure both socially and within the research context to approach the topic empathetically. I chose to disclose this rather than discuss or position myself as an active drug user within the community. In the recruitment thread enacting published disclosure, members asked me to share my drug-use experience, perhaps as a way to figure out my value field in relation to drug use. My position on this was to share my experience of being connected to social networks of people who used drugs recreationally (indicating drug use did not hold a social stigma for me), and that I support harm reduction approaches that include the transparent discussion of drug use and drug safety practices. In this way I attempted to situate myself not as an insider or outsider but as a person who is familiar with drug user practices and aligned with a harm reduction approach rather than a prohibition-based agenda. In some ways, this broad statement backfired, with one forum poster suggesting that because I had access to an offline network of recreational drug users, I did not 'need them'. While membership was open and the community clusters diverse, the community surrounding the platform held insider-outsider dynamics. Masson and Bancroft (2018, 82) identify from their research that the us-vs-them mentality held by participants stemmed from two places, first in response to negative stereotyping of drug users and second through shared motivations, experiences and vested interests. This community dynamic was familiar to me and I argue that it is characteristic more broadly of stigmatised communities. For the purposes of research design, research practice fits into the range of vested interests that constitute the community.

Participant Anonymity

Researchers in the field need to work within clear protocols for maintaining their participants' anonymity in their data collection and reporting process. Embedding privacy practices into the choices of technologies researchers use and engage with reduces the risk of implicating their participants. The second rule of netnographic ethics put forward by Kozinets is that the researcher should ensure confidentiality and anonymity of informants. Unlike ethnography conducted in-person with drug user communities, engaging with participants in an online-only manner enables the researcher to protect participants involved in illegal practices by working with, rather than against, their desire to hide their real-world identities. There has been significant methodological consideration given to the legitimacy of data gained from online populations. Within online drug user populations, this consideration is mostly focused on the rationale that a researcher can never take an online identity as a participant's real-world identity, but that what is shared can still be authentic experiences and perspectives (Barratt, 2011b, 2012). The affordance of engaging the communities surrounding cryptomarkets is that the researcher can engage with anonymous participants without needing to take additional measures to protect their real-world identity. Within our research, Monica and I acknowledged that most participants would be far more aware of how to construct an anonymous persona than us, therefore we attributed to them this agential characteristic in the research process. Consequently, I argue that acknowledging the agency of participants in managing their privacy should also be embedded in research protocols, with the researcher considering the possibility for unintended consequences.

Within the cryptomarket space and online research more generally, ensuring the confidentiality and anonymity of informants must move from the researcher management of participant identities and narratives to wider data management practices and reporting protocols. It must also be considered in the finer detail of how the technologies of data capture have the capacity to reveal identity elements in ways unintended by the researcher. Consequently, data confidentiality and participant anonymity require nuanced ethical practices for ethnographically sensitised research within cryptomarkets. As discussed by Monica and me in our article reporting the methodological workflow of our study (Barratt & Maddox, 2016), this can be challenging if confidentiality and anonymity is not implemented at the technological as well as procedural level. We discussed that, within the Australian context, our research materials could be subpoenaed by law enforcement, as they had been for a researcher in the UK under similar jurisdictional regulations (Garrett, 2014). This potential meant all the collected data that was not gathered from public-access group discussions, such as the interviews we conducted and group chats within community spaces, needed to be anonymised prior to being saved. In line with this endeavour, I did not keep conventional field notes (an immersion journal). Instead, I consistently recorded the public conversations and posts that surrounded events and narratives that held my gaze or were meaningful for my interview participants and community members. Where this occurred in direct conversations, through online chat and email, I copied and anonymised the discussion, showing the participant what I had done and asking for their permission to save the transcripts. These practices formed the body of my journaling and provided circumstantial experiences that spoke to what I was doing, learning and thinking about at the time. The technology set-up phase of our research included ensuring that while the data we collected had utility for the research aims, the data collection practices and technologies deployed did not record additional and unintended identifying or incriminating information outside the scope of the research. In addition to ensuring technical practices that support participant anonymity at the time of data collection, Ferguson (2017, 690) observes that the permanence of both participant and researcher digital footprints intensifies the challenge of identity protection at the point of data collection and retrospectively.

Conducting Member Checks

The third rule of netnographic ethics discussed by Kozinets is that researchers should seek and incorporate feedback in the form of member checks. Within the context of cryptomarkets, this can be done in the forum spaces and chat channels and during interviews. Within the practice of my study, I found utility in conducting a member check with a homologous and related community in person, the community surrounding cryptocurrencies (Barratt & Maddox, 2016). One rationale for engaging with them in person was that there was no direct implication as they were removed enough from the illicit practices but deeply familiar with the technologies. Given that I was drowning in the specialised terminologies relating to operational security (OpSec) and cryptography, they were extremely helpful in setting me straight on my facts, term use and sense-making processes. Presenting to this group also enabled me to give back some of the early findings of the research without implicating the audience. It also meant that I was able to have the presentation filmed and uploaded to YouTube as a shareable link, which I subsequently distributed amongst cryptomarket users in my forum posts and through Twitter. Thus, the member-check process served many purposes, from building research rigour to wider audience engagement and the production of sharable digital objects evidencing the research in action for online audiences.

The Public–Private Dichotomy

The fourth rule of netnography, a consideration of the public and private nature of posts made by users in discussion forums and whether using this material requires informed consent, applies most closely to the study conducted by Kowalski et al. (2019). However, this study is currently ongoing and the full suite of reported findings is yet to be published. It is therefore perhaps too soon to interrogate how this specific aspect of research ethics has been conducted. Within the broader literature speaking to forum monitoring and observation, there are a variety of stances towards whether forum data can be considered public content requiring no consent to use or private text requiring consent to report (Martin & Christin, 2016). However, recent changes in the Australian National Statement on Ethical Conduct in Human Research (NHMRC, 2018) point to an increasing movement for ethics boards to require user consent for the reporting of content and quotes produced in social media. The question here often comes down to one of scale, feasibility and likelihood consent will be granted. For netnographic practice incorporating large datasets of forum posts, for example, these variables are also at play and must be navigated thoughtfully by the researcher.

THEMATIC RESONANCE

Now that we have reviewed the ethical principles brought into focus through the structured approach of netnography, it is time to turn to the study of some of the more endogenous and unstructured elements of the cryptomarkets context. In bringing this context into focus, we can explore how the netnographic method alters and transforms over time in response to dynamic environmental and individual level conditions. In order to identify clusters of experience and research practice endogenous to cryptomarkets, I turn to the development of the themes previously introduced in this chapter as a way to engender context specific structure to netnographic methods.

The following sections will explore the themes of construction, disruption (with the addition of its root word *rupture*), contention, redirection, obsolescence and iteration. These themes begin with the notion of construction. This discussion will unpack how the cryptomarket can be understood as a form of constructive activism and how researchers construct their technical set-ups to engage with cryptomarket participants and data sites. The second theme is that of disruption or rupture. Cryptomarkets have been argued to be a form of socio-technical disruption, which this section will unpack. As the opening of this chapter illustrates, they also experience rupture through law enforcement activities to seize and shut down these marketplaces.

Because of the illicit nature of drug use and drug sales, alongside the loss of the sense of untouchability which the privacy and security technologies imbued, these environments are very contentious for both the researcher and the user. This section will unpack how this directly affects the design and conduct of ethnographic research in this space. The theme of redirection speaks to the smoke-and-mirrors nature of the environment, where nothing and no one is quite who or what they seem. This theme is associated with the applied concerns of privacy and anonymity for the user, site administration and within research practice. Users can hold several identities within a single forum or across cryptomarkets, and consider a broad range of OpSec measures for preserving their anonymity, from the privacy technologies they use, the information they provide about themselves, even to the way they write and what they say. In order to maintain site security and retain users, cryptomarkets are in a constant process of redirection, driving users to an updated. onion link or redirecting users from recently shut down cryptomarkets to alternative spaces. It also speaks to the contentious nature of the environment, which is pervaded by scams and deceit. Through this theme, and its wayward tendrils, we can see that the thematic categories are not mutually exclusive in practice.

Finally, the chapter closes out with the somewhat flip-sided themes of obsolescence and iteration. Technologies for private communication and collective conversations become obsolete depending on their perceived and actual security with each law enforcement activity. Each new cryptomarket touts 'new and improved' privacy and security technologies and e-commerce affordances that iterate on previous versions. Technologies mediating value exchange, such as cryptocurrencies and escrow systems, iterate and acquire features to smooth the pathways towards networked adoption, secure transfer and usability. We will now explore how the research practices within the five studies articulate these themes.

CONSTRUCTION

The theme of construction is based upon the collaborative act of building things, whether they be cryptomarkets or data capture techniques. The original nature of the term construction that we put forward based on the Silk Road study findings was positioning the collaborative construction of cryptomarkets as a form of online activism (Maddox et al., 2016). Cryptomarkets are founded upon a radical libertarian and opportunistic premise of a 'freed market', including grey- and black-market practices, as a means to sabotage or dismantle the state (Munksgaard & Demant, 2016, 78). The free movement of drugs facilitated by privacy technologies contravenes the regulation and prohibition-based policy responses to pharmaceutical and recreational drugs in many countries or states. Sotirakopoulos (2018) argues that we may see early cryptomarkets such as Silk Road as a libertarian counter-conduct of resistance towards state regulation of drugs, and prohibition-based policies. When we coined the term constructive activism, we extended Bennett and Segerberg's (2012) notion of connective action from personalised clicking and sharing behaviours to collaborative coding behaviours. Thus, the foundational community of Silk Road could be seen as a cyber-libertarian open source culture. They shared a vision to build a secure and anonymous e-commerce platform that could operate as a free market beyond state regulation. In addition to characterising the founding culture of the community, we also wanted to highlight that not all forms of online activism are about public engagement. In this instance, activism was about disengagement with the state and a form of exit politics (Burrows, 2019). They sought to build a new world in the shell of the old as a way to bring about social change. As discussed above, constructive activism is a form of social resistance in which communities disengage with the state and use emerging technologies to build more permissive realities. The study findings by Masson and Bancroft (2018) resonate with the theme of construction in that they argue that cryptomarkets inhabit and construct a new space of exchange through behaviours associated with gift exchange, in which cryptomarket transactions are imbued with similar relational motivations, obligations and interactions. Their finding, similar to ours, points to activism through collaborations in code and incorporating emerging technologies to build an alternative space of value exchange.

The association between cryptomarkets and the construction of a new space of exchange mirrors the way the authors identify secure and technically appropriate ways to engage with cryptomarket participants and data sites. Through their engagement with encryption technologies and accessing the Silk Road, the authors constructed technical protocols for site access. For example, Ferguson discusses downloading the Tor browser, signing up for a Silk Road account and then spending several weeks on the site, for hours every day. This is likely the first step that all authors took. The next step was to learn how to use the cryptocurrency facilitating sales at the time, with authors reporting on cryptocurrencies such as Bitcoin and Monero. Then comes learning how to use the channels of communication through which to directly engage with participants. Van Hout and Bingham (2013a) report learning how to use the private messaging systems on the cryptomarkets under study in order to achieve a certain level of competence. Further, we report learning how to use public key cryptography and encrypted text chat (Barratt & Maddox, 2016), this is also a likely step most authors undertook as they were prevalent communication and identity verification practices in the environment. Additionally, we report exploring anonymising technologies such as the Tails operating system in order to understand the additional technologies our participants would likely use to remain anonymous. Familiarity with these technologies constructed the basic requirements for field work practice, upon which most authors introduced other platforms and tools. While there are usual steps that a researcher will undertake in the environment, how these are done may look different over time; more on this will be discussed in the theme of obsolescence.

DISRUPTION/RUPTURE

Disruptive innovation relates to the ways emerging technologies alter the business models, production and distribution mechanisms and at times customer base of an industry. When conducting netnographic research approaches within this context, these alterations also reflect changes in the conceptual model of the field site the researcher holds in their mind's eye and a step-change in the available data sites, data types, data collection practices and who the research participant is alongside how they can be reached. This section unpacks the ways the authors have viewed cryptomarkets as a form of socio-technical disruption within the drug market context and then points to the ruptures in research practice and field site conceptualisation that have paralleled this innovation arc.

Socio-Technical Disruption

There are many ways to frame what cryptomarkets are; however, from most perspectives they represent a form of socio-technical disruption in which emerging technologies are utilised to create an online drug marketplace that offers drug sellers and consumers both visibility and anonymity within the context of circumventing legislative controls and providing a 'free market' experiment. Despite their small share of the drug market, Masson and Bancroft (2018) argue that cryptomarkets' significance is in the greater efficiency they bring to some aspects of the middle market and retail market in illicit drugs. Ferguson (2017) describes the unique nature of cryptomarkets as providing a platform-based infrastructure similar to that of eBay or Amazon Marketplace, which act as decentralised operations or 'middlemen services' connecting sellers and buyers in a communal space. Drug vendors and consumers utilise the P2P online transaction infrastructure of cryptomarkets to review each other's reputations and establish the availability and quality of products in ways that assist in member transaction decision-making. Ferguson observes that darknet marketplaces (DNMs), a commonly used name for cryptomarkets, incorporate mechanisms to handle disputes, a feedback system and forums where the community discusses buyers, vendors, drugs and drug use, and everyday life. To this definition Masson and Bancroft (2018) add that cryptomarkets are a hybrid of several technical systems including where they are hosted (the darknet or Dark Web), how payments are made using peer-to-peer cryptocurrencies such as Bitcoin and Monero, and how drugs are delivered through public postal services and private couriers. They also identify a wider social infrastructure of supporting discussion forums in the darknet and clearnet. The most significant feature or affordance for users of drug cryptomarkets is the ability to browse the available listings provided by both local and international vendors and read the reviews.

Rupture

Through the initial findings of the Van Hout and Bingham studies as well as those conducted by Barratt and me, participants encountered cryptomarket platforms and these affordances with a sense of wonder and joy, framing the Silk Road experience as like being in a sweet shop (Van Hout & Bingham, 2013a) or cake shop (Barratt et al., 2016). This sense of rupture from the current status quo appeared to be fairly universal for both researchers and users alike (Barratt & Aldridge, 2016). As this chapter attests, it has also brought about a rupture to research practice.

The transformative wave of digital data collection has been disruptive in both e-commerce contexts and research methodology, with the two inextricably linked within the cryptomarket context. Within this context, we can see the transparency surrounding drug market mechanisms and user/consumer behaviours is unprecedented. One reason for this is the hitherto inaccessible forms of user behaviours in illicit drug markets that leave behind digital traces and enable researchers to engage directly with anonymous drug users. This insight is reinforced by Martin et al. (2019, 77) who identify the extensive range of components within the cryptomarket system that generate novel sets of data for researchers. A second reason for this is the dynamic nature of the environment in which sites disappear, users are scammed, doxxed and blackmailed, and people and sites are hacked or attacked. This produces data loss, field site loss, disrupted data, complex technical set-ups and additional requirements to ensure user anonymity, confidentiality and researcher privacy and security.

CONTENTION

This section considers how the theme of contention wove through the very first study conducted by Van Hout and Bingham and continued on through the study I was involved in. Through this theme, I explore the concept of contentious visibility and how this affects the researcher.

In their longitudinal study, Van Hout and Bingham acknowledge that research interest in this space is both of public health and law enforcement concern (Van Hout & Bingham, 2013a, 385). They also identify that study findings would be of interest to drug policy makers, law enforcement, customs and excise, postal service providers, scientists and researchers, clinical, health and social professionals and those involved in computer security (Van Hout & Bingham, 2013b, 528). Here we can already see the contention that weaves through the research field with its diverse focus on drug consumerism, harm reduction and law enforcement. In a recent analysis of 120 related publications indexed in Web of Science and Scopus, works have appeared in drug policy journals, criminology, psychiatry, computer science, pharmacology, medical, legal and other publications (Martin et al., 2019, 82). The co-existence of study applications across these fields affects the reception of researchers amongst the communities surrounding cryptomarkets. All five studies point to the contentious nature of the social environment surrounding cryptomarkets where researchers are held in suspicion. The disrupted market spaces, sometimes suspended by law enforcement, competitors or DDOS attacks from hackers, for example, also impede a researcher's capacity to engage with research cohorts and their data sites. From the diverse range of research orientations towards cryptomarkets, research messages are mixed and simplistically perceived: do we want to 'save' them, prosecute them or scalp new market insights from them? For example, the communities tend to perceive researchers in terms of an advocate or threat and often conflate research practice with law enforcement activities, while embroiling research within disruptive market competition.

For the study conducted by Barratt, myself and collaborators, I was the active researcher in the field (Barratt et al., 2016; Barratt & Maddox, 2016; Maddox et al., 2016) and navigated the six-month preparation phase, recruitment process and interviews. The lead researcher, M.B., had already gained ethics approval for the project prior to my engagement, leveraging the experience of the Curtin University ethics board in reviewing previous ethnographic studies conducted through the National Drug Research Institute (Moore, 1993; Moore et al., 2009). Prior to the law enforcement seizure of the Silk Road cryptomarket, I had conducted a single interview. The site seizure was a rupture for the fieldwork and necessitated a return to ethics and a reframing of the project scope to a retrospective discussion of users' experiences of purchasing on the now defunct the Silk Road. We felt that this situation was actually of benefit to our participants in that we were talking about past behaviours rather than current ones. Subsequent to approval of our amendment application to pursue users' experiences of purchasing on the cryptomarket retrospectively, I conducted a further 16 semi-structured interviews, mostly via encrypted IRC. Unlike the Van Hout and Bingham study, interviews were conducted via anonymous synchronous text chat rather than within forum-based communication channels. Given that law enforcement gained administrator access to the Silk Road site upon its seizure, upon our return to the field site we treated forum communications as unsecure.

Contentious Visibility

The site seizure event introduced a central issue of the study for both myself and participants: personal visibility was cloaked to avoid vulnerability in a highly contentious (and performatively so) social context. In an associated publication, I identify this central theme as contentious visibility (Maddox, 2020). I argue that contentious visibility is engendered by the playful and purposive splitting of online identities and movement of users between multiple sites. These associated activities make forum banning and blocking practices a blunt tool in the moderation of the forthright, combative and at times voluminous communication style of cryptomarket forums, with flame wars being an example of this (Maddox et al., 2016, 117). In this chapter, I focus on researcher visibility and vulnerability in a contentious environment.

In their second phase study, Van Hout and Bingham (2013a) report monitoring the site and forums, capturing screenshots of postings. They also inserted more interactive probes into the forums in the form of creating 'taster question' discussion threads. They suggest this approach stimulated participant interest and produced resultant discourse. At the time I re-entered the field, and posted a recruitment thread on the Hub forums, trust and engagement with strangers or outsiders was at an all-time low. The recruitment thread responses were polarised between those who distrusted researchers and those who felt that the research could be an advocate for the normalisation of recreational drug use. While posting a recruitment thread, and bumping it through responding to comments is, as Van Hout and Bingham observed, a way to engage the community, it can be a location where researchers are targeted by the community. The thread puttered along with polarised responses from forum members until a known troll took deep offence at my presence as a researcher on the forum and issued a series of threats, culminating in a death threat.

At the time of the death threat, I was blithely chatting away to community members on an associated IRC chat channel when one of the users asked me if I had seen the post. I immediately checked in to the forum and saw the threat had been posted both in the public space and further elaborated on by direct message. While I took a series of preventative actions to deal with these personal attacks, including informing the site moderators, these initial negative experiences continued to shape the ways in which I raised the visibility of the work in the environment. As a result of this experience, Monica and I went through a review process at Curtin University and developed a set of risk reduction recommendations for other researchers who were looking to conduct research with online communities. As Ferguson (2017, 687) suggests, this threat had to be taken seriously, given the potential links between cryptomarkets and organised crime. Second, we had made the decision to connect our researcher identities to the identities that we used to navigate the site in the hope that transparency would add credibility to the research.

REDIRECTION

This section considers the theme of redirection and how it relates to netnographic practice. In this section I will discuss the utility of netnographic practice to redirect the researcher's gaze. The cryptomarket researcher must also account for the ways that participants obscure their identities through forms of redirection such as attention to writing style and the multiplicity of identities they use. These forms of redirection challenge the ability of the researcher to define the population under study, which Pires (2003) points out is actually an argument for netnography.

Redirecting the Researcher's Gaze

Following the approach argued for previously by Barratt and Lenton (2010), we sought to engage with drug users directly in order to understand the impact that online access to a diverse range of drugs had upon their drug consumption trajectory. The unanticipated advantage of being active within the environment was that we were able to experience the rupture and changing community perspectives towards risk and outsiders prior to and after the law enforcement activity of seizing the site and shutting down the associated forums. First, it exposed the level of grief and loss (both financial and emotional) experienced by the community. Second, in response to the digital migration to other marketplaces and forums, we were able to move with the population, eventually ending up at the newly constructed forums-only site, the Hub. The resilience of ethnographic approaches and netnography as a practice in online environments is that it occurs within the sense-making and redirection process of a community during times of upheaval and rupture. In essence, what the researcher observes during immersion can directly inform the direction taken in the research practice.

This principle of redirection in research practice is also clearly articulated in how two of the studies used their immersion observations to refine the scope of their study. For example, Ferguson's (2017) study examined trust and was later refined into an examination of how vendors and buyers assess one another under conditions of anonymity and in the absence of access to direct sanctions. In terms of redirection, Ferguson used the forums in a similar way as the community members themselves, as a space through which to understand immediate issues as they arose. Consequently, she was able to refine and redirect the cryptomarkets component of her study to focus on changes within the Silk Road's feedback system.

Within netnographic practice the spectrum of forms of engagement do not necessarily include any direct social interaction between researcher and researched. This observational spectrum can incorporate access to far larger datasets than can be obtained in offline fieldwork (Ferguson, 2017, 694). For Kowalski et al. (2019), a substantial amount of data was collected, which they observed as providing a challenge to ethnographic synthesis. They report observations as carried out at the two highest-rated drug cryptomarkets at the time, the complementary drug cryptomarket fora hosted on the darknet, the complementary drug cryptomarket fora hosted on the clearnet, and related subreddits such as the now defunct /r/darknetmarkets. This practice resulted in roughly a thousand ethnographic documents, capturing data generated by more than 227 contributors across the fora and trading sites, dozens of field notes, and user profiles constructed from information shared on the fora. Where does one start with data of this scale? Kowalski's answer was to turn to her analytic memos to look for new lines of inquiry. In doing this she identified that she had been irritated by a set of seemingly non-generative posts. This process allowed for the space to identify these 'non-generative' posts as an interesting subset of data. She was thus able to move beyond the recounting of instructions given to newbies on how to access cryptomarkets and provide insight into her overarching research question as to why cryptomarkets weren't more widely used. In this sense, redirection occurred amidst the distributed possibilities raised within the dataset through the use of her own emotional responses to point to areas of tension within the community.

Identity Redirection

This anonymous population also provides challenges to conventional methods in that it is difficult to define the population either demographically or metrically. The gender of anonymous online participants or a forum population may be inferred through writing style analysis, referred to technically as stylometry (Peersman, Daelemans, & Van Vaerenbergh, 2011), while geography may be inferred through time zone alignments with the time of day that members are posting (La Morgia, Mei, Raponi, & Stefa, 2018). This was evident in the Silk Road forum by references to 'when the ozzies [Australians] get on'. However, these determinates are estimates and can be undermined intentionally by participants who wish to stretch operational security and anonymity to these aspects. Ferguson (2017, 694) points out that a limitation of crawling forum data is the inconsistency of language and terminology used within the cryptomarket environment. She argues that while this variation can be due to the global nature and cultural variation across the population, it may also be an intentional form of linguistic OpSec. Ferguson observed that individuals may completely 'throw out grammatical correctness' as a form of deflection or redirection to reduce any potential for forensic linguistics to uncover the links between their online and offline identities. Establishing metrics of how many people are involved in the population under study is usually done by accessing membership lists, for example. This data is somewhat publicly available in online forums when the membership numbers are made visible as a way to indicate that the site is popular. While the number of forum members was available for Silk Road, interview participants in my study discussed how a group of friends would use a shared single identity for the marketplace. Further to this, it was common practice for a person to have more than one forum identity within a single site or across sites, as evidenced to me in a discussion with a site moderator, and in the work of Ekambaranathan (2018) and Rossy and Décary-Hétu (2017). However, just because there is a clear element of identity redirection, this does not mean that researchers should not engage with social questions of how gender, for example, plays out in these environments. As Fleetwood, Aldridge, and Chatwin (2020) incisively point out, the assumption that most actors in this environment are male has led to the marginalisation of enquiry about women and gender in existing scholarship of online illegal drug markets. Thus, a truism emerges that just because an environment is shaded by a smoke-and-mirrors set of deceptions around identity presentation and visibility, this does not mean that the social factors shaping the environment should be ignored or not engaged with by researchers.

OBSOLESCENCE

The process of maintaining anonymity in the cryptomarket environment is presented as being engaged in a technical game of cat and mouse between operational security measures that users see as the price of admission and law enforcement activities (Bancroft & Scott Reid, 2017, 500). Privacy technologies and operational security tactics quickly become obsolete as the community dissects how they are constructed and attempts to hack them, alongside attentive investigation of the latest law enforcement activities.

For their in-depth case study of a single user experience, Bingham recruited an active Silk Road member through a lengthy relationship-building phase on the Silk Road chat forum. Their intention was to undertake interviews; however, it appears that their recruitment of site users was 'hampered by negative and suspicious reactions by forum participants'. Consequently, the low-trust nature of the forum space impeded the ability of the researchers to complete their original study design (Van Hout & Bingham, 2013a, 385). This issue of being able to engage participants within the contentious environment of the cryptomarket affected all four studies, particularly after the seizure of Silk Road. For data collection, the authors report that the conversational-style interview lasting 70 minutes was conducted via video-deactivated Skype, with online pseudonyms used and no names or personal identifiers requested. In addition to these anonymising measures (technical anonymity), the participant was actively advised not to verbalise any potentially identifying names or places (social anonymity). This protocol was followed in the subsequent research discussed below. While this is excellent practice in ensuring social anonymity throughout the conduct of the interview, the use of Skype may not ensure technical anonymity within specific use cases (Microsoft, 2020). Consequently, it behoves the researcher to check the current security concerns, hacks and breaches relating to their communication software of choice. In doing so, they are able to establish whether it is perceived as secure and trustworthy in the public domain and the ways it can be used as a secure channel of communication at the time of research.

The second phase clearly gained more traction with the community, involving systematic online observations, monitoring of discussion threads on the site during four months of fieldwork and online interviews with 20 adult Silk Road users. In addition to this, they mention some of the preparation time they invested in learning the technology prior to starting data collection. They report practising the use of Tor, bitcoin (the cryptocurrency commonly used to pay for the drugs) and private messaging on Silk Road in order to achieve a certain level of competence. For the third phase, Bingham had been active on the Silk Road site for 12 months prior to data collection, and had used this time to establish rapport and build trust with potential study participants, in this case vendors. Ten vendors completed an online interview consisting of a series of open-ended questions that they could complete in their own time. These questions were sent to the interviewee via direct messaging on the Silk Road forum and/or via Tor mail. Within the same study, over the course of 12 months, we can see the shift away from the use of Skype and towards technologies of engagement more endogenous to the field site, more interactive and participative, and perhaps more trusted by the participants.

Technological Obsolescence

Further innovations and recursive practice can be seen across the other studies with the introduction of other emerging and community-vetted technologies for secure communication at the time of research. Monica and I chose to conduct synchronous text interviews through encrypted IRC, but also gave our participants the option to use alternative interfaces should they feel these were more secure, with two people taking up this option. Ferguson (2017) incorporated Signal, a secure chat application that had more recently become popular amongst privacy-conscious individuals. Similarly, Masson and Bancroft (2018) report the use of Skype video calling, and using the encrypted 'self-erasing' chat app Wickr. This iteration of communication tools illustrates that what was used six years ago when Van Hout and Bingham began their study, may no longer be in common use, with Skype being the exception. For all researchers, following the operational security discussions on the forums is a key way to understand the preferred modus operandi endorsed by the broader community.

ITERATION AND INNOVATION

In addition to the platforms of engagement, the five studies illustrate iteration of practice that forms a distinct rupture between the first and the latter studies in terms of connecting the online-offline identities of participants. In this section, we explore how iteration and innovation of engagement tactics lead to a break in prior conventions.

From Ferguson's study onwards, a broader array of cryptomarkets were incorporated into the field site, with researchers also following the movement of drug retail into social media. Masson and Bancroft (2018) reported complementing interview data with overt non-participatory observation of the discussion forums linked to the top five cryptomarkets at the time. In contrast, the Kowalski et al. (2019) study reported including observational data of the two most prominent drug cryptomarkets at the time. From the interview data, additional cryptomarkets were incorporated as data sites based upon which ones participants used, thereby customising the boundaries of the field site through the activities of participants. Further data sites were also incorporated based upon digital locations that were frequently referenced at sites already included for observation. This approach resulted in a mix between sites hosted on the darknet and sites hosted on the clearnet. Both of these studies conceptualised cryptomarkets as multi-sited and occurring within and beyond cryptomarkets themselves. Consequently, it is through user practices and data site trails that these researchers extended their concept of the cryptomarket beyond the darknet and into the clearnet.

Breaking 'the Rules'

Of the five studies reviewed, two studies reported conducting in person interviews. In addition to observational work at data sites, Masson and Bancroft (2018) reported that the interview formats were selected based upon what the interviewer and interviewee thought was the best approach. This approach resulted in nine interviews with users of drug cryptomarkets incorporating a combination of interview modes including in person, Skype video calling, and the encrypted 'self-erasing' chat app Wickr. The second study to report the use of in-person interviewing was a later study by Kowalski et al. (2019), which drew data from seven face-to-face semi-structured qualitative interviews with participants who had a history of cryptomarket engagement. A pivotal innovation within these two study approaches was the agency participants held in the research process. For one study, it was in deciding how their interview would be conducted and that this led to in-person interviews for some. In the other it was how the researchers used the practices of their participants as a way to define the scope of their field site. Both studies broke with the prior convention of only working with anonymous online participants by connecting with their participants in 'meatspace'. This practice in and of itself is a form of rupture from previous studies.

As stated at the outset of this chapter, the fact that the community surrounding cryptomarkets already practised online anonymity was a contributing argument for the use of netnographic practices. Engaging with participants through their existing technically and socially constructed anonymous online identity was considered a way to reduce the risks of implicating participants. However, as these most recent studies highlight, this is not the only argument for netnographic practices, and new insights can be produced through the obsolescence of previous conventions. This dichotomy of practice surrounding approaches to participant anonymity and confidentiality presents one of the most powerful alterations of netnography across the studies. The empathetic and agential approach taken by the researchers led to the opposite tendency to engage in interactions both in the digital and in the physical world, with participants breaking the norm of anonymity.

CONCLUSION

This chapter has considered the hallmarks of the netnographic method across five studies that implemented structured, ethically nuanced and ethnographically sensitised methods for the study of cryptomarkets. These studies, crossing a broad range of disciplines, cover a very active period within the cryptomarket environment. Their research trajectories and encounters demonstrate the capacity of netnographic practices to transform alongside the fluid cultural conditions characterising the dynamic social and technological contexts of the online environment.

The chapter initially considered the question of 'why netnography' and in responding to this, conducted a deep dive into the ethical terrain covered by the five studies. We encountered the diverse disclosure practices taken, including direct disclosure of their researcher identity to participants, nodal disclosure of the research agenda to site admins and moderators and published disclosure of the research activity to community members through the forums. This discussion illustrated how researcher disclosure practices, such as sharing prior research publications, were subverted through the playful purposive information-seeking practices of participants and community members. Through the consideration of their approaches to ensuring participant anonymity at a technical and social level (Barratt, 2011a), it becomes evident that ensuring confidentiality and anonymity of informants must move from the researcher management of participant identities and narratives to wider data management practices and reporting protocols. The researcher must also consider the permanence of both participant and researcher digital footprints as an aspect of identity protection, both at the point of data collection and retrospectively. In considering the five domains of ethical practice within netnography, further insights generated include the utility for member checks to support research rigour and also to support the capacity of the researcher to engage a wider audience through the production of sharable digital objects. The discussion on the blurred boundaries between public and private data highlighted the increasing demand by ethics boards to require consent for the use of quotes and narratives published by users online.

Moving from an analysis of the structured elements of netnographic practice evident in the study, the chapter then deployed a thematic approach to unpack the more context specific aspects of research practice. From the theme of construction, the authors followed a similar series of initial steps. Through their engagement with encryption technologies and accessing the cryptomarket data sites, the authors constructed technical protocols for site access. Familiarity with these technologies constructed the basic requirements for field work practice, upon which most authors introduced other platforms and tools. This theme also signalled the moveable feast of privacy enhancing communication tools that become available over time. Similarly, within the theme of obsolescence we encountered the notion that maintaining anonymity in the cryptomarket environment is a technical game of cat and mouse between operational security measures that users see as the price of admission and law enforcement activities.

From this discussion I argue that as researchers, we need to incorporate technologies that have the capacity to deliver the kinds of data we seek. For example, they must be able to produce valid and ethical data. This includes ensuring that our participants feel comfortable using them and that these technologies will offer the confidentiality and security required. The example discussed demonstrates a key principle that particular software platforms are more or less suited to particular kinds of investigation. The researcher in the field must be flexible yet informed, allowing participants to direct the selection of communication approaches while ensuring that how communication is conducted will enact confidentiality and anonymity.

The theme of disruption explored how socio-technical disruption resulted in the rupture of research methodologies. Specifically, this rupture was illustrated in how the methods used reflect a step-change in the available data sites, data types, data collection practices and who the research participant is alongside how they can be reached. The five studies also demonstrated the versatile ways that researchers adapted around processes of data loss, field site loss, disrupted data, complex technical set-ups and additional requirements to ensure user anonymity, confidentiality and researcher privacy. The thematic discussion also highlighted how the disrupted nature of the cryptomarket environment pushed researchers to respond to forms of contentious visibility and identified how the anonymity of community members limited the researchers' ability to define community composition and boundaries.

These challenges notwithstanding, and following the argument of Fleetwood et al. (2020), there is future scope for researchers to engage with the social factors imbued in this environment despite its smoke and mirrors nature. In a final stroke, this chapter has illustrated how the authors of later studies broke with normative conventions by connecting with their participants in 'meatspace' and collapsing their identities across the online and offline contexts of cryptomarket practices. Through the ethical consideration and thematic lens, this chapter has dived into the intricacies of cryptomarket research and shown how the use of netnography to investigate this cultural realm has been applied, subverted and transformed. Perhaps the study of cryptomarkets is not typical netnography or ethnography. Like the markets themselves, research in this space acts as a critical mirror and reveals the fractures and liminalities within normative practices. Through this chapter I argue that the sharpened and emergent aspect of this research field has much to contribute to broader discussions and applications of netnographic practice.

REFERENCES

Bancroft, A., & Scott Reid, P. (2017). Challenging the techno-politics of anonymity: The case of cryptomarket users. *Information, Communication & Society, 20*(4), 497–512.

Barratt, M. J. (2011a). *Discussing illicit drugs in public internet forums: Is pseudonymity necessary or sufficient?* Paper presented at the Communities and Technologies 2011, Brisbane, QUT.

Barratt, M. J. (2011b). Discussing illicit drugs in public internet forums: Visibility, stigma, and pseudonymity. In J. Kjeldskov & J. Paay (Eds.), *C&T '11. Proceedings of the Fifth International Conference on Communities and Technologies, Brisbane, Australia* (pp. 159–168). New York, NY: ACM.

Barratt, M. J. (2012). The efficacy of interviewing young drug users through online chat. *Drug and Alcohol Review, 31*, 566–572.

Barratt, M. J., & Aldridge, J. (2016). Everything you always wanted to know about drug cryptomarkets* (*but were afraid to ask). *International Journal of Drug Policy, 35*(1), 1–6.

Barratt, M. J., & Lenton, S. (2010). Beyond recruitment? Participatory online research with people who use drugs. *International Journal of Internet Research Ethics, 3*(1), 69–86.

Barratt, M. J., Lenton, S., Maddox, A., & Allen, M. (2016). 'What if you live on top of a bakery and you like cakes?'—Drug use and harm trajectories before, during and after the emergence of Silk Road. *International Journal of Drug Policy, 35*, 50–57.

Barratt, M. J., & Maddox, A. (2016). Active engagement with stigmatised communities through digital ethnography. *Qualitative Research, 16*(6), 701–719.

Becker, H. S. (1973). *Outsiders; studies in the sociology of deviance.* New York: Free Press of Glencoe.

Bennett, W. L., & Segerberg, A. (2012). The logic of connective action. *Information, Communication & Society, 15*(5), 739–768.

Bourgois, P. I. (1995). *In search of respect: selling crack in El Barrio.* Cambridge: Cambridge University Press.

Burrows, R. (2019). Urban futures and the darkeEnlightenment: A brief guide for the perplexed. In K. Jacobs & J. Malpas (Eds.), *Philosophy and the city: interdisciplinary and transcultural perspectives* (pp. 1–22). London, UK ; Lanham, Maryland: Rowman & Littlefield International.

Cromie, J., & Ewing, M. (2008). Squatting at the digital campfire. Researching the open source software community. *International Journal of Market Research, 50*(5), 631–653.

Dwyer, S. C., & Buckle, J. L. (2009). The space between: On being an insider-outsider in qualitative research. *International Journal of Qualitative Methods, 8*(1), 54–63.

Ekambaranathan, A. (2018). *Using stylometry to track cybercriminals in darknet forums.* (Masters thesis). University of Twente, the Netherlands.

Ettorre, E. (2017). Feminist autoethnography, gender, and drug use: 'Feeling about' empathy while 'storying the I'. *Contemporary Drug Problems, 44*(4), 356–374.

Feldman, H. W., & Aldrich, M. R. (1990). *The role of ethnography in substance abuse research and public policy: Historical precedent and future prospects.* US Department of Health and Human Services (HHS), National Institutes of Health (NIH), National Institute on Drug Abuse (NIDA).

Ferguson, R. H. (2017). Offline 'stranger' and online lurker: Methods for an ethnography of illicit transactions on the darknet. *Qualitative Research, 17*(6), 683–698.

Fleetwood, J., Aldridge, J., & Chatwin, C. (2020). Gendering research on online illegal drug markets. *Addiction Research & Theory*, 1–10: https://doi.org/10.1080/16066359.2020.1722806.

Garrett, B. (2014, June). Place-hacker Bradley Garrett: Research at the edge of the law. *Times Higher Education*, p. 2014. Retrieved from https://perma.cc/L2VR-TTQH

Gehl, R. (2016). Power/freedom on the dark web: A digital ethnography of the Dark Web Social Network. *New Media & Society, 18*(7), 1219–1235.

Gehl, R. (2018). *Weaving the dark web: Legitimacy on freenet, Tor, and I2P.* Cambridge, MA: The MIT Press.

Kowalski, M., Hooker, C., & Barratt, M. J. (2019). Should we smoke it for you as well? An ethnographic analysis of a drug cryptomarket environment. *International Journal of Drug Policy, 73*, 245–254.

Kozinets, R. V. (2002). The field behind the screen: Using netnography for marketing research in online communities. *Journal of Marketing Research, 39*(1), 61–72.

Kozinets, R. V. (2010). *Netnography: Doing ethnographic research online.* Thousand Oaks, CA: Sage Publications.

Kozinets, R. V. (2020). *Netnography 3E: The essential guide to Qualitative Social Media Research*: Thousand Oaks (CA): SAGE.

La Morgia, M., Mei, A., Raponi, S., & Stefa, J. (2018). *Time-zone geolocation of crowds in the Dark Web.* Paper presented at the 2018 IEEE 38th International Conference on Distributed Computing Systems (ICDCS).

Maddox, A. (2016). *Research methods and global online communities: A case study.* London: Routledge.

Maddox, A. (2020). Disrupting the ethnographic imaginarium: Challenges of immersion in the Silk Road cryptomarket community. *Journal of Digital Social Research, 2*(1), 31–51.

Maddox, A., Barratt, M. J., Lenton, S., & Allen, M. (2016). Constructive activism in the dark web: Cryptomarkets and illicit drugs in the digital 'demimonde'. *Information Communication and Society, 19*(1), 111–126.

Martin, J. (2014). *Drugs on the dark net: How cryptomarkets are transforming the global trade in illicit drugs.* Basingstoke: Palgrave Macmillan.

Martin, J., & Christin, N. (2016). Ethics in cryptomarket research. *International Journal of Drug Policy, 35*, 84–91.

Martin, J., Cunliffe, J., & Munksgaard, R. (2019). *Cryptomarkets: A research companion*. Bingley, West Yorkshire: Emerald Publishing Limited.

Masson, K., & Bancroft, A. (2018). 'Nice people doing shady things': Drugs and the morality of exchange in the darknet cryptomarkets. *International Journal of Drug Policy, 58*, 78–84.

Microsoft. (2020). Does Skype use encryption. Retrieved from https://perma.cc/87QJ-BFKJ

Moore, D. (1993). Ethnography and illicit drug use: Dispatches from an anthropologist in the "field" *Addiction Research & Theory, 1*(1), 11–25.

Moore, D., Dray, A., Green, R., Hudson, S. L., Jenkinson, R., Siokou, C., … Dietze, P. (2009). Extending drug ethno-epidemiology using agent-based modelling. *Addiction, 104*(12), 1991–1997.

Munksgaard, R., & Demant, J. (2016). Mixing politics and crime – The prevalence and decline of political discourse on the cryptomarket. *International Journal of Drug Policy, 35*, 77–83.

NHMRC. (2018). *National Statement on Ethical Conduct in Human Research 2007 (Updated 2018)*. National Health and Medical Research Council Retrieved from www.nhmrc.gov.au/about-us/publications/national-statement-ethical-conduct-human-research-2007-updated-2018

Peersman, C., Daelemans, W., & Van Vaerenbergh, L. (2011). *Predicting age and gender in online social networks*. Paper presented at the Proceedings of the 3rd international workshop on Search and mining user-generated contents.

Pires, G. (2003). Identifying and reaching an ethnic market: Methodological issues. *Qualitative Market Research: An International Journal, 6*(4), 224–235.

Race, K. (2017). Thinking with pleasure: Experimenting with drugs and drug research. *International Journal of Drug Policy, 49*, 144–149.

Rossy, Q., & Décary-Hétu, D. (2018). Internet traces and the analysis of online illicit markets. In Quentin Rossy, David Décary-Hétu, Olivier Delémont, & Massimiliano Mulone (Eds.), *The Routledge International Handbook of Forensic Intelligence and Criminology* (pp. 249–263). London: Routledge.

Sotirakopoulos, N. (2018). Cryptomarkets as a libertarian counter-conduct of resistance. *European Journal of Social Theory, 21*(2), 189–206.

Southgate, E., Shying, K., & Grandy, G. (2014). Researchers as dirty workers: Cautionary tales on insider-outsider dynamics. *Qualitative Research in Organizations and Management: An International Journal, 9*(3), 223–240.

Van Hout, M. C., & Bingham, T. (2013a). 'Silk Road', the virtual drug marketplace: A single case study of user experiences. *International Journal of Drug Policy, 24*(5), 385–391.

Van Hout, M. C., & Bingham, T. (2013b). 'Surfing the Silk Road': A study of users' experiences. *International Journal of Drug Policy, 24*(6), 524–529.

Van Hout, M. C., & Bingham, T. (2014). Responsible vendors, intelligent consumers: Silk Road, the online revolution in drug trading. *International Journal of Drug Policy, 25*(2), 183–189.

Weppner, R. S. (1977). *Street ethnography: Selected studies of crime and drug use in natural settings*. Beverly Hills; London: Sage Publications.

3

Netnography to Explore Gambling Practices

Situating and Advancing Discourse and Method

Killian O'Leary

NETNOGRAPHY TO EXPLORE GAMBLING PRACTICES: SITUATING AND ADVANCING DISCOURSE AND METHOD

Like most, I expect, I have friends that enjoy gambling. Each has their own particular vice, some like horse racing, others play poker, while many of us on occasion will have a punt on the lottery. However, over years of conducting gambling research, both online (O'Leary & Carroll 2013) and offline (O'Leary et al., 2018), I've witnessed the trials and tribulations associated with the activity. I've seen the pacing and panic in anticipation of an outcome. The elation and glow from a win and the dour sour reality of a big loss. This 'pleasurable-painful' duality (Bergler, 1957) is what draws people to gambling. The potential for monetary gain as well as the risk of significant loss is endemic to its appeal. The activity creates what Bakhtin (1993) terms an 'eventness of being', a heightened exhilarating consumption experience. It's not unique in this respect. Many other activities do this; however, the normalisation, legitimation and pervading presence of gambling in contemporary consumer culture makes it a particularly easy activity to engage in for those partial to amplified releases of dopamine.

The purpose of this chapter is to offer a reading of the contemporary landscape of digital gambling, and position how netnography must evolve and advance to understand this. To do so the evolution of the digital gambling marketplace is discussed. From here I move towards outlining the merits and particular utilities of netnography in examining online gambling, discussing my previous work on online poker. This contextualises the utility of netnography in understanding gambling but also highlights its scant utilisation by social scientists. Remarking upon this I embark on a discussion of new gambling contexts and groups that have emerged, pointing to research potentialities for future netnographers. I comment on variant methods that can be employed as well as put forward some innovations that might be made.

THE EVOLUTION OF DIGITAL GAMBLING

If, like me, you are old enough to remember the bombardment of banner advertising during the dot com boom, you'll remember that gambling has been a perpetual feature of the internet. From the very early days of the digital revolution, online casinos emerged through flashing images atop of our screens. In 1994, Antigua and Barbuda was the first nation to legalise gambling passing a 'Free Trade and Processing Act', which offered licences to online

Table 3.1 Seminal Moments in the Evolution of Digital Gambling

1994	Antigua and Barbuda legalise the licensing of online casinos. The gambling software powerhouse Microgaming is established.
1996	The first digital gambling casino, Intercasino, is launched. Intertops, the first sports betting website is also launched.
1998	Planet Poker launches the first online poker site.
2000	Betfair is launched, the first peer to peer or exchange gambling site.
2002	Live betting is introduced by various sports betting platforms
2003	eCommerce and Online Gaming Regulation Act (eCOGRA), an independent standards authority is created. An accountant, Chris Moneymaker, wins the World Series of Poker Main Event for $2.5million via a $40 tournament on Pokerstars, launching a global poker boom.
2006	The United States passes the Unlawful Internet Gambling Enforcement Act (UIGEA) freezing millions of online accounts. Poker site Full Tilt is subsequently exposed as operating a Ponzi scheme.
2008	Apple's app store is launched, gambling sites are made available via smartphones.
2014	Bitcoin emerges as an established crypto-currency. Online casinos begin to accept and pay out in Bitcoin.
2018	Omnia Casino, the world's first ever 100% artificial intelligence-built online casino, is launched.
2019	Betting on E-sports and fantasy sports emerges. Carnegie Mellon University and Facebook develop an AI poker bot (Pluribus) that defeats established professionals.

Source: Compiled from various sources: Casinos.co, onlinecasinoreports.ie, gamblingsites.com, pokernews.com, wired.com.

casinos to operate from their jurisdiction, globally. This paved the way for other territories such as Canada, Costa Rica and the Isle of Man to recognise the profitability's associated with licensing the activity. Over 25 years later, with many twists and turns (see Table 3.1), most notably the United States' banishment of all online gambling activities through its 'Unlawful Internet Gambling Enforcement Act' (UIGEA), the digital gambling industry is flourishing.

It is estimated that by 2024 the gambling industry worldwide will be worth 94 billion dollars, that figure doubling from a current worth of 46 billion dollars (Zion Market Research, 2018). In economic terms digital gambling is a bull market. No longer limited to casino games such as roulette, blackjack and slots, online gambling now offers the opportunity to wager on a host of global events and practices. Elections, reality TV shows, whether it snows or not at Christmas, among a multitude of other happenings are all now catered to by digital gambling platforms. Arguably the biggest innovation, however, has been the advent of sports betting online. Traditionally, a staple of gambling purists, digital sport betting has grown and evolved exponentially. Mobile technologies, live and handicap betting as well as peer-to-peer marketplaces such as Betfair, where consumers can simultaneously act as both bookkeeper and punter, have changed the sports betting landscape.

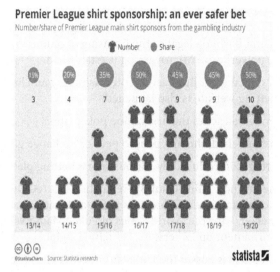

Figure 3.1 Growth of Gambling Shirt Sponsorship in the English Premier League.
Source: Statista.

Indeed, as a marker of just how prevalent, as well as valuable, sports betting and digital gambling more generally is, half of the teams that will line up for the English Premier League in 2020[1] will be sponsored by online gambling operators (see Figure 3.1)

In terms of visibility, gambling advertising is now commonplace and normative across the global marketplace. Credibility and legitimacy of the activity has been manufactured by the industry through high-profile sponsorships and celebrity endorsements. For example, Usain Bolt, Rafael Nadal, Neymar, Mike Tyson, Ray Winstone, Clive Owen and Samuel L. Jackson, among others, have all thrown their sizeable image behind online gambling sites. Humphrey's (2010) notes that such endorsements create cultural legitimacy for gambling, dissociating and destigmatising the activity from its illicit antecedents, and making it appeal to those who not otherwise would have considered it. The resultant effect of this is that vulnerable consumers such as children are now more than ever susceptible to gambling, and thus the development of gambling problems. In fact, a recent study by the Gambling Commission (2018) outlined that 450,000 children in the UK aged 11 to 16 bet regularly, a figure that is significantly higher than those in the same age group who have taken drugs, smoked or drunk alcohol. There are undoubted issues that surround the pervasiveness of gambling in contemporary consumer culture and the social costs this incurs onto broader society. Yet, in spite of this, the industry seems to be, as mentioned, ever expanding.

NETNOGRAPHY AND GAMBLING

In the main, digital gambling has been approached from psychological, economic and institutional perspectives (see Williams et al., 2012). Markedly cultural perspectives,[2] which netnography and its innate humanistic orientation caters to aptly (Kozinets, 2016), remain limited in the canons of gambling studies. Given that 'some of the most interactive and textually rich parts of the internet are numerous gambling and gaming forums' (Griffiths 2010, 12) this is surprising. Especially when we consider the concern to expand the epistemic spectrum of gambling studies towards more socio-cultural approaches (see Gordon et al., 2015). Beyond Giebelhausen et al.'s (2009) study of penny auctions, Wang's (2018) investigation of female gamblers and previous work on online poker (O'Leary & Carroll 2013), there remains a dearth of netnographic explorations of online gambling cultures. With gambling increasingly occupying, and characterising, the consumption of various virtual contexts (which I will explore in the next section), there is an opening for willing netnographers to further social-cultural understandings of the activity.

As method and methodology, netnography embraces qualitative techniques to study 'cultures and communities that manifest through communications and exchanges mediated by information technologies' (Kozinets, 2017, 378). These techniques include participant and non-participant observation, interviewing, as well as introspection, both on the part of participants as well as researchers (Kozinets, 2015; Villegas, 2018). Significantly different in orientation and practice than more positivistic methods traditionally used to study gambling, such as national surveys (Abbott and Volberg 1996; Cox et al., 2005; Griffiths et al., 2009) or data modelling (Lee et al., 2007; Doran & Young 2010; Back et al., 2011), netnography always retains a humanistic focus. In the current information age of technology where institutions, marketers and scholars seem preoccupied with big data and analytics (Thompson, 2019), the emic-agentic locus of netnography runs counterintuitive, and importantly so. As Thompson (2019) comments, the increasing digitisation of consumer culture and the fascination with big data is shrouded in a myth that large data sets can provide higher forms of consumer intelligence understanding and knowledge. Yet while aggregate statistics formed from digital analytics may inform us of the geographic dispersal of online gamblers and how this links to certain socio-economic factors, e.g. national legislation or poverty rates, big data and more positivistic methods towards gambling research can't capture the emotions or social interactions that people encounter when gambling online. Evocative representation and commentary on the hedonistic, illicit, problematic or otherwise behaviours of gambling consumers cannot be adequately expounded upon from large quantitative data sets. Instead, these need to be informed from personal and social accounts of gambling consumption, those that attend to evoking nuanced understandings of human engagement with online gambling activities.

Herein lies a particular utility of netnography towards the study of online gambling. 'Performing a netnography means maintaining an anthropological preoccupation with the human' (Kozinets, 2017, 377). This preoccupation helps scholars unpack the complexities that occupy and govern the consumption of certain online activities or contexts. For example, in seeking to understand Facebook, Anderson et al. (2016) use netnography to provide an evocative account of the arduous labours that in involved in maintaining a presence on the platform, e.g. producing conspicuous content and liking posts. Similarly, in recent research I conducted on social media (O'Leary & Murphy, 2019), netnography allowed us to engage with and capture an abundance of ephemeral interactions on anonymous apps. This afforded an understanding of how these apps, which are much maligned in the broader media, operate as crucial outlets of sociality and catharsis for post-millennials. Other uses of netnography, as illustrated in this volume, have also been used to decode complex online cultures, practices and rituals.

In terms of gambling, one of the greatest benefits of netnography is its non-obtrusive nature and capability to capture an abundance of thick description not readily available offline (Kozinets, 2015). Gamblers can be quite secretive and even antagonistic towards the questioning approaches of researchers (Wood & Griffiths 2007). Therefore, covert research can be a necessary part of gambling study (Spradley, 1980). Covert approaches to data collection are a contentious issue. On the one hand, they are vilified for being unethical or unprofessional (Beauchamp et al., 1982; Herrera, 1999), while on the other, advocates argue that it can offer researchers the ability to gather information that would have not otherwise been available to them (Calvey, 2000; Miller, 2001). Lugosi (2006) demonstrates that covert research should not be thought of as the antithesis to open and overt research, but instead thought of in terms of context. He posits that the nature of the study, the character of the fieldwork context, and the relationship between informants and the ethnographer determines whether research should be overt or covert. When conducting research on gambling contexts covert research is often required. Even if the practice has become increasingly normalised, there remains a stigma attached to the activity, particularly for certain demographics. For example, when studying female gamblers, Li (2008) found that covert observation was essential in garnering access to the true feelings of casino patrons. This became particularly evident when, in feeling uneasy with the nature of her initial approach, Li (2008) chose to reveal her presence to gamblers, subsequently finding a marked removal of participation and a successive inhibition from patrons to disclose insights to her. Yet while covert approaches may be necessary, so too are well established ethical and moral guidelines in representing findings. Netnographers should at all times support individual privacy rights, with anonymity regarding identities and commentary a best practice approach (Boellstroff et al., 2012). Kozinets (2015, 141) provides a pertinent maxim 'when we know that data can be traced, we are obligated to gain informed consent, or attempt to make the data truly untraceable'.

Beyond accessing rich data, however, covert approaches to gambling research also has other benefits. For example, it can help reduce research bias. Overt monitoring and recording of gambling practices may influence gamblers to inflate or reduce their bets and exaggerate or minimise narratives pertaining to their betting practices. When I previously studied Irish road bowling (O'Leary et al., 2018), a subculture that is pervaded by excessive gambling practices, covert data collected during initial observations in the field was crucial to minimising research bias. It allowed me to address the gap between what road bowlers said in interviews and what they actually did in practice. Covert research is also highly important to the netnographic process in studying gambling. Lurking, which involves the observing online practices, interactions and conversations in a covert manner, can facilitate the process of cultural entrée, the procedure of identifying communities and contexts to observe and learning about their unique characteristics. Catterall and Maclaran (2002) outline that the significance of lurking cannot be understated. It is an essential component in gaining knowledge on the rules, norms and rituals of online communities. When investigating online poker, I found that lurking was crucial in becoming attuned to, and acculturated in, the world of hardcore online poker players. Lurking facilitated the following in the study of the Online Poker Subculture (see Figure 3.2).

As outlined, lurking facilitated an in-depth engagement with, and learning of, various facets of the online poker community. The identification of a key forum to study as well understanding poker parlance was crucial in collecting and subsequently interpreting data. The importance of lurking in this respect to studying gambling contexts, where idiosyncratic languages very often dominate discourse, is vital. This mechanism of the netnographic toolkit, facilitates what Kozinets (2019) terms *cultural engagement*, the attunement to the symbolic modalities of online communities, such as language, symbols and acronyms but also rituals, etiquettes and hierarchies. Lurking affords a period of lieu in considering, and more importantly learning, cultural engagement strategies. Netnographers can thus become adept at speaking in the vernacular of those that they wish to study, a process that is crucial to the netnographic process and participant observation.

The usefulness of netnography in fostering and enabling participant observation can also not be understated. As mentioned, very often those engaging in gambling activities are guarded about their practices and as such they will only divulge or allow a researcher to observe what they are doing if they feel at ease with his/her presence (Neal, 1998). When hidden behind an avatar or screenname, people are less inhibited, they reveal more (Suler,

1. **Cognisance of the broad online poker landscape, including**:
   - Online poker sites, e.g. Pokerstars, PartyPoker, 888.com
   - Online poker and training forums, e.g. 2+2, Cardrunners, Deuces Cracked
   - Online magazine/media sites, e.g. Cardplayer.com, Pokernews.com, Pokertube.com
   - Poker reporting and tracking sites, e.g. PokerTableRatings, Sharkscope, Pokerlistings
2. **Identification of 2+2 as the world's premier poker forum for serious online poker players.**
3. **Understanding of how 2+2 worked, including**:
   - Knowledge of its hierarchy and social structure. This depended on the number of postings individual members had made and statuses awarded for such, e.g. 'Newbie' for 15–50 postings up to 'Pooh-Bah' for over 3,000 postings.
   - Understanding of the parlance online poker players used to converse with one another and mathematical terms used to interpret the game, e.g. VPIP% (Voluntary Put In Pot), HH (Hand History), LAG (Loose Aggressive Player).
   - Awareness of the rituals that characterised the practices of those on the forum, e.g. flaming practices used by high status 'Pooh-Bah's' against ' 'Newbies', or collaborative conversations on optimum game theory strategies.

Figure 3.2 Netnographic Study of the Online Poker Subculture.

2004), and in doing so they offer rich data that might otherwise take months of developing a rapport with an informant offline. Additionally, participants that might not have ordinarily taken part in the research if it were offline are also more likely to engage (Griffiths, 2010) significantly reducing research costs and time. Here the utility of netnography to gambling studies lies in its ability to facilitate *social engagement*; interacting, communicating and exchanging ideas with participants (Kozinets, 2019), which might otherwise be difficult to achieve. Netnography thus holds many potential advantages for gambling scholars. At a juncture where more socio-cultural elucidations on digital gambling are required, its usage and adoption can extend insight into the codified and complex practices of new online gambling contexts and communities that are emerging online. Its orientation and application is particularly suited to advancing gambling discourse in many areas. Next, I point to some ways forward.

THE FUTURE FOR NETNOGRAPHY AND GAMBLING RESEARCH

Online gambling today is a burgeoning consumption activity. Marketed across the globe in various guises, e.g. lotteries, online poker and bingo, to name a few, it finds itself approaching a zenith of legitimatisation and social acceptance. Aiding this is the prevalence of the activity in permeating new contexts and social groups online, e.g. E-sports and Facebook communities. Given this advancement, as netnographers we must now ask, and seek to answer, a number of questions. Among these: What new digital worlds have gambling infiltrated or created? How can these contexts and their communities be approached and studied? How must netnography evolve to capture the dynamisms of contemporary online gamblers? And, finally, how might netnography inform marketers, scholars and policy makers alike, about the implications of the escalation in the activity? While all of these questions and more need to be attended to by various scholars across a broad range of academic disciplines, I attempt now to provide some initial thoughts and guidance on the future of netnography and gambling research in the hope of initiating discourse around the above questions and imbuing others to follow suit.

While this chapter has established the evolution of digital gambling, I offer in Table 3.2 a typology of contemporary digital gambling contexts and how netnography might be applied towards their study.[3] These contexts and their settings highlight a diverse and expanding spectrum of online gambling activities, occupied by distinct communities of online gamblers. They may serve as fertile exploratory bases of enquiry, both to gambling researchers and netnographers alike.

Notwithstanding the potentialities of seeking to understand and document such diverse communities of gambling practitioners, netnographers must also identify how best to study and represent such contexts. Whilst the utility of netnography towards the study of online gambling is established via the proficiencies of its lurking and participant observation capacities. Similarly, these two methods have been the primary means through which both broader netnographic studies, as well as the limited netnographic studies of gambling, have collected data. The consumption patterns of internet usage, as well as online gambling practices, are constantly evolving and changing at accelerated rates. In seeking not to be left behind, netnographers must now consider how they can advance their methods of study and representation (see Kozinets et al., 2018). The same is true of those that wish to employ netnography as a basis to further discourse on gambling. I propose that there are a few avenues worth pursuing in this respect.

First, in terms of understanding and representing online gambling, netnography must move to consider the socio-material nature of the internet. In other words, while netnography retains a humanistic orientation we must supplement this with a consideration of how non-human elements craft and contribute to online gambling practices. Algorithms and artificial intelligence now play crucial roles in servicing, targeting and communicating with online gamblers. Chatbots pervade gambling platforms, while gaming companies target susceptible and vulnerable consumers through advanced data tracking methods (GambleAware, 2019). Not only this, but increasingly online gamblers are reliant upon highly advanced software packages. Poker players for instance use tracking software to analyse, in game, the betting tendencies of players they are competing against. They also avail of what are known as 'solvers', computer programs that run highly complex statistical analyses, in order to determine game theory optimal decisions for any given scenario (see Figure 3.3).

Increasingly, similar technologies are being used for other gambling activities such as online casinos and horse racing. This human non-human dyadic has created a new gambling landscape, one in which there is a humanistic push to be non-human, or re-assign oneself as a virtual entity that relies on technology to make best practice decisions. Rationality and optimal play through statistical analysis are lauded as the best way to exploit positive variances, and ultimately make money. And perhaps it is. However, this is paradoxical to the motivations of traditional gambling activities, where sociality, human interaction and hedonism were key. Therefore, might the humanistic orientation of netnography not be limiting in understanding such an increasingly technologically focused domain? I contend not. It is precisely because of the increasing prevalence and reliance on technology that gambling research needs to affirm how human interaction and understanding of gambling has changed. For example, how are contemporary gamblers attuned to non-human actors? How does interaction with chatbots affect online experiences? Are gamblers aware of their susceptibility to predatory automated advertising practices? And what are the changing manifestations of online gambling identities in face of new mathematically and technologically focused practices?

Table 3.2 Contemporary Digital Gambling Contexts and Applying Netnography

Online gambling contexts	Archetypes and advancements	Applying netnography
Lotteries Examples: Euromillions, Postcode Lottery, R Kings Competitions.	A forerunner for establishing gambling in broader public consciousness, lotteries traditionally have been a staple of consumer culture. Governments, charities and increasingly private companies operate lotteries on a daily, weekly, bi-weekly or monthly basis. A new phenomenon in terms of lotteries is the diffusion of raffles on social media platforms. Both private companies as well as individual sellers runs pools that offer participants who purchase tickets the chance to win high value items such as cars, phones, computers and even houses.	Netnography can advance the study of lotteries by assessing how governments and NGOs promote online gambling practices. Very often, these organisations endorse positive social causes, yet the dissemination of their promotional material through automated and specific targeting measures could be viewed as predatory. Additionally, there is much potential in assessing how unregulated, privately organised lotteries run on contemporary social media platforms. The non-obtrusive nature of netnography can advance insight around issues surrounding gambling normalisation, consumer vulnerability and the precarity of draws.
Online casinos Examples: Skybet, Ladbrokes casino, 32Red.	A perpetual feature of the internet, online casinos are still hugely popular worldwide. Digital slots, blackjack, roulette, bingo and progressive jackpots occupy this domain. However, advancements in gamblification processes, such as loyalty programs, attractive welcome bonuses as well as 'play money games' on social media platforms (which can rely on real money purchases), have helped grow the appetite for casino-game type gambling. Worryingly, children have been found to be particularly susceptible to 'play money games'.	More socio-cultural elucidations on the social aspects of online casino gambling can be advanced by netnography. Behavioural, health and risk studies dominate research discourse, but little is known about the communities that surround online casino gambling. Netnography can be used to understand how casino gamblers coalesce and operate as communities of practices in order to strategize against corporate entities. It may also aid in affecting insights into the increasing role A.I. is playing in managing casino gambling. Analysis of human and non-human interactions can be recorded through screencast videography. Autonetnographic accounts of casino subscriptions may also lend insight into the pervasive advertising practices of casino operators.

(continued)

Table 3.2 (Cont.)

Online gambling contexts	Archetypes and advancements	Applying netnography
Online poker Examples: Pokerstars, PartyPoker, Zynga poker.	Still hugely popular worldwide, but perhaps not as culturally vogue as it once was, online poker sites have expanded into new markets. For example, Pokerstars now offer sports and casino betting, and Zynga poker caters to offering online poker games through Facebook.	Netnography can advance research into the evolving online poker landscape. The activity is witnessing a period of burgeoning innovation and deregulation. Many poker sites now offer broader betting practices. For example, Pokerstars, and many sports betting websites similarly offer poker games such as Skybet. Netnography can capture the nuances of the game acting as 'gateway' or 'supplementary' activity to other gambling practices.
Sports betting Examples: Bet365, Paddypower, Unibet.	A major advancement in online gambling, sports betting now occupies a premier position in the digital gambling landscape. It caters to every conceivable sporting event from athletics to drone racing. Peer-to-peer sports betting platforms are also hugely popular. In terms of advancement, the recent legalisation of sports gambling in 11 US states, as well as the seeming applicability of betting practices towards E-sports and fantasy sports, is continuing to grow the popularity of the activity worldwide.	In today's global marketplace sports betting's presence is widely established, particularly in terms of its representation on social media platforms. Netnography can access global audiences across various platforms, collecting data on how organisations, influencers and gamblers disseminate information on the activity. In doing so, netnography has the potential to advance discourse on contemporary methods of sports betting advertising, their normalisation and associated issues of consumer vulnerability. Alongside this, netnography can be applied as a means to capture the ecstasy or turmoil that sporting betting consumers encounter. Emotionally charged exchanges are regularly posted online.
E-sports Examples: Betway, Thunderpick, HERO E-sports.	Competitive video gaming has grown exponentially in recent years. Streaming of online tournaments garner viewers in the tens of millions and viewership is estimated to surpass that of sports such as basketball and baseball by 2021. Sports betting companies now offer bets on E-sports events and peer to peer marketplaces, where gamers can wager on the outcome of competing against one another, are emerging.	The potentialities of netnography towards the study of E-sports lies in multiple domains. Socio-cultural elucidations on the comparative characteristics of E-sports communities can be captured. Here discourse on the rituals, hierarchies and practices of E-sports communities can be advanced. Additionally, how strategy is enacted in various games, how fans interact on streaming sites such as Twitch, and how fandom culture develops around E-sports celebrities can all be presented by embracing netnographic tools.

Fantasy Sports Examples: Fantasy Football, Fantasy Premier League, Fantasy Bet, FantasyDraftKings, FootballIndex.	Different to E-sports, fantasy sports relate to the assemblage of virtual teams that comprise a selection of sports professionals. Traditionally known as rotisserie leagues, and hugely popular with NFL, soccer, basketball and baseball fans, teams are awarded points on the basis of the statistical performance of their chosen players in real-game settings. Increasingly, betting practices have come to occupy this sphere of fandom, with peer-to-peer marketplaces emerging, as well as stock exchanges that focus on the potential future successes of real life sporting stars.	The value of fantasy sports to gambling operators will increase exponentially in the near future. Netnography has the potential to capture an abundance of rich data on these activities, documenting the unique nuances of fantasy sports practices and experiences. In doing so, it also has the potential to communicate how fantasy sports has changed the evaluation metrics of sporting performances more broadly, enamouring a new era of statistical orientation and obsession in sporting analysis. Additionally, netnography can document how competing ideologies regarding fandom are raised through fantasy sports consumption, and how issues of addiction and emotional distress are experienced by players.
Board games Examples: Chessmoney, Playjava, GSN Games.	Traditionally reserved to offline platforms of engagement, huge online communities now play, converse and gamble on games such as Chess, Checkers, Go and Scrabble. Betting on professional games as well as peer-to-peer wagers are now increasingly facilitated by various websites.	An understudied area of gambling research, the potential of netnography to capture thick description on the interactions and practices of board game gamblers is noteworthy. It can provide insight into the dynamics of strategy focused communities that are adapting and leveraging their understanding of a game in order to make monetary gains. In particular, netnography can redress how participants and communities shift and move towards gambling, how they transition in this process and what changes they witness or become susceptible to.

3-way/8bb

BTN AllIn SB strategy

⇌ RANGE*CONVERTER*

■ Fold (77.98%)
■ Call (22.02%)

AA Call 100.0%	AKs Call 100.0%	AQs Call 100.0%	AJs Call 100.0%	ATs Call 100.0%	A9s Call 100.0%	A8s Call 100.0%	A7s Call 100.0%	A6s Call 100.0%	A5s Call 100.0%	A4s Call 100.0%	A3s Call 100.0%	A2s Call 100.0%
AKo Call 100.0%	KK Call 100.0%	KQs Call 100.0%	KJs Call 100.0%	KTs Call 100.0%	K9s Call 100.0%	K8s Fold 100.0%	K7s Fold 100.0%	K6s Fold 100.0%	K5s Fold 100.0%	K4s Fold 100.0%	K3s Fold 100.0%	K2s Fold 100.0%
AQo Call 100.0%	KQo Call 100.0%	QQ Call 100.0%	QJs Call 100.0%	QTs Call 100.0%	Q9s Fold 100.0%	Q8s Fold 100.0%	Q7s Fold 100.0%	Q6s Fold 100.0%	Q5s Fold 100.0%	Q4s Fold 100.0%	Q3s Fold 100.0%	Q2s Fold 100.0%
AJo Call 100.0%	KJo Call 100.0%	QJo Fold 100.0%	JJ Call 100.0%	JTs Call 100.0%	J9s Fold 100.0%	J8s Fold 100.0%	J7s Fold 100.0%	J6s Fold 100.0%	J5s Fold 100.0%	J4s Fold 100.0%	J3s Fold 100.0%	J2s Fold 100.0%
ATo Call 100.0%	KTo Call 100.0%	QTo Fold 100.0%	JTo Fold 100.0%	TT Call 100.0%	T9s Fold 100.0%	T8s Fold 100.0%	T7s Fold 100.0%	T6s Fold 100.0%	T5s Fold 100.0%	T4s Fold 100.0%	T3s Fold 100.0%	T2s Fold 100.0%
A9o Call 100.0%	K9o Fold 100.0%	Q9o Fold 100.0%	J9o Fold 100.0%	T9o Fold 100.0%	99 Call 100.0%	98s Fold 100.0%	97s Fold 100.0%	96s Fold 100.0%	95s Fold 100.0%	94s Fold 100.0%	93s Fold 100.0%	92s Fold 100.0%
A8o Call 100.0%	K8o Fold 100.0%	Q8o Fold 100.0%	J8o Fold 100.0%	T8o Fold 100.0%	98o Fold 100.0%	88 Call 100.0%	87s Fold 100.0%	86s Fold 100.0%	85s Fold 100.0%	84s Fold 100.0%	83s Fold 100.0%	82s Fold 100.0%
A7o Call 100.0%	K7o Fold 100.0%	Q7o Fold 100.0%	J7o Fold 100.0%	T7o Fold 100.0%	97o Fold 100.0%	87o Fold 100.0%	77 Call 100.0%	76s Fold 100.0%	75s Fold 100.0%	74s Fold 100.0%	73s Fold 100.0%	72s Fold 100.0%
A6o Call 100.0%	K6o Fold 100.0%	Q6o Fold 100.0%	J6o Fold 100.0%	T6o Fold 100.0%	96o Fold 100.0%	86o Fold 100.0%	76o Fold 100.0%	66 Call 100.0%	65s Fold 100.0%	64s Fold 100.0%	63s Fold 100.0%	62s Fold 100.0%
A5o Call 100.0%	K5o Fold 100.0%	Q5o Fold 100.0%	J5o Fold 100.0%	T5o Fold 100.0%	95o Fold 100.0%	85o Fold 100.0%	75o Fold 100.0%	65o Fold 100.0%	55 Call 100.0%	54s Fold 100.0%	53s Fold 100.0%	52s Fold 100.0%
A4o Fold 100.0%	K4o Fold 100.0%	Q4o Fold 100.0%	J4o Fold 100.0%	T4o Fold 100.0%	94o Fold 100.0%	84o Fold 100.0%	74o Fold 100.0%	64o Fold 100.0%	54o Fold 100.0%	44 Call 100.0%	43s Fold 100.0%	42s Fold 100.0%
A3o Fold 100.0%	K3o Fold 100.0%	Q3o Fold 100.0%	J3o Fold 100.0%	T3o Fold 100.0%	93o Fold 100.0%	83o Fold 100.0%	73o Fold 100.0%	63o Fold 100.0%	53o Fold 100.0%	43o Fold 100.0%	33 Call 100.0%	32s Fold 100.0%
A2o Fold 100.0%	K2o Fold 100.0%	Q2o Fold 100.0%	J2o Fold 100.0%	T2o Fold 100.0%	92o Fold 100.0%	82o Fold 100.0%	72o Fold 100.0%	62o Fold 100.0%	52o Fold 100.0%	42o Fold 100.0%	32o Fold 100.0%	22 Fold 100.0%

Figure 3.3 Poker Solver.
Source: Rangeconverter.com.

These are all pertinent questions that netnography can answer. To do so, the work of Lugosi and Quinton (2018) and their conceptualisation of 'More-than-human netnography' should be considered. They provide an excellent account of some key considerations in moving netnographic research forward in light of the complexities surrounding technology-mediated social practices, where human as well as non-human agencies play decisive roles. Foremost among these is the call to embrace relational and relativistic lenses of analysis, where emphasis shifts from individuals to socio-material networks of interaction. In particular, I see potential in Actor Network Theory (ANT). It has the capability to elucidate on the comparative agencies, symbiosis and conflicts of human and non-human elements in digital gambling contexts.

ANT explores the relational ties and disparities between 'actants', seeking to identify how the interdependencies of multiple agencies hold together (Law, 2009). Here, description of the relational contingencies that inform networks allow for an understanding of how networks subsist (Latour, 2005). Emphasising a human non-human dyadic in the consumption of contexts (Bajde, 2013), ANT's orientation aligns with the current character of the online gambling landscape and the humanistic orientation of netnography. Its application offers netnographers the potential to recognise how actors and/or objects rely on one another in virtual networks, but similarly how they can decentre the importance of the other. For example, software packages are only useful, once applied and advanced by human embodiment in a virtual context, yet these packages also reduce the agency of humans in consuming gambling, predetermining behavioural responses to stimuli, e.g. folding a hand of poker based on statistical percentages assigned to possible outcomes (see figure 3). ANT can potentially be used to understand the contingencies and complexities involved in this network. To date such theoretical orientation has been limited in gambling research. Netnographic data, framed by ANT, can advance gambling research in novel ways, situating how individuals and their behaviours are informed by and predicated on social-material networks.

However, such theoretical extension may also require methodological innovation. Novel approaches to data collection, interpretation and subsequent demonstration of findings should be considered. As mentioned, the internet and the digital gambling landscape are mutable entities. For example, how can netnographers capture non-human elements in gambling consumption or provide evocative accounts of gamblers increasingly engagement with socio-material networks. Here, video-based approaches may provide a way forward. These come in varying formats, e.g. video ethnographies, documentary films, experimental non-fiction accounts and videographies (see Rokka et al., 2018). Visual methods are a staple of the netnographic tradition, both informing data sets and aiding in their evocative representation (Kozinets, 2002; Tenderich et al., 2019; Rambe & Mkono, 2019). In particular, the recent work of Kawaf (2019) and screencast videography offers rich potential. Encompassing the recording of digital activity via screencasts (videos of users on-screen activities), screencast videography attempts to chart digital journeys of consumers in-situ experiences. Documented evidence of behaviour is thus provided through footage and/or soundtracks of how consumers engage with digital content, navigate virtual settings and participate with others.

Applicable to mobile, desktop and laptop technologies, screencast videography can be applied to most online consumption activities, e.g. shopping, online dating, gaming, etc. Its utility in examining online gambling, however, has a number of advantages. First, if a broad sample of screencasts are compiled from individual gamblers, it may prove useful in observing gamblers in as naturalistic settings as possible. This may be useful in capturing the dynamic nature of how gamblers interact and converse with one another online, e.g. in discussion forums, Twitter communities or in-game settings. Additionally, it may also be useful in capturing and identifying how gamblers go on 'tilt' and excessive or problematic gambling behaviour manifests. Second, and speaking to the aforementioned discussion, it can track gamblers interactions online with non-human entities. For example, the monitoring of on-screen activities can highlight how gamblers traverse websites and their variant designs, how they communicate with chatbots, how susceptible they are to advertisements and special offers that are communicated via automated technologies, e.g. emails or push notifications, and how they use specialised software programs to supplement and advance their gambling experiences, e.g. training or tracking programs. In these instances and others, such data can only further gambling discourse through more evocative representations of its practice and the networks that constitute its contemporary character. A limitation of this method, however, is the necessity to gather participants that are willing to record their on-screen activities and subsequently allow a researcher to view their interactions and online behaviours. For netnographers where this is an issue, autonetnographic accounts of screencast activity may prove useful. In particular, there is a dearth of researcher centric or introspective accounts of online gambling consumption.

CONCLUSION

In sum then, netnography has undeniable potential to study and capture the future of gambling consumption online. In particular, employing netnography to facilitate more evocative socio-cultural representations of gambling will both advance discourse on gambling, and in time position it as a key methodological framework for gambling researchers. In an era where social motives for gambling are increasing across consumer culture, netnographers are well placed to unpack how the normalisation and legitimisation of gambling online has reduced the likelihood of those experiencing gambling problems to seek treatment (Sztainert et al. 2014). This can help inform social policy on gambling, its regulation as well as possible legislation. While some initial guidelines, areas of enquiry and possible methods have been presented here, the mantle of onus is on future netnographers, me included, to advance this undertaking. Netnography currently suffers from scant adoption in gambling research; however, the odds of gambling netnographies focusing on E-sports, fantasy sports and augmented and virtual realties, etc., soon appearing in top-tier journals are favourable.

NOTES

1 The English Premier League is shown in over 200 countries to over 600 million people annually.
2 Cotte (1997), Cotte and Latour (2008), Humphreys (2010) and Humphreys and Latour (2013) are notable exceptions.
3 What is presented in Table 3.2 isn't intended to serve as an exhaustive listing, rather its purpose is to illustrate some traditional and emerging online gambling markets. It is hoped others can advance this undertaking.

REFERENCES

Abbott, M.W. & Volberg, R.A. (1996) 'The New Zealand national survey of problem and pathological gambling', *Journal of Gambling Studies*, 12(2), 143–160.
Anderson, S., Hamilton, K. & Tonner, A. (2016) 'Social labour: Exploring work in consumption', *Marketing Theory*, 16(3), 383–400.
Back, K.J., Lee, C.K. & Stinchfield, R. (2011) 'Gambling motivation and passion: A comparison study of recreational and pathological gamblers', *Journal of Gambling Studies*, 27(3), 355–370.
Bajde, D. (2013) 'Consumer culture theory (re) visits actor–network theory: Flattening consumption studies' *Marketing Theory*, 13(2), 227–242.
Bakhtin, M. (1993) *Toward a Philosophy of the Act,* Liapunov, V. and Holquist, M., eds., translated by Liapunov, V., Austin, TX: University of Texas Press.
Beauchamp, T., Faden, R., Wallace, J. & Walters, L. (1982) *Ethical Issues in Social Scientific Research*, Baltimore: John Hopkins University Press.
Bergler, E. (1957) *The Psychology of Gambling*, New York: Hill & Wang.
Boellstorff, T., Nardi, B., Pearce, C. & Taylor, T.L. (2012) *Ethnography and Virtual Worlds: A Handbook of Method*, Princeton: Princeton University Press.
Calvey, D. (2000) 'Getting on the door and staying there: A covert participant observational study of bouncers', In Lee-Treweek, G. and Linkogle, S., eds., *Danger in the Field: Risks and Ethics in Social Research*, London: Routledge, 43–60.
Catterall, M. & Maclaran, P. (2002) 'Researching consumers in virtual worlds: A cyberspace odyssey', *Journal of Consumer Behaviour: An International Research Review*, 1(3), 228–237.
Cotte, J. (1997) 'Chances, trances, and lots of slots: Gambling motives and consumption experiences', *Journal of Leisure Research*, 29(4), 380–406.
Cotte, J. & Latour, K.A. (2008) 'Blackjack in the kitchen: Understanding online versus casino gambling', *Journal of Consumer Research*, 35(5), 742–758.

Cox, B.J., Yu, N., Afifi, T.O. & Ladouceur, R. (2005) 'A national survey of gambling problems in Canada', *The Canadian Journal of Psychiatry*, 50(4), 213–217.

Doran, B. & Young, M., (2010) 'Predicting the spatial distribution of gambling vulnerability: An application of gravity modeling using ABS Mesh Blocks', *Applied Geography*, 30(1), 141–152.

GambleAware (2019) 'Interim Synthesis Report – The effect of gambling marketing and advertising on children, young people and vulnerable adults', compiled by Ipsos MORI.

Gambling Commission (2018) 'Young People and Gambling 2018: A research study among 11–16 years olds in Great Britain', Gambling Commission, available: www.gamblingcommission.gov.uk/pdf/survey-data/young-people-and-gambling-2018-report.pdf

Giebelhausen, M., Robinson, S. & Cotte, J. (2011) 'Shopping+ gambling= shambling: The online context of penny auctions', *ACR North American Advances*, 39, 174–175.

Gordon, R., Gurrieri, L. & Chapman, M. (2015) 'Broadening an understanding of problem gambling: The lifestyle consumption community of sports betting', *Journal of Business Research*, 68(10), 2164–2172.

Griffiths, M.D. (2010) 'The use of online methodologies in data collection for gambling and gambling addiction', *International Journal of Mental Health and Addiction*, 8(1), 8–20.

Griffiths, M.D., Wardle, H., Orford, J., Sproston, K. & Erens, B. (2009) 'Sociodemographic correlates of internet gambling: Findings from the 2007 British Gambling Prevalence Survey', *CyberPsychology & Behavior*, 12(2), 199–202.

Herrera, C. D. (1999) 'Two arguments for "covert research" in social research', *British Journal of Sociology*, 50(2), 331–341.

Humphreys, A. (2010) 'Semiotic structure and the legitimation of consumption practices: The case of casino gambling', *Journal of Consumer Research*, 37(3), 490–510.

Humphreys, A. & Latour, K.A. (2013) 'Framing the game: Assessing the impact of cultural representations on consumer perceptions of legitimacy', *Journal of Consumer Research*, 40(4), 773–795.

Kawaf, F. (2019) 'Capturing digital experience: The method of screencast videography', *International Journal of Research in Marketing*, 36(2), 169–184.

Kozinets, R.V. (2002) 'Can consumers escape the market? Emancipatory illuminations from burning man', *Journal of Consumer Research*, 29(1), 20–38.

Kozinets, R.V. (1997) 'I want to believe: A nethnography of the "X-philes" subculture of consumption', *Advances in Consumer Research*, 24, 470–475.

Kozinets, R.V. (2015) *Netnography: Redefined*, London: Sage.

Kozinets, R.V. (2017) 'Netnography: Radical Participative Understanding for a Networked Communication Society', In Willig, C. and Stainton-Rogers, W. eds., *The SAGE Handbook of Qualitative Research in Pschyology* (pp. 374–380), London: Sage.

Kozinets, R.V. (2019) *Netnography: The Essential Guide to Qualitative Social Media Research*, London: Sage.

Kozinets, R.V., Scaraboto, D. & Parmentier, M.A. (2018) 'Evolving netnography: How brand auto-netnography, a netnographic sensibility, and more-than-human netnography can transform your research', *Journal of Marketing Management*, 34(3–4), 231–242, doi: 10.1080/0267257X.2018.1446488

Latour, B. (2005) *Reassembling the Social: An Introduction to Actor–Network Theory*, Oxford, UK: Oxford University Press.

Law, J. (2009) 'Actor–network theory and material semiotics', In Turner, B.S. ed., *The New Blackwell Companion to Social Theory*, (pp. 141–159), Oxford, UK: Wiley-Blackwell.

Lee, H. P., Chae, P. K., Lee, H. S., & Kim, Y. K. (2007) 'The five-factor gambling motivation model', *Psychiatry Research*, 150(1), 21–32.

Li, J. (2008) 'Ethical challenges in participant observation: A reflection on ethnographic fieldwork', *The Qualitative Report*, 13(1), 100–115.

Lugosi, P. (2006) 'Between overt and covert research: Concealment and disclosure in an ethnographic study of commercial hospitality', *Qualitative Inquiry*, 12(3), 541–561.

Lugosi, P. & Quinton, S, (2018) 'More-than-human netnography', *Journal of Marketing Management*, 34(3–4), 287–313.

Miller, J. M. (2001) 'Covert participant observation: Reconsidering the least used method', In Miller, J.M. and Tewksbury, R., eds., *Extreme Methods: Innovative Approaches to Social Science Research*, Boston: Allyn & Bacon, 13–21.

Neal, M. (1998) 'You lucky punters! A study of gambling in betting shops', *Sociology*, 32(3), 581–600.

O'Leary, K. & Carroll, C. (2013) 'The online poker sub-culture: Dialogues, interactions and networks', *Journal of Gambling Studies*, 29(4), 613–630.

O'Leary, K. & Murphy, S. (2019) 'Moving beyond Goffman: The performativity of anonymity on SNS', *European Journal of Marketing*, https://doi.org/10.1108/EJM-01-2017-0016

O'Leary, K., Patterson, M. & O'Malley, L. (2018) 'Road bowling in Ireland: Social space and the context of context', *Consumption Markets & Culture*, 22(5–6), 598–616.

Rambe, P. & Mkono, M. (2019) 'Appropriating WhatsApp-mediated postgraduate supervision to negotiate "relational authenticity" in resource-constrained environments', *British Journal of Educational Technology*, 50(2), 702–734.

Rokka, J., Hietanen, J. & Brownlie, D. (2018) 'Screening marketing: Videography and the expanding horizons of filmic research', *Journal of Marketing Management*, 34(5–6), 421–431.

Spradley, J.P. (1980) *Participant Observation*, New York: Holt, Rinehart and Winston.

Suler, J. (2004) 'The online disinhibition effect', *Cyberpsychology & Behavior*, 7(3), 321–326.

Sztainert, T., Wohl, M.J., McManus, J.F. & Stead, J.D. (2014) 'On being attracted to the possibility of a win: Reward sensitivity (via gambling motives) undermines treatment seeking among pathological gamblers', *Journal of Gambling Studies*, 30(4), 901–911.

Tenderich, A., Tenderich, B., Barton, T., & Richards, S. E. (2019) 'What are PWDs (people with diabetes) doing online? A netnographic analysis', *Journal of Diabetes Science and Technology*, 13(2), 187–197.

Thompson, C.J. (2019) 'The "big data" myth and the pitfalls of "thick data" opportunism: On the need for a different ontology of markets and consumption', *Journal of Marketing Management*, 35(3–4), 207–230.

Villegas, D. (2018) 'From the self to the screen: a journey guide for auto-netnography in online communities', *Journal of Marketing Management*, 34(3–4), 243–262.

Wang, Y.S. (2018) 'Addiction by design: Using netnography for user experiences in female online gambling game', *International Journal of Human–Computer Interaction*, 34(8), 774–785.

Williams, R.J., Wood, R.T. & Parke, J. (2012) *Routledge International Handbook of Internet Gambling*, London: Routledge.

Wood, R.T.A. & Griffiths, M.D. (2007) 'Online data collection from gamblers: Methodological issues', *International Journal of Mental Health and Addiction*, 5, 151–163.

Zion Market Research (2018) 'Size of the online gambling market in 2017 and 2024 (in billion U.S. dollars)', *Statista*, available: www.statista.com/statistics/270728/market-volume-of-online-gaming-worldwide/

4

In the Public Interest
Netnography to Impel Policy and Regulatory Change

Robert V. Kozinets, Rossella Gambetti, Ulrike Gretzel,
Maribel Suarez, and Caroline Renzulli

THE NEED FOR THE RESEARCH

Informing public policy and regulatory decisions are important roles that social science can fulfill. According to Sprott and Miyazaki's (2002) content analysis of publications in the *Journal of Public Policy and Marketing*, only 7.9 percent of its articles were positioned as providing scientific inputs to the policy-making process. In this chapter, we will explain how netnography has recently been adapted for use in the context of regulatory investigation and public policy advocacy in the United States, how this work is continuing, and how more research work in this area is clearly needed.

The story begins in 2015 in the capital city of the United States. A Washington, DC-based non-profit advocacy organization working to reduce tobacco use around the world named the Campaign for Tobacco-Free Kids (CTFK) began noticing social media feeds were increasingly containing various depictions of tobacco consumption. Focusing their efforts on the social media feeds of consumers in the low- and middle-income countries where more than 80 percent of the world's smokers live, they began collecting content, conducting their own type of investigative netnographic research. Although it was difficult for them to determine whether or not this was "organic," or naturally occurring word-of-mouth, or prompted influencer or "word-of-mouth" marketing (Kozinets et al., 2010), there were certain recurring patterns. The brands that appeared most tended to be owned by the world's four largest private tobacco companies (Philip Morris International, British American Tobacco, Imperial Brands, and Japan Tobacco International). However, if these were organic posts, this might be expected. Nonetheless, the people at CTFK strongly suspected, from the quantity and nature of these social media posts, that Big Tobacco was using established influencer marketing methods to appeal to young people, recruit them, and have them promote a variety of combustible and e-cigarette products. This violated international agreements to limit such advertising. However, CTFK wanted more data, more methodological rigor, and more certainty in their findings before they could take these findings to the level of a public policy recommendation. To achieve these goals, they reached out to someone who understood netnography. That person was the lead author of this chapter.

THE REQUIREMENTS OF THE STUDY

It quickly became apparent that the project CTFK wanted to conduct was complex. It required a multi-site, multi-researcher, multi-language netnography. CTFK had a list of countries that they wanted to investigate further that included social media in Brazil, Uruguay, Italy, Indonesia, the Philippines, Russia, the Ukraine, Egypt, Moldova, South Africa, and India. The research itself would require an extensive netnography that involved investigative social media data collection combined with observations of online broadcast media and promotions, immersive observation of events, and then enhanced with online and face-to-face interviews to obtain a "behind-the-scenes" perspective that would allow us to connect the dots regarding what we were seeing in social media and on other online sources.

This was the first public policy type assignment that the first author was engaged in, and he identified four major challenges requiring adaptations and extensions of netnography. The first was obtaining a culturally sophisticated understanding of 10 countries, their languages, and their cultures. Although CTFK's efforts established that there were online social media tobacco posts, without cultural insiders the project could only offer an incomplete understanding of their contents' meanings, connotative nuance, and contexts. The project needed people on the ground in these countries. As well, there were numerous algorithms that limited what we could see in local social media from remote locations (even using VPNs). Second, we needed cultural insiders who could reach out to influencers in their own language and gain an understanding of their motivations and actions for the posts, and in particular any training or compensation they might be receiving for these actions. Third, the project needed high-quality and experienced researchers who could thoroughly document what they were finding and adjust course as necessary to complement the multinational operations of the team. Finally, the project and its researchers needed to be very careful about ethics and confidentiality concerns. Because tobacco marketing was illicit, if not borderline illegal in some of these nations, we needed to design data collection protocols that not only met the highest standards of ethical research, but also provided ironclad protection for the people we contacted.

CONDUCTING THE NETNOGRAPHY

With some effort and old-fashioned networking, the first and third author working together were able to assemble a team of outstanding researchers and ensure that they were trained in the appropriate netnographic procedures and ethical operations, and that they understood our interview guide and preferred recruitment techniques. That team included the first four authors of this paper along with Silvia Biraghi (Italy), Eni Maryani (Indonesia), Ruxandra Trandofoiu (Moldova), Jerome Cleofas (Philippines), Abu Elnasr Sobaih (Egypt), Antonina Anisimovich (Ukraine and Russia), Verónica Olivera Sapienza (Uruguay), and Mridula Dwivedi (India). Our South African researcher was unable to finish the project due to political and social unrest in the country that particularly affected the higher education system there. The members of our research team were all trained as academic researchers, and we approached the project with the highest regard for methodological rigor and ethical standards. However, we were aware that the goal of the netnography was not knowledge creation or journal publication (although CTFK held this out as something that could follow the project's completion). Instead, we knew that our task was to provide thorough investigation and documentation for the purposes of policy change. We were always aware that our work might be covered in the news in the various countries affected by our work. The work of an advocacy group like CTFK involves working with journalists to affect public opinion and gain public support, and often this meant shaming tobacco companies who were engaging in sordid activities.

The actual research work was more like detective work or investigative journalism than most of us were used to. Although some of it resembled the rigorous netnographic data collection we had done before, there was always an air of irregularity, as the influencers we contacted usually seemed hesitant or even frightened to speak to us, as if they knew that what they were doing was wrong. As well, very little information was out in the open. We found that tobacco marketing campaign related events were given new names loosely related to the brands they promoted and featured designs that resembled brand logos in their shapes and colors, but removed trademarked names. Photographs and promotions never contained the names of the big tobacco companies. On Instagram, posts contained evocative hashtags such as #YouDecide, #DecideYourFlow, #FreedomMusic, or #PartyLikeUs but, again, rarely named tobacco brands. We had to follow a trail of hashtags, looking for similarities, to find patterns in use and track down common causes. We also tracked clues such as the agency names stamped on photographs and posts of promotional material like boxes of tobacco products received by Instagram influencers. Through our efforts, we were able to identify various digital marketing agencies, event marketing companies, and public relations firms, and found patterns in their connections to global tobacco companies. Although they were cloaked and obscured in different ways, we were able to gather enough complementary information from multiple countries, with enough corroborations between them, that we could draw reasonable conclusions about the sophisticated interrelation of these campaigns as well as their organization, intention, and structure.

THE FINDINGS OF THE NETNOGRAPHY

Our findings left little doubt that Big Tobacco companies had rolled up a potent blend of social media marketing and event marketing whose intention was to attract young people into the world of smoking and e-cigarettes. We found sophisticated and interconnected strategies, extravagant events with names like "K-Player," "BestNightEver" and "TastetheCity" in which alcohol, live music and attractive hosts intermix with young influencers who were invited online to these ostensibly underground parties, treated lavishly from the moment they entered, and then encouraged in different ways and by different paid actors at the parties to post about the tobacco brand related events, using the tobacco brand hashtags that we were able to trace.

Some of the parties seemed to contain private rooms with attractive backgrounds for influencers to pose against for selfies that also contained special displays with cigarette brands and boxes. Interviews with influencers later confirmed these inferences. Figure 4.1 shows a Brazilian influencer's public post showing her with a friend adopting a familiar selfie pose in one such private party section. Her post contains the word "Ahead," which is a British American Tobacco brand hashtag and account. Her use of the hashtag "#quemteinspira" ("what inspires you?") draws on the marketing in the ahead-br.com. br web-page, which links curiosity, nonconformity and energy with the Kent brand's color scheme and signature shapes. Finally, the Kent brand is clearly visible, twice in the background of the selfie (one is also visible at the bottom of the photo between the two influencers).

We also found promotions that used young micro and nano-influencers posting both with and without the required #ad or #sponsored designations (see Kozinets et al., 2019). As well, we found that groups like the "Night Hunters" recruited young people who also promoted products such as alcohol and fashion. They were hired to post pictures of themselves with cigarettes and the requisite hashtags. All of these tactics indicated to us that Big Tobacco was using social media and event marketing in sophisticated ways to target young people in the countries we investigated.

Most of the sponsoring tobacco companies hid behind public relations and digital agencies to keep their tobacco advertising under the radar of existing regulation. But in Indonesia, we

Figure 4.1 Public Brazilian influencer post promoting Kent brand.
Source: Researcher immersion journal notes and annotations.

Figure 4.2 Generation G Brand Ambassador Account Posting About Their "Chosen Interns," Young Indonesians Who Are Paid Tobacco Product Influencers.

found active accounts that openly promoted the brands of Gudang Garam—an internationally traded Indonesian tobacco company whose market capitalization is close to $6 billion—and their "Generation G" brand ambassadors such as the one whose post is in Figure 4.2. Social media content creators with the right number of followers were invited to apply for a few coveted spots as members of Generation G. If they were lucky enough to be chosen, they attended training camps in hotels in large Indonesian cities. During the camps (which were documented on Instagram, see Figure 4.2), the boys and girls of Generation G brand ambassadors were taught about cigarette brands, how to photograph them, when to post them to their social media audiences, and how to interact on social media. After attending these camps, the young nano-influencers were paid generous fees for posting tobacco-related images. Often, the money these young people were able to make as tobacco influencers amounted to more income than their parents earned in full-time jobs.

PRESENTING AND APPLYING THE RESEARCH FINDINGS

In early 2017, the lead author presented the results of the netnography to CTFK in their Washington, DC, offices. The research helped shine a light not only onto Big Tobacco's unchecked use of social media, but also on the lack of regulation of social media companies that were allowing tobacco companies free access to use the platforms to promote tobacco use to youth. There was little, if any, accountability, and the tech companies tended to respond reactively to complaints rather than acting proactively as good corporate citizens. Technology companies were, in many ways, as responsible for what was happening in these cases as the tobacco companies and public relations agencies who were educating youth about how to post tobacco messages and then were directly compensating them for doing it. As Kary and Wagner (2019) point out, there are social media influencer related "loopholes" in technology company policies that have been allowing "posters on Facebook, Instagram, Twitter and Snapchat [to] advertise tobacco products despite the sites' own policies against it."

After over a year of careful preparation on the part of CTFK and affiliated agencies, the *New York Times* published an article about the practice entitled "Big Tobacco's Global Reach on Social Media" (Kaplan, 2018). The article contained numerous examples from the netnography study (which it mentioned by name), as well as an influencer contract drawn from the netnography project (see Figure 4.3 for a screenshot of the contract, translated from Italian into English) that we were able to obtain in our research investigation. As the excerpt provided in Figure 3 reveals, British American Tobacco was using third parties to contract with influencers to promote their products through lifestyle marketing linked to their LikeUs (which sounds similar to "luckies") Facebook page and the #lus and #likeus_ party hashtags.

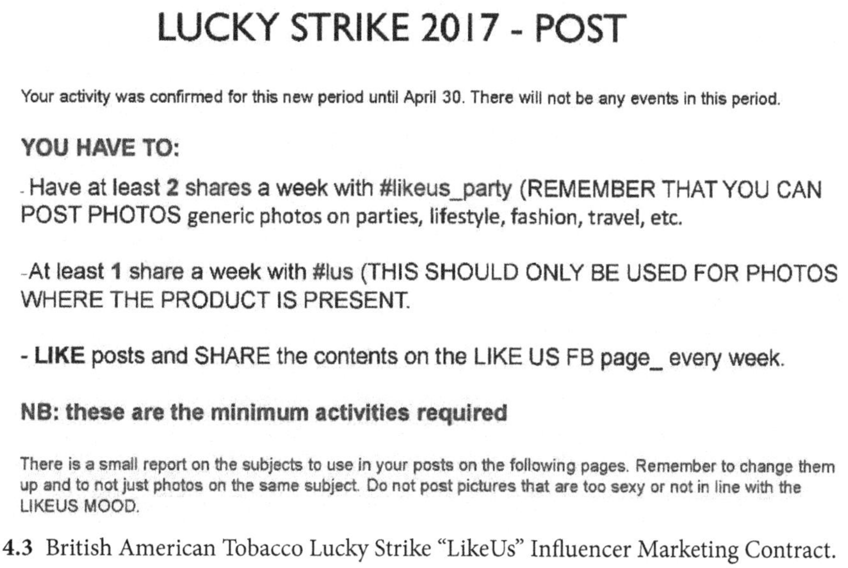

LUCKY STRIKE 2017 - POST

Your activity was confirmed for this new period until April 30. There will not be any events in this period.

YOU HAVE TO:

- Have at least **2** shares a week with #likeus_party (REMEMBER THAT YOU CAN POST PHOTOS generic photos on parties, lifestyle, fashion, travel, etc.

-At least **1** share a week with #lus (THIS SHOULD ONLY BE USED FOR PHOTOS WHERE THE PRODUCT IS PRESENT.

- **LIKE** posts and SHARE the contents on the LIKE US FB page_ every week.

NB: these are the minimum activities required

There is a small report on the subjects to use in your posts on the following pages. Remember to change them up and to not just photos on the same subject. Do not post pictures that are too sexy or not in line with the LIKEUS MOOD.

Figure 4.3 British American Tobacco Lucky Strike "LikeUs" Influencer Marketing Contract. *Source*: Original research.

THE PUBLIC POLICY PETITION

On the same day that the *New York Times* article was published, CTFK, along with eight other non-profits (including the American Academy of Pediatrics, the American Cancer Society, and the American Heart Association), filed a petition with the US Federal Trade Commission. The petition is extensive, and combines the research we conducted with a large amount of other information collected and commissioned by CTFK, all of it carefully organized in the 60-page document. Demonstrating the value of interactional methods such as interviews, the petition relies particularly heavily on the disclosures we carefully collected during anonymous interviews with social media influencers in the ten countries we investigated.

The following quote from the FTC Petition describes some of CTFK netnography, and emphasizes the important role of the interviews in being able to connect the dots between the social media posts and the actions by tobacco companies and their agencies.

> Certain confidential and anonymous (to Petitioners) interviews of influencers paid by Respondents or their agents in Brazil, Italy, and Uruguay, conducted by the netnography market research firm Netnografica, with financial support from the Campaign for Tobacco-Free Kids, revealed examples of how certain Respondents, via their marketing firms, worked with digital influencers to promote their cigarette brands. Across countries, the various interviews suggest that the youngest influencers, with the largest potential audience for advertising tobacco products, were recruited and used as influencers for certain Respondents' deceptive advertising campaigns.
> (Request for Investigative and Enforcement Action to Stop Deceptive Advertising, 2018, 41)

You may note in this quote the special attention to the anonymous nature of the interviews. The petition specifies that we kept secret the identities of the social media influencers we interviewed, and did not reveal them to CTFK. In fact, after ensuring that the data was reliable, we destroyed all records that could identify the people we interviewed. Although several journalists wanted to speak to them, we were unable to comply because we had guaranteed that they would never be identified. These procedures were a necessary adaptation of netnography and its ethical standards to this highly sensitive international context. We expect that, just as with other studies in this volume such as those of cryptomarkets (Chapter 2, this volume) and military personnel (Chapter 6), these high security methods of assuring confidentiality or anonymity will be important procedures for future policy-related netnographies.

AFTER THE PETITION

Another outcome of this research project was policy change from Facebook and Instagram. The research was used by CTFK over the past several years to publicly and private pressure Facebook, Instagram, and Twitter to ban influencer marketing of tobacco on their platforms. In December 2019, Facebook and Instagram finally announced that influencers will no longer be allowed to promote products related to vaping, tobacco, and weapons on their sites.

The research project with CTFK was a milestone but, in many ways, it was just the beginning of our commitment. After the *New York Times* article and the Federal Trade Commission petition, we continued to be involved in the research and the issue of social media regulation. All of us have been interviewed by journalists and our work continues to be featured in the press. In March, 2019, the lead author wrote and published an article for *The Conversation* online (Kozinets, 2019). That article, which received coverage in the press in the US and other countries, was translated into other languages, and was turned into a class reading for students in grades 8–12. Working with journalists is not something that netnographers or other academic researchers are trained for and, as a result, we all found that we needed to adapt our skillsets to ensure that we could effectively communicate the message of our research. This meant moving out of our own comfort zones and thinking about how our research could be most effectively leveraged to help inform public opinion about the current need for more regulation of social media.

Our work also has involved maintaining contact with CTFK and other non-profit organizations and groups that are interested in initiating changes in tobacco policy. Several of us have given seminars and workshops, and others have been active participants in meetings to help educate and inform the members of these organizations so that they can more effectively help to direct policy makers in making decisions to protect the public interest. Some of us have also continued researching the use of social media to promote smoking. In particular, we have been carefully following the use of young social media influencers by e-cigarette companies like JUUL (a brand now connected to Philip Morris/Altria). For example, the Instagram post from the "juul is the ruul" account in Figure 4.4 shows three young people, two of them with e-cigarettes (one with smoke coming from his mouth), a range of different JUUL-related hashtags, and a reference to their high school prom. Keeping an eye on the role of social media in e-cigarette promotions is very important if we are to tackle what Jerome Adams, the Surgeon General of the United States, has called an "e-cigarette epidemic among youth" (Surgeon General's Advisory on E-cigarette Use Among Youth, 2019).

THE OUTLOOK

Limited, corporate, and exchange focused thinking has led to marketing causing significant social harm (Hill & Martin, 2014). The use of social media marketing for e-cigarettes appears to have been enormously effective, for instance. Just 11 years after their introduction in 2007, more than 3.6 million US youth use them, including 1 in 5 high school students and 1 in 20 middle school students (Cullen et al., 2018). When combined with

Figure 4.4 Instagram Post of a "JuulGang" of Young Influencers.

the lack of effective regulation and enforcement, the example of e-cigarettes demonstrates the serious potential harmfulness of influencer and affiliate marketing today. Not only do social media content creators wield consequential power, they also have a record of deception that has gone unpunished. The "noncompliance of individual influencers and affiliate networks with affiliate link disclosure requirements continues at an alarming rate and escapes FTC scrutiny" (Bladow, 2018, 1163). Importantly, these social media transgressions are having some of their most profound negative effects upon young people. But they affect us all.

As social media platforms increasingly harbor and influence our culture and public discourse, and as social media marketing that uses this access continues to expand, it is transforming practically every element of our lives and societies (see Chapter 1). Better research and regulation are therefore needed not only for tobacco regulation, but also to inform social media policy and regulation more broadly. Facebook's Mark Zuckerberg seems to agree. In public statements, he recently asked for the US government to start developing a "new type of regulator" (an agency) to oversee social media enforcement (Bloomberg, 2020). This public relations blitz on the part of Zuckerberg followed Facebook's release of a white paper that attempted to delineate "a way forward" for "online content regulation" (Facebook, 2020). However, the social media companies should not be allowed to write the regulations that govern them. Informing these regulations is where academic and social scientists must be able to bring their expertise to bear. And advocacy groups and other organizations must get involved to influence public opinion so that governments will finally wake up and use their power to protect the public.

Today, many social scientists, free market economists, and marketing scholars operate under the neoliberal assumption that all regulations are bad, that they inevitably distort the market, inhibit freedom, or are just plain ineffective and expensive to enforce. But regulations are just rules. Rules can be well-informed, based on science, and effective, blind and useless, or positioned somewhere in between these two extremes. What we do know is that without adequate regulations about social media or their enforcement, these media operate as little more than a lawless anarchy. If public agencies fail to adequately regulate water use, its people get filthy, polluted rivers and lakes and corporate exploitation. If public agencies fail to regulate social media and technology companies, the people ostensibly served by those agencies get filthy, polluted communication channels, rich tech companies, abuse by bad actors like Big Tobacco and foreign governments, mass mistrust, and endless opportunities for manipulation.

We believe that there is a very important role for netnography in the world of public policy and regulation, especially as it regards social media. This chapter provided an in-depth look at a recent netnography project with a non-profit advocacy group that demonstrated the value of the method and its implementation. Netnography was used to decipher a tangled web of online content and relationships in order to reveal the use of advanced influencer marketing practices by Big Tobacco on the world's most popular social media platforms. The findings of the netnography resulted in policy change by Facebook and Instagram, served as the basis for a regulatory petition, were covered in the press in a number of nations, and have served as the basis for ongoing research, consultation, discussion, and training. This netnography can serve as a template for much-needed future research that might present coherent and fact-based cases for public regulation of the use of social media by companies, and of the technology companies who run these platforms for their own profit, sometimes to the detriment of society.

REFERENCES

Bladow, L. E. (2018). Worth the click: Why greater FTC enforcement is needed to curtail deceptive practices in influencer marketing. *William & Mary Law Review*, 59, 1123–1164.

Bloomberg (2020). Facebook needs, wants, must have regulation, Zuckerberg says. *Los Angeles Times*, February 17.

Cullen K. A., Ambrose B. K., Gentzke A. S., Apelberg B. J., Jamal, A., & King, B. A. (2018). Notes from the field: Increase in use of electronic cigarettes and any tobacco product among middle and high school students – United States, 2011–2018. *MMWR Morbidity & Mortality Weekly*, 67 (45), 1276–1277.

Facebook (2020). Charting a Way Forward: Online Content Regulation. *Facebook White Paper*, February.

Hill, R. P., & Martin, K.D. (2014). Broadening the paradigm of marketing as exchange: a public policy and marketing perspective. *Journal of Public Policy & Marketing*, 33 (1), 17–33.

Kaplan, S. (2018). Big Tobacco's global reach on social media. *New York Times*, August 24.

Kary, T. & Wagner, K. (2019), Philip Morris influencer tobacco ads on social media under fire. Bloomberg.com, May 22.

Kozinets, R. V. (2019). How social media is helping Big Tobacco hook a new generation of smokers. *The Conversation*, March 27.

Kozinets, R. V., Gambetti, R., Suarez, M., Dewhirst, T., Gretzel, U., & Renzulli, C. (2019). Activationism: How tobacco marketers hacked global youth culture. In Marie-Agnès Parmentier and Zeynep Arsel, eds., Research in Consumer Culture Theory, Vol. 2, Proceedings of the 2019 Consumer Culture Theory *Conference*, Montréal, PQ, 1–6.

Kozinets, R. V., de Valck, K., Wojnicki A., & Wilner, S. (2010). Networked narratives: Understanding word-of-mouth marketing in online communities. *Journal of Marketing*, 74 (March), 71–89.

Request for Investigative and Enforcement Action to Stop Deceptive Advertising (2018), *Federal Trade Commission Petition*, August 24.

Sprott, D. E., & Miyazaki, A.D. (2002). Two decades of contributions to marketing and public policy: An analysis of research published in *Journal of Public Policy & Marketing*. *Journal of Public Policy & Marketing*, 21 (1), 105–125.

Surgeon General's Advisory on E-cigarette Use Among Youth (2019), *Centers for Disease Control and Prevention Web-site*, April 9.

Section 2
Netnography Territorialized

5

Netnography in the Healthcare and Nursing Sector

Martin Salzmann-Erikson and Henrik Eriksson

SOCIAL MEDIA'S EVOLUTION INTO HEALTHCARE SETTINGS

As depicted in other chapters in this book looking into how social media and the web have changed our opportunities to socialize with others, we will examine how social media have evolved as regards health-related matters. As the Internet and all the resources connected to a virtual community were becoming one of the public's main sources of health information, a shift in the relation between health-seekers and health professionals was becoming a fact. Health professionals and the institutions they worked in were no longer the first authorities people reached out to when they wanted information on their health concerns. As the resources grew on Internet forums, a plethora of social media "experts" entered the arena previously dominated by elite professional nurses, whose point of departure is an institutional healthcare setting. Suddenly, the Internet had created possibilities for people to become their own nurse and health expert. It not only enabled people to gather information for themselves and on their own health issues, but it also, more importantly, allowed people to make sense of their experiences and to become self-perceived, self-lived "experts" on their own conditions. The Internet and new open-access policies made scholarly information on health available to everyone connected to these resources. On the Internet, this new kind of expert could use scholarly information, facts, and figures to give advice as well as the first-hand experience of a self-perceived notion of illness/sickness to share with anyone who would listen. For the first time, it is now possible to anonymously reach out to others in a similar situation without first passing through an association or an institution. For healthcare institutions and their agents, decentralization of information is often conceived of as a threat to their hegemonic position. How many times haven't we seen health professionals on TV delegitimize freely available information, advice, and remedies?

How Are Social Media Relevant to Nursing?

For healthcare, in general, and nursing, in particular, this paradigmatic shift from analog to digital care also meant trying to get a grip on what knowledge to share, how and when health-seekers should receive information as well as trying to maintain perceptions of health professionals as the experts by creating their own social media platforms. In parallel, health-seekers built their own health resources in the public domain of social media. This new situation was eventually brought to light by scholars in the nursing field. During the past decade, the Internet as a tool for distributing surveys and conducting interviews has been elaborated upon, but the overall scope of nursing research concerned what was happening in clinical and healthcare institutions. When the trajectory and patterns of the new experts that organized themselves through social media also revealed a distinct power shift, a growing interest in these new arenas was also starting to appear in nursing practice as well as research. To understand the use of netnography in nursing and healthcare and its implications, we believe we must first clarify and look at some of the roots in nursing as well as put things in context. Nursing research is framed by four cornerstones: human, environment/space, health, and care/caring/nursing. Given that all four of these concepts are inherent in activities on social media and the Web, why on earth would it not be relevant for nursing to use netnography as a methodology?

HISTORY OF ETHNOGRAPHY AND NETNOGRAPHY IN HEALTHCARE

While other disciplines saw the potential of adopting the epistemological orientation from anthropology already in the 1950s (Spindler & Spindler, 2000), in the wake of this nursing was still occupied with serving the medical tradition and its anthropocentric ideas. One of the first nursing researchers to incorporate the tenets of anthropology into nursing was Madeleine Leininger, with her publication from the late 1960s entitled "Ethnoscience: a promising research approach to improve nursing practice" (Leininger, 1969). During the following years, more researchers in the field published ethnographies (Field, 1983; Parker & Germain, 1980). Messerschmidt (1982) saw the potential of taking turns in anthropology by conducting ethnographic work "at home," which has the advantages of easier access to the field, requiring fewer resources, and making translation easier. Thus, ethnographic work in nursing has been published, with topics including the privacy and dignity of cancer patients, nursing in a pediatric intensive care ward, and nursing on an acute stroke ward. This being said, nursing has struggled for some time to try to separate itself from medical dominance. Even so, the breakout meant that other methodologies, such as ethnography, were beginning to be used, but entering the digital world and netnography posed yet another challenge. One might think the step from ethnography to netnography is small, perhaps even a natural step? In our view, this is correct; nursing has historically been skeptical about the artificial.

Nursing and Technology

Thus, as we addressed previously, for decades nursing has invested its rhetoric and research in the pronounced conservative world of ideas of a medical paradigm. Nursing has regarded research as a complement to this medical gaze, seeking to unveil the natural order and the origin of caring. In this quest, cultural development in general technological advancement specifically has been thought to work against this "natural care." This orientation toward "nature" and the idea that there is a nature governing the interactions and laws of caring relations has had many consequences for the research. One of them is a pronounced ambiguous relation to technology and technological development. For this reason, everything related to the Internet, cyberspace, and digitalization has been given very low priority by nurses in their practice as well as in their research. The idea that what happens in cyberspace cannot be genuine or authentic was the stance taken by nursing researchers long into the 2000s.

Understanding Human Interactions Online

During our initial and tentative steps into the world of netnography, we did not share the general view of resistance to digitization. In our view, there is a giant leap for mankind occurring in "cyberspace," involving equally paradigmatic changes in our relations as occurred to "space" itself. This must apply to nursing and health research as well. Marketing researchers, criminologists, sociologists, and pedagogues are busy building up expertise in and around interactions in cyberspace to incorporate what they know from their fields. Our posture was that nursing researchers cannot be meant to ignore this, because we were convinced of that alongside cyber-bullying and all forms of cyber-violence, there must also be different forms of cyber-nursing at hand on these virtual arenas. We wanted to capture this phenomenon and thought that netnography could give us a set of principles with which to do so. How people live their lives online, socialize on social media, and how they use the Web to inform themselves in a way that may affect their health have been vastly overlooked in our field. Researchers in nursing have been left behind, and are still only on the verge of seeing the value of investigating what is happening online – even though nursing claims to adopt a holistic and person-centered approach. As we previously mentioned with regard to the cornerstones of nursing, we argue that natural settings also need to include spaces in which people act and live: cyberspace.

OUR CONTRIBUTION TO AND PATH TOWARD NETNOGRAPHY IN NURSING

We began planning a joint study. One mantra in research is that the research question should guide the choice of methodology and methods, but in this case, we did just the opposite. Our intention was to conduct an original study based on "ethnographic observations" on an Internet forum, but we did not have a specific research question or a topic. During this time, the French Poly Implant Prothese (PIP) scandal was being fueled in the mass media. Briefly, the scandal concerned the rupturing silicone breast implants made of cheap materials that had been used for over 20 years in plastic surgery. One prominent issue for the women involved was their uncertainty as to where to turn to discuss their worries. Some voices argued that this issue should not burden the public healthcare budget. On the contrary, the women were responsible for their own "bad decision" to alter their bodies. This was our ontological point of departure for further investigating where the women turned for support. Although Sweden has a public healthcare system that is accessible to all citizens on equal terms regardless of income or insurance, reconstructive surgery (i.e., implants) is not considered a healthcare matter, as long as it is not related to pathology or malignancy. Thus, women who were emotionally affected by the PIP scandal and wanted to remove implants were not able to turn to the public healthcare system. Furthermore, a review of the literature showed that little research had been done on women's emotional health in relation to plastic surgery. Hence, in our determination to use the "novel" research approach of netnography, this was our point of departure. When we presented our study, we concluded and framed our understanding from first netnographic work by introducing the concept of torrenting into a healthcare and nursing. The torrenting concept is commonly used in computer science to refer to peer-to-peer applications that contribute to distribute vast data traffic over the Internet. Torrenting is a kind of peer-to-peer sharing technology where a number of users can connect and share their files rather than being dependent on a source. The strength of such protocols is that they enable information to swarm in multiple directions, in direct contrast to traditional, nonmultitasking one-to-one communication protocols. We saw a similar structure in the information flow among the posters in health forums and used this concept as an overall term for the flow or swarm of information among posters. These seemingly technical terms were very applicable to describing what happens through the self-care activity in the forum. For example, culturally specific knowledge of how to complain when a surgery fails, for example, was seeded by first-hand experience, and this knowledge could be further reproduced among other posters. By linking personal experiences of treatment and healthcare – strategies used to gain greater anecdotal knowledge about different situations – the posters learned from each other through this torrenting activities. In doing this, they also developed the courage to take the steps needed regarding their own procedures (Salzmann-Erikson & Eriksson, 2011). We also understood that the torrenting primarily was a tenet of self-care activity but also has considerable value for observers in the forum and that it this was an important mechanism to describe. The intermittent nature and irregularity of the forum activities means that a posted question generates answers from other posters along different timelines according to their own experience of the phenomenon in focus. Torrenting meant that users simultaneously can be the agents and the objects of action that came. This came to be important for the further advancement of our insight that we will speak more about later in the chapter. Understanding the great potential of applying netnography in our field, we were ready to take the step of introducing our understanding to a broader public.

Strategies for Moving Netnographic Method into the Field of Nursing

Nursing research is a very closed field of knowledge production; one might call it a gated community. The trust and interest in what is going on outside, especially in the social and human sciences, is rather low, and there is great skepticism when it comes to conceptual and methodological development. There are remarkable processes that must be completed before netnography can be fully adopted in nursing research, where new methods often need to be blessed by the nursing community before being adopted to their full potential. As we described earlier, throughout history nurses have been supervised, mentored, and disciplined by the predominant medical/positivist paradigm. With this history in mind, nursing researchers are constantly rehearsing how to count correctly, dose correctly, read manuals correctly, and behave correctly in general. This is part of the academic training that, over time, becomes a fully integrated part of who a nurse is. This training also applies to us, and sometimes, for example when writing this chapter, we have become acutely aware of it. These ideas about "the proper way" of doing things spill over into the scientific work as a whole as well as the scientific methods chosen. In nursing, when papers are being peer-reviewed there is a fetish-like attraction to the methods sections; comments abound concerning whether a given method has been used in the proper manner.

Proper Ways of Doing Nursing Research

With this said, we knew that moving a method developed by Kozinets (2002) in consumer and market research into the field of nursing and health would undeniably raise many questions for nursing researchers, who tend to scrutinize papers in relation to well-known and "correct" methods manuals in the field. This was a problem for us, and we discussed how to further popularize the ideas of Kozinets in the field of nursing, while developing our knowledge at the same time. We knew from previous scholarly work that one way to do this was to engage with a method developed within this gated community. We also knew that the rite of passage for new methods was that they often needed to pass be employed by nursing scholars before being used by other researchers in the field. Overall, we tend to think that this is also related to the fact that the work nurses perform is licensed. Nurses are registered; they have a duty to promote health, address health concerns, and minimize chronic health conditions. For this reason, nursing as a field of knowledge, a set of methods and a research discipline is influenced by the perception that nursing is an "extended arm" of the physician and medical knowledge. Experimenting with these questions concerning netnography as a method and what our next step would be to advance it in nursing, we came up with a standard concept to bring netnography inside our gated community. We wrote our own methods article (Salzmann-Erikson & Eriksson, 2012). We might have been the first to do this, but we did not want to be the last. We were soon followed by Witney, Hendricks and Cope (2015), who made a step-by-step contribution to nursing by explaining Kozinets' framework and how it should be used in nursing research. We made a new attempt in 2014, expanding our discussion on cyberspace as a source of data, including the ethical, ontological, and epistemological issues related to nursing (Salzmann-Erikson & Eriksson, 2015). We were later followed by Burles and Bally (2018). So, the rite of passage for netnography follows a standard pattern. Netnography is in the process of being adopted by nursing researchers – a process in which they implement and rewrite the concepts themselves.

CONVERSATIONS ABOUT HEALTH ON SOCIAL MEDIA

In real-time or off-line discussions, one naturally replies, answers, reacts, or responds immediately. This is not necessarily the case in forum discussions, as long time intervals may occur pass between a post and a reply. Based on our analysis of interactions, we noticed that some topics of conversations were answered rather immediately, while others remained totally unanswered. However, the third type of replies or threads was especially interesting, because they did not follow the sequential logical order expected in conversations or discussions. As explained earlier, we address this phenomenon using the term torrenting activities in what we have labeled as cyber-nursing. Traditional off-line nursing is associated with words such as compassion, caring, commitment, competence, courage, and communication. We began to understand that netnography might increase our understanding of how people express caring and support online. In the next section, we will present some insights gained through these netnographic understandings.

Caring Support on Social Media

To begin with, one of the most interesting questions for the nursing researcher is support. Our initial question when approaching the plethora of healthcare websites and communities therefore concerned support: What kind of support is offered on these forums that traditional offline advice does not address? Almost a decade after first framing this question, we can conclude that the "support studies" conducted have addressed new patterns with regard to why people seek support on the Internet. For example, looking at the support new fathers offer each other in cyberspace, we concluded that sharing concerns is very different from contacts with formal healthcare providers:

> What should I do? It feels a bit like whatever I do and
> whenever I do it – it just turns out wrong, wrong,
> wrong. The only positive thing to come of this is that I
> have a wonderful son who I love more than life. He is
> so wonderful, so happy, so spirited and mischievous!
> "Erik_the_DAD"
> Reply:
> You are a great partner and father who gives everything
> for his family!
> "Hyde"
> (Eriksson & Salzmann-Erikson, 2013b, 3)

To analyze these types of communication between "Erik_the_DAD" and "Hyde," one has to put oneself in their position, both using one's own experiences but also bracketing preconceptions about proper forms of support based on strict nursing manuals. As illustrated in the above conversation, the requested and received support was focused on handling caregiving in everyday life. For some of the fathers, sharing their concerns was also a way of "letting off steam." A lot of things are happening that might not occur in traditional support. Interpreting the human world of health and illness in relation to support is related to the methodological task of searching for clues in human interaction. Caring support in cyberspace can be understood as communicated encouragement, confirmation, and advice, whereas the reciprocity of skillfulness, as a *pay-it-forward principle*, is crucial to understanding the motivation underlying support connected to self-care in digital arenas. Staying abreast of activity on an Internet support forum even after one's own health concerns have been addressed gives expert status that was previously non-existent. By presenting oneself as a role model for others, one can use self-perceived experiences to promote one's expert status within the realm of social media support. Further, we have also shown how social media offer a link to resources "outside the home" that should not be underestimated as a vital ingredient when taking part in health forums (Eriksson, Salzmann-Erikson, & Pringle, 2014). In Bridges, Howell and Schmied's (2018) study of breastfeeding support in Facebook groups, similar results concerning sought and given support were found to validate and elaborate on the same elements. Alongside information, there is an emotional and authentic presence approach that online environments provide that is unique in relation to traditional analog support. From netnography, we have learned that cyber-nursing overcomes the inherent limitations that a nurse-patient relation can never escape, owing to the idea of "a professional stance" – also a legacy from the positivist idea of *keeping a distance*.

Different Styles of Expressing Caring and Support Among Peers in Cyberspace

The licensed nurse is educated, trained, and has years of clinical practice in addressing patients in need of support. Nurses can be humble, caring, comforting as well as rude, paternalistic, and insensitive. But what characterizes peers who discuss health issues online? Are there any similarities with educated registered nurse? Or does it even matter? One characteristic is seen in those who reply to posts by saying how things ought to be and providing straight answers; they are driven by solutions and write long posts about their opinions. We call them "the keyboard cowboys." Perhaps the readers have met one? These keyboard cowboys educate others, act superior, are highly visible and sometimes use capitals to stress their "outstanding expertise." There are also other ways to express one's expertise, for example by being a cyber-aid. This archetype could be said to be the opposite of the cowboy. The cyber-aid is an active listener, humble and understanding, spreading warmth, and acknowledging concerns. In some sense, cyber-aids create a kind of You-I relationship and enforce their engagement by adding emoticons:

Oh dear! Poor you, tough break! Broke out in a cold sweat as I was reading, what an ordeal you are going through right now. Hope your tummy has calmed down a bit now. Stay calm and at home and let the healing process do its job. Then I must say that it is incredibly beautiful and inspiring to read your posts. Thanks for letting us go along for the ride. ☺
(Eriksson & Salzmann-Erikson, 2013a, 338)

Table 5.1 Key Features of Cyber-Nursing Archetypes

Keyboard cowboy	*Cyber-aid*	*Health interest trader*
Solution-driven	Humble	Objective
Objective/subjective	Confirming	Intermediate knowledge
Confident	Subjective	Educational
Active writer	Listening	Gives perspectives
Expressing their own view, based on their own preferences	Acknowledges others' view	Provides a balanced position
Wordy	Soothing	Instructive
Self-oriented	Relation-driven	Fact-driven

In addition to the cowboy and the aid, there is a third archetype who expresses expertise by trading health interests. They use themselves as links between the online discussion and the plethora of available information sources on other parts of the Web. They use themselves as a link to transform information from somewhere else and contextualize it to the specific health issue (see Table 5.1).

We can think of virtual communities and virtual self-care as a platform and an environment for those seeking health guidance. But who will one meet? Will questions be answered by a keyboard cowboy? If one is seeking someone who can confirm fears, is it worth taking the chance of getting a reply from an insensitive keyboard cowboy? Just as when one seeks help at a hospital, the encounters with others on social media will likely be the result of random events. As previously described, we coined the concept "torrenting" to capture these activities, the flow of exchanging information. Torrenting elaborates on how cyber-nursing users can simultaneously be the agents and the objects of action as well as on how one's own nursing expertise is built into the virtual environment by offering support, confirmation, and encouragement. By constructing these three archetypes, we not only developed our own understanding of caring in cyberspace, but we also began to question the notion of support, which is a key concept in nursing.

Understanding support in online environments is and has been a crucial ontological starting point for nursing research. In fact, this is the crucial motivation for embracing and utilizing netnography in the discipline. Support is to nursing research what the consumer is to marketing research when it comes to social media cultures and nursing science's understanding of online human behavior. We have consciously elaborated on this in relation to the concept of cyber-nursing to advance our understanding, and by doing so we address the health patterns of this digital era (Eriksson & Salzmann-Erikson, 2016). We believe that the concept of cyber-nursing frames nursing competence in relation to the "self" and others, something that is ongoing on social media via the Internet; we also believe that our understanding of this phenomenon is still very premature and that much remains to be done.

PARADIGMATIC CHANGES FOR NURSING

By elaborating on this further, we can also predict what the vast digitalization of healthcare in everyday life and in health institutions means in relation to paradigmatic changes for nursing. For example, the utilization of smart phones, tablets, and computers with social media programs, the online availability of medical journals, SMS, e-mail, cameras, and GPS functions in healthcare all provide opportunities for people to take action in an effort to optimize their health without any healthcare providers present. We can also predict that the use of technology has a generational aspect. The so-called digital generation, born around or after the millennium, has grown up surrounded by digital devices. This generation does not have any reference to a time before this paradigm of digital living and, on a whole, possesses computer technology knowledge that surpasses that of older generations. For this reason, the interest in technological and digital aspects of caring/nursing is likely to increase on its own. When addressing these evolving technological and digital aspects of health and nursing, netnography will be a crucial tool in the methodological toolbox.

Netnography in the Nursing Toolbox

When overviewing the bulk of the research on health and nursing research during the past decade, we conclude that a range of questions has been addressed utilizing netnography. The topic of concern can be positioned in relation to different ambitions and contexts. There is also a forceful and subversive element of the netnography method to consider, beyond it merely being another method in the researcher's toolbox. Netnography is taking up a new aspect of forecasting previously unknown to this field. We now live in a time where changes and ideas are moving very rapidly around the globe and where the distance from idea to implementation can be very short. For this reason, shared perceptions and attitudes on social media now have, more than ever before, an important impact on perceptions of care and caring practices. By monitoring Twitter discussions on social media, coming trends can be predicted. For example, there is an ongoing discussion in social media about nursing robotics in care of the elderly. Based on our analyses of these discussions, we concluded that most postings come from metropolitan areas around the globe, focusing on market-driven, science fiction solutions for elderly care and the functional, psychological, and social aspects of robots in nursing care (Eriksson & Salzmann-Erikson, 2018). From this, many conclusions can be drawn. Regarding methods, and most importantly in relation to this presentation, using netnography to monitor social media can provide valuable insights into current attitudes as well as forecast coming trends. We found that Twitter users overall seem to have positive attitudes toward using various nursing robots in elderly care, and we will soon see robots in nursing care practice (Salzmann-Erikson & Eriksson, 2018a). Netnography offers a window through which to study a foreseeable future, as social media are forums on which corporations, healthcare institutions, researchers, and universities as well as private citizens worldwide share thoughts, links, and pictures. Our experience, based on conducting multiple netnographic studies, is that social media offer a great opportunity for nursing science to proactively position a critical attitude toward upcoming technological changes before they are implemented (Eriksson & Salzmann-Erikson, 2017).

I Share, Therefore I am

"I share, therefore I am" has a core meaning on social media that is important to understand in relation to ongoing digitalization. Based on our study (Salzmann-Erikson & Eriksson, 2018b) of messages PhD students from all over the world shared about their life, we concluded that social media provide a "metacurriculum" that exists above and beyond any locally defined PhD syllabus and that is active in the PhD students' global social communities and culture. This is one example of how netnography provides opportunities to analyze power structures and space claims on social media. By sharing and comparing social discipline and conformity, any local setting can be reflected upon and sometimes challenged. This sharing, as exemplified among PhD students above, is the same among people sharing health concerns on social media. Social discipline and conformity in relation to how to act as a patient and/or what to expect in relation to services are challenged by the shared meta-understanding that is developed through the comparison enabled by social media. The support given and taken on social media therefore also includes questions about how the power structures operating in everyday life are reinforced or challenged by structures within the realm of social media. For example, we have seen how a forum dominated by men can also be a marketplace of homosocial competition, tending to assume an "all-male world" in discussions among participants (Eriksson et al., 2014). Similarly, Salzmann-Erikson's (2016a) netnography studying YouTube videos of nursing homes concluded that residents' spaces are not value-neutral, but rather artifacts and milieus where ways of exercising discipline according to hierarchical power orders are played out. By developing these understanding about power structures, netnography has made a crucial contribution to the ability of nursing and health researchers to grasp and analyze different, diverse, and coexisting power structures within virtual reality itself, but also those existing within institutions and their analog arenas. We have also seen how health professionals in psychiatric intensive care adopted a dominant position on Twitter postings, while patients and relatives could use Twitter to share their negative experience as well as geotagging to express their continued existence and to provide relief from the burden of confinement and boost their own self-position in relation to the institution through self-disclosure (Salzmann-Erikson, 2016b). The analysis of power structures in relation to significant phenomena in nursing is an area of development as we move forward with netnographic approaches in nursing.

Social Media and Suffering

We know that suffering is an important phenomenon in nursing. Nursing care is continually connected to suffering and work to alleviate suffering in various forms. There is a large body of knowledge on caring and how to alleviate suffering that relates to practices in institutional and analog arenas. Especially the Nordic countries have made crucial contributions to understanding suffering within healthcare and nursing sciences (Eriksson, 1994). However, the downsides of advanced media technologies are that they also include new forms of ill health and suffering that emerge due to the increased prevalence of a digital lifestyle. These new forms of suffering, often called "mediated" and "distant" suffering, will be an increasingly important part of netnographic research within the healthcare and nursing sciences. There is a greater need for new insights into the experiences of distant suffering that advanced media technologies create. For example, one benefit of media technologies is that the younger generations were able to coordinate a global strike protesting climate change. Their anxiety about their dystopian future living on a much hotter planet and the health burdens and suffering connected to global warming – including strategies for mitigating it – are questions that need a great deal of attention from the nursing and health sciences during the decades to come to address this broader picture of health in a digital world. In the following section, we present some suggestions for those who wish to get started doing social media research in nursing.

GET STARTED WITH SOCIAL MEDIA RESEARCH: SIX SUGGESTIONS

First of all, we encourage you to reflect on whether your area of interest corresponds to the focus of institutions or to lived experiences. Is your interest in focusing on people's attitudes and experience of care or is it the experience of a given condition, symptom, coping strategies, burden, or experience of loss that you wish to investigate? Is your research question a matter of institutional interest? Or are your questions more related to the domain of self-care?

What are your intentions? What or who will be the "subject" of the study? It may be that a researcher wants to explore online discussions of mental health among refugees during their period of arrival in the destination country. However, if a home healthcare scholar in nursing wishes to contribute to the theory of hope and suffering among patients on a palliative ward, netnography may not be appropriate to this research question. Thus, although we do encourage all nursing scholars to expand their use of netnography, all research questions are not suitable for this methodology.

Next, based on your established objectives and research questions, it is time to locate the digital arena for your specific inquiry. Depending on the nature of your topic, you may wish to study the phenomena of interest in a specific geographic area, or on a global level. Social media analytics software can be highly useful in locating where your specific topic is actively discussed online, and what social media platforms are the most active. Moreover, Sentiment Analysis can provide you with information on attitudes and thus guide you in the research process. Is Twitter, Tumblr, or Instagram the most probable platform for your topics to be posted and discussed on, or is it more likely you will find it on vlogs on YouTube or in old-fashioned blogs? Even though an influencer might have more followers on Instagram, the reciprocity of exchanged information and responses might be found in YouTube comments.

Yet another key aspect of research design is ethical considerations. There are numerous publications discussing and debating the ethical considerations to be made in netnographic studies. One good piece of advice is to adhere to national and universal regulations and to seek approval from an ethics committee if the research is to be considered human subjects research. Regarding, regarding ethical considerations, clarity regarding the following areas is recommended: (a) to what extent the site, postings, and the avatar should be exploited, (b) will there be any kind of interaction between you, the researcher, and the posters, (c) will the data comprise personal information that may be associated with the posters, and (d) will the data concern the posters' health. Lastly, always do careful preparation before investing time and resources in a research project.

Six Bullet Points to Consider Prior to a Netnographic Inquiry in Nursing and Health

- What area of nursing are you interested in?
- Is the matter local or global?
- Where can you locate the information? What kinds of platforms will you use?
- What are the ethical aspects to take into consideration?
- What are your objectives? Subjective experiences or institutional matters?
- Who are the stakeholder(s)?

The Future of Netnography in Nursing

As depicted in our overview of netnographic studies in health and nursing, the contexts in which netnographies are conducted vary from diabetes care and mental health to elderly care. However, nursing specializations are numerous, and on a list from *Nurse Journal*, no fewer than 106 specializations are presented ("100+ Awesome Nursing Specializations," n.d.). While most of these specializations have not been the subject of netnographic inquiries, there are plenty of opportunities, for example, in rheumatology, rheumatology nursing, refugee nursing, private sector nursing, infection control nursing, and legal consultant nursing, to mention a few. Moreover, we suggest that netnography is suitable when: (1) studying support in regulated self-care digital arenas, (2) investigating healthcare and nursing, (3) deepening knowledge in the healthcare information shared on digital arenas, (4) describing healthcare and nursing depictions in viral communities, (5) analyzing structures/power within institutions, (6) analyzing implications for institutional practices, and, lastly, (7) when researchers wish to extend knowledge in education and forecasting studies of institutional changes due to digital developments. Whether all of the above seven areas are applicable in all 106 specializations is beyond our ability to determine. Thus, we encourage nursing researchers to reflect on and evaluate whether their specializations and fields of research could benefit from an Internet-based approach, as this would make a substantial contribution to the existing body of knowledge.

REFERENCES

100+ Awesome Nursing Specializations. (n.d.). Retrieved October 12, 2019, from https://nursejournal. org/articles/awesome-nursing-specialities-you-should-know/

Bridges, N., Howell, G., & Schmied, V. (2018). Exploring breastfeeding support on social media. *International Breastfeeding Journal*, 13(22), 1–9. https://doi.org/10.1186/s13006-018-0166-9

Burles, M. C., & Bally, J. M. G. (2018). Ethical, practical, and methodological considerations for unobtrusive qualitative research about personal narratives shared on the Internet, 17, 1–9. *International Journal of Qualitative Methods*. https://doi.org/10.1177/1609406918788203

Eriksson, H., & Salzmann-Erikson, M. (2013a). Cyber nursing-health "experts" approaches in the post-modern era of virtual performances: A nethnography study. *International Journal of Nursing Studies*, 50(3), 335–344. https://doi.org/10.1016/j.ijnurstu.2012.09.014

Eriksson, H., & Salzmann-Erikson, M. (2013b). Supporting a caring fatherhood in cyberspace – an analysis of communication about caring within an online forum for fathers. *Scandinavian Journal of Caring Sciences*, 27(1), 63–69. https://doi.org/10.1111/j.1471-6712.2012.01001.x

Eriksson, H., & Salzmann-Erikson, M. (2016). Cyber nursing: A conceptual framework. *Journal of Research in Nursing*, 21(7), 505–514. https://doi.org/10.1177/1744987116661378

Eriksson, H., & Salzmann-Erikson, M. (2017). The digital generation and nursing robotics: A netnographic study about nursing care robots posted on social media. *Nursing Inquiry*, 24(2). https://doi.org/10.1111/nin.12165

Eriksson, H., & Salzmann-Erikson, M. (2018). Twitter discussions about the predicaments of robots in geriatric nursing: Forecast of nursing robotics in aged care. *Contemporary Nurse*, 54(1), 97–107. https://doi.org/10.1080/10376178.2017.1364972

Eriksson, H., Salzmann-Erikson, M., & Pringle, K. (2014). Virtual impossible men: Privacy and invisibility as forms of privilege in online venues for fathers during early parenthood. *Culture, Society and Masculinities*, 6(1), 52–68. https://doi.org/10.3149/CSM.0601.52

Eriksson, K. (1994). *Den lidande människan [Eng. The suffering human]*. Åbo: Liber.

Field, P. A. (1983). An ethnography: Four public health nurses' perspectives of nursing. *Journal of Advanced Nursing*, 8, 3–12. https://doi.org/10.1111/j.1365-2648.1983.tb00284.x

Kozinets, R. V. (2002). The field behind the screen: Using netnography for marketing research in online communities. *Journal of Marketing Research*, 39(1), 61–72, https://doi.org/10.1509/jmkr.39.1.61.18935

Leininger, M. (1969). Ethnoscience a peomising research approach to improve nursing practice. *Image*, 3: 2–8. https://doi.org/10.1111/j.1547-5069.1969.tb01066.x

Messerschmidt, D. A. (1982). On anthropology "at home." In D. A. Messerschmidt (Ed.), *Anthropologists at home in North America: Methods and issues in the study of one's own society* (pp. 3–15), Cambridge: Cambridge University Press.

Parker, R., & Germain, C. (1980). The cancer unit: An ethnography. *The American Journal of Nursing*, 80(10), 1897–1898. https://doi.org/10.2307/3462480

Salzmann-Erikson, M. (2016a). Space invaders – A netnographic study of how artefacts in nursing home environments exercise disciplining structures. *Nursing Inquiry*, 23(2), 138–147. https://doi.org/10.1111/nin.12125

Salzmann-Erikson, M. (2016b). Virtual communication about psychiatric intensive care units: Social actor representatives claim space on Twitter. *International Journal of Mental Health Nursing*, 26(4) 366–374. https://doi.org/10.1111/inm.12253

Salzmann-Erikson, M., & Eriksson, H. (2011). Torrenting values, feelings, and thoughts – cyber nursing and virtual self-care in a breast augmentation forum. *International Journal of Qualitative Studies on Health and Well-Being*, 6(4). https://doi.org/10.3402/qhw.v6i4.7378

Salzmann-Erikson, M., & Eriksson, H. (2012). LiLEDDA – a six step forum-based netnographic research method for nursing and caring sciences. *Aporia*, 4(4), 8–19. https://doi.org/10.18192/aporia.v4i4.2903

Salzmann-Erikson, M., & Eriksson, H. (2015). Research data from cyberspace: Analyses and guidelines from caring science epistemology. *Nordic Journal of Nursing Research*, 35(2), 91–97. https://doi.org/10.1177/0107408315571501

Salzmann-Erikson, M., & Eriksson, H. (2018a). Absorbability, applicability and availability in nursing and care robots: A thematic analysis of Twitter postings. *Telematics and Informatics*, 35(5), 1553–1560. https://doi.org/10.1016/j.tele.2018.04.001

Salzmann-Erikson, M., & Eriksson, H. (2018b). PhD students' presenting, staging and announcing their educational status – an analysis of shared images in social media. *Computers and Education*, 116, 237–243. https://doi.org/10.1016/j.compedu.2017.09.012

Spindler, G., & Spindler, L. (2000). *Fifty years of anthropology and education, 1950–2000: A Spindler anthology*. Mahwah, NJ: Lawrence Erlbaum 202 Assoc. Publishers.

Witney, C., Hendricks, J., & Cope, V. (2015). The specialist breast care nurse's role in the identification and minimisation of distress in a members' only, breast cancer focused online support community. *International Journal of Nursing & Clinical Practices*, 2, 139. https://doi.org/10.15344/2394-4978/2015/139

6

Netnography in a Military Context
Ethical Considerations

Donna L. Schuman, Donald L. Schuman,
Natalie Pope, and Amy Johnson

The military is globally recognized for having a distinct and highly unique culture. Service in the Armed Forces permeates many aspects of life, not only for its members but for all connected to the military community. The military has embraced the digital sphere, using social media networks to communicate with others, seek support, and tell stories of their experiences. Unique aspects of military culture influence how members engage online. Previous research has shown the military community can be challenging to access directly, and, as such, the study of the military through online methods has proven appealing. Kozinets' (2020) netnography provides a useful framework for studying the digital interactions of military-connected communities.

Netnography, introduced by Kozinets (1997) when the Internet was still inchoate, has grown exponentially over the past two decades to solidify into a well-formed method of inquiry with clear guidelines and practices for understanding culture-sharing groups through their social media interactions and artifacts, or online "social traces" (Kozinets, 2020, p. 317). This chapter defines military netnography as the application of netnographic methods to military populations. Despite the benefits of a military netnography approach, a literature search revealed only five published studies applied a true netnographic method, and a sixth is in progress. This chapter explores these six studies in detail, paying particular attention to the ethical aspects of the studies. One of the most defining elements of netnography lies in its focus on ethical considerations.

Attention to research ethics is especially important for those studying military populations due to the vulnerability of military communities, the prevalence of insider researchers, and concerns regarding cybersecurity. This chapter explores the literature on the use of netnography as a method of inquiry for understanding military communities through online social traces. It critically discusses the steps undertaken by military researchers to address ethical considerations, drawing on global studies and examples. The chapter demonstrates that despite the key role ethics plays in netnographic projects and the higher degree of risk associated with the military population, few researchers discuss their ethical considerations in planning and undertaking netnography. Building on this, the chapter discusses ethical issues and recommendations in the context of military netnography: recruitment and enrollment of participants, informed consent, protection of privacy and confidentiality, deception and avoidance of harm, participant safety, and researcher risk. This chapter makes suggestions for researchers engaging in military netnography based on the findings of the literature search as well as the authors' own experience in the field.

MILITARY CULTURE

Cultural understanding and awareness are defining aspects of the ethnographic method, whether traditional or digital. As such, it is critical to reflect on military culture. While military communities around the world differ in ways that reflect the peoples, subcultures, values, and governments of individual countries, military communities across the globe share many commonalities. Military service profoundly shapes the world views of those who serve and their family members who support them during training, relocations, and deployments. Even within the overarching military culture, each military unit has a distinct subculture, mission, history, and set of core values, but all share the common goal of instilling strong character and promoting morale and wellbeing in military members (Department of Veterans Affairs [VA], 2013).

In many aspects, military members can relate to each other in ways that cut across international boundaries and differ from their civilian counterparts. For example, unlike U.S. civilians who may hold Western individualistic values, such as prizing freedom and self-reliance, U.S. military communities are based on tightly knit, cohesive groups who prize performing one's duty, giving up individual liberties for the good of the mission, and selfless service (non-Western values).

Such a strong military culture requires its members to follow both explicit and implicit expectations that permeate all aspects of life for its members. The military adopts a "Warrior Ethos" – a universally understood code that ensures group cohesion, and therefore, survival (Department of the Army, 2013; Pressfield, 2011). This credo includes placing the mission first, displaying mental and physical toughness and courage, not letting one's nation, unit, leaders, or subordinates down, and showing willingness to sacrifice their lives for love of country. Adherence to military attitudes is strong in part because failure to conform to the rules and expectations of military service may jeopardize the mission, risk harm to comrades, or result in expulsion (Kuehner, 2013).

Service members are far more likely than civilians to form their identities around their jobs and roles in their units. The military is organized hierarchically around a chain of command, with a "commander" at the helm, charged with fulfilling the mission and maintaining good order and discipline in the troops. In civilian sectors, an employer may have authority over a person during working hours, but for active-duty service members, their commander has a paternalistic authority over them and is responsible for their conduct, whether they are on duty or not. Active military members, who are called upon to separate their civic rights from the uniforms they wear, are limited in individual freedoms afforded civilians. For example, although U.S. service members are encouraged to vote, they are prohibited from active engagement in partisan politics and attending such events in uniform (Peterson, 2019). Likewise, the perception of Australian Defence as an impartial and non-political force is considered sacrosanct, as was demonstrated by the level of public support given to Australian Defence Chief Angus Campbell when he moved military officers away from a televised political discussion (Greene, 2019).

Military family members often incorporate the values and principles of military service and display high levels of resilience, patriotism, and civic duty (Hall, 2016). Military authority over members also indirectly extends to the service members' families due to the commander's influence over the service member who can be held accountable for their family members' conduct (Halvorson, 2010). Command paternalism is one factor that contributes to loss of an individual civilian identity for military partners (Higate & Cameron, 2004; Jessup, 2000). Even after leaving active military service, veterans and their families may continue to uphold the deeply engrained values, principles, and codes of conduct to which they adhered during military service. Some may also continue to struggle with lingering effects of combat or other forms of military-related trauma that can manifest in various ways across the lifespan.

Although military service confers a plethora of benefits to those who serve, including opportunities for travel and adventure, education, enhanced maturity, discipline, leadership skills, resilience, and camaraderie (VA, 2015), it also entails significant hardships due to the unique challenges associated with military life, such as deployments and relocations. Compared to their civilian counterparts, military populations are at higher risk for physical (Levy & Sidel, 2009) and behavioral health disorders (Bein et al., 2019), as well as for multiple forms of social isolation (Wilson et al., 2018). During service, military personnel are subject to difficulties that may include physical exertion in extreme environments, austere living conditions, exposure to chemical hazards, threats of injury and death, and geographical separations from family, friends, and community. Family members may experience frequent and extended separations, relocations, deployment-related stressors, illness/injury/death of a loved one, and vicarious traumatization (i.e., indirect trauma occurring through exposure to combat-related memories and emotions; Hall, 2016). In a study of 56 wives of veterans with posttraumatic stress disorder (PTSD) in Croatia, one-third met criteria for secondary traumatic stress (Frančišković et al., 2007).

Distinct aspects of offline military culture, as outlined here, influence how members of military communities around the world engage using social media. Broadly, the military community has embraced digital technology for the many advantages offered by Internet communication. Next, we will expand on our discussion of military culture to consider how the unique features of this culture shape the way service members engage with others via social media.

MILITARY AND SOCIAL MEDIA

The Internet emerged from work during the 1950–1960 Cold War Era to ensure the U.S. Department of Defense (DOD) could maintain communications during the event of a nuclear war (Bryant, 2016). Unparalleled in its power as a research tool, the Internet contains a vast repository of data that researchers can use to gain a deeper understanding of culture-sharing groups previously difficult to access. The historical convergence of the advent of Web 2.0 (the "social" web characterized by user-generated content and social media) in the early 2000s with the U.S.-initiated Global War on Terror in 2001, has ignited interest into the study of the social media traces of military communities.

Service members, veterans, and their families use the Internet and various forms of social media to connect with others, seek support, cope with the demands of military life (Talkington, 2011), and share their experiences, as well as to communicate with friends and loved ones during times of separation (Robbins, 2007; Schuman et al., 2018). Also, members of the Armed Forces have used social media networks to provide accurate portrayals of war or to maintain electronic war diaries (Robbins, 2007). More recently, war veterans are using the Internet to engage in outreach and advocacy on topics of concern to the military community, such as military suicide and the lack of mental health services for veterans (Schuman et al., 2018).

Persons not counted among the military population may also seek out online groups formed around a military interest, becoming members of a military-focused community. These groups are popular among persons who may have worked as civilian contractors during war or worked on a military installation in the U.S. or overseas (e.g., *Landstuhl LRMC, Landstuhl Regional Medical Center Alumni and Friends*). Many others are open to like-minded persons who have an interest in the topic (e.g., *Civil War Relic Hunters, Vietnam War Memorials in America*).

Not only do individual members of military communities make heavy use of social media, but military organizations around the world also maintain a strong social media presence. In efforts to reach potential recruits who are increasingly younger and more tech-savvy (Wooten et al., 2014), the DoD is on Facebook, Twitter, Instagram, YouTube, LinkedIn, Flickr, and Second Life (Department of the Army, 2013). The Australian Army Facebook page is reputed to have ten times as many followers as the country has military members (Ryan & Thompson, 2016). Social media also provides benefits to military organizations, including connecting global professional military communities, breaking through generational gaps between senior and junior military personnel, fostering greater transparency, enhancing understanding of military members' experiences, recognizing achievement, sharing operational lessons learned, and providing digital training, education, and military doctrine (Ryan & Thompson, 2016). Galvanized by mounting public health concerns around mental health challenges and escalating suicide rates in military populations, DoD and VA leaders in the U.S. are encouraging social media use as a platform for information and support (e.g., realWarriors app and forums). Also, U.S. military leaders are using social media to promote understanding and connection between civilians and their military communities and bridge the "civilian-military divide." One example of this is the DoD sponsored social media initiative (identified by the *#knowyourmil* hashtags), aimed at helping U.S. citizens get to know their military better and clear up misconceptions about military life (Lange, 2019).

Despite the positive benefits of social media, the use of social media networks by service members and families presents a threat to military organizations around the world. In addition to being a tool to wage and defend against war (Doffman, 2019) and influence political processes (Isaac & Wakabayashi, 2017), operationally sensitive information can be easily distributed. For example, social media activity reportedly compromised a planned training event in Australia when soldiers posted geotagged content on social media platforms that enabled opposing forces to ascertain their location (Wroe, 2016). This ever-persistent cybersecurity threat is ingrained in the military community and significantly impacts their online behavior and their attitudes towards researchers. With social media networks providing a rich repository of information on a population that has historically been difficult to access, researchers are turning to methods like digital ethnography to help them capture, categorize, and understand the military community.

In sum, the Internet serves a multitude of purposes for military personnel and organizations. Social media in particular provides a vehicle for service members to connect with their friends and family while abroad, supports the advocacy and outreach efforts (e.g., recruiting and public health campaigns) of military organizations, and offers a means of social support for members of various military communities. Next, we will discuss how researchers are using netnography as a strategy to understand the shared meanings and culture of military communities. Ethical considerations of conducting a military netnography are also addressed in the following sections.

MILITARY NETNOGRAPHY

Virtual communities have formed around a sense of shared meaning using a rapidly evolving array of social media platforms. Ethnographic research methods rooted in anthropology have co-evolved with technology to study the social media traces (i.e., online visual, textual, and auditory artifacts) of these culture-sharing groups. Netnography is a "form of cultural research that uses qualitative techniques to investigate social media," emphasizing the use of a set of clear, differentiated techniques and ethical practices (Kozinets, 2020, p. 6). According to Kozinets (2020), netnography differs from other forms of online ethnography in its cultural focus, reliance on social media data, immersive engagement, and praxis, as well as in its emphasis on ethical rigor. *Military netnography* is the application of netnographic research methods, as described by Kozinets (2015, 2020), to the social media traces of military communities. Owing to the proclaimed importance of ethics in netnography, this chapter looks at the ethical elements of existing studies that have applied a military netnography methodology.

Traditionally, because of the difficulty accessing military populations within the community, researchers interested in studying military populations were limited mainly to clinical samples in health care settings (Pedersen et al., 2015). Previously, researchers focused on computer-mediated communication (CMC) mainly gathered data from online forums (Im & Chee, 2012). CMC research on military communities has focused on the adjustment of military spouses to overseas posts (Blakely et al., 2014); stressors experienced by women in Marine Corps families (Jennings-Kelsall et al., 2012); relational uncertainty in military life (Knobloch et al., 2018); and advice-giving in military forums (McAninch et al., 2018). Military forums, along with Facebook, are frequently used sites of study for theses and dissertations, primarily because online data is perceived to be freely accessible. This assumption is flawed however, as this chapter will outline.

Web-based diaries known as "blogs," "vlogs," social networking sites like Facebook, and microblogging sites, such as Twitter, are rich social mediascapes for studying military culture (Highfill, 2019; Schuman et al., 2018; Sugiura et al., 2017). However, few of these studies are true netnographies focused on studying a culture-sharing group through immersion in their online interactions and artifacts. Netnographic research within military populations is still quite nascent. To date, only a handful of studies with a military focus are actually Internet ethnographies, and even fewer have explicitly identified a netnographic methodology.

A literature search reveals five studies using a netnographic methodology, as defined by Kozinets (2015), and a sixth study underway. These are investigations of an Israeli remembrance community (Gal-Ezer; 2012), Israeli ex-Prisoners of War (POWs) of the Yom Kippur War (Gal-Ezer, 2014); war heritage sites (Irimiás, & Volo, 2018), social media use by persons with PTSD (Salzmann-Erickson & Hicdurmaz, 2017), the sharing of war trauma stories on YouTube (Schuman et al., 2018), and thematic and content analyses of vlogger interviews and commenter responses to war trauma stories shared on YouTube (Schuman et al., in progress; see Table 6.1).

This chapter discusses each of these studies in terms of primary sites, aims, netnographic procedures, and ethical considerations.

In the first of these studies, Gal-Ezer (2012) utilized multimodal ethnographic and netnographic methods to examine online and offline participation and cultural artifacts from a memorial website honoring the Israeli 14th Tank Brigade veterans of the Yom Kippur War. Data included texts, artifacts, and in-depth interviews with veterans and historians. Despite the use of verbatim quotes, the researcher did not include an explicit discussion of the ethical steps undertaken in the study.

Further to this, using data collected from 2008–2014, Gal-Ezer (2014) conducted a case study of Israeli ex-POWs from the same war era. Virtual data were extracted from blogs of the ex-POWs and included a wide array of texts and artifacts. Reflecting the evolution of ethical standards within the netnographic method and emerging guidelines for making ethical decision-making more explicit, in this study, the author expressly indicated adherence to strict ethical standards for offline interviews and taking steps to protect bloggers' identities by omitting user names from quotes (Gal-Ezer 2014).

In the third study examined in this literature review, Irimiás & Volo (2018) investigated the processes through which members of history-driven Italian Facebook communities shared knowledge of World War I heritage sites located in the Triveneto region of Italy. The researchers compared user-generated content to official narratives published by destination

Table 6.1 Netnography and Military Populations

Authors	Study population	Study purpose	Data collection methods	Netnography data	Findings and future directions
Salzmann-Erikson & Hiçdurmaz (2017)	Individuals with PTSD (one participant was a Vietnam Veteran).	How social media is used to communicate narratives of their daily lives?	Netnography.	16 YouTube videos from 12 different posters, eight blogs from different persons, and nine large threads in social forums – all containing first-hand experience of PTSD.	How stories of PTSD are structured and narrated; strategies for coping with PTSD; how PTSD restricts daily living. Future directions: description of online interactions between posters and commenters.
Irimias & Volo (2018)	Official and unofficial websites on military sites in Northern Italy connected with World War I	How is information about military communicated within virtual communities as compared with promotional material from destination marketing organizations (DMOs)?	Observation, in-depth interviews, netnography.	Two user-generated virtual communities focused on war heritage sites and three regional DMOs' websites and war heritage itinerary websites.	Findings related to language style, engagement, content, audience, interaction with tourists, etc. Future directions: how information communicated online compares between official and unofficial websites for other military web sites.
Schuman, Lawrence, & Pope (2018)	Iraq and Afghanistan veterans who self-published stories on military-related trauma to YouTube.	How do combat veterans communicate narratives of their combat-related trauma via military video web blogs?	Netnography.	Publicly available milvlogs of 17 veterans published by 17 unique vloggers on YouTube.	Veterans' motivation for publishing milvlogs and themes related to combat trauma (e.g., loss, help-seeking, managing symptoms, guilt, and shame). Future directions: how interactions with commenters affect PTSD symptoms.

(Gal-Ezer, 2012)	Israeli 14th Tank Brigade veterans, who fought in the 1973 Yom Kippur War.	How do these veterans narrate their traumatic war experiences and incorporate it into the nation's collective memory?	In-depth interviews, in-person observation, discourse analysis of texts and artifacts, netnography.	Online observation of the 14th Brigade website from October 2007 – 2012. Observation included texts and artifacts, forums, documents, speeches, songs, letters, images, audio, video, and visual presentations. Observation also included independent linked websites of the brigade units.	Website promotes remembrance and provides historically accurate information for veterans and their families; helps communicate Brigade's contribution to Israeli national security; functions as a digital web library and media center including documentation such as government war protocols, battle maps, photographs, poems, and diaries. Future directions: use of remembrance sites by Veterans, families, and bereaved as "holding" places for grief and how interactions with other visitors affect remembrance and grief.
(Gal-Ezer, 2014)	1973 Yom Kippur War Israeli ex-POWs (Prisoners of War).	How do generations (over a 40-year period) interact specifically related to use of media, acknowledgment of PTSD, and recognition of POWs on a national level?	In-depth interviews, in-person observation, analysis of texts and artifacts, netnography.	Official blog of the ex-POWs, texts and artifacts available online (e.g., speeches, songs, letters, images, audio, video presentations), and other official and user-generated websites connected to the study topic.	Online mediums have enabled ex-POWs to connect to each other and communicate their stories to the public; websites now function as historical archives for students, researchers, and the general public. Future directions: Former POWs perceptions of events and the captivity experience over their life trajectories; how remembrance sites can be used to reverse stigma for Veterans of "unpopular" wars.

sites. However, even though the study team members undertook actions requiring ethical decision-making, they provided no discussion of such decisions in the article.

The work of Salzmann-Erickson and Hicdurmaz (2017) is the fourth netnographic study included in this review. Their study included a subsample of Vietnam veterans in their examination of posttraumatic stress disorder using blogs, YouTube vlogs, and online forum discussions. The authors found that the sharing of narratives online functioned as a self-care activity for war-affected veterans by giving them a vehicle through which to share their feelings. The authors indicated "no ethical vetting was necessary as all data were gathered from publicly accessible venues and were strictly archival and cross-section observational, without any intervention or interaction with the posters," (p. 3) though the authors did explicitly describe taking steps to protect the anonymity of posters by suppressing forum names, usernames, and URLs.

In the fifth and sixth studies identified in this review of military netnography, Schuman et al. (2018) investigated Iraq/Afghanistan veterans' use of YouTube as a vehicle to share "milvlogs" (military vlogs) about war trauma using a netnographic method described by Kozinets (2015). Data were collected from 17 unique milvlogs including verbatim transcripts, milvlog characteristics, and analytics. Findings illustrated how veterans were using vlog sites to draw attention to military suicide. Schuman et al. (2018) included a detailed description of ethical considerations including IRB approval, concealing usernames and URLs, checking the reverse searchability of quotes, and seeking permission from vloggers who left contact information for the use of direct quotes.

Following the observational portion of the study (which was the subject of Schuman et al., 2018), 7 of 12 vloggers who provided contact information on their sites agreed to complete an online survey that included demographic questions and several open-ended interview questions. A netnographic analysis of the interviews and interactions between vloggers and commenters is currently in progress and will be the subject of a future publication.

The studies highlighted above used netnographic methods to study military culture, although the authors explicitly focused on culture in varying degrees. Topics covered in these military netnographies included war heritage sites, the communication of war trauma stories on YouTube, and an Israeli remembrance community. All, save one, of the studies offered at least some explication of their ethical practices. For researchers professing to follow the netnographic method, ethical planning must occur during all phases of the research and the researchers must clearly articulate ethical decision-making; else, the study may be an online ethnography, but not truly a netnography (Kozinets, 2020). Next, we will turn our discussion to ethical issues particularly relevant to military netnography methods.

REFLECTION ON GAPS IN THE LITERATURE

This examination in the extant literature on military netnography raises several critical points of reflection and suggests gaps that should be addressed, all pertaining to ethical concerns. While ethical considerations are a critical component of all netnographic studies, such concerns are of the utmost importance in online ethnographies conducted on the social traces of vulnerable or sensitive populations, of which the military community can be considered owing to the hardships faced as a result of service (Hall, 2016; VA, 2015). As such, the remainder of this chapter will focus specifically on the ethical issues relating to netnographic studies on military populations.

Given that military populations have higher degrees of risk associated with social media use than civilians, it follows that researchers (who often also have some military affiliation) may also incur heightened risk in conducting social media research with military populations. Because there seems to be confusion and variability across military netnographies published thus far, and discussion of issues related to researchers' obligations to warn or protect and researcher risk are largely absent from the existing literature, a more in-depth analysis of ethical considerations pertinent to the conduct military netnography is highly relevant.

ETHICAL CONSIDERATIONS

The second half of this chapter will discuss research ethics pertaining to the conduct of netnographic studies of military communities. For more general guidance, readers are referred to a systematic review conducted by Golder et al. (2017) on ethical concerns in conducting social media research and to Kozinets (2020) for one of the most comprehensive discussions of conducting online ethnographic research to date. This chapter cautions potential digital researchers that although online spaces offer fertile fields for research, the Internet is an electronic landscape fraught with ethical perplexities. Specific areas of concern for online research include *ethical approval and participant recruitment*; *informed consent*; *protection of privacy and confidentiality*, *deception*, and *avoidance of harm* (Weeden & Williams, 2012). This chapter applies these ethical areas of concern to a military netnography framework and further examines issues related to a *duty to warn/protect* and *researcher risk*. The chapter makes recommendations for researchers engaging in military netnography based on findings of a literature review and the authors' own experience in the field.

ETHICAL APPROVAL AND PARTICIPANT RECRUITMENT

In deciding to conduct research online, researchers are immediately required to establish whether they consider interactions to be data or human subject research. Regarding social media research, such a determination can be a complicated and contested issue (Golder et al., 2017; Roberts, 2015). Assuming the latter approach is adopted, IRB approval is required before commencing data collection. Although IRBs are becoming more familiar with the study of online human behavior, researchers cannot be complacent and rely solely on the advice provided by these boards, particularly as military communities have unique risks, as will be outlined further in this chapter. Researchers should also note studies including military participants may require the approval of military IRBs and entities, in addition to those of the researchers' affiliated university (Wooten et al., 2014). It is worthwhile noting that of the six studies investigated in this literature review, only three declared having IRB approval. In the study by Salzmann-Erikson and Eriksson (2012) that examined how experiences of PTSD were communicated via social media, the authors did not seek out ethical approval for their study because data came from publicly available sources and involved solely archival and cross-sectional data retrieval. Publishing details regarding IRB status will assist emergent researchers in their decision-making.

Previous researchers have struggled with recruiting service members, veterans, and their families for studies. Military communities often show skepticism towards outsiders, and there is a heightened sense of privacy relating to cybersecurity concerns, as will be examined in detail later in this chapter. Military netnographers must first steep themselves in the history, culture, and jargon of the participants, and their particular military subculture during the immersion phase of research. The netnographer may declare their presence to the military community during this phase, or they may choose to remain unobtrusive. Without sufficient time spent in immersion, researchers risk violating unspoken norms of military culture and could very well be met with distrust and outright rejection at the interaction phase, jeopardizing the ability to achieve the depth necessary to answer the research question(s) fully. Researchers should also include team members who are themselves members of a military-connected community, not only to increase the likelihood of gaining access to the social data of nonpublic military groups, but also to ensure the credibility of the research findings. The role of an insider in the community has proven pivotal owing to the unique military culture outlined earlier. Even if one or more members of the research team are military-connected, netnographers should prepare themselves for adverse reactions from administrators and community members. Johnson et al.'s account of being challenged in the research space (2018) provides a warning for other researchers who fail to appreciate the complexity of issues, such as negotiating access and insider/ outsider status.

Based on this and similar experiences, researchers should avoid approaching group members directly and instead enlist the support of a gatekeeper as entrée is more likely if gatekeepers and community members understand the researcher's motivations and demonstrate an understanding of military culture. Researchers should also demonstrate knowledge and adherence to group norms and practices related to research requests. The adoption of these practices reduces the risk of the researcher being rejected from the field in the preliminary stages of research before moving forward to collecting consent from participants.

PROTECTION OF PRIVACY AND CONFIDENTIALITY

One of the critical debates in netnography is the question of whether online spaces are public or private. According to Westin's (1967) theory of privacy, privacy is the claim to determine *when, how*, and *to what extent* information is communicated to others. Self-disclosure on the Web, as in real life, can increase the level of intimacy between persons, leading to greater benefit in the form of social support; the tradeoff, however, is the risk to personal privacy. Internet users may hold the mistaken assumption that their online disclosures are private and by extension constitute privileged communication (Taddicken & Jers, 2011; Taddicken, 2013). However, privacy issues are complex. Users may perceive some degree of privacy on forums that require registration to view posts. Cautions to consider the space as private relates more so to closed online spaces where membership is required or where access has been afforded to privileged insiders. Researchers rarely include their rationale for determining the public-private status of the online spaces they study (Johnson et al., 2018). As such, new researchers may not receive the guidance they need to navigate the field.

Although users have the option of employing privacy settings to conceal their profile from public view, studies have shown that most users of social network sites do not use or do not understand privacy settings (MacDonald et al., 2010; Tufekci, 2008). Research suggests that users may provide extensive personal data in online profiles, such as date of birth, romantic status, sexual preference, political views, religion, and offline contact information (MacDonald et al., 2010).

Confidentiality is a separate concept from privacy. In many cases, group members' real-world identities and off-line behaviors can link to their online activity. Concerning the need to protect the anonymity of research participants online, Kozinets (2015) warned, "With sophisticated, and potentially ethically contentious, methods of tracking, many of the supposedly anonymous and invisible activities of social media members can be linked to an actual identity" (p. 659). Loss of anonymity poses particular concerns for some active duty service members whose online posts might place them at risk of incurring legal sanctions or expose them to other forms of risk, such as becoming targets of anti-military cyberbullies (Hilton, 2017).

Researchers must remain mindful of the reverse searchability of online content that could potentially identify the author of messages. Loss of anonymity is a particular cybersecurity concern for military communities. In some cases, military netnographies have shared exact participant quotes without declaring their considerations of privacy and confidentiality, in contrast to advice that cautions researchers against this practice (Weeden 2012). In their study of pro-anorexia online forums, Gavin et al. (2008), elected not to identify the name of the forum from which they collected study data, although they did utilize verbatim quotes in their article. While these authors obtained IRB approval for their study, the feasibility of reverse searching quotes could potentially compromise the assumed anonymity of study participants. Cloaking, or concealment of participants' identities (such as through the use of pseudo names or websites, and other means), is a technique that could ensure participants remain anonymous (Kozinets, 2015). The European Union's General Data Protection Regulation (GDPR) contains a comprehensive set of privacy regulations enacted by the European Parliament, effective May 2018, that includes not only what personal data can be collected, but also governs data collected for research purposes (including data scraped from online accounts and websites). By conducting research per the ethical principles embedded in netnography, researchers will comply with safeguards required by the GDPR, which are currently the most restrictive privacy standards affecting social media data (Kozinets, 2020). Privacy and confidentiality are critical concerns in obtaining informed consent from participants. Researchers are obligated to ensure the protection of participants from the potential impacts of their involvement in the research process.

INFORMED CONSENT

In the conduct of netnography, Kozinets (2015, 2020) emphasizes the importance of revealing one's identity as a researcher and obtaining informed consent by contacting potential participants directly. Some argue that the Internet is a public space, and online community members know their message posts are public and can be read by anyone, so consent is impractical and unnecessary (Hudson & Bruckman, 2004). However, even though members may know the public can freely read their online forum posts, they likely do not intend their posts to be used for research purposes (Finn, 1999). As highlighted previously, participants need to be made aware of the study in order to counteract potential risks. Indeed, Hudson and Bruckman (2004) reported that after divulging their identities as researchers, they were removed from over 60 percent of the Internet chatrooms they attempted to study.

Collecting informed consent from those interacting online is problematic for many researchers (Hudson & Bruckman, 2004); however, every effort should be made to obtain consent from individual participants, even if the forum is public and does not require registration. Consent is especially important in cases of the use of direct quotes, as any information shared outside the group could jeopardize members' emotional or physical safety. The "leakage" of information from these groups can negatively impact participants owing to the interconnection of the military community (Johnson, Williams-Veazey, & Archer, 2019). Physical safety could also be affected due to operational or personal security concerns. In contrast to the Salzmann-Erikson and Eriksson (2012) study mentioned, even when not required, we would encourage those doing research with online communities to consider contacting site administrators and posters whenever possible. Even when information is accessible online, likely the creators of the online content never intended its use for research purposes.

DECEPTION AND AVOIDANCE OF HARM

When considering the risks of disclosure, including removal from the field, researchers may succumb to the temptation to collect data covertly. Kozinets cautions against using deception (Kozinets, 2015). Deception involves concealing the study's actual purpose from participants. Debriefing of online participants may be inadequate in cases of deception; one reason why researchers should avoid deceiving participants is that it could lead to possible harm (Weeden, 2012). One of the fundamental principles of the Ethics Working Committee of the Association of Internet Researchers (AoIR), Version 2.0 is based on the degree of participant vulnerability – the greater the vulnerability of the participant, the higher the obligation of the researcher to provide protection (Markham & Buchanan, 2012). The AoIR encourages researchers to ask whether analysis, publication, redistribution, or dissemination of content could harm the subject in any way and if information was revealed outside the venue, whether harm could result.

Around the world, countries are enacting social media policies for military members to guard against the release of information that could compromise national security or jeopardize the safety of service members and their families. In the U.S., social media misconduct is punishable under the Uniform Code of Military Justice (UCMJ). Misconduct can include releasing sensitive information on a social media platform, partisan political banter, making disrespectful or negative statements about superiors, posting or linking to obscene or material deemed inappropriate, and using social media to engage in harassment, bullying, hazing, stalking, discrimination or retaliation. Punishment can range from a Letter of Reprimand or Article 15 to a Court Martial (Rodewig, 2012), resulting in possible loss of pay, rank, and freedom. In 2012, a Marine Corps Sergeant received an "other-than-honorable" discharge after creating a Facebook page that endorsed a political party and included an epithet aimed at the sitting U.S. president (James & Taylor, 2012).

The U.S. is not alone in establishing sanctions for social media behavior perceived to jeopardize national security. Some countries have even more restrictive policies (Peck, 2019), and more countries are developing them. This year, Russian lawmakers voted to stop their military personnel from posting anything online about their military service after soldiers' social media traces revealed troop positions (Nechepurenko, 2019).

Not only can the online communication of military personnel result in adverse consequences if deemed to violate social media policies, but the online activities of family members may also result in sanctions for the service member. In consideration of this, Internet research on military populations carries increased responsibilities for the researcher to protect individual identities. Netnographers must consider factors unique to military cultures in all phases of research to prevent inadvertent harm. Another factor to consider is that military populations are more likely to have vulnerabilities arising from their service that may contribute to increased safety risks. Compared to civilians, members of the military community not only face greater degrees of vulnerability due to increased risks of behavioral health disorders, substance misuse, interpersonal violence, and other stressors related to military service (Short, Dickson, Greenberg, & MacManus, 2018), but they also are subject to an increased likelihood of becoming targets of harassment, blackmail, and terrorism. In light of these issues, netnographers must consider the implications that could arise from including information (such as URL addresses and geotagged locations) that could reveal the online and offline identities of military personnel or their family members.

PARTICIPANT SAFETY

In arguing that military communities are a vulnerable population (owing to the gravity of the influence of military service on well-being), participant safety is a crucial concern. Throughout the conduct of netnography, particularly with military populations who are in crisis or have mental health conditions, the researcher may discover social media content suggesting a poster is at-risk of harm to self or others. Such discoveries raise questions regarding researchers' responsibility to warn and protect. What considerations might influence any actions the researcher might take? Certainly, researchers have a moral, ethical, and professional duty to respond, even in the absence of any legal requirements. However, in most cases, the identity of the poster is unknown to the researcher and the post made at some point in the past, further complicating decisions about the right actions to take.

Major social media sites have recently developed procedures for responding to address safety concerns. For example, Facebook (2020) uses machine learning tools and a random forest learning algorithm to identify individuals at risk of self- or other-harm. Facebook's policy is to work with law enforcement and first responders in cases it determines to pose a genuine risk of imminent harm, to include those involving suicide, self-injury, or threat to public safety. Salzmann-Erickson & Hicdurmaz (2017) highlighted a critical issue where posters may seek out social media venues in a state of crisis and may require professional support. The authors propose that forums that attract persons in crisis could be continuously monitored by helping professionals who could provide referrals. They further suggest the need for providing contact information for helping professionals on "official" versions of support forums maintained by universities or professional organizations. Additionally, studies conducted on war-affected populations with PTSD (Salzmann-Erikson & Eriksson, 2017; Schuman et al., 2018) recommended posting crisis contacts on websites where vulnerable individuals were likely to post. For social media sites without established procedures, the researcher could contact the site administrator to express concerns. The researcher could also upload crisis resources on public sites, and request approval from site administrators to post resources on private/closed sites.

RESEARCHER RISK

Not only are research participants vulnerable to potential risks arising from having their data included in a research study, but hazards also exist for researchers. Few guidelines exist for handling risks encountered by social media researchers. Maintaining that the topic of danger for researchers who immerse themselves in the online field is infrequently discussed, Johnson et al. (2018) published a reflexive account of the social and emotional harm experienced when she sought consent from group administrators of a closed Facebook group for military spouses to which she already belonged. Concerns about social isolation from a community that provided her personal support resulted in the researcher withdrawing from the social media research project.

Military netnographers may also be exposed to graphic descriptions of combat and traumatizing experiences during war, resulting in vicarious traumatization (McCann & Pearlman, 1990). As is already common for members of the military who have found themselves targeted by cyberbullies and hackers because of their military status or connection (Collier, 2019), military netnographers may also find themselves similarly harassed online by individuals hostile to the researcher's particular military-focused research topics. Risks for netnographers is an important future area of study. Some tools to help researchers who are following the netnographic method to manage emotional reactions are engaging in reflexivity, self-care, consultation, and the use of an immersion journal during the research process (Kozinets, 2020).

CONCLUSION

While ethics are important in all research projects and especially crucial in studies professing to apply a netnographic methodology, this chapter demonstrates how critical ethical considerations are for military netnographers. Because netnography has a well-defined method that addresses the ethical conduct of research and takes into account the unique cultural aspects of vulnerable populations, it is a particularly well-suited approach for studying how military-connected individuals seek and build community through social media venues. This chapter has demonstrated how distinct aspects of offline military culture influence how members of military communities around the world engage using social media and discussed the resulting impact on researchers. A literature review of existing studies applying a military netnographic methodology highlighted gaps, revealing confusion on the part of researchers, and variability in ethical approaches. As a result, the remainder of the chapter focused on addressing typical questions asked by online researchers through the specific context of military research. These were related to ethical approval and participant recruitment, informed consent, protection of privacy and confidentiality, deception and avoidance of harm, a duty to warn and protect, and concepts of researcher risk. Recommendations were made based on findings of the literature review and the authors' own experience in the field. This chapter argues that by following a netnographic method, researchers can rest assured they are meeting rigorous standards for ethical research practices with vulnerable/sensitive populations, such as the military. Further investigation is required in the field of military netnography, particularly to better understand its use and practicality as a method for capturing the unique worldview of military organizations around the globe.

REFERENCES

Bein, L., Grau, P. P., Saunders, S. M., & deRoon-Cassini, T. A. (2019). Military mental health: Problem recognition, treatment-seeking, and barriers. *Military Behavioral Health, 7*(2), 1–10. https://doi.org/10.1080/21635781.2018.1526147

Blakely, G., Hennessy, C., Chung, M., & Skirton, H. (2014). Adaption and adjustment of military spouses to overseas postings: An online forum study. *Nursing & Health Sciences, 16*(3), 387–394.

Bryant, B. (2016). How the Internet was constructed 60 years ago. *Newsweek Special Edition.* www.newsweek.com/making-internet-tim-berners-lee-world-wide-web-arpanet-438018

Collier, K. (2019, September 18). *US veterans and service members targeted by foreign entities online, report finds.* CNN Politics. www.cnn.com/2019/09/18/politics/veterans-foreign-influence-online-campaigns/index.html

Department of the Army. (2013). *The warrior ethos and soldier combat skills.* https://fas.org/irp/doddir/army/tc3-21–75.pdf

Department of Veterans Affairs (VA). (2015). *Veterans employment toolkit: Positive outcomes of military service.* www.va.gov/VETSINWORKPLACE/docs/em_positiveChanges.asp

Department of Veterans Affairs (VA). (2019, December 13.). *Understanding military culture: Structure and branches.* www.mentalhealth.va.gov/communityproviders/docs/structure_branches.pdf

Doffman, Z. (2019, August 1). Cyber warfare: Army deploys 'Social Media Warfare' division to fight Russia. *Forbes.* www.forbes.com/sites/zakdoffman/2019/08/01/social-media-warfare-new-military-cyber-unit-will-fight-russias-dark-arts/#205a65ec4f6e

Facebook. (2020). *Suicide prevention: Overview.* www.facebook.com/safety/wellbeing/suicide prevention

Finn, J. (1999). An exploration of helping processes in an online self-help group focusing on issues of disability. *Health & Social Work, 24*(3), 220–231.

Frančišković, T., Stevanović, A., Jelušić, I., Roganović, B., Klarić, M., & Grković, J. (2007). Secondary traumatization of wives of war veterans with posttraumatic stress disorder. *Croatian Medical Journal, 48*(2), 0–184.

Gal-Ezer, M. (2012). From "silent generation" to cyber-psy-site, story and history: The 14th Tank Brigade battles on public collective memory and official recognition. *Cyberpsychology: Journal of Psychosocial Research on Cyberspace, 6*(2), Article 4. https://doi.org/10.5817/CP2012-2-4

Gal-Ezer, M. (2014). Forty years: From 'silent generation' to 'Homeland' awards. *Participations: Journal of Audience & Reception Studies, 11*(2), 274–319.

Garamone, J. (2019, May 16). *DOD official cites widening military-civilian gap.* U.S. Department of Defense. www.defense.gov/explore/story/Article/1850344/dod-official-cites-widening-military-civilian-gap/

Gavin. J., Rodham, K., Poyer, H. (2008). The presentation of "pro-anorexia" in online group interactions. *Qualitative Health Research, 18*(3), 325–333. https://doi.org/10.1177/1049732307311640

Golder, S., Ahmed, S., Norman, G., & Booth, A. (2017). Attitudes towards the ethics of using social media: A systematic review. *Journal of Medical Internet Research*, 19(6), e195.

Greene, A. (2019). Defence chiefs desert Christopher Pyne in awkward press conference. *ABC Online*. www.abc.net.au/news/2019-03-28/defence-chiefs-desert-christopher-pyne-in-press-conference/10949250

Hall, L. K. (2016). *Counseling military families: What mental health professionals need to know* (3rd ed.). New York: Routledge.

Halvorson, A. (2010). Understanding the military: The institution, the culture, and the people. [PDF document]. *Substance Abuse and Mental Health Services Administration*.

Higate, P., & Cameron, A. (2004). Looking back: Military partners reflections on the traditional military. *Journal of Political and Military Sociology*, 32(2), 207–218. www.samhsa.gov/sites/default/files/military_white_paper_final.pdf

Highfill, M. C. (2019). *Exploring reactions of stakeholders to military-connected spouse abuse disclosure: An online observational approach* (Thesis). https://rc.library.uta.edu/uta-ir/bitstream/handle/10106/28588/HIGHFILL-THESIS-2019.pdf?sequence=1&isAllowed=y

Hilton, J. (2017, December 6). The Pentagon, misogyny, and cyber bulling. www.huffpost.com/entry/the-pentagon-misogyny-and-cyber-bullying_b_7065266?guccounter=1&guce_referrer=aHR0cHM6Ly93d3cuZ29vZ2xlLmNvbS88&guce_referrer_sig=AQAAAIJgfMTXhuO5Kd0E4_wpSn863nUaU4LVQ2bmMWQQTi4Oh1Gb0JJkYO17UJwHjlf4ByWaX1cUwErn-_CQBV03s7xJ69rA5y4FDyWbkXHFKmzkkQiOwzpZoc7Z6f5cmVATfjPtkmKp2-hvc_ts4JvwFNQHyeeiha0JkOovq7DHRzmB

Hudson, J. M., & Bruckman, A. (2004). "Go away": Participant objections to being studied and the ethics of chatroom research. *The Information Society*, 20(2), 127–139.

Im, E. O., & Chee, W. (2012). Practical guidelines for qualitative research using online forums. *Computers, Informatics, Nursing: CIN*, 30(11), 604.

Irimiás, A., & Volo, S. (2018). A netnography of war heritage sites' online narratives: User-generated content and destination marketing organizations communication at comparison. *International Journal of Culture, Tourism and Hospitality Research*, 12(1), 159–172. https://doi.org/10.1108/IJCTHR-07-2017-0079

Isaac, M. & Wakabayashe, D. (2017, October 30). Russian influence reached 126 million through Facebook alone. *The New York Times*. www.nytimes.com/2017/10/30/technology/facebook-google-russia.html

James, M. S. & Taylor, M. (2012). *Marine Sgt. Gary Stein gets 'Other Than Honorable' discharge over anti-Obama Facebook comment*. ABC News. https://abcnews.go.com/US/marine-sgt-gary-stein-honorable-discharge-anti-obama/story?id=16216279

Jennings-Kelsall, V., Aloia, L., Solomon, D., Marshall, A., & Leifker, F. (2012). Stressors experienced by women within Marine Corps families: A qualitative study of discourse within an online forum. *Military Psychology*, 24(4), 363–381.

Jessup, C. (2000). Transforming wives into spouses: Changing Army attitudes. In Strachan, H (ed.). *The British Army, manpower and society into the twenty-first century* (pp. 87–104). London: Frank Cass.

Johnson, A., Lawson, C., & Ames, K. (2018). Are you really one of us? Exploring ethics, risk and insider research in a private Facebook community. In *Proceedings of the 9th International Conference on Social Media and Society* (pp. 102–109). New York: Association for Computing Machinery. http://doi.org/10.1145/3217804.3217902

Johnson, A., Williams-Veazey, L., Archer, C. (2019). Is privacy in closed Facebook groups only an illusion? Investigating intimacy, leakage and researcher ethics in Facebook communities [panel presentation]. *Digital Intimacies Conference 5.0.*, Melbourne, Australia.

Knobloch, L., Basinger, E., Abendschein, B., Wehrman, E., Monk, J., & McAninch, K. (2018). Communication in online forums about the experience and management of relational uncertainty in military life. *Journal of Family Communication*, 18(1), 13–31.

Kozinets, R. V. (1997). "I want to believe": A netnography of the X-Philes' subculture of consumption. *Advances in Consumer Research*, 24, 470–475.

Kozinets, R. V. (2010). *Netnography: Doing ethnographic research online*. Los Angeles, CA: Sage Ltd.

Kozinets, R. V. (2015). *Netnography redefined* (2nd ed.). Los Angeles, CA: Sage Ltd.

Kozinets, R. V. (2020). *Netnography: The essential guide to qualitative social media research* (3rd ed.). London: Sage Ltd.

Kuehner, C. A. (2013). My military: A Navy nurse practitioner's perspective on military culture and joining forces for veteran health. *Journal of the American Academy of Nurse Practitioners*, 25(2), 77–83. https://doi-org.ezproxy.uta.edu/10.1111/j.1745-7599.2012.00810.x

Lange, K. (2019, December, 26). DoD launching initiative to get to #KnowYourMil Better. *DoDLive*. www.dodlive.mil/2018/01/17/dod-launching-initiative-to-get-to-knowyourmil-better/

Levy, B. S., & Sidel, V. W. (2009). Health effects of combat: A life-course perspective. *Annual Review of Public Health*, 30, 123–136. doi:10.1146/annurev.publhealth.031308.100147

MacDonald, J., Sohn, S., & Ellis, P. (2010). Privacy, professionalism and Facebook: A dilemma for young doctors. *Medical Education*, 44(8), 805–813.

Markham, A., & Buchanan, E. (2012). *Ethical decision-making and internet research: Recommendations from the AoIR Ethics Working Committee* (Version 2.0). https://aoir.org/reports/ethics2.pdf

McAninch, K., Wehrman, E., & Abendschein, B. (2018). Identifying sequences of advice-giving in online military discussion forums. *Communication Quarterly*, 66(5), 557–575.

McCann, I. L., & Pearlman, L. A. (1990). Vicarious traumatization: A framework for understanding the psychological effects of working with victims. *Journal of Traumatic Stress*, 3, 131–149.

Nechepurenko, I. (2019, February 19). Russia votes to ban smartphone use by military, trying to hide digital traces. *The New York Times*. www.nytimes.com/2019/02/19/world/europe/russia-military-social-media-ban.html

Parrott, S., Albright, D., Dyche, C., & Steele, H. (2019). Hero, charity case, and victim: How U.S. news media frame military veterans on Twitter. *Armed Forces & Society*, 45(4), 702–722.

Peck, M. (2019, April 6). "Slander" the Chinese military online and you'll go to jail. *The National Interest*. https://nationalinterest.org/blog/buzz/"slander"-chinese-military-online-and-you'll-go-jail-51112

Pedersen, E. R., Helmuth, E. D., Marshall, G. N., Schell, T. L., PunKay, M., & Kurz, J. (2015). Using Facebook to recruit young adult veterans: Online mental health research. *JMIR Research Protocols*, 4, e63.

Peterson, P. (2019, December 14). Election season calls for caution, professionalism among military. *DoDLive*. www.dodlive.mil/2012/07/24/election-season-calls-for-caution-professionalism-among-military/

Pressfield, S. (2011). *The warrior ethos*. Los Angeles: Black Irish Entertainment LLC.

Robbins, E. L. (2007). Muddy boots IO: The rise of soldier blogs. *Military Review*, 87(5), 109.

Roberts, L.D. (2015). Ethical issues in conducting qualitative research in online communities. *Qualitative Research in Psychology*, 12(3), 363–381.

Rodewig, C. (2012). Social media use punishable under UCMJ. www.army.mil/article/73367/social_media_misuse_punishable_under_ucmj

Ryan, M. & Thompson, M. (2016, August 21). *Social media in the military: Opportunities, perils and a safe middle path*. https://groundedcuriosity.com/social-media-in-the-military-opportunities-perils-and-a-safe-middle-path/

Salzmann-Erikson, M., & Eriksson, H. (2012). LiLEDDA: A six step forum-based netnographic research method for nursing science. *Aporia: The Nursing Journal*, 4(4), 7–18. http://urn.kb.se/resolve?urn=urn:nbn:se:oru:diva-26336

Salzmann-Erikson, M., & Hiçdurmaz, D. (2017). Use of social media among individuals who suffer from post-traumatic stress: A qualitative analysis of narratives. *Qualitative Health Research*, 27(2), 285–294.

Schuman, D. L., Lawrence, K. A., & Pope, N. (2018). Broadcasting war trauma: An exploratory netnography of Veterans' Youtube vlogs. *Qualitative Health Research*, 29(3), 357–370.

Short, R., Dickson, H., Greenberg, N., & MacManus, D. (2018). Offending behaviour, health and well-being of military veterans in the criminal justice system. *PLoS One*, 13(11), e0207282.

Sugiura, L., Wiles, R., & Pope, C. (2017). Ethical challenges in online research: Public/private perceptions. *Research Ethics*, 13(3–4), 184–199.

Taddicken, M., & Jers, C. (2011). The uses of privacy online: Trading a loss of privacy for social web gratifications? In Trepte, S., Reinecke, L. (eds.). *Privacy online* (pp. 143–156). Berlin: Springer. https://doi.org/10.1007/978-3-642-21521-6_11.

Taddicken, M. (2013). 13 privacy, surveillance, and self-disclosure in the social web. *Internet and Surveillance: The Challenges of Web 2.0 and Social Media*, 16, 255–272.

Talkington, B. K. (2011). *Communicating support: Where and how Army spouses seek community*. (doctoral dissertation). ProQuest Theses and Dissertations. (UMI NO. 3459129).

Tufekci, Z. (2008). Grooming, gossip, Facebook and Myspace. *Information, Communication & Society*, 11(4), 544–564.

5en, M. R. (2012). Ethics and on-line research methodology. *Journal of Social Work Values and Ethics*, 9(1), 40–51.

Weeden, M. R., & Williams, G. (2012). Ethics and on-line research methodology. *Journal of Social Work Values and Ethics*, 9(1), 40–51.

Westin, A. (1967). *Privacy and freedom*. New York: Atheneum.

Wilson, G., Hill, M., & Kiernan, M. D. (2018). Loneliness and social isolation of military veterans: Systematic narrative review. *Occupational Medicine, 68*(9), 600–609.

Wooten, N., Al-Barwani, M., Chmielewski, J., Buck, J., Moore, L., & Woods, A. (2014). A case study of social media and remote communications in military research: Examining military and deployment experiences of Army women. *SAGE Research Methods Cases.* doi:10.4135/9781446273050145540257

Wroe, D. (2016). Australian soldiers social media could be inadvertently helping the enemy. *The Sydney Morning Herald.* www.smh.com.au/politics/federal/australian-soldiers-social-media-could-be-inadvertently-helping-the-enemy-20160905-gr900h.html

7

Political Netnography
A Method for Studying Power and Ideology in Social Media

Dino Villegas

INTRODUCTION

Netnography (Kozinets, 2006; R. Kozinets, Scaraboto, & Parmentier, 2018) offers important opportunities for academics and practitioners to study a diverse range of social science phenomena. Netnography has been adapted and utilized to study online fan communities (Kozinets, 1998), market segments (Xun & Reynolds, 2010), exotic tourism (Mkono & Markwell, 2014), education in the wild (Kulavuz-Onal & Vásquez, 2013), online dating (Wang, 2019), role play (Wang, Lee, & Hsu, 2017), and many other relevant contemporary phenomena. At the same time, the method has many extensions and variations, including auto-netnography (Villegas, 2018), more-than-human netnography (Lugosi & Quinton, 2018), or the use of netnography in conjunction with videography (Belk & Kozinets, 2017) or digital diaries (Biraghi & Gambetti, 2018).

In this chapter, I will argue for the need to develop a novel subcategory of netnography that I term political netnography. The chapter aims to contribute to the general literature on netnography by defining the political netnography concept, categorizing a sample of the current research, and proposing different ways to advance it. To understand the need to develop the concept, we first will explore some aspects of political ethnography, paying special attention to the ethnographic definition of politics. After defining politics in an ethnographic sense, we will examine the symbiotic relationship between different dimensions of politics and social media, including in political campaigns, social movements, effects on democracy, and fake news. After establishing the need for a political netnography approach, we will categorize a sample of current politically related studies that utilize netnography. The chapter will advance on two political relevant issues: (1) the analysis of power, complementing netnography with critical discourse analysis and elite ethnography, and (2) the study of ideology. Finally, the chapter will discuss the possibility of using political netnography in order to inform political strategies in the real world.

POLITICAL ETHNOGRAPHY, OR THE ETHNOGRAPHIC UNDERSTANDING OF POLITICS

To explore the need for a political netnography, we first should briefly discuss its offline version: political ethnography. In the literature, we can find many different definitions and approaches of political ethnography that we can summarize as the use of ethnography in the political field. However, gaining a precise consensus regarding exactly what this means is far more complex. It must start with even simpler questions. What do we mean by politics? What do ethnographers understand "the political" to signify? Certainly, the definitions of politics and the political are complex and contain many meanings. It is not the intention of this chapter to cover all of those meanings but, rather, to explore some of the current explanations that are most relevant to an understanding in the domain of netnography.

From a discourse analysis perspective, for example, Gee (2010) defines politics as "any situation where the distribution of social goods is at stake" (124). In Gee's definition, we can see clearly how institutions such as political parties and governments are included in the sphere of the political as they set rules and have discussions about the distribution of social goods. In this context, "ethnography is uniquely equipped to look microscopically at the foundations of political institutions and their attendant sets of practices" (Auyero, 2006, 258).

A different approach, yet in some ways one consistent with the idea of the political as the "distribution of social goods," is the understanding of political ethnography as the study of power relations in society (Baiocchi & Connor, 2008) and "the structures, institutions, movements, and collective identities that both maintain and challenge it" (140). A key concept in this definition is the idea of challenging and maintain the power structure. This challenge moves the concept of politics beyond official institutions and opens it to everyday citizens, grassroots social movements, and other actors that may not be considered formal political institutions. More specifically, according to Benzecry and Baiocchi (2017, 234), political ethnographers commonly "focused on a few main questions revolving around the nature of the political bond, such as how it is organized, and whether people invest their sense of sovereignty in other citizens and organizations, or in state institutions."

The participant-observational practices of ethnography provided some important benefits for politically related studies. First, the type of small but thick data used by ethnographers can shed light on the more human side of political issues. Second, the immersion required during ethnography enables the researcher to see social and political currents before they can be detected by other methods. In this context, political ethnographers are interested in details that are not yet solidified but can become emerging trends into traditional politics (Luhtakallio & Eliasoph, 2014).

According to Baiocchi and Connor (2008), political ethnography can be divided into three different types of studies.

1. First are ethnographies of political actors and institutions. In this category are any ethnographies that focus on traditional political institutions such as political parties, governments, and/or formal social movements.
2. The second type of study is encounters with formal politics. In this second category are studies regarding encounters of non-political actors with formal political institutions, for example, investigations regarding how government policies can affect every-day lives or how citizens interact with formal political structures via, for example, resistance or consent.
3. The third type of political ethnography study is research on the lived experience of the political. This type of research focuses on everyday life and its relations to politics even when there no apparent relationship. This type of ethnography has "often highlighted how some of the most seemingly mundane aspects of life become rooted in politics of the state or nation" (Baiocchi & Connor, 2008, 148).

When pursuing any of these approaches, ethnographers use a diverse range of qualitative methods of data collection. Tilly (2006, 410), for example, mentions that many political ethnographies apply a mix of some of these approaches:

- In-depth interviews
- Conversation
- Participant observation
- Passive observation of interactions
- Covert observation of interactions
- Unobtrusive observation of the residues and consequences of interaction.

Thus far, we have discussed how we understand politics and how we understand political ethnography, as well as having a quick look at its benefits and approaches. The question that remains, however, is why do we need a political netnography? According to Luhtakallio and Eliasoph (2014), one of the greatest current challenges of political ethnography today is the exploration of the new virtual communications. In this context, we can see how the online world and especially social media have transformed modern-day political dynamics. Because of the depth and amount of these changes, I strongly believe that we need a method specifically suited to understand these realities from an ethnographic perspective. The reason for this is because of the many important ways that social media impacts politics, a topic that the next section of this chapter now turns towards.

SOCIAL MEDIA AND THE NEED FOR A POLITICAL NETNOGRAPHY

In 2013, when I worked as the campaign manager for a presidential candidate in Chile, Facebook and Twitter were at the center of our strategy. Because of our active participation in social media, we established a competitive position for the candidate and reached a new generation of voters that had been resistant to traditional political activities. Together with the pragmatic effect of social media in this campaign, I also witnessed how relevant social media was in the larger realm of politics. We certainly were not unique in this way. In today's world, political marketers "use social media to create and disseminate symbolic content that introduces candidates to voters and performs their political personas" (Kreiss, Lawrence, & McGregor, 2018, 22).

We can easily see how social media has shaken electoral politics to their core around the world. For example, studies have analyzed how social media had a very important role to play in the elections of Barack Obama (Cogburn & Espinoza-Vasquez, 2011) and Donald Trump (Enli, 2017) as well as in many other elections around the world (Davis, Bacha, & Just, 2016; Nulty, Theocharis, Popa, Parnet, & Benoit, 2016). The same strong social media influence phenomenon has been located in other democratic decisions, such as the Brexit result in the United Kingdom (Hall, Tinati, & Jennings, 2018). Social media does not just impact elections, either. Researchers of the political also draw social media into questions about the influence of populism today (Engesser, Ernst, Esser, & Büchel, 2017) or the contemporary political practices of government officials and candidates (Svensson, 2012).

Beyond elections, inquiries about concerns on how social media may affect democracy are another focus of attention. For example, some authors have discussed ways that social media can promote democracy (Jha & Kodila-Tedika, 2019) while others claim that even though they can promote participation, platforms such as Facebook also can facilitate the spread of misinformation (Gerbaudo, 2018; Valenzuela, Halpern, Katz, & Miranda, 2019). Another issue related to the topic of social media and democracy is the phenomenon of fake news (Allcott & Gentzkow, 2017; Bradshaw & Howard, 2018; Morgan, 2018). Fake news is not just a concept that is part of an academic conversation but also an important debate on the press and an everyday dilemma.

Social movements that challenge power and resource distribution also have arisen around the world using social media to facilitate their political efforts (Castells, 2012; Valenzuela, 2013). In Chile, between 2011 and 2013, different situations and social movements were gaining traction in the social media discussion; examples of these are "Patagonia Sin Represas" ("Patagonia without dams"), which stopped the construction of a dam in Aysén in the Chilean Patagonia (Silva, 2016) and No+AFP, a resistance to a pension scheme that has become a major flash point in recent national politics. Years earlier, in what was called then the "Penguin Revolution" (Barahona, García, Gloor, & Parraguez, 2012), high school students armed with mobile phones and using social media made demands for free education. These demands became so relevant in Chilean politics that they guided the agenda for many years afterwards. In the context of this protest, studies have found "a positive relationship between the use of both Facebook and Twitter and participation" (Scherman, Arriagada, & Valenzuela, 2015, 167).

Of course, Chilean politics are just one example. We can find similar patterns demonstrating how social media has sparked massive discussion on social and politically relevant themes in many places around the world. Studies have shown that social media now serves as a tool for collective action and that it helps social movements to (a) spread information leading to the coordination of social movement activities, (b) engage in emotional and motivational messages that aid mobilization, and (c) generate a network structure that has a role in informational exposure benefiting the movement (Jost et al., 2018).

This is just a small sample of the many changes triggered by social media on the political dimension. This chapter could go further in each of them or mention other areas; however, I believe that the main point here is made, that is, that social media has revolutionized the political arena and thus its study must also revolutionize, to some extent, the practice of political studies.

If we want to explore politics today – as it exists in the distribution of social goods and/ or in the arena of power relations – or in any of its forms, we ignore social media at our own peril as scholars, and to the disadvantage of our own work. Currently, we can argue that some of these issues can be researched from many other perspectives, especially with the current opportunities in quantitative methods and big data, and this is certainly true. However, de Volo and Schatz (2004, 268) remind us of a crucially important fact, that "far from becoming outmoded as quantitative data are increasingly available, ethnographic methods remain critical to political analysis." As political realities alter because of social media, it is important to understand them on a human scale, in reality, rather than through methods that are based on distancing techniques of prediction and control. Because of this, it is important to develop an ethnographic method specially designed to explore the impact of social media in the political sphere. And this is exactly where the new field of political netnography is positioned.

UNDERSTANDING POLITICAL NETNOGRAPHY

So far in this chapter, I have discussed political ethnography and why it is important to adapt ethnographic methods to the presence of social media, moving it toward what I herein term a specialized sub-field of political netnography. In this important subsection of the chapter, I will explain the concept, develop it, and propose some of its possible uses. In order to achieve this, I will begin by defining political netnography so that we can subsequently compare related current research in light of the definition.

The most current definition of netnography tells us that netnography "adapts the method of ethnography and other qualitative research practices to the cultural experiences that encompass and are reflected within the traces, networks, and systems of social media" (Kozinets, 2019a, 19). At its core, netnography is an empirical method born from the field of anthropology (Kozinets, 2002). Ethnography, in general, is "empirically embedded; this is its signature element" (Kozinets, 2019a, 150).

Under this, it is important to mention that netnography is not limited only to some sort of online ethnographic practice, but is a specific and growing set of methods and processes that can be applied to social media contexts, many of which are native to digital fields and areas (Ibid.). In this context, I see political netnography as a sub-category of netnography that focuses on the study of political issues affected by or affecting social media. More specifically, I understand political netnography to mean the use of the netnography approach to study a particular sub-set of cultural practices in social media that are related to discussions about challenging or maintaining the distribution of resources and/or power. As discussed above, in social media those issues can extend from political campaigns to social movements or the effects of social media discourse on democracy or democracies.

The idea of political netnography as a sub-category of netnography can be useful in the development of new data gathering and interpretation methods specifically designed for that purpose. Up until now, we haven't formalized political netnography as a concept. This does not mean, however, that netnographers are not studying politics. In fact, research using netnography or some type of on-line ethnographic or another qualitative method to study politics is diverse.

In the following part of the chapter, I will discuss some of the extant research done on social media and politics using netnography. For this, I selected a sample of research in the area and categorized them in an adaptation of Baiocchi and Connor's (2008) categorization of political ethnography. Based on their work, I call these categories: (1) netnography of formal politics, (2) netnography of political encounters, and (3) netnography of lived political experiences.

Netnography of Formal Politics

In this category of political netnography, a netnography of formal politics is used to examine the practice of formal political actors. This examination can range a concentration on political candidates, political parties or social movements that are looking to generate a change in power or resources distributions. This type of political netnography category is evident when used to study a clear political figure such as a political candidate. For example, Laaksonen et al. (2017) use what they call *augmented online ethnography* to explain candidate-to-candidate interaction during election time. In another example, Svensson (2012) used participant-observational netnographic methods to study the use of social media by a candidate in Swedish elections.

Not all the formal politics are as evident as these, however. Some groups can be considered to be political or not depending on their context. This is the case for the study of Biddix and Park (2008) that used netnography to explore the campus living wage movement among college students in the United States. A similar research situation was presented by the netnographic investigation of an online skinhead newsgroup in order to understand talks and perceptions about racism (Campbell, 2006).

Netnography of Political Encounters

Netnographies of political encounters include research studies that use qualitative social media research methods to investigate citizens' reactions to formal political institutions. For example, consider the research into political accountability from a public perspective in

Canada in a moment of political crises that was conducted by Aung et al. (2017). Another example is the work of Scullion, Jackson, and Molesworth (2013) that combined netnography with focus groups in order to explore the ongoing public word-of-mouth "talks" that occurred during the political debates of the British General Election of 2010. Other research in this category could explore particular communities to understand political perceptions. An example of this is Svensson's (2015) participant–observational netnography of political discussion, motives, and participation in Qruiser, a Swedish queer online community.

Sometime citizens will organize themselves, but do not necessarily engage in centralized protest behavior. In these cases, people in social media join a cause to challenge, or perhaps to support, the established configuration or system of power or resource distribution. Some prior netnographies can fit into this category of political ethnography. For example, in this context Bonilla and Rosa (2015) used netnography to explore online protest for the police shooting of unarmed African American teenager in summer of 2014. I would also include the study of the use of hashtags in digital protest in this category.

Netnographies of Lived Political Experiences

Other netnographies focus on behaviors that may not be considered political, but which are political under the definition previously discussed. These types of netnography explore how people interact using social media and how that interaction behavior may be in ideologically motivated to challenge or confirm existing power and resource distribution structures. Two studies in this categories reveal that this type of netnography is possible. In only the second published netnography, R. V. Kozinets and Handelman (1998) explored early online boycotting behaviors on Internet newsgroups. Their results showed how participants were not only members of a collective effort to alter corporate behavior, but also engaged in this consumer protest as an act of individual, emotional, and even spiritual self-expression. In a more recent netnography, Kozinets (2019b) looked into contemporary YouTube video comment discourse around three different capitalist and utopian entrepreneurs. His interpretation of that corpus of data revealed public discourses of consumer utopianism, a "YouTube utopianism," that alternately reaffirmed as well as challenged the ideological underpinnings of contemporary capitalism.

A Summary of the Three Perspectives

During this section, we have seen how many published netnographies have political interest and can be classified as political netnographies. Also, we have divided a sample of netnographic research studies into three different sub-sections: (1) netnographies of formal politics, (2) netnographies of political encounters and (3) netnographies of lived political experiences.

Table 7.1 provides a summary of prior studies sorted in these sub-categories. At the same time, Table 7.1 shows how netnography was used. As we can appreciate, all of the researchers employed some type of participatory or non-participatory engagement. At the same time, most of them use other traditional qualitative research methods such as interviews or focus groups. If we go back to the political ethnographic methods discussed before in this chapter, the only method absent from these descriptions is covert observation of interactions (Tilly, 2006). This is understandable, as netnography's ethical procedures are very clear in their strictures regarding the imperative of no deception when doing interactive engagement.

To advance a political netnography approach, in the following part of the chapter I describe and develop two research topics that, in my view, are important not just to politics, but also which can help us advance new data collection methods or procedures. These research topics are (1) the study of power and (2) the understanding of ideology. After that, the chapter will

Table 7.1 Sample of Political Related Research Using Netnography

Political netnography category	Authors	Study description	Method
Formal politics	Laaksonen et al. (2017)	Study candidate-to-candidate interaction during election time.	Online observation of Facebook and Twitter complemented by big data analysis. They called the method a Big-Data Augmented Online Ethnography.
	Svensson (2012)	Research in how a Sweden political candidate used social media during elections.	Netnography participant observation, the researcher followed all the candidate social media accounts and interacted on them. Online interviews to the candidate and other campaign members.
	Biddix & Park (2008)	Exploration of the campus living wage movement among college students in the United States.	Network ethnographic analysis complemented with online interviews.
	Campbell (2006)	Exploration of an online skinhead newsgroup.	Ethnographic exploration of an online skinhead newsgroup.
Encounters with politics	Svensson (2015)	Review of political discussion in a queer online community to understand motives of participations.	Netnography, participant observations in a political forum discussion on Qruiser plus participant interviews.
	Aung et al. (2017)	Explore the public perception on accountability during a political crisis.	Netnography of five social media sites, in each of the sites content analysis was perform.
	Scullion, Jackson, and Molesworth (2013)	The research focuses on talk or discussions that emerge as result of political TV debates.	Netnography observation of the political discussions in a non-political forum after a TV debate, together with the use of focus groups.
	Bonilla & Rosa (2015)	Digital protest, using hashtags, for the police shooting of unarmed African American teenager in summer of 2014.	Theorizing on how hashtags can become a form of activism and how can be studies from an ethnographic perspective.
Live political experiences	Kozinets & Handelman (1998)	Exploration of boycotting behaviors in newsgroups.	Netnography of 11 online newsgroups, plus 14 online interviews.
	Kozinets (2019b)	Explore how social media related with different forms of consumer utopianism and its potential activism.	Ten-month netnography in three YouTube-based data sites.

consider how all of these topics and approaches can be valuable for theoretical development as well also for informing the strategic approach of the political practitioner.

THE STUDY OF POWER AND POLITICAL DISCOURSE

The political discussion is always in part a discussion about power. Thus, it is unsurprising that, in some way or another, all of the research studies portrayed in Table 7.1 are, to some extent, about power relations. Because of this and to transcend the focus of current netnographies, the political netnographer can extend their current data collection methods (see, for example, Table 7.1) with the use of specific other approaches related to the study of power.

As these discussions are mediated in social media mostly, and oftentimes in textual format, one of these approaches is discourse analysis (DA), especially variations of DA such as critical discourse analysis (CDA) that can assist in politically related issues. An understanding based in CDA can help the political netnographer achieve better insights not just into the understanding power discourses but also in another political element as is the concept of ideology.

To explore power relations of groups in social media, CDA in conjunction with netnography can advance practice, first because of the legacy of studies from CDA on politically related issues and, second, because, at its core, CDA aims to analyze social problems, social abuse, and power inequality (Van Dijk, 2014). When approaching netnography from a critical discourse perspective the researcher wants to get "insight into the crucial role of discourse in the reproduction of dominance and inequality" (Van Dijk, 1993, 253). In this context, the researcher has to ask the text if the use of the language by the group or actor in question provides signs of power inequality or abuse to other groups.

It's important to remember that discourse is not just text and images. Videos and podcasts are discourses. Even silence can be a discourse, as, for example, when a political figure fails to respond to some questions while attending to others. This type of silence can signify a power inequality in social media as well. It is important to mention that even though CDA can be used to reveal power relations, it is mostly used for the study of those who hold power. Used in this manner, CDA in political netnography can be beneficially applied to what Boswell et al. (2019) called "elite ethnographies." Examples of elite ethnographies would be an ethnography of a member of the government, parliament or any other formal political actor that holds a power position. The focus of elite ethnographies are on "campaigning and governing practice" (58). We might consider whether a study such as that of Ott (2017), who studies the "politics of debasement" of Donald Trump and highlights how Twitter "privileges discourse that is simple, impulsive, and uncivil" might be further developed using netnographic techniques (59).

Boswell et al. (2019) present a few data collecting methods to study the powerful that can adapt well to netnography and that at the same time can benefit from the CDA perspective. Three of these methods that I believe are relevant to the topic of political netnography are:

- **Memoirs:** These include autobiographies or first-person reflections of the politician on power or government. Using social media, the researcher could try to analyze politician content about these issues, for example to analyze a politician's Twitter feed, look at memoir-type campaigning messaging on Facebook or Instagram, or follow personal writing on a politician's personal blog.
- **Elite Focus-Groups:** Group discussions can encourage elite members to discuss different views. Today's technology allows us to conduct this type of focus groups online to confront views about power or resource distribution.

- **Para-ethnography:** Boswell et al. (2019) present para-ethnography as interviews that focus on a specific document or artifact. Political netnography could focus on particular content made by the politician that is used by the researcher to challenge a specific view.

With CDA and elite ethnography, we have discussed power from the perspective of study of the powerful. However, netnography and other ethnographic methods have a strong history of being deployed for studying underrepresented groups and giving them a voice. These methods are especially useful for understanding sensitive topics and vulnerable or underprivileged populations (Langer, & Beckman, 2005). Relying upon insider research, however, requires awareness of the need to apply ethical research precautions to the process (Greene, 2014; Zinn, 1979).

NETNOGRAPHY AND THE DISCOURSES OF IDEOLOGY

Related with power, relevant for political studies, and accessible from discourse analysis is the concept of ideology. Netnographers have already embraced the concept of ideology. For example, R. V. Kozinets (2019b), studies citizen-consumers' responses to technological utopias as a form of realized social media ideological practice that may be part of the foundation of the global culture. As well, R. V. Kozinets and Handelman (1998, 2004) used netnographic investigation and social media data to examine how consumers expressed and challenged ideology in online contexts. From a discursive point of view, we might understand ideology using a broader view. Van Dijk (2006, 115), for instance, explains the concept of ideology as relating to the "system of ideas" of particular group members that is related to the shared social cognition of that group.

Ideology can serve as the structure of the social representations shared by a collective at the same time as it serves as the basis of a group self-image and influences members of that groups' image of others (Van Dijk, 2006). From a political netnography/discourse perspective, the researcher can inquire about the identification ideological elements of a certain group or community in social media. In other words, researchers can investigate how group members define themselves versus how they define others. To access a certain group's ideology in social media, following Van Dijk (2001), I proposed a series of questions that the netnographer can ask themselves when interpreting field data:

- How do the members define themselves? Do they have identity devices that discriminate who belongs to the group versus who does not belong? Do members define themselves using gender, ethnicity, appearance, national or other factors or categories that could be discriminatory or exclusionary?
- What specific actions define the group?
- Do group members posit a specific reason for the group to exist?
- Can we interpret group norm and values? What do group members define as good and bad? Many times, strong ideologies in groups define particular behaviors, beliefs, or peoples to be good versus the bad behaviors, beliefs, or peoples of others.
- Do they have a particular position in society? How do they relate to other groups?
- How they define the resources of the group? What resources do they value the most?

The netnographic researcher can ask these questions not just when collecting data from social media sites, but also as they are applying and using interviews, focus groups or any of the previously mentioned methods for data collection as a part of their research project or netnography. At the same time, inquiry about ideologies from a netnographic perspective can be applied to consolidated formal political groups, such as political parties or activist organizations. It could also be used to elaborate and develop emerging ideologies or in a conflict-attuned intersectional fashion as members of diverse groups converge in online interaction or conversation.

UTILIZING POLITICAL NETNOGRAPHY TO INFORM A POLITICAL STRATEGY

Ethnographic methods have an impressive history of informing the development of a marketing strategy by providing "rich stories infused with the tensions, contradictions, and emotions of people's everyday lives" through which "executives are better able to grasp the complexity of consumer cultures" (Cayla & Arnould 2013, 1). Applied ethnographies can be especially useful to determine unmet needs and wants, create ideas, and inform strategies (Mariampolski, 2006). Thus far in this chapter, we have mainly discussed applying netnography from an academic perspective in order to generate theory about politics or other social sciences. However, as a former political campaign manager myself, I am convinced that the use of political netnography can become an important asset for political strategy generation – a type of "applied political netnography." This use of applied political netnography is a logical extension and development of netnography's success as an applied business and marketing research method across a wide variety of global industries, as other chapters in this volume clearly demonstrate.

Consider some of the following applications. Political campaigns, public organizations, and politicians use social media to create and promote certain messages about parties and candidates. Political brands often focus on storytelling and emotional resonance, providing political narratives as well as life stories from voters and citizens. The degree to which politicians truly listen to and interpret these individual stories can make a significant difference in their popular reception. To study this day-to-day political content and the varieties of its popular reception, a topic that fills much of the global news cycle, netnography can study the stories, the responses that people provide, and the various interactions and ripplings of this political discourse throughout social media and social life. This narrative analysis, which would utilize user-generated content, might offer important insights into how people live and how they collectively and individually interpret the world (Patterson & Monroe, 1998). This sort of analysis can give the applied political netnographer a look into potential emerging political themes. It might be useful as an early warning system, adding rich contextual elements to the public relations and social media monitoring dashboards applied frequently by managers in industry and in the political sphere.

When doing political netnography, just as with any other type of netnography, the applied campaign manager / researcher would focus upon particular sites or social media platforms such as Twitter feeds or hashtags, Facebook pages or groups, Reddit groups, and so on. In this scenario, the political advisor will choose a site or number of sites to participate in and to study. At the same the netnographer may want to focus upon a particular political online communities (Lin & Himelboim, 2018; Velasquez, 2012). For example, we can see that different types of political community might relate differently to a particular candidate or political party. These types of political community might include some of the following:

1. *Official online political communities:* Consider first the online community created by an official political actor. A political netnographer strategist conducting ongoing

netnography of one of its own online sites, such as a Facebook group, might want to identify the level of interaction between members, the quality of the relationships inside the community, as well as the levels of identification and the overall quality of the communication (Brogi, 2014). In official political communities, a researcher or team of netnographers who interact with other users could be used, as they would likely encounter a friendly space. This is helpful because the disclosure of an official position or representation of the campaign should not be a problem in these cases. These researchers can become a type of authorized and official voice and ears for the community, generating a bridge between volunteers, users, and campaign officials.

2. *Supporter-initiated online political communities.* Online groups can be initiated from the official political actor, or they can also be created by citizens. The latter organizations is a non-official online political communities. These communities can support a candidate, party or organization and are often initiated and maintained by citizens who are followers of the political brand. In many cases, the behavior of these communities is similar to that of a fan group. For example, online groups from a specific region or area, demographics groups such as students or women in favor of the candidate, or others tend to show considerable enthusiasm for topics or candidates. For example, Alexandria Ocasio-Cortez has inspired an enthusiastic fan base on social media in the United States (Barnes 2020). Although netnographers can actively participate in these communities, this participation should be undertaken only with the support of the administrator of the page and with all the group's users being very clear about the researcher's intentions. Such an approach is in line with netnographic precepts. It offers researchers the opportunity to mirror the actions of influencers, in that they will interact in the name of the brand and disclose the relationship. However, instead of sharing opinions, they will be there to gather ideas, discourses, and observations.

3. *Opposition research in oppositional political online communities:* A more controversial possibility is the use of netnography to study oppositional online communities, that is, sites that support the opposite candidate or party. Opposition research is an important part of a political marketing campaign as a way to find opponents' weak spots (Strömbäck, 2009). In marketing, netnography has already been used to understand brand rivalry and community conflicts. The findings of Ewing, Wagstaff, and Powell's (2013) study suggest that rivalry between brand communities can manifest in different ways as humor, ridicule, and even hostile behavior. Accordingly, we hypothesize that this type of conduct could be popular among rival political brands due to the high emotions between them.

The participation of a netnographer in these types of communities is subject to an ethical dilemma, as a netnographer should never misrepresent him- or herself when researching (Kozinets, 2015, 2019a). As well, there may be a practical impossibility regarding disclosing their presence without affecting the outcome. However, where these groups are public or have public elements, their study becomes far simpler and not subject to these restrictions. A more observational netnography where the researcher collects data can be performed as long as they are situated in public communities or forums.

4. *Anti-brand political communities:* As mentioned before, rivalry can lead to hostile confrontations or even to a radicalizing of the competition or those who follow them. A version of this type of conduct exists in political anti-brand communities, sites where most of the content is in opposition or attacking a candidate or party. These attacks need not be direct, but could also be in the form of parodies, memes, songs, or similar tactics. In marketing, anti-brand communities have been studied in different scenarios.

For example, Hollenbeck and Zinkhan (2010) used netnography to study an anti-Walmart community. These types of communities could generate a narrative that can pollute the brand meaning, generating what is called a doppelgänger image (Thompson, Rindfleisch, & Arsel, 2006), a concept that might become more widely applicable in political discourse and study. Political netnographers can collect data from public opposition sites and use this data to look for clues to understand how their image can be affected and what themes or doppelgänger images might be emerging. In such cases, it is particularly important to "closely monitor popular culture for signs that their brand is beginning to develop a doppelgänger brand image" (Thompson et al., 2006, 61).

5. *Activist Political Online Communities:* Another type of community that the netnographer can follow consists of forums specifically developed for activists to promote or further activism. These can be formal non-profit sites or areas that have pursued an activist theme that can be of significant influence in politics. We will discuss online activists later in this chapter as a relevant issue for political netnographers.

6. *Non-political online communities:* Finally, we must acknowledge that many political discussions actually take place on non-political sites (Svensson 2015; Wright, Graham, & Jackson, 2016). These could be news sites such as those of magazines, newspapers, or television channels, or even other thematic sites, where, from time to time, people discuss politics. Jenkins (2016) found political discussions occurring often on fan-related sites, such as among Harry Potter or Superman fans. There may be no limit to the kinds of sites and social media discussions that involve power and political topics and concerns. The researcher also may want to understand the structure of each of these online groups: what is the emerging theme? Can we apply some of the ideology or power analyses discussed earlier to these groups and their interactions?

CONCLUSIONS

The aim of the chapter was to explore, discuss and expand the possibilities of developing the novel concept of political netnography both for scholars and practitioners. In this context, we interpreted political ethnography as a qualitative research method that can give us deep insights about conversations related to power and resource distribution. Today, many of these conversations have moved to social media. Therefore, political netnography takes advantage of the largely untapped opportunity to understand these political conversations using a rigorous and well-defined methodological technique, and to use this technique in order to make sense of them in context by an empathic and immersed human researcher.

This chapter classified current netnographies in the political vein into three different category, revealing how current research interest in the political arena can be structured. Methods and tools specifically developed to study social media can be of great help in the field. This chapter examine the concepts of power and ideology, noting how importing methods from other interpretive and qualitative methods can benefit the development of political netnography. In the last part of the chapter we also examine how the concept of political netnography can be applied not only for theory develop but also for informing the strategy making of political institutions and actors.

Finally, I believe that the use of political netnography as a research method could be usefully applied by some obvious suspects such as political scientists or political strategists, and can also be used for other non-so-obvious research purposes. Every day, politics become more relevant, urgent, and embedded within social media. Any discipline that requires careful investigation of the relationship between power and the discourses reflected and originating in social media can benefit from political netnography. For example, one area of personal interest to me (as a politically inclined marketing professor), is how companies and brands interact with the political sphere. One recent salient example is the 2019 Nike campaign starring Colin Kaepernick, which combined notions of politics, sports, exclusion, nationalism, and race. Many other brands have entered or contributed to social media discourses of ideology, politics, and power. In closing, let me note that this chapter is certainly not the final word on the inter-relation of social media, research, and the political sphere. It is intended to be just the first brick in the political netnography house of ideas. By introducing the political netnography concept, I partake in the long open source tradition of netnography. I sincerely hope that many other scholars, practitioners, and thinkers will come forth to help develop, refine, and contribute both to the political netnography method and to the body of work which is represents.

REFERENCES

Allcott, H., & Gentzkow, M. (2017). Social media and fake news in the 2016 election. *Journal of Economic Perspectives*, 31(2), 211–236.

Arnould, E. J., & Wallendorf, M. (1994). Market-oriented ethnography: Interpretation building and marketing strategy formulation. *Journal of Marketing Research*, 31(4), 484–504. doi:10.2307/3151878

Aung, M., Bahramirad, S., Burga, R., Hayhoe, M.-A., Huang, S., & LeBlanc, J. (2017). Sense-making accountability: Netnographic study of an online public perspective. *Social and Environmental Accountability Journal*, 37(1), 18–32.

Auyero, J. (2006). Introductory note to politics under the microscope: Special issue on political ethnography I. *Qualitative Sociology*, 29(3), 257–259.

Baiocchi, G., & Connor, B. T. (2008). The ethnos in the polis: Political ethnography as a mode of inquiry. *Sociology Compass*, 2(1), 139–155.

Barahona, M., García, C., Gloor, P., & Parraguez, P. (2012). *Tracking the 2011 student-led movement in chile through social media use.* Paper presented at the Collective Intelligence 2012.

Barnes, Christopher C. (2020). Democratic socialists on social media: Cohesion, fragmentation, and normative strategies. *tripleC: Communication, Capitalism & Critique. Open Access Journal for a Global Sustainable Information Society*, 18(1), 32–47.

Belk, R., & Kozinetz, R. (2017). Videography and netnography. In K. Kubacki & S. Rundle-Thiele (Eds.). *Formative research in social marketing* (pp. 265–279). Singapore: Springer.

Benzecry, C. E., & Baiocchi, G. (2017). What is political about political ethnography? On the context of discovery and the normalization of an emergent subfield. *Theory and Society*, 46(3), 229–247. doi:10.1007/s11186-017-9289-z

Biddix, J. P., & Park, H. W. (2008). Online networks of student protest: the case of the living wage campaign. *New Media & Society*, 10(6), 871–891. doi:10.1177/1461444808096249

Biraghi, S., & Gambetti, R. C. (2018). How to use digital diaries in data collection to engage networked consumers. *Mercati & Competitività*, 4, 109–127.

Bonilla, Y., & Rosa, J. (2015). # Ferguson: Digital protest, hashtag ethnography, and the racial politics of social media in the United States. *American Ethnologist*, 42(1), 4–17.

Boswell, J., Corbett, J., Dommett, K., Jennings, W., Flinders, M., Rhodes, R., & Wood, M. (2019). State of the field: What can political ethnography tell us about anti-politics and democratic disaffection? *European Journal of Political Research*, 58(1), 56–71.

Bradshaw, S., & Howard, P. N. (2018). Challenging truth and trust: A global inventory of organized social media manipulation. *The Computational Propaganda Project*.

Brogi, S. (2014). Online brand communities: A literature review. *Procedia-Social and Behavioral Sciences*, 109(0), 385–389.

Campbell, A. (2006). The search for authenticity: An exploration of an online skinhead newsgroup. *New Media & Society*, 8(2), 269–294.

Castells, M. (2012). *Redes de indignación y esperanza.* Madrid: Alianza Editorial.

Cayla, Julien, and Eric Arnould (2013). Ethnographic stories for market learning. *Journal of Marketing*, 77 (4), 1–16.

Cogburn, D. L., & Espinoza-Vasquez, F. K. (2011). From networked nominee to networked nation: Examining the impact of Web 2.0 and social media on political participation and civic engagement in the 2008 Obama campaign. *Journal of Political Marketing*, 10(1–2), 189–213. doi:10.1080/15377857.2011.540224

Davis, R., Bacha, C. H., & Just, M. R. (2016). *Twitter and elections around the world: Campaigning in 140 characters or less.* New York, NY: Routledge.

de Volo, L. B., & Schatz, E. (2004). From the inside out: Ethnographic methods in political research. *PS: Political Science & Politics, 37*(2), 267–271.

Engesser, S., Ernst, N., Esser, F., & Büchel, F. (2017). Populism and social media: How politicians spread a fragmented ideology. *Information, Communication & Society, 20*(8), 1109–1126.

Enli, G. (2017). Twitter as arena for the authentic outsider: exploring the social media campaigns of Trump and Clinton in the 2016 US presidential election. *European Journal of Communication, 32*(1), 50–61. doi:10.1177/0267323116682802

Ewing, M. T., Wagstaff, P. E., & Powell, I. H. (2013). Brand rivalry and community conflict. *Journal of Business Research, 66*(1), 4–12.

Gee, J. P. (2010). *How to do discourse analysis: A toolkit.* London: Routledge.

Gerbaudo, P. (2018). Social media and populism: an elective affinity? *Media, Culture & Society, 40*(5), 745–753. doi:10.1177/0163443718772192

Greene, M. J. (2014). On the inside looking in: Methodological insights and challenges in conducting qualitative insider research. *The Qualitative Report, 19*(29), 1–13.

Hall, W., Tinati, R., & Jennings, W. (2018). From Brexit to Trump: Social media's role in democracy. *Computer, 51*(1), 18–27.

Hollenbeck, C. R., & Zinkhan, G. M. (2010). Anti-brand communities, negotiation of brand meaning, and the learning process: The case of Wal-Mart. *Consumption, Markets and Culture, 13*(3), 325–345.

Jenkins, H. (2016). Youth voice, media, and political engagement: Introducing the core concepts. In H. Jenkins, S. Shresthova, L. Gamber-Thompson, N. Kligler-Vilenchik, & A. Zimmerman (Eds.). *By any media necessary: The new youth activism* (pp. 1–60). New York: New York University Press.

Jha, C. K., & Kodila-Tedika, O. (2019). Does social media promote democracy? Some empirical evidence. *Journal of Policy Modeling.* doi:https://doi.org/10.1016/j.jpolmod.2019.05.010

Jost, J. T., Barberá, P., Bonneau, R., Langer, M., Metzger, M., Nagler, J., ... & Tucker, J. A. (2018). How social media facilitates political protest: Information, motivation, and social networks. *Political Psychology, 39*, 85–118.

Kozinets, R. V. (1998). On netnography: Initial reflections on consumer research investigations of cyberculture. *Advances in Consumer Research, 25*(1), 366–371.

Kozinets, R. V. (2002). The field behind the screen: Using netnography for marketing research in online communities. *Journal of Marketing Research, 39*(1), 61–72. doi:10.1509/jmkr.39.1.61.18935

Kozinets, R. V. (2006). Click to connect: Netnography and tribal advertising. *Journal of Advertising Research, 46*(3), 279–288. doi:10.2501/S0021849906060338

Kozinets, R. V. (2015). *Netnography: Redefined.* London: Sage.

Kozinets, R. V (2019a). *Netnography: The essential guide to qualitative social media research.* London: SAGE Publications Limited.

Kozinets, R. V. (2019b). YouTube utopianism: Social media profanation and the clicktivism of capitalist critique. *Journal of Business Research, 98*, 65–81.

Kozinets, R. V., & Handelman, J. (1998). Ensouling consumption: A netnographic exploration of the meaning of boycotting behavior. In Joseph Alba & Wesley Hutchinson (Eds.). *Advances in consumer research*, Vol. 25 (pp. 475–80). Provo, UT: Association for Consumer Research.

Kozinets, R. V., & Handelman, J. M. (2004). Adversaries of consumption: Consumer movements, activism, and ideology. *Journal of Consumer Research, 31*(3), 691–704.

Kozinets, R. V., Scaraboto, D., & Parmentier, M.-A. (2018). Evolving netnography: How brand auto-netnography, a netnographic sensibility, and more-than-human netnography can transform your research. *Journal of Marketing Management, 34*(3–4), 231–242. doi:10.1080/0267257X.2018.1446488

Kreiss, D., Lawrence, R. G., & McGregor, S. C. (2018). In their own words: Political practitioner accounts of candidates, audiences, affordances, genres, and timing in strategic social media use. *Political Communication, 35*(1), 8–31.

Kulavuz-Onal, D., & Vásquez, C. (2013). Reconceptualising fieldwork in a netnography of an online community of English language teachers. *Ethnography and Education, 8*(2), 224–238.

Laaksonen, S.-M., Nelimarkka, M., Tuokko, M., Marttila, M., Kekkonen, A., & Villi, M. (2017). Working the fields of big data: Using big-data-augmented online ethnography to study candidate–candidate interaction at election time. *Journal of Information Technology & Politics, 14*(2), 110–131.

Langer, R., & Beckman, S.C. (2005). Sensitive research topics: Netnography revisited. *Qualitative Market Research An International Journal, 8*(2), 189–203.

Lin, J.-S., & Himelboim, I. (2018). Political brand communities as social network clusters: Winning and trailing candidates in the GOP 2016 primary elections. *Journal of Political Marketing*, 1–29. doi:10.1080/15377857.2018.1478661

Lugosi, P., & Quinton, S. (2018). More-than-human netnography. *Journal of Marketing Management, 34*(3–4), 287–313.

Luhtakallio, E., & Eliasoph, N. (2014). Ethnography of politics and political communication: Studies in sociology and political science. *The Oxford handbook of political communication*. Oxford: Oxford Handbooks Online, 1–11.

Mariampolski, H. (2006). *Ethnography for marketers: A guide to consumer immersion*. Thousand Oaks, California: Sage.

Mkono, M., & Markwell, K. (2014). The application of netnography in tourism studies. *Annals of Tourism Research, 48*, 289–291.

Morgan, S. (2018). Fake news, disinformation, manipulation and online tactics to undermine democracy. *Journal of Cyber Policy, 3*(1), 39–43. doi:10.1080/23738871.2018.1462395

Nulty, P., Theocharis, Y., Popa, S. A., Parnet, O., & Benoit, K. (2016). Social media and political communication in the 2014 elections to the European Parliament. *Electoral Studies, 44*, 429–444.

Ott, B. L. (2017). The age of Twitter: Donald J. Trump and the politics of debasement. *Critical Studies in Media Communication, 34*(1), 59–68.

Patterson, M., & Monroe, K. R. (1998). Narrative in political science. *Annual Review of Political Science, 1*(1), 315–331. doi:10.1146/annurev.polisci.1.1.315

Scherman, A., Arriagada, A., & Valenzuela, S. (2015). Student and environmental protests in Chile: The role of social media. *Politics, 35*(2), 151–171. doi:10.1111/1467-9256.12072

Scullion, R., Jackson, D., & Molesworth, M. (2013). Performance, politics, and media: How the 2010 British general election leadership debates generated "talk" among the electorate. *Journal of Political Marketing, 12*(2–3), 226–243.

Silva, E. (2016). Patagonia, without dams! Lessons of a David vs. Goliath campaign. *The Extractive Industries and Society, 3*(4), 947–957.

Strömbäck, J. (2009). Selective professionalisation of political campaigning: A test of the party-centred theory of professionalised campaigning in the context of the 2006 Swedish election. *Political Studies, 57*(1), 95–116. doi:10.1111/j.1467-9248.2008.00727.x

Svensson, J. (2012). Negotiating the political self on social media platforms: An in-depth study of image-management in an election-campaign in a multi-party democracy. *eJournal of eDemocracy & Open Government, 4*(2), 183–197.

Svensson, J. (2015). Participation as a pastime: Political discussion in a queer community online. *Javnost-The Public, 22*(3), 283–297.

Thompson, C. J., Rindfleisch, A., & Arsel, Z. (2006). Emotional branding and the strategic value of the doppelgänger brand image. *Journal of Marketing, 70*(1), 50–64.

Tilly, C. (2006). Afterword: Political ethnography as art and science. *Qualitative sociology, 29*(3), 409–412.

Valenzuela, S. (2013). Unpacking the use of social media for protest behavior: The roles of information, opinion expression, and activism. *American Behavioral Scientist, 57*(7), 920–942. doi:10.1177/0002764213479375

Valenzuela, S., Halpern, D., Katz, J. E., & Miranda, J. P. (2019). The paradox of participation versus misinformation: social media, political engagement, and the spread of misinformation. *Digital Journalism, 7*(6), 802–823. doi:10.1080/21670811.2019.1623701

Van Dijk, T. A. (1993). Principles of critical discourse analysis. *Discourse & Society, 4*(2), 249–283.

Van Dijk, T. A. (2001). Discourse, ideology and context. *Folia Linguistica, 35*(1–2), 11–40.

Van Dijk, T. A. (2006). Ideology and discourse analysis. *Journal of Political Ideologies, 11*(2), 115–140.

Van Dijk, T. A. (2014). Discourse, cognition, society. *The discourse studies reader: Main currents in theory and analysis, 388*, 121–146.

Velasquez, A. (2012). Social media and online political discussion: The effect of cues and informational cascades on participation in online political communities. *New Media & Society, 14*(8), 1286–1303.

Villegas, D. (2018). From the self to the screen: A journey guide for auto-netnography in online communities. *Journal of Marketing Management, 34*(3–4), 243–262. doi:10.1080/0267257X.2018.1443970

Wang, Y.-S. (2019). Virtual cohabitation in online dating sites: A netnography analysis. *Online Information Review, 43*(4), 513–530. https://doi.org/10.1108/OIR-11-2016-0338

Wang, Y.-S., Lee, W.-L., & Hsu, T.-H. (2017). Using netnography for the study of role-playing in female online games. *Internet Research*, *27*(4), 905–923. https://doi.org/10.1108/IntR-04-2016-0111

Wright, S., Graham, T., & Jackson, D. (2015). Third space, social media, and everyday political talk. In A. Bruns, G. Enli, E. Skogerbø, A. O. Larsson, & C. Christensen (Eds.). *The Routledge companion to social media and politics* (pp. 74–88). New York: Routledge.

Xun, J., & Reynolds, J. (2010). Applying netnography to market research: The case of the online forum. *Journal of Targeting, Measurement and Analysis for Marketing*, *18*(1), 17–31.

Zinn, M. B. (1979). Field research in minority communities: Ethical, methodological and political observations by an insider. *Social Problems*, 27(2), 209–219.

8

Netnography in Public Relations

Margalit Toledano

INTRODUCTION

There are major debates about the definition and function of public relations. The Public Relations Society of America defines the profession as "a strategic communication process that builds mutually beneficial relationships between organizations and their publics" (http://prdefinition.prsa.org/index.php/2012/03/01/new-definition-of-public-relations/). Other definitions focus on public relations as sustained efforts to establish and maintain goodwill and mutual understanding and see practitioners acting as the intermediaries between organizations and society. Less positive viewpoints align public relations with organizational and managerial biases that shape unethical manipulative practices with the pejorative title of "spin."

Since the 1990s, public relations scholarship has increasingly developed diverse approaches to the profession's role in society. Critical scholars, for example, attend more to practitioners' abuse of power when communicating on behalf of organizations, to public relations promotion of exclusive elite and corporate interests, and to its use of unethical strategies and tactics (L'Etang, McKie, Snow & Xifra 2016). Even mainstream public relations scholars have called for a shift from organization-centered practices to more community-based ones. Heath (2013, 368) called for a "fully functioning society" approach to public relations that reasons that "for organisations to be successful they need to contribute to society, its dialogue quality, its sense of community, the quality of its structure and functions for collaborative decision making, the correction of meaning, and the alignment of interests." As the field matures, more public relations scholars are advocating for a shift of focus from one based on individual practitioners serving organizations to one that challenges organizations and their practitioners to serve the community (Heath, 2018).

In this respect, public relations differs from marketing communication. Unlike marketers, public relations professionals not only serve all sectors – business, government, and non-profit organizations – but are less focused on such organizational interests as increasing sales and enhancing customer relations. Public relations seek to build relationships with internal as well as diverse external stakeholders. While marketing professionals use market research to inform strategic decisions and employ advertising in paid media, public relations professionals use uncontrolled media and publicity earned via media relations in addition to lobbying, events, fundraising, and crisis and issue management. Similarly, community relations and the management of socially responsible projects are considered the responsibility of public relations. However, as Kozinets (2010) observes, boundaries between marketing communication and public relations are not always clear. Moreover, conflicts between the two, over strategy, budget, and ethics, often surface although cooperation is expected, especially in the context of responsibility for the organization's social media sites (Toledano, 2010). According to Kozinets (2010, 25) the strategy of social media should be the space for marketing and public relations to meet.

One major responsibility of public relations practitioners is building trustworthy relationships with diverse organizational stakeholders who can range from community activists to institutional investors. Each group of stakeholders is based on different socio-cultural norms and meanings that should be gauged and understood via formative research to enable effective communication and relationships with different publics. Stakeholders are, as Macnamara (2018a, 5) put it: "not only the recipients of messages and influence but also active agents in response and impact." Formative or planning research that identifies stakeholders' attitudes, information gaps, interests, and needs is an essential part of the practice of public relations. This remains true, even though it is often "skipped over by practitioners – particularly by those trained as *technicians* rather than strategic *managers*" (Macnamara, 2012b, 330). Studies have identified cost, lack of time, and especially lack of expertise and knowledge of appropriate research methods as major factors that explain the low use of research in public relations. Macnamara (2012b, 332) also attributes this to "a large number of PR practitioners ... [having] no training in research." Macnamara (2012b) further suggests that, to lower the cost of research, public relations would benefit from joining or "piggy-backing" marketing, brand or reputation research projects by, for example, adding specific questions to marketing surveys to serve public relations strategic planning decisions.

In order to augment the use of research in public relations, especially formative research, this chapter identifies opportunities in the particular social media research known as netnography. Netnography adapts the methods of ethnography and other research practices "to the cultural experiences that encompass and are reflected within the traces, networks, and systems of social media" (Kozinets, 2020, 19). The chapter suggests that netnographic explorations of organizational stakeholders and communities in their social and cultural contexts has the potential to provide vital insights for public relations practitioners on challenges that go beyond financial benefits for the organizations they serve. In addition, it argues that netnography offers both an appropriate method for better understanding public relations as a social phenomenon, and for comprehending the changing socio-cultural environment in which the profession functions.

This chapter overviews a limited number of ethnographic and netnographic studies in the public relations literature and shares experiences from two studies that demonstrate the value of netnography in providing relevant insights on cultures and social trends. In addition, it uses content from an interview with an expert on the use of research by the public relations industry. The interviewee, Ngaire Crawford, is Head of Insights NZ at Isentia (www.isentia.com/about-us/), a leading media intelligence and data technology company in the Asia Pacific. The online interview was held via Zoom, recorded, and transcribed with permission from Ms. Crawford. Based on her extensive experience in communication and media research – both as analyst and consultant to the PR industry for over 12 years – Ms. Crawford observed that "Social media analytics is currently used by the PR industry mainly to gauge Return on Investment (ROI)." Practitioners are interested in the potential numbers of people who could see or share the message, the total number of followers, the recording of "likes" and "shares." From a communication research perspective, this is a narrow view (Crawford, 2019).

Drawing from the interview evidence, the chapter presents public relations' current fascination with social media analytics as an embodiment of its functionalist paradigm designed to serve organizational interests. To demonstrate the potential of netnography to augment pro-social public relations research in alignment with its wish to contribute to fully functioning society, this chapter shares the author's experiences from two published netnographic studies on specific communities and their relevance to public relations. The two netnographic studies were concerned with community action, activism, and the spanned boundaries of the profession in the digital. Both studies also demonstrate how social media has enabled amateur civilians to perform public relations tasks successfully.

LITERATURE REVIEW

In an overview of the evolution of public relations measurement and evaluation since the beginning of the twentieth century, Watson (2012) identified the following major periods and themes. He found that, up to the 1950s, the emerging function of public relations used opinion polls and media analysis; while the second half of the century saw an expansion of media analysis until around 1975 when "the academic voice began to become more prominent in the discussion and development of methodologies and in nationally-based education programmes aimed at practitioners. The internet and social media also began to change practices" (390). He concluded that, in the new century, corporate communication requires the development of communication strategies "more closely related to organisational objectives where KPI are measured rather than outputs from communication activity" (396).

In 2010, the public relations industry accepted for the first time a new benchmark of standards for public relations measurement at the International Association of Measurement and Evaluation of Communication (AMEC) conference in Barcelona. The Barcelona Principles are designed to guide practitioners to measure, among other components, outcomes rather than outputs and to recognize the value of social media sources. The updated 2015 version of the Barcelona principles states that social media should be measured consistently with other media and focus on engagement (https://amecorg.com/how-the-barcelona-principles-have-been-updated/).

However, the industry continues to use evaluative research that is centered on the organization and is less interested in community or other stakeholder engagement. Stacks' (2017) widely used book, *The Primer of Public Relations Research*, states that public relations research goal is "to evaluate public relations outcomes and present them to the client (internal or external), thus adding to our impact on research return on investment" (p. vi). This functionalist organization-centered approach is echoed in other publications that are interested in measuring and proving public relations success only in the context of its contribution to an organization's goals. Macnamara (2012b, 206) criticizes the narrow functionalist view of public relations for its effort "to prove effectiveness and how these elements serve the need of the system – with the system usually defined as the organisation or the PR function itself." The narrow functionalist approach might be used by business, government, and non-profit organizations when they pursue what they identify as best for the organization at the cost of ignoring communities and the environment.

A group of public relations scholars, who advocate for a critical approach to the study of the field, has positioned itself against narrow functionalist approaches that refer to traditional systems theory. L'Etang (2008, 17) distinguishes between the key questions that inspire functional and critical approaches in public relations: Functional questions would be: "How can I measure media content? How can I evaluate this PR campaign? Which psychological models could be used to structure a persuasive campaign?"; critical questions would be: "Does PR impede or assist democracy? Is public relations another term for propaganda? Is public relations a profession?" This chapter argues that the dominance of the narrow functionalist paradigm in public relations explains the use of organization-centered evaluative research rather than ethnographic and netnographic formative research. This deficiency is especially regrettable in relation to public relations use of social media.

According to DiStaso, McCorkindale and Wright (2011), one Social Media Understanding Group conducted 25 interviews with public relations and communication executives about the opportunities and challenges their organizations faced using social media and how they measured the impact of social media on their organizations. Their study identified a clear wish for measurement of impact and behavioral outcomes designed to show how communicating with stakeholders via social media contributed to achieving organizational goals. Macnamara (2018a, 3) recently highlighted key omissions in those strategies: "even when evaluation of strategic communication is conducted at outcomes and impact stages, a key step that is missing in many projects and programs is identifying the full impact of decisions and activities on stakeholders and on society." He also identified the neglect of any "provision for identifying and reporting how the views, needs, and interests of stakeholders and publics might impact the organization and require it to change." This neglect highlights the narrow public relations industry's focus on social media communication that continues to be inspired by the organization-centered functionalist approach whereby the industry's measurement standards give "no recognition to impact on others beyond the intended impact specified in the organization's objectives or to broader contextual issues such as the social, cultural, and political environment" (Macnamara, 2018a, 2).

Social Media and Public Relations: Potentials and Practices

Social media has the capacity to move beyond current practices by providing public relations practitioners with extensive opportunities to reach, interact and build relationships with a wide range of organizational stakeholders. The interactive and participatory characteristic of social media supports, at least in theory, a paradigm of public relations able to assume social obligations, undertake dialogue with stakeholders on equal terms, and contribute to meaningful community engagement. In practice, however, social media is underused for this kind of research.

This emerges clearly in Macnamara's (2010) interviews with 15 Australian senior public relations executives designed to gauge their usage and opinions about the impact of social media on their organizations. They identified " 'Creating conversations,' 'dialogue,' 'engaging stakeholders,' 'listening' and 'building community' as important aspects of using social media" (Macnamara, 2010, 33). However, the research also noticed how public relations practice was not using all the benefits of social media and especially the opportunity to use social media for "listening" to stakeholder communities. Crawford (2019) confirms that practitioners tend to use social media analytics for evaluative research, mainly to measure the impact of public relations campaigns and messages on organizational objectives.

This need not be the limit of social media use. Brand and Beall (2017) call for "the application of cognitive listening theory to public relations in new media contexts" (56) and the use of analytic instruments as "listening tools" (58). They argue that "a cognitive listening model can serve as an effective means to connect current research threads on new media and public relations" (63). Similarly, while, Macnamara (2010, 24–25) found some "professional public communicators … [deployed] social media and social networks in naive and even deceitful ways" other cases found "some organisations engaging in productive ways with their stakeholders using interactive social media and social networks."

Concerns about the impact of public relations activities on social media on the community and society and the implications for democracy continue to be relatively neglected. Kent (2010, 650) has argued that public relations scholars have mistakenly evaluated social media as dialogic while practitioners used it as "just another tool of organizational marketing initiatives and exploiting publics." Kent (2013, 344) advocates for a more responsible use of social media that would not exploit publics, would be genuinely social and committed to the democratic ideals of public relations:

> For decades, we have argued that our communication technologies will connect us, but that connectivity to our "friends" on social media comes at the expense of isolation from our fellow human beings who live next door or down the hall.

He concludes that "social media are a tool that can be used better."

Augmenting PR Research

Professional communicators could, should and do utilize social media data to improve organizations' intelligence since online platforms play a major role in stakeholder communications and interaction. Nevertheless, that utilization is skewed. According to Wright and Hinson's (2015) report on a ten-year longitudinal study on the use of social media in the practice of public relations in the US, only about half of the professionals said their organizations (or their clients) were measuring social media for research. Although there is a constant growth in this number from year to year with a focus on measuring the effect of public relations activities on stakeholders, this and other similar reports from Europe showed no evidence for the use of netnography in public relations.

In the US, Jiang, Luo and Kulemeka's (2016) study conducted in-depth interviews with 43 senior communication managers from 15 top-tier corporations and 28 non-profits based in the US to examine how they evaluate social media engagement and how they cultivate as well as measure social media engagement during crises. Their findings indicate how social media analytics provide key information on: "numbers of page visits," "how long people stayed," "how many people responded and how many people liked, but also how many people looked at this one particular thing" (685). They identified "engagement" as a buzzword that consisted of social media users' involvement, interaction, intimacy, and influence that are measured via numerical parameters. They also identified the benefit of social media analytics for monitoring issues as part of crisis management which is a crucial function of public relations (687). Nevertheless, the practitioners still emphasized the future trend for social media analytics as "establishing dollar value of social media exposure" (686). In conclusion, it is evident that social media analytics is used for evaluating organization's self-centered goals whereas options for using netnography for better understanding of stakeholders, communities and social issues remain rare.

The rationale for using netnography in public relations research also builds on earlier, albeit limited, calls for the use of its predecessor ethnographic research. Public relations scholars who have championed ethnographic research are relatively scarce (Daymon & Holloway, 2011; Macnamara, 2012a; Stacks, 2011). L'Etang (2010) commented that not many public relations scholars "have invested the necessary time and practice" (149) to do ethnographic work despite ethnographic methods being particularly useful for the examination of "public relations work in various cultural settings" (L'Etang, 2012, 170). Daymon and Holloway (2011) also foreground the relevance of these methods to public relations in observing that traditional ethnography is concerned with "how social realities are seen from the perspective of those who live and work in them" (145). Their description of ethnographic research as "the study of a way of life (the culture) of a group, community or organization ... [that] relies on extended period of fieldwork" (163) also fits public relations needs. Although Pieczka (2002) did use them effectively in studying the culture of public relations professionals, her research approach has not been taken up by many others in the field.

One rare exception was Macnamara's (2012a) application of ethnographic analysis to the state of public relations education and practice in Australia through "a broad exploratory study … using ethnography and elements of autoethnography to provide reflective insights into the nature of and influences on PR scholarship and practice in the region" (367). Macnamara's (2018b) later and more ambitious ethnographic study was conducted internationally over two years to examine recently developed evaluation frameworks and models and accompanying implementation guidelines. It involved "First-hand observations and active participation was undertaken in a number of significant initiatives by organizations involved in attempting to develop standards and best practice models for evaluation of public communication during the period of the study" (Macnamara, 2018b, 183).

Given the inroads of ethnographic research into public relations, and the explosion of social media, this chapter argues that public relations is now well-placed to go to the next stage of research through the use of netnography as "the ethnography of online network actors and interactions" (Kozinets, 2020, 15). Both ethnography and netnography are interested in the investigation of cultures via participation, observation, and analysis of groups communication and behavior. However, this must be done with care because, as Kozinets (2020) has found, "netnography is not merely ethnography done online" (14) and "all netnographies involve collecting, participating, and interpreting online traces" (16). Online traces that people leave when they post texts, visuals, videos and so on are used for researching group cultures and this is one feature that helps distinguish netnography from other online ethnographic studies. These online traces are of special interest for public relations practitioners who would benefit from netnography when investigating online communities of stakeholders and social issues that impact the profession.

Using Netnography in Public Relations Research

Despite the potential benefits, examples of netnographic research in public relations are rare. Johns (2014) used netnography for analyzing the role of social media for agenda setting by the Australian government during a period of conflict. His content analysis of social media messages showed how a government authority was able "to connect with their previously alienated stakeholders and meet the needs of the community" (866). These findings were based on qualitative interviews and content analysis of media and agency reports. Data was also collected via netnographic observation of the social media pages posted by the Australian government authority – including its Facebook, Twitter, and YouTube channels. Johns' (2014) study provided insights relating to the use of social media, particularly in enhancing relationships with the communities.

Other Australian researchers used netnography for a study on bloggers (Archer & Harrigan, 2016, 4). They derived their data from three years of "ethnographic study between 2012 and 2015, both online and offline, of female (mainly 'mum') bloggers in Australia and the marketers and PR practitioners they liaise with." Their research explored the relationships between public relations practitioners and bloggers by a process that included blog contents that were downloaded "into word documents at regular intervals and coded thematically" (Archer & Harrigan, 2016, 4). They concluded, as if the terms were interchangeable, that their "study could be termed netnography (Kozinets, 2010) or digital ethnography (Underberg and Zorn, 2013)" (Archer & Harrigan, 2016, 4), although netnography is a specific set of research practices, rather than a general idea to take ethnography online. In order to provide more textured specifics, the next two sections offer critical reflections on the author's own research involving netnography: The first recounts experiences around the important public relations function of event management; the second looks at collective action involving fundraising, which is another common public relations role.

EXPERIENCES FROM A NETNOGRAPHIC STUDY (1): EVENTS MANAGEMENT AND THE MEETUP ORGANIZERS

Netnographic research can involve different levels of researcher participation in stakeholder communications and can range from mere observations to intensive engagement in the observed group's online deliberations. A high level of engagement requires a researcher "to establish trust and rapport with members of online platforms, fit in with the group, record data diligently but also ethically, and reflect upon their role in the research" (French & Gordon, 2015, 291). The following case shares the author's unplanned experience with members of an online community during an empirical netnographic study on the role of public relations practitioners in facilitating community networks. The study (Toledano & Maplesden, 2016) aimed at tracing the involvement of public relations in online networks and focused on facilitators of community networks who used an online platform called *Meetup* to manage offline community face-to-face interactions. Inspired by the centrality of community and community building concepts in the public relations literature (Hallahan, 2013), the study found that current democratic and inclusive networks might operate with no help from professional public relations services, but network facilitators, who were not trained in public relations, used public relations skills.

The portal Meetup enables the formation of local, community-based groups that set periodic, face-to-face, social meetings via Meetup's online system. Meetup groups use local meetings to share information and experiences, to pursue a cause they feel strongly about, to support political candidates, to act on environmental or community matters, or just go to the movies together. Each group has a different profile, topic of interest, size, and policies. What they have in common is that they all use the framework provided by Meetup and the group organizer pays a small fee for Meetup's administrative services on behalf of the group.

The sheer size of Meetup operations (currently 35 million Meetup users) and the role of Meetup organizers in this system, presented an opportunity to study the role of public relations in online networks and to reflect on its significance for the profession and society. The published study (Toledano & Maplesden, 2016) identified Meetup as an example of a developing trend in which untrained "amateur PR" users, such as Meetup organizers, might be taking over traditional public relations work in facilitating community networks.

The researchers obtained data from several sources: quantitative data from responses to an online questionnaire; qualitative data from ethnographic observations as well as netnographic observations of the organizers communication in their online forum; and email and Skype interviews with staff at Meetup headquarters and a small number of meetup organizers. The survey responses were analyzed with SPSS and netnographic content from the organizers' online discussions with each other on their designated Meetup forum was analyzed thematically.

To understand how the organizers of Meetup groups work, the researchers first conducted face-to-face pilot interviews with two organizers of groups. They conducted an email interview with Meetup's Senior Community Relations Specialist from Meetup's New York headquarters. The authors also participated in three different group meetings to observe the way they worked. It was not possible to carry out the extended period of insider observations recommended in the ethnography literature because the groups did not welcome an observer. However, the researchers obtained information from observing the three open groups and used that to design a questionnaire for an online survey that targeted the online group of Meetup group organizers. The researchers posted the questionnaire by emails to the organizers in February 2015. Meetup's Community Relations Specialist gave permission via email to contact Meetup people.

The Meetup website provided a list of 125 Meetup groups in the US that were designated to organizers who wanted to share their experiences as organizers with other organizers. The Meetup organizers actually formed an online community of event managers and the authors were able to use their archived materials from the Meetup website to identify the issues and challenges they faced.

A full list of organizers of Meetup organizers' groups was available on the Meetup website with email addresses. The researchers sent a link to an online questionnaire (powered by Qualtrics) to organizers of large organizers' groups in the US with a detailed introduction about the research goal. Twenty-nine organizers provided valid responses to the online questionnaire, and although a small sample drawn from a small population of experts, the nature of the questionnaire allowed for meaningful descriptive analyses.

Surprisingly, and not at all according to the research plan, the organizers who received the invitation to participate in the research started a discussion not just about the research, but about the researchers on their designated online community space on Meetup's website. At first, the organizers suspected the researchers' motivation. That changed because one organizer found on the author's university's website an application that was submitted to the school's research scholarship committee and shared the detailed research plan with the organizers on their online discussion forum. The detailed research plan, although not intended for anybody outside the university, contributed to building trust and increased some organizers' engagement in the data collection. In practice, obtaining detailed description on the research project from the university sources ignited organizer excitement around it. The fact that they "hacked" it themselves to verify the researchers' genuine interest in Meetup organizers provided a sort of objective credibility and convinced the organizers to take part in the project that they could identify as sincere and valuable.

On their online discussion forum, organizers became intrigued by the questionnaire suggestion that they were using public relations skills. In their communication with each other, they admitted it was an accurate description of what they did and that it would probably be good for them to gain some training in public relations and event management. Some organizers used the emailed invitation to communicate directly with the researchers and provided detailed insights into their role as organizers of Meetup groups. The organizers' dialogue on their own forum created the netnographic opportunity for this project and eventually added valuable data to the findings.

Among other findings relating to the organizers' operations, the post-survey netnographic study found that though Meetup groups were not supposed to include any commercial activity, some organizers who organized several Meetup groups benefited from commercial sponsorship. They sometimes used the Meetup social network to promote their professional business and other interests and to build relationships in their industry and with commercial sponsors. The organizers provided insights into their relationships with sponsors and their event management challenges and solutions. Based on these findings the authors identified new ethical concerns for the industry in the online environment. They concluded that public relations practitioners should not exploit online/offline networks to influence the network members by promoting organizational interests in ways that may mislead communities.

The process of data collection in this study involved the researchers' participation as subjects of the investigated community. It demonstrates the realities of the relationships between researchers and participants in the new online environment. Denzin and Lincoln's (2011) editorial summary of Gaston's (2011) chapter reflects the experience of the researchers involved in the Meetup organizers' study. According to Denzin and Lincoln (2011, 418), Gaston presented a new space:

> where online subjects talk back, interact with us, read our research, criticize our work, all while eroding the walls we build around ourselves as objective outsiders studying the virtual worlds of others. We have become the subject. In this space, it is essential to reflect carefully on the ethical issues framing our studies.

Building trustworthy relationships between researchers and participants is essential since, as Daymon and Holloway (2011, 235) point out: "If you are able to establish rapport from the beginning of the research process, the evidence you collect will be valuable and insightful. Issues to consider in the interviewer-participant relationship concern status, trust and your 'communicative competencies.'"

This experience might be well described by the features of netnography, especially with regard to the relationships between researchers and participants. It provided valuable insights unlikely to have been obtained in any other way. One cautionary note is the need to pay particular attention to ethics in the new spaces "where online subjects talk back, interact with us, read our research, criticize our work, all while eroding the walls we build around ourselves as objective outsiders studying the virtual worlds of others" (Denzin & Lincoln, 2011, 418).

EXPERIENCES FROM A NETNOGRAPHIC STUDY (2): COMMUNITY ACTION BY BUYING A BEACH TOGETHER

Doan and Toledano's (2018) study – published under the title "Beyond organization-centred public relations: Collective action through a civic crowdfunding campaign" – combined netnography and thematic analysis of interviews with the major players involved. It provided an account of how two amateur activists initiated and managed a remarkably successful fundraising campaign that raised US$1.5 million within three weeks to buy a private beach in New Zealand and gift it back to New Zealanders. By analyzing the online campaign, the study identified success factors for civic crowdfunding campaigns and accounted for a different kind of activist and community-based public relations that goes beyond organization-centered approaches to offer gratifying community-centered work. The article suggested that the campaign addressed a promising but neglected intersection in the public relations literature, namely, the integration of online crowdfunding, collective action, and community activism.

The January–February 2016 Awaroa / Abel Tasman beach campaign in New Zealand attracted international media attention when it succeeded in raising money to buy what was then a private beach in order to open it to perpetual public access. The campaign was eventually taken up by almost 40,000 individuals, groups, and institutions through the civic crowdfunding platform Givealittle.co.nz (Givealittle, 2016). Because the Awaroa beach fundraising campaign ran exclusively online, netnography was selected as the most appropriate research method.

The research was based on five online resources. The first was the campaign Facebook page, with 127 messages posted by the campaign organizers and 1,435 comments posted by the public from January 22, 2016 – the launch day – to March 17, 2016 when the organizers received the certificate of change of the beach ownership. This source also included written and audio-visual materials such as video clips produced by the campaign organizers to provide updates and links to online media, radio, and TV clips. Additional data was gathered from the campaign's Givealittle page, which consisted of an overview, 36 updates, and 91 questions and answers; an analysis of a random sample of 372 comments that was drawn from 11,000 comments made by pledgers when they contributed on the platform Givealittle. co.nz; 51 archival media articles about the campaign on New Zealand's most popular news sites, stuff.co.nz and nzherald.co.nz, and from three blog posts specifically about the Awaroa beach by a protagonist in the campaign. In addition to the online sources, the researchers conducted five interviews with major players: the campaign organizers, the Givealittle platform's Chief Giving, a media representative, and the tender lawyer. An email interview was conducted with a communication representative of the New Zealand government's Department of Conservation (DOC). Data was transcribed and imported into NVivo for thematic analysis of content.

Doan and Toledano's (2018) study demonstrated the potential of netnography to enable effective public relations research on topics such as current community activism and donors' motivations. In doing so, it identified both a deeply rooted expectation for fairness, and an opposition to private ownership of a pristine beach, as major factors that enlisted masses of New Zealanders to participate in the huge civic crowdfunding campaign. New Zealanders' culture of giving money and time as volunteers for social causes placed them consistently on the top of a list of the most charitable countries around the globe (www.cafonline.org/about-us/publications/2016-publications).

The expectations for fairness, which became evident from the netnographic analysis of the pledgers' online messages, align with the country's traditional values. The selling of state-owned assets, and the scrapping of state control over wages, prices, rents etc., that were introduced to New Zealand's new neo-liberal markets in the 80s and 90s, resulted in high income inequality and poverty that did not match New Zealanders' previously well-rooted egalitarian values. Historically, New Zealand's "fundraising was informed by transnational precedents, but was also shaped by the early co-existence of state and voluntary welfare, and by its elaboration in a small-scale, egalitarian society" (Tennant, 2013, 47). Currently, the gap between the poor and wealthy does not reflect an egalitarian society but some cultural values and expectations were still there and ignited New Zealanders to act against private ownership of the beach.

Similar to the findings from the research on Meetup groups organizers, the Awaroa beach campaign was initiated and run by amateurs. In fact, two Christchurch brothers-in-law, Adam Gardner, a tennis coach, and Duane Major, a church community coordinator, came across the news about the beach being on sale on Christmas Day 2015 and started to banter about the beach, which they and their families have visited several times before. A couple of weeks later, when Major saw breath-taking pictures of the Awaroa beach that his friend posted on Facebook, the pair decided to start a civic crowdfunding campaign to prevent it from going to private hands and to ensure free public access to this pristine beach (Gift Abel Tasman Beach, 2016). The two amateurs were able to conduct the most successful fundraising (civil crowdfunding) campaign in New Zealand history with no support from professional public relations thanks to the nature of social media, their authentic appeal, and the power of the community cause.

Crowdfunding, as a digital form of the public relations function of fundraising, deals and communicates with community, a foundational concept in public relations; collective action explains human action in producing and achieving common goals; and activism tackles social issues. In conjunction, they help public relations scholars and practitioners understand how to mobilize financial and non-financial resources beyond organizational boundaries and contribute positively to society. As the campaign illustrates, individuals as well as public relations practitioners can use crowdfunding as a tool that enables a shift from organizational goals to a focus on the promotion of social causes and to leading a fully functioning society (Heath, 2018).

ETHICAL CONCERNS

Even in this clearly pro-social example, and in computerized content analysis of social media conversations, ethical concerns remain. Reid and Duffy (2018, 280) ask two useful questions: "how do we approach participant observation and informed consent?" and "how do we ensure the anonymity of our research subject?" The legal rules around online privacy keep changing and Kozinets, Scaraboto, and Parmentier (2018, 240) expressed a key concern for the future of open research while profit-motivated business organizations actually own and control "most of the data, most of the platforms, and most of the data analysis tools in the world."

To counter the growing influence of platforms and potential abuse of the system for profit the European Union recently introduced a new code of ethics and regulations that require informed consent from content contributors and full transparency. The new ethical code GDPR (General Data Protection Regulation) has been in force in Europe since May 2018 and will "fundamentally reshape the way in which data is handled across every sector, from healthcare to banking and beyond" (EU GDPR https://eugdpr.org/).

Ngaire Crawford (2019) commented that

Following the Cambridge Analytica server violation of privacy rights and abuse of social media, data authorities have been limiting access to social media data in order to protect online privacy. It limited the ability of monitoring and accessing data on how people engage with brands or issues. We cannot gauge "closed" groups where people share content that companies are interested to see and analyse. Infiltrating closed groups is illegal.

The meetup case presented in Toledano and Maplesden (2016) raised concerns around different ethical challenges, mainly in gaining the investigated online community's trust and agreement to participate in the research based on informed consent. The outcome suggests that researchers who conduct online surveys, either as academics or practitioners, should be prepared for suspicious respondents using the Internet to access details about the research project that may not have been intended for them. In the case of the Meetup research, this eventually had a positive impact as it built the researchers' credibility and participants were able to trust the survey following their own investigation on the researchers and the research goal. On the strength of this experience, it is possible to conclude that transparency and cooperation between researchers and the research subjects at the earliest stage of the research is essential for building trust and engaging participants in the data collection. This is true in both traditional research methods as well as such newer qualitative methods as netnography.

Netnography was indeed an appropriate approach to the study of the specific occupational group of Meetup event managers and the specific nation-wide activist movement that bought a beach together via a crowdfunding campaign. In both cases ethical codes were respected. The researchers used only open content and only engaged with interviewees who agreed to participate in the study. However, conducting social media analytics as well as netnographic studies present ethical challenges that have also to be taken into consideration.

DISCUSSION AND CONCLUSION

This chapter discussed the potential of netnographic research to support the evolution of the public relations practice and scholarship into more socially responsible and respected activities that contribute to a fully functioning society. The traditional functionalist approach to public relations predominantly emphasizes and measures outputs and outcomes that are limited to the organizational mission. Heath (2018) explained the shift in PR research focus from serving organization self-interests to a broader socio-cultural and community perspective on its role in society:

> the goal became increasingly not only to understand the means by which organizations either bend society to serve them or bend themselves to serve society, but also to develop the assessments by which to determine which strategic options and outcomes serve society best.
>
> (2)

Netnography enables public relations to go beyond the standard evaluation of outcomes that benefit only the employing organizations; netnography allows access to new types of data drawn from observations of online communities and analyses of their conversations with each other. The two research experiences shared in this chapter provided evidence for the potential use of netnography in public relations studies.

The Meetup research (Toledano & Maplesden, 2016) highlighted contemporary realities in the online research environment and the need for a mix of research methods likely to benefit from the inclusion of netnography. It studied a community of online event managers that used public relations skills with no training or affiliation with the profession. The findings exposed how currently online/offline communities were organized by amateurs who might not be familiar with the profession's code of ethics and, therefore, act against it unconsciously. This was actually evident in the findings about financial sponsors of meetup groups and the lack of transparency around their relationships with the event organizers.

Through this study it was clear that the suggested netnographic approach to public relations research would be useful for describing professions from "the perspective of those who live and work in them" (Daymon & Holloway, 2011, 145). As a result, studies on the culture or values of public relations practitioners, for example, could be based on analysis of practitioner conversations with each other on their professional association forum and benefit from the advantages of netnographic research.

The second research project examined a crowdfunding campaign organized successfully by amateurs. Over a decade ago, Lewis, Williams, and Franklin (2008) examined the influence of public relations on the news media in the UK and identified one case of amateur success that led them to conclude that "'amateur' PR success is clearly not the norm" (14). It seems that during the decade the growth of social media has enabled amateur successes though with no specific ethical guidelines. Bruckman (2002) argued that "internet users are amateur artists. The internet can be seen as a playground for amateur artists creating semi-published work" (217). This different topic deserves further investigation.

The crowdfunding study looked at the motivations for community action and suggested that civic crowdfunding might serve as a foundational technological platform for resource-limited activists to gain more capabilities and funding. It demonstrated how civic crowdfunding could be used for pro-social activism and could be developed as a public relations practice contributing to a fully functioning society.

Neither of the two cases attempted to measure communication impact that might benefit self-interested organizations. Both studies aimed to understand the new communities' dynamics and their implications for the profession. The studies serve as an example for the potential of netnography to enable the growth of the public relations body of knowledge beyond organizational contexts. However, it was noted that the use of research in general and netnography in particular is not prevalent in the industry of public relations. According to Ms. Ngaire:

> Public relations practitioners want data that relate to their clients' reputation and the impact of their messages. Only few are using online data to gain understanding of stakeholders. We should be interested in how stakeholders understand issues, their feelings about it, the lenses they use to interpret general issues. We need to use human judgement of sentiments and relate to nuances. I advocate for human-based research that is able to identify nuances and discrepancies in discourse.

The chapter provided evidence for the contention that the public relations industry is underutilizing netnography as a research tool that can provide insights into the environment, social and cultural issues affecting organizations' stakeholders, and the profession. Big Data, social media, and social network analytics are becoming part of public relations practitioner toolkits and the topic of special courses included in public relations curricula whereas netnographic studies capable of better serving the community and social approach to public relations have not yet become a core component of the mainstream research toolkit or featured in public relations degree courses.

Reid and Duffy (2018) deal with the difference between netnography and social media content analysis by defining "netnographic sensibility" as an approach that "marries the nuanced, rich understanding of consumer garnered through netnography (Kozinets, 2015, 263), with the scale and depth facilitated through social listening practices." They suggest this concept as a bridge between netnography and social media monitoring "while the automation of the data through social media monitoring tools is one way of categorising and classifying data, there remains a need for human insight to understand the nuances behind behaviours" (Reid & Duffy, 2018, 271).

Following on from that research, this chapter concludes that social media analytics provides useful but limited understanding on organizations and stakeholder communications and relationships. Public relations research would benefit from going beyond social media monitoring and analytics to embrace netnography as a method that enables deeper insight into the social and cultural environment in which stakeholders live. According to the contextual insight of Edwards (2012, 18), "PR is shaped by the cultures and societies in which it operates [and so the] … effects of PR work must be measured in social and cultural terms, as well as in terms of organizational interests." On these grounds, as well as for its intrinsically distinct and contemporary research capabilities, netnography is both a useful and appropriate method to be included in the contemporary public relations research toolkit and a way to assist public relations to fulfil its social role.

REFERENCES

Archer, C., & Harrigan, P. (2016). Show me the money: How bloggers as stakeholders are challenging theories of relationship building in public relations. *Media International Australia, 160*(1), 67–77.

Brand, J. D., & Beall, M. L. (2017). Cognitive listening theory and public relations practices in new media. In S. Duhé (Ed.), *New media and public relations* (pp. 56–66) (3rd. ed.). New York, NY: Peter Lang.

Bruckman, A. (2002). Studying the amateur artist: A perspective on disguising data collected in human subjects research on the Internet. *Ethics and Information Technology, 4*(3), 217–231.

Crawford, N. (2019). Personal communication with the author on 11 Nov, 2019, via Zoom online conversation. Wellington and Hamilton, New Zealand.

Daymon, C., & Holloway, I. (2011). *Qualitative research methods in public relations and marketing communications* (2nd. ed.). Abingdon, UK: Routledge.

Denzin, N. K., & Lincoln, Y. S. (Eds.). (2011). *The Sage handbook of qualitative research* (4th. ed.). Thousand Oaks, CA: Sage.

DiStaso, M. W., McCorkindale, T. & Wright, D. K. (2011). How public relations executives perceive and measure the impact of social media in their organizations. *Public Relations Review, 37*(3), 325–328.

Doan, M., & Toledano, M. (2018). Beyond organization-centred public relations: Collective action through a civic crowdfunding campaign. *Public Relations Review, 44*(1), 37–46.

Edwards, L. (2012). Defining the "object" of public relations research: A new starting point. *Public Relations Inquiry, 1*(1), 7–30.

French, J., & Gordon, R. (2015). *Strategic social marketing.* Thousand Oaks, CA: Sage.

Gaston, S. N. (2011). The methods, politics, and ethics of representation in online ethnography. In N. K. Denzin & Y. S. Lincoln (Eds.), *The Sage handbook of qualitative research* (pp. 513–527). (4th. ed.). Thousand Oaks, CA: Sage.

Gift Abel Tasman Beach. (2016). Retrieved 17 October from www.facebook.com/saveatb/

Givealittle. (2016). Retrieved 17 October, from: https://givealittle.co.nz/project/abeltasmanbeach2016/share

Hallahan, K. (2013). Community and community building. In R. L. Heath (Ed.), *Encyclopedia of public relations, Vol. 1* (pp. 166–169) (2nd. ed.). Thousand Oaks, CA: Sage.

Heath, R. L. (2013). Fully functioning society theory. In R. L. Heath (Ed.), *Encyclopedia of public relations, Vol. 1* (pp. 368–371) (2nd. ed.). Thousand Oaks, CA: Sage.

Heath, R. L. (2018). Fully Functioning Society. In R. L. Heath & W. Johansen (Eds.), *The international encyclopedia of strategic communication.* Hoboken, NJ: John Wiley & Sons. https://doi-org.ezproxy.waikato.ac.nz/10.1002/9781119010722.iesc0078

Jiang, H., Luo, I. & Kulemeka, O. (2016). Social media engagement as an evaluation barometer: Insights from communication executives. *Public Relations Review, 42*(4), 679–691.

Johns, R. (2014). Community change: Water management through the use of social media, the case of Australia's Murray-darling Basin. *Public Relations Review, 40*(5), 865–867.

Kent, M. L. (2010). Directions in social media for professionals and scholars. In R. L. Heath (Ed.), *The SAGE handbook of public relations* (pp. 643–656). Thousand Oaks, CA: Sage.

Kent, M. L. (2013). Using social media dialogically: Public relations role in reviving democracy. *Public Relations Review, 39*(4), 337–345.

Kozinets, R. V. (2010). Social media vision: Marketing and the threat of public relationships. *Finance, Marketing and Production, XXVIII*(4), 21–27. doi: 10.1400 / 199967.

Kozinets, R. V. (2015). *Netnography: Redefined.* London, UK: Sage.

Kozinets, R. V., Scaraboto, D. & Parmentier, M. A. (2018). Evolving netnography: How brand auto-netnography, a netnographic sensibiltiy, and more-than-human netnography can transform your research. *Journal of Marketing Management, 34*(3–4), 231–242.

Kozinets, R. V. (2020). *Netnography: The essential guide to qualitative social media research.* London, UK: Sage.

L'Etang, J. (2008). *Public relations: Concepts, practice and critique.* Thousand Oaks, CA: Sage.

L'Etang, J. (2010). "Make it real": Anthropological reflections on public relations, diplomacy, and rhetoric. In R. L. Heath (Ed.), *The SAGE handbook of public relations* (pp. 145–162) (2nd. ed.). Thousand Oaks, CA: Sage.

L'Etang, J. (2012). Public relations, culture, and anthropology: Towards an ethnographic research agenda. *Journal of Public Relations Research, 24*(2), 165–183.

L'Etang, J., McKie, D., Snow, N. & Xifra, J. (Eds.). (2016). *The Routledge handbook of critical public relations.* Abingdon, UK: Routledge.

Lewis, J., Williams, A. & Franklin, B. (2008). A compromised fourth estate? *Journalism Studies, 9*(1), 1–20. doi: 10.1080/14616700701767974

Macnamara, J. (2010). Public relations and the social: How practitioners are using, or abusing, social media. *Asia Pacific Public Relations Journal, 11*(1), 21–39.

Macnamara, J. (2012a). The global shadow of functionalism and excellence theory: An analysis of Australian PR. *Public Relations Inquiry, 1*(3), 367–402.

Macnamara, J. (2012b). *Public relations: Theories, practices, critiques.* French Forest, Australia: Pearson.

Macnamara, J. (2018a). Impact Assessment. In R. L. Heath & W. Johansen (Eds.), *The international encyclopedia of strategic communication* (pp. 1–9). Hoboken, NJ: John Wiley & Sons. https://onlinelibrary-wiley-com.ezproxy.waikato.ac.nz/doi/10.1002/9781119010722.iesc0078

Macnamara, J. (2018b). A review of new evaluation models for strategic communication: Progress and gaps. *International Journal of Strategic Communication, 12*(2), 180–195.

Motion, J., Heath, R. L. & Leitch, S. (2015). *Social media and public relations: Fake friends and powerful publics.* Abingdon, UK: Routledge.

Pieczka, M. (2002). Public relations expertise deconstructed. *Media, Culture & Society, 24*(3), 301–323. https://doi.org/10.1177/016344370202400302

Reid, E., & Duffy, K. (2018). A netnographic sensibility: Developing the netnographic/social listening boundaries. *Journal of Marketing Management, 34*(3–4), 263–286.

Stacks, D. W. (2011). *Primer of public relations research* (2nd. ed.). New York, NY: Guilford Press.

Stacks, D. W. (2017). *Primer of public relations research* (3rd. ed). New York, NY: The Gilford Press.

Tennant, M. (2013). Fun and fundraising; The selling of charity in New Zealand's past. *Social History, 38*(1), 46–65.

Toledano, M. (2010). Professional competition and cooperation in the digital age: A pilot study of New Zealand practitioners. *Public Relations Review, 36*(3), 230–237.

Toledano, M., & Maplesden, A. (2016). Facilitating community networks: Public relations skills and non-professional organizers. *Public Relations Review, 42*(4), 713–722.

Underberg, N., & Zorn, E. (2013). *Digital ethnography.* Austin, TX: University of Texas Press.

Watson, T. (2012). The evolution of public relations measurement and evaluation. *Public Relations Review, 38*(3), 390–398.

Wright D. K., & Hinson, D. M. (2015). Examining social and emerging media use in public relations practice: A ten-year longitudinal analysis. *Public Relations Journal, 9*(2), 1–26.

9

Netnography in Tourism Beyond Web 2.0
A Critical Assessment

Rokhshad Tavakoli and Paolo Mura

INTRODUCTION

Since its development by Tim Berners-Lee in 1989, the World Wide Web (WWW) has been continually evolving. The WWW, often referred to simply as the 'Web', is the hub of information, such as texts, images and videos that are shared using the Internet. By accessing the Web, users from around the world can connect and interact instantly (Berners-Lee, 2000). Originally conceived as a space for storing information that could be accessed and shared using Hypertext Transfer Protocol (HTTP), the Web has undergone many changes over the last two decades. Among these changes are technological advances that enhance user involvement by offering greater opportunities for interactive and immersive experiences.

The different stages of the Web throughout its evolution have been categorised using the naming pattern 'Web X.Y'. The origins of the Web lie in Web 0.5, which covers the earliest technical developments in the late 1980s (Weber & Rech, 2010). Other categories followed, each of which advanced the Web in terms of what it was able to offer to users. These categories were Web 1.0, which referred to static or read-only pages; Web 2.0, a social Web with bidirectional interaction; and Web 3.0, a semantic Web, or a Web of data (Choudhury, 2014). Interim categories were also recognised, namely Web 1.5, Web 2.5 and Web 3.5. Following on from these, two further categories have subsequently been identified as the Web has continued to grow and develop, namely Web 4.0 and Web 5.0 (Patel, 2013).

The development of the Internet – alongside the evolution of the Web – has contributed to produce new socio-cultural trends in the tourism industry, which have been a subject of interest by tourism scholars and practitioners since the 1990s. According to Buhalis and Law (2008), the growth of Information Communication Technologies (ICTs) and the expansion of the Internet have changed the tourism industry drastically. The whole travel decision-making process, for example, has been affected by the possibility of potential travellers to acquire information about destinations online. Likewise, while assembling the different components of holiday packages (e.g. transportation, accommodation, excursions) were under the exclusive control of tour operators and travel agencies in the past, they can now be purchased directly by consumers at a relatively lower cost. As such, since the Internet has allowed tourists not to rely necessarily on professional service providers to organise a trip, it has increased consumers' involvement and decisional power during the pre-holiday experience. This has also been possible through the creation of websites and applications (e.g. Booking.com, TripAdvisor, Trivago) that allow tourists to purchase flights, hotel rooms and other tourist services. Moreover, tourists have increasingly gained significant power in influencing other potential tourists through the sharing of reviews and photos on different platforms during and after the tourism experience (see Liang & Corkindale, 2019; Wu & Pearce, 2014). In this regard, tourists should be regarded as both consumers and producers of holiday experiences.

The advent of the Internet and the evolution of the Web led to the emergence of a new subculture known as cyberculture. It is becoming increasingly difficult to ignore the influence of digital culture and the role of citizens as netizens. In this regard, MacKinnon (2012) argues that

> it is no longer sufficient for people to assert their rights and responsibilities as citizens of nation-states. If the goals of global social justice and accountable governance are to be served, people now also need to assert their rights and responsibilities as netizens: citizens of a globally connected Internet.
>
> (p.1)

As such, these developments highlight the need to explore online and digital culture.

Many attempts have been made to address the need to know more on cybercultures and online virtual experiences. One of the approaches employed to cast additional light on online communities is netnography, which was conceptualised at the end of the 1990s by Kozinets (1997). This qualitative approach helps researchers to study online communities through an ethnographic lens. Netnography provides patterns of online behaviour of people who are surfing the Internet. The importance of this approach has been acknowledged by many researchers in different disciplines (Bartl, Kannan & Stockinger, 2016; Bengry-Howell, Wiles, Nind & Crow, 2011; Nind, Wiles, Bengry-Howell & Crow, 2013), including tourism (Mkono & Markwell, 2014; Tavakoli & Mura, 2018; Tavakoli & Wijesinghe, 2019). Netnography is a highly beneficial method for understanding the complexity and implications of tourism. However, Mkono and Markwell (2014), alongside Tavakoli and Wijesinghe (2019), believe that despite attracting the attention of tourism scholars, netnography has not yet been fully utilised within tourism academic circles. A possible reason for this hiatus could be a lack of awareness of – and limited confidence about – this approach among tourism scholars. Taking a more holistic view, another potential cause could also be related to the fact that in tourism quantitative methods are still more popular than qualitative research (Wilson, Mura, Sharif & Wijesinghe, 2019).

Drawing upon Tavakoli and Wijesinghe (2019), most of the previous studies have focused on Web 2.0, particularly on tourism-related social media. This could be attributed to a lack of knowledge about the other levels of the Web. Moreover, their research unveils the existence of several knowledge gaps in netnographic studies in tourism, such as communication focus, type of participant, researcher standpoint, researcher reflexivity, and data analysis techniques. Their analysis also shows that in terms of communication focus, a high percentage of researchers only focused on textual communications, and in many cases, they only analysed the comments quantitatively. As Kozinets (2002) points out, netnography should not only involve analysing quantitative data but should also have ethnographical components. To date, netnographers have shown more interest in studying travel consumers rather than other tourism stakeholders. In addition, most researchers have taken a passive position in their netnographic research since the lack of reflexivity in these papers is evident.

To address these gaps in knowledge, this chapter discusses the different levels of immersion produced by online platforms as well as the opportunities they provide to overcome research-related barriers. This also sparks new epistemological, methodological and ethical debates concerning online relational approaches in tourism. More specifically, the employment of more advanced Web platforms in research may raise the following questions, among others: How does the presence of the researcher influence the research process in the cyberworld? How does netnography shape the relationship between researchers and participants? What is the role of researchers' reflexivity in netnographic approaches to research?

The chapter consists of three main parts. In the first, a brief literature review of the evolution of the Web is presented to provide an overview of the existing online platforms. The second part casts light on the different dimensions of conducting netnography beyond Web 2.0 in tourism studies and suggests possible future research avenues. The final part discusses the opportunities that netnography can offer to ethnographers to overcome some of the obstacles related to conducting fieldwork. By focusing on this relatively new approach in tourism, this work contributes to the expansion of knowledge and understanding of research methodologies/methods in tourism in general and netnographic approaches in particular.

THE EVOLUTION OF THE WEB AND NETNOGRAPHY IN TOURISM

Web 1.0, introduced by Tim Berners-Lee in 1989, involved static, read-only pages. During this stage, there was little interaction between developers and users. As this Web was read-only, users were not permitted to add, alter or otherwise manipulate any data on a Web page (Patel, 2013). The purpose of the Web at this time was to store and present information with no two-way communication (Murugesan, 2010). Web 1.0, in the form of websites and email communication, became very popular as a promotional tool among various sectors under the tourism umbrella and is still typical in the tourism industry, especially among small–medium enterprises (SMEs). However, designing a Web page for a destination or any other SMEs is not only a matter of having specific computer skills. It also requires an in-depth understanding of people's desires and experiences, which are the subject of interest by social scientists in general and ethnographers in particular. In this regard, netnography can provide information about the challenges experienced by Web page owners in creating Web content and keeping the information updated all the time. This is very important from a financial perspective as Web page owners are required to pay a maintenance fee to software companies, which usually design Web pages for them. Moreover, within this context, netnography can also be employed to analyse the content of Web pages, such as texts and photos, to understand how it was designed and how tourists interpret it.

Towards the end of the 1990s, the Web started to become less static with the introduction of Web 1.5. This phase saw the like of Microsoft, eBay and Amazon enter the market, and Web pages introduced content management systems. Increasing knowledge of Hypertext Mark-up Language (HTML) made it easier to refresh and update content, leading to more dynamic experience. Advertising and selling online fixed tourism packages and online ticketing became fashionable among tour operators and tourists, while the problem of open interaction remained. Studying this missing interaction component through a netnographic approach could reveal the consumers' experiences on the first version of online booking and money transaction. During this phase consumers often experienced online fraud cases, such as the case of tourists paying for hotel rooms that did not exist at the destination. In these specific circumstances, tourists were not able to communicate easily and instantly with the service providers. Therefore, the need for all the online stakeholders to be able to interact more easily and efficiently led to the development of Web 2.0.

With the introduction of Web 2.0 in 2004, the Web moved away from its read-only origins and enabled users to interact with websites and other users. In this sense, it is often referred to as 'the social Web' (Weber & Rech, 2010). O'Reilly and Musser (2006) described it as a more mature version of the Web, characterised by user participation and creating a network of users who could interact in a series of economic, social, and technological trends. In comparison to earlier forms of the Web, Web 2.0 was more user-centric, more participative, and created a relationship between itself and the user (Patel, 2013). Its read-write nature fostered a collaborative element that was previously lacking, allowing consumers to contribute content to websites. Importantly, the tourism industry benefits considerably from this evolution by using global social media platforms (Facebook and Instagram) and social networks that are specially designed for tourism purposes (Lonely Planet, TripAdvisor and Travello). Web 2.0 receives much attention from tourism netnographers (Tavakoli & Wijesinghe, 2019) due to its popularity among users. This platform provides an opportunity for different stakeholders to communicate. For example, a netnographic study could explore the experiences faced by property owners when they receive fake reviews and their strategies to overcome them.

The social Web led, in turn, to the Mobile Web, also known as Web 2.5. It could be said that this version was defined by its users; they were 'always-on', in the sense that they always carried their mobile devices and were always connected to the Internet (Weber & Rech, 2010). In the Web 2.5 era, the amount of data gathered about users increased, including that which was voluntarily offered as well as information extracted by persuading people to relate personal information (Miah, 2011). The sharing of information became more effective and usage began to change rapidly from desktop devices to mobile ones. User-generated content also became more prevalent (Kaplan, 2012). Clement (2019) provides information on the number of apps available in leading app stores as of the second quarter of 2019. Google Play, with 2.46 million apps, is leading the market, followed by Apple's App Store with 1.96 million. Tourism-related applications are contributing to this overwhelming number as many airlines, hotel chains and destinations produce their own applications. In this case, the result of a netnographic study on tourists' use of particular apps (specifically designed for tourism and hospitality purposes) will help the industry to decide whether or not investing on these apps, considering their temporary usage during the trip.

Following on from the Mobile Web, Web 3.0 has been termed the 'Semantic Web' (Patel, 2013). As opposed to the user-orientated previous generation, the focus of Web 3.0 was on computers themselves, including the interaction between machines and computer content recognition (Vieira & Isaia, 2015; Mistilis & Buhalis, 2012). In keeping with all versions, however, the reason for this focus was to provide ever better services. In this version of the Web, artificial intelligence grew in prominence, allowing searches that provided recommendations and gave personalised suggestions (Viera & Isaia, 2015). As a knowledge-based Web, new semantic technology offered machines the capability to gather data related to users' situations and, as a result, predict their needs (Eftekari, Barzegar & Isaai, 2010). This is made possible by technological advances enabling 'large quantities of existing data to be analysed and processed' (Gutierrez, Hurtado, Mendelzon & Perez 2011; p. 250). Examples of Web 3.0 are online and virtual shopping, smart searches and smart advertising. Virtual worlds, such as *Second Life*, also took hold as a result of Web 3.0. There is no doubt that the tourism industry, like other business-oriented industries, gains substantial benefits from smart marketing tools as these can unconsciously convince potential customers to purchase their products. However, there is less awareness of the public of virtual tourism experiences. For example, many may not be aware of the virtual destinations and virtual hotels existing in cyberspace. Exploring this level of the Web by conducting netnography has been relatively neglected by tourism scholars. A netnographic study could explore the experiences of tourists buying packages through smart tourism advertisements or experiencing virtual destinations. Moreover, virtual tourism could provide more opportunities for understanding the experiences of people having different constraints to travel, such as those who are physically challenged or senior citizens.

Between Web 3.0 and 4.0 came the transitional period of Web 3.5, in which artificial intelligence and semantic technologies that used reasoning were employed to introduce interactive, fully pervasive services that aimed to bring the virtual world closer to the real one (Weber & Rech, 2010). Examples of Web 3.5 include 3D virtual social networks, such as vTime. Artificial Intelligence continued to play a part in Web 4.0, also known as the 'Symbiotic Web' (Kurgun, Kurgun & Aktas, 2018). In Web 4.0, the lines between humans and machines became blurred. Computers were able to run applications without programmes having to be installed. In terms of creativity, Web 4.0 brought together both human and artificial intelligence to create a symbiotic alliance (Wu & Unhelkar, 2010). It was content-exploring, self-learning and collaborative, enabling machines to generate content as well as humans (Weber & Rech, 2010). Powerful hardware and software were utilised for the analysis of content and decision-making purposes. Increasing high bandwidths also facilitated the creation of rich visual content (Martínez-López, Anaya-Sánchez, Aguilar-Illescas & Molinillo, 2016). Web 3.5 and 4.0 are relatively advanced and costly to implement for SMEs. However, artificial human museum guides (Traum et al., 2012) and the Hilton concierge robot (Prentice, Lopes & Wang, 2019) are two examples of attempts to humanise the relationship between machine and visitor in the context of tourism. Moreover, Japan is getting ready for the next Tokyo Olympic Games by providing robots as translators, guides to access venues and helpers to carry bags for disabled people and the elderly. Netnographic studies in tourism are mostly focussed on human interactions and online application user experiences, while the interaction between humans and robots is yet to be explored. It would be interesting to investigate how translator robots can change tourists' experiences as they can help overcome language barriers among different cultures on holiday.

Parvathi and Mariselvi (2017) categorised the 'Web of Hologram' as Web 4.5. The hologram is a 3D display technology that uses different techniques to present a virtual copy of an actual object/human or virtual subject through the Web. This technology can be used in tourism for promotional or educational purposes. For example, Ogawa and Fujimoto (2018) explained how they train tourists making origami as an intangible culture through hologram technology. Moreover, they also used hologram as a sightseeing promotion tool by using a smartphone.

The latest generation of the Web, namely Web 5.0, is also known as the 'Web of Thought' or 'sensory-emotion Web'. Continuing the progression of interactivity between human and machine, Web 5.0 adds an emotional dimension (Parvathi & Mariselvi, 2017). It does so by enabling the Web to recognise users' emotions and reactions. Previously, the Web had been emotionally neutral. Web 5.0 allows machines to recognise and react to facial expressions. These emotions can then be adapted and used, for example, in avatars in order to facilitate interaction between humans and virtual humans (Llargues Asensio et al., 2014). These developments transform the Web into a more personalised experience for users. This advancement is the ultimate utopia of the virtual reality environment as it allows robots and machines to express emotions and interact with humans more effectively. The interactions between robots and guests at the front office of a hotel or during tour guiding would be a great topic to explore through netnography. Perhaps, the most exciting topic could be conducting a netnography on robots and analyse their reactions to the questions and experiences of tourists.

Web 5.0 is still in its infancy and has yet to be explored thoroughly by scholars. The current generation of users practises a mixture of the previous versions, such as Web 2.0 and Web 4.0. Over time, continuing technical advances are making it possible, both financially and technologically, for the average user to regularly experience the more highly advanced capabilities of Web 4.0, such as artificial intelligence and virtual worlds. Commercialising multisensory VR masks increases the level of immersion through simulations of smells, hot and cold winds, water mist, vibrations and punches (e.g., FeelReal). This new technology, which was the primary concern of virtual tourists on Web 3.5 platforms, may enhance virtual tourism experiences (Mura, Tavakoli & Sharif, 2017).

These examples are representative of the implications of the evolution of the Web for tourism and help to generate ideas for conducting netnographic studies. However, netnographers' gaze should not focus exclusively upon the customer/tourist experience, as other stakeholders' points of view are also valuable. In this respect, the following section will discuss the different perspectives that netnographers can consider for their research.

NETNOGRAPHY BEYOND WEB 2.0 IN TOURISM: PARTICIPANTS AND RESEARCHERS' INVOLVEMENT

According to Tavakoli and Wijesinghe (2019), most tourism-related netnographic studies published in the last decade have focused on forms of text-based communication generated by tourists on social media platforms (mostly in Web 2.0). Moreover, they pointed out that the majority of researchers have taken a rather passive/unreflective role in their research, with most of them not having a robust ethnographic standpoint in their papers. Based on these two primary concerns, this section will discuss these issues from three perspectives. First, the level of participants' (tourists, enterprises, etc.) involvement with the Web. Second, participant–researcher interaction and engagement in the field. Finally, the level of researchers' involvement in the research process.

Tourists as Participants

The nature of the Web after Web 2.0 changed the structure of netnographic research design. The advent of new technologies has increased the involvement and participation of users; yet, the representation of consumer experience is less textual because these services are (mobile) device oriented. The lack of empirical studies in this area could be related to a deficiency of knowledge among tourism scholars. Therefore, this section discusses how tourists are involved in these new technologies.

Most of the applications in Web 2.5 and Web 3.0 provide excellent free services in exchange for collecting vast amounts of data, all of which is produced by users. For instance, one may search for a destination using the Google search engine and immediately receive advertisements of that particular destination or hotel recommendation in his/her social media. The reason behind this lies in the fact that Google, as a search engine, records not only the keywords employed in the online search but also the result links, time, location and other details. This provides in-depth information about the users, their habits and interests, and their browsing style, which in turn creates reach profiles and user tagging (Murugesan, 2010). The same process, with even more details, also occurs on social networks. These platforms are selling users' data for these purposes. Therefore, they are free to use.

This process can be perceived positively as it creates a win-win situation. Technology is beneficial to the tourist experience, as it can help potential tourists to access relevant information faster by tailoring search results to their individual needs. In addition, it also gives tourism businesses the opportunity to target potential customers faster and easier, a process known as smart marketing. However, many users do not perceive these services positively and are not willing to share their personal information, as they believe it raises ethical concerns. Kokolakis (2017) argued about the privacy paradox phenomenon based on the privacy attitudes and privacy behaviour of the users by asking this question if 'people really care about their privacy?' (p. 122). A netnographic study would help to understand in greater detail whether individuals and corporations (especially SMEs) are aware of these ethical concerns and how they feel about them. More specifically, deep engagement with online communities could shed additional light on netizens' views about their rights as research participants, including privacy, anonymity, consent to participation and permission to use material published online for research purposes. This could contribute to strengthening ethical research practices while conducting netnography since different interpretations concerning ethical research procedures in cyberspaces are currently debated in the tourism literature (see Whalen, 2018; Wu & Pearce, 2014).

Moreover, the number of tourism-related applications is increasing. Since tourism planning involves various apps, such as transportation, accommodation and entertainment applications, there are a few questions that may arise. For example, whether the increased involvement of customers in the planning process through applications will help them to save on resources (money and time), or whether they prefer traditional travel agencies when they buy pre-organised packages. The other question is since travelling is not a daily activity for many, would the selection of applications be confusing for them? As mentioned earlier, if every service provider (e.g., transport, accommodation, and F&B) creates its own application, then the number of apps would be overwhelming. A timely and necessary netnographic study may answer these questions by providing in-depth information about consumers' use and experience of tourist applications, the obstacles faced while using these applications and their suggestions to develop more user-friendly online platforms. Potentially, Web 3.5, 4.0, and 5.0 could improve application usage by introducing robots and personal assistants' apps.

Web 3.5 and 4.0 services try to bring the virtual and non-virtual worlds closer together through artificial intelligence (AI). These advanced semantic technologies provide interactive and pervasive platforms, such as real-time translators, 3D immersive virtual worlds and networks, and fully interactive environments. With real-time translator applications, language barriers are decreasing, a point that could make tourism experiences smoother. The input of these apps can be text, voice or image. For example, camera translators enable users to translate a text directly from the camera. Google Assistant is a voice translator that can assist users in translating 27 languages. Kwet (2019) explains how US economic domination works based on corporate colonisation and monopoly of power through digital technology.

Augmented and virtual reality are other technologies under Web 3.5. 3D immersive virtual reality technology is widely used in the leisure industry, and since it is considered trendy by members of generation V, other sectors – such as marketing and education – have also planned and implemented practical strategies. Over the last decade, the tourism industry has been using augmented and virtual reality to market destinations. These technologies help to enhance tourists' experiences in many destinations. For instance, a new type of amusement for thrill-seekers is the mix of realities in theme parks by using VR head mounts on rollercoasters. Another example is *Rift*, a virtual theme park opened in Malaysia that offers a range of games and virtual experiences for visitors. These AR/VR recreational activities can provide rich data on visitors' experiences of virtual imaginary environments. This kind of studies could explore experiences of escapism in the cyberworld.

More immersive technologies will offer complex sensory experiences by adding other features, such as smells, hot and cold winds, and vibration (e.g., Feelreal). This advancement may increase perceptions of authenticity in virtual tourism, based on the idea that users expect experiences that are more 'real' in virtual environments (Mura, Tavakoli & Sharif, 2017). But why do most users wish to have virtual experiences closer to actual ones? It would be fascinating to explore VR users' experiences through netnographic studies in virtual destinations, their new identities, their experiences of freedom, intimacy and relationships, or any other issues relevant to the sociology of tourism.

All the above examples show that, although the focus of many netnographic studies was on tourists, a vast gap exists in the literature when it comes to tourists' behaviour and experiences regarding the usage of the Web beyond Web 2.0. More specifically, two groups have been overlooked by netnographers, namely passive netizens, and non-netizens. Passive netizens are those who use the Internet and different layers of the Web but do not interact with other stakeholders. They do not provide comments, likes, feedback, or interact with other users and service providers. There could be various reasons for this; they may think it would be a waste of time, or they may perceive that their feedback would not be valuable. There may also be other reasons, which netnographic studies could help to discover.

The other group, which can be labelled as non-netizens, are those who have constraints that stop them from using the Internet, or who intentionally refuse to go online. The first group can be categorised into a few subgroups. First, users may face government restrictions that stop them from using the Internet either fully or partially (e.g., North Korea, China). Second, there are those, such as senior citizens, who have access to the Internet but cannot use it because of a lack of information and communication technology literacy. Third, there is a lack of accessibility for many users with disabilities (physical and mental), which excludes them from this dimension of modern life. A netnographic study would help us to understand their needs and give us some hints on how we can include them in the new digital realms. The other non-netizen group is the minority who has decided to fight against digital colonisation. They have no wish to be part of the digital world and deliberately refuse to use the Internet. The question arises as to whether and how they are successful in fighting against this wave of digital colonisation.

Tourism Service Providers as Participants

In the field of hospitality, guests/tourists tend to be the centre of attention in the tourism cycle. Therefore, their experiences are perceived as being more important than those of other stakeholders. This view could be one of the reasons why tourism scholars tend to focus more on tourists' experiences rather than those of service providers. The evolution of the Web had a considerable influence on the performance of tourism service providers. For example, Web 2.0 gave customers a chance to raise their concerns about or show their appreciation of the services they received. Service providers may not agree with all the comments, and some of them may even be perceived as attacks from competitors. However, the feedback offered by these platforms also increases service providers' sensitivity to and awareness of problems, enabling them to seek to provide better services in order to achieve higher customer satisfaction scores. For this reason, new jobs have been created to keep an eye on social media comments, to respond to them constructively, and also to create fresh and engaging content for social media. The challenges SMEs are facing to survive in the digital market, in a context where the larger companies have strategies to grow their markets online, could be an interesting topic to explore through a netnographic study.

After the implementation of Web 2.5 and Web 3.0, the competition between service providers to attract more customers grew ever more fierce. Smart marketing falls under this category as it gives service providers a chance to target specific potential tourists. Booking air tickets is one example that shows how airlines can target specific tourists. When individuals use their devices to search for a flight ticket, cookies will be created in the system. The airline software realises that a specific customer is looking for a specific destination, and it increases the prices slightly to create a fear of missing out on the deal, a move that makes people more likely to buy the ticket immediately. For this to be effective, users should be connected to their applications or already logged into the system with their details. As a consequence of these practices, users may feel cheated or may perceive this process as unethical. A netnographic study may help us to understand how service providers apply different techniques to attract more customers and whether these techniques are ethical.

More specifically, netnography could explore service providers' intentions behind the development of certain apps alongside their knowledge of – and willingness to respect – consumers' rights. Moreover, it could offer insightful information about consumers' experiences of smart marketing, their knowledge of cookies and their sensitivity to privacy issues. A netnographic study, for example, may explore whether customers would compromise their rights to privacy to have more efficient services. In this regard, some customers may perceive smart marketing as intrusive and partly questionable from an ethical perspective; yet, others may also value the useful and tailor-made information provided (mainly based on their preferences) while planning a trip.

Marketing under Web 3.5 has become more creative, as the existence of virtual worlds has enabled service providers to compete within them. For instance, many hotel brands exist in *Second Life*, and tourists are able to go and experience holidays there. The use of AR/VR enhances these experiences, and many virtual worlds are adaptable to these technologies. AR in restaurants has created new experiences for customers, turning them into tourist attractions (e.g. Le Petit Chef). VR has become trendier than AR, and many destinations try to market their products through VR applications. In this respect, a netnographic study may help to explore how AR/VR apps can increase the level of engagement of tourists in historical or urban places, and whether and how they could replace the tour guides.

Finally, robots have become smarter and can now process information and even think and learn by themselves. The advanced technologies employed in Web 4.0 are exerting an influence on the tourism industry. Many people associate the word 'robot' with a physical, programmable machine that can accomplish a series of tasks automatically. *Alibaba* opened 'the future hotel', which, with the help of AI, serves tourists. The Hilton group came up with the idea of a robot concierge at their hotels that acts as a guide for customers. While robots as machines have become very advanced, at the same time software robots, which do not have physical representations, have also grown smarter. Many companies are using robots to deal with customer service through online chats. The technology behind this uses machine learning to provide customers with the best answers. Google Assistants and Siri are examples of robots that help users to find information by working out the best possible search results. For example, these robots can reserve tickets, hotel rooms or restaurants for users, and plan and remind the user when and where they need to go. These technologies have also been used in museums for guided tours (e.g. virtual humans in Boston Museum). The accuracy and reliability of these assistance devices and applications can be a topic of exploration through a netnographic study.

All these technologies are undeniably contributing to the general wellbeing of societies, but as they continue to grow a few questions may be raised. Does AI, in general, promote capitalism and imperialism? Does everyone under the tourism umbrella benefit from these advances? Many SMEs feel that reviews are susceptible to distortion, as they believe marketing intimidators manipulate the way data is presented to customers. The main issue is to understand how SMEs feel threatened by these technologies. Will they actually help them, or will they end up paying more to be seen by potential customers?

Programmers and Producers as Participants

To date, netnographic researchers in tourism have tended to focus on tourists and service providers rather than technology producers. An enormous amount of effort lies behind each stage of producing an application. A general perception exists that the production of an application is a very scientific task, which is the job of computer software engineers. Application production is not an individual task; usually, a team of people is involved. Programming and designing an application requires a deep understanding of the social setting before the idea is coded and implemented. Therefore, any application production team needs the assistance of a netnographer or a social scientist in order to produce a successful application.

Nowadays, these applications contribute to social settings and the changing of norms in regard to tourism experiences. For instance, location-based tourism applications (Web 2.5) increased the possibility of interaction among tourists, and between tourists and locals (e.g., *Couch Surfing, Travello*). The result of a netnographic study on programmers' experiences in designing these applications may reveal the level of their social science knowledge for implementing the applications.

By the time Web 3.0 and 3.5 were implemented, users themselves were able to become developers. For example, in some virtual worlds (e.g., *Secondlife*), the platform designers allow users to co-create the environment. This aspect of content creation changed the notion of virtual tourism, as the environment may not necessarily be a replication of the actual physical place. This means that virtual tourists can travel to imaginary places or travel to simulated places from the past or future. Moreover, the creation of avatars helps users to experience and explore various dimensions of their identities. The co-created environment would be a fantastic field for a netnography to explore the experiences of the users and programmers working together to create a new reality.

Web 4.0 and 5.0 are not yet well developed, particularly in relation to tourism. Only a few implemented applications have been commercialised. A perception has been created in human minds that robots and computers will eventually replace them, and they will lose their jobs. At first glance, it may seem true; robots are able to take over repetitive tasks and perform them better than humans, as they are consistent in performance and do not get tired. Whereas it was once seen as fancy or uncommon in the tourism and hospitality industry, technology is becoming more practical and commonplace. Robots have replaced waiters and housekeeping in a few outlets (e.g., the Alibaba hotel in China), and autonomous driving offers another method of transportation for tourists (e.g., auto-drive taxes at the Tokyo Olympic Games 2020). However, the risk management of these fully technology based systems are complicated as these robots and virtual humans may be spoilt by computer viruses or hackers. Finding out the various dimensions of risk could be accomplished by a netnography on cybersecurity specialists.

A netnographic study of developers' experiences of producing an application would be useful for other programmers and providers. These kinds of netnographic studies may raise a few questions: How do their experiences lead them to create platforms or applications? What are the challenges they face during and after offering the services? And, do they face any restrictions when marketing their products, such as governmental, religious or local constraints? Does any authority lead or fund this programming? Could the current structures of power lead society to new areas of digital colonisation?

Researchers' Involvement

According to Tavakoli and Wijesinghe (2019), tourism netnographers did not show a strong positionality in their studies. Indeed, their work found that most of those studies were based on analysing publicly available online data, and the majority of them were conducted on Web 2.0. Conducting netnographic research beyond Web 2.0 requires a higher level of information technology literacy, which may not be very common among social scientists. Moreover, access to data in Web 2.5 to 5.0 is more difficult as the associated applications are designed in individualistic ways. Also, in some cases where data is available online, ethical procedures are required to be taken into consideration. The main issue is that most netnographers limit themselves to analysing text, photos and videos, while different types of information and methods of data collection exist and require analysis.

Web 2.5 and 3.0 are characterised by integration, mobility and the provision of a highly interactive environment that may not be solely based on textual communication. Online communities are more focused than they were in Web 2.0, and researchers need to access these groups through applications. Location-based applications, in which users are given the opportunity of connecting with people in the surrounding area, also fall under this category. For instance, *Couchsurfing* matches tourists and hosts based on their location. Researchers need to be part of the community to create a relationship of trust in order to study user behaviour; therefore, it becomes a more complicated process than simply analysing secondary data.

As user involvement increases on Web 3.5, so does the involvement of netnographers in the field. In platforms such as virtual worlds, researchers need to create avatars, enter the field and experience the communities first hand in order to have a fruitful netnography. In Web 4.0 and 5.0, the level of immersion is increased, and researchers could also use AR/VR gadgets to understand users' experiences. However, researchers can also still take a passive position and simply interview participants without becoming involved in the field.

Netnography and Ethnography

Tavakoli and Wijesinghe (2019) found that the majority of netnographic papers published during the last decade in tourism did not report the ethnographic portions of their research in the papers. As such, they fail to highlight the opportunities that netnography may bring to ethnographers. Traditionally, ethnographic studies have been grounded on researchers' fieldwork, namely a relatively long period of time during which ethnographers often have to travel to far-away lands, immerse themselves in the culture under investigation, adapt to a different lifestyle and, in most circumstances, learn a new language. Being *in situ* is regarded as one of the main foundational principles of ethnography as it guarantees researchers' first-end involvement in the field, which in turn increases the possibility to build rapport and establish relationships of trust with the participants. More specifically, fieldwork's propensity to create empathy in relationships enhances researchers' understanding of a cultural group.

Nevertheless, conducting ethnographic fieldwork also involves a number of problems as it may be time-consuming, relatively expensive, and environmentally unsustainable, especially if it requires travelling extensively to faraway locations. Importantly, there have been many instances in which fieldwork has jeopardised researchers' physical and psychological safety (see Adler, 1993; Mura, 2015; Whyte, 1956). The issue of researchers' personal safety may be particularly pronounced if ethnographers decide to explore sensitive topics in dangerous contexts (see Jamieson, 2000; Liamputtong, 2007).

While some of the above-mentioned issues may also affect netnographers (even interactions in cyberspace may lead to psychological distress for researchers, especially in netnographic approaches that go beyond Web 2.0), in general, virtual involvement in netnographic studies may be relatively safer, less expensive and less time-consuming than physical experiences in traditional ethnographic approaches. Indeed, netnography often does not involve researchers' physical mobilities as the empirical material can be co-produced through online interactions. Moreover, traditional ethical issues concerning participants' anonymity and confidentiality may be relatively easy to address in netnographic approaches to research as netizens may decide to opt for online profiles and/or avatars without displaying their identity and personal information. This may encourage participants' openness in sharing experiences and emotions.

Despite this, netnography presents limitations. Conducting studies in contexts and social groups where the Internet cannot be accessed or is not commonly used may be problematic and unfeasible. Furthermore, the employment of Web 3.0, Web 4.0 and Web 5.0

technologies is still limited and not available in the market. As such, fully immersive online experiences and interactions between researchers and participants are difficult to experience in cyberworlds. This raises concerns about the depth of relationships characterising current netnographic encounters and questions netizens' rapport and relationships of trust. In this scenario, whether interactions *in situ* help to build relationships of trust more than cyberinteractions is still a subject of contentious debates. Also, observing patterns of behaviour and bodily reactions online may be challenging if more advanced technologies are not developed and employed. This may lead to issues concerning the exploration of emotional reactions (although the increasing use of emoticons among the younger generations may partly address this concern).

Rather than establishing whether ethnography or netnography may be the best approach to research, it is important to regard the two as complementary approaches. It is becoming increasingly difficult to ignore the Internet and virtual realities in our daily routines. Virtual reality applications are becoming more immersive and are perceived as more real than before. As Tavakoli and Mura (2015) have argued, virtual reality is part of reality, and today, the line between these two is blurred or simply inexistent. Therefore, we are floating between citizenship and netizenship in everyday life. Being a netizen became naturalised so quickly during the last 20 years that it is hard for individuals to ignore it. At the same time, being a netizen requires people to follow the norms and cybercultures of online communities. These cybercultures and norms do not necessarily follow individuals' citizen cultures, as the Internet does not have geographical borders. Moreover, cyberculture, like other cultures, evolves over time and also changes based on the different levels of the Web. Since these online and offline cultures may vary from one community to another, a netnographic study would be more meaningful when blended with ethnographic research.

CONCLUSION

This chapter mapped the evolution of the Web – from Web 1.0 to Web 5.0 – to discuss how the advent of new technologies may contribute to more advanced netnographic approaches to research (Table 9.1). This work has highlighted how the implications of the evolution of the Web not only apply to tourists but also to tourism service providers, tourism applications' programmers and tourism researchers. Overall, the chapter has highlighted the limitations of the existing netnographic approaches in tourism due to the emphasis placed by tourism scholars on textual analysis and Web 2.0 platforms.

One of the implications of this chapter concerns a reconceptualisation of the notion of netnography, one that encompasses more advanced technologies and a broader spectrum of tourism stakeholders. Moreover, this work paves the way for more reflective netnographic approaches to research by tourism scholars as it encourages matters of positionality in cyberspace. In other words, the foundational principles of ethnography should not be overlooked in netnography based on the idea that the latter is an extension of the former.

The points discussed in this chapter may also have implications for the tourism industry as they suggest ways of blending virtual and non-virtual experiences to enhance tourists' experiences. In this regard, the discussions presented in the text highlight the important role of netnography in exploring netizens' tourist and leisure experiences in both cyberspace and mixed realities environments. Netnography could also provide important information to tourism and hospitality managers and marketers, which in turn could offer feedback to programmers and scientists in terms of consumers' technological preferences and future technological advancements to target.

Table 9.1 The Evolution of the Web in Tourism and Its Opportunities for Netnography

Evolution of the Web	Characteristics and use in tourism	Opportunities for netnography
Web 1.0	Static, 'read-only Web'. Websites and email communication – popular as promotional tools in tourism.	Relatively scarce due to little interaction among users, developers and researchers. Mainly analysis of static texts and images. Analysis of the experience of service providers (as user) for designing, updating and maintaining the Web pages.
Web 1.5	'Dynamic Web' but not interactive. A more dynamic experience yet no interaction among users. Online booking websites, advertising and selling online fixed tourism packages became fashionable among tour operators.	Relatively scarce due to little interaction among users and between developers and users Service providers' experience of overbooking. Cybersecurity issues such as customers' experience of phishing.
Web 2.0	'The social Web' – users can interact with websites and other users. Read–write nature, collaborative (co-creation with users). Social media platforms (Facebook and Instagram) and social networks specifically designed for tourism purposes (Lonely Planet, TripAdvisor).	Good due to the opportunities for interaction among users, developers and researchers. Analysis of the interactions between different stakeholders. Analysis of UGCs to understand the reconstruction of destination image.
Web 2.5	The 'Mobile Web' – from desktop devices to mobile ones Sensorial experiences and level of immersion still relatively scarce. Tourism-related applications for airlines, hotel chains and destinations	Good due to the opportunities for interaction among users, developers and researchers. Understanding the experience of tourists using apps designed for a destination knowing the temporary nature of it and overwhelming number of mobile apps.
Web 3.0	The 'Semantic Web' – interaction between machines and computer content recognition. Sensorial experiences and level of immersion potentially good but still limited. Hotels and destinations in virtual worlds (e.g. *Second Life*), smart marketing tools for the tourism industry.	Very good due to the increased opportunities for interaction among users, developers and researchers. Analysis of the experience of virtual tourism, avatar behaviour. Understanding of the smart marketing effects on the SMEs.

(continued)

Table 9.1 (Cont.)

Evolution of the Web	Characteristics and use in tourism	Opportunities for netnography
Web 3.5	The 'Ubiquitous Web' Artificial intelligence and semantic technologies using reasoning introduce interactive, fully pervasive services. Sensorial experiences and level of immersion potentially good due to the production of primordial gadgets (e.g. *Oculus Rift*). 3D virtual social networks (e.g. vTime)	Very good due to the increased opportunities for interaction among users, developers and researchers. Analysis of the experience of designers and users of immersive 3D virtual social worlds. Analysis of the potential imaginary tourism destinations, simulation of past and future in 3D virtual words.
Web 4.0	The 'Symbiotic Web' – Human and artificial intelligence brought together to create a symbiotic alliance – content-exploring, self-learning and collaborative. Sensorial experiences and level of immersion advanced but not utilised in tourism due to lack of advanced gadgets easily available in the market. Artificial human museum guides, the Hilton concierge robot, robots as tourism service providers	Excellent due to the increased opportunities for interaction among users, developers and researchers. Analysis of the interaction between humans and virtual humans as concierge in a hotel or a guide in a museum Exploring the experiences of robot services in the hotels and restaurants.
Web 4.5	'Web of Holograms' – teleporting objects and humans. Sensorial experiences and level of immersion advanced but not commercialised yet. Tele business tourism, teleconferences and using for tourism marketing.	Good due to the increased opportunities for interaction among users, developers and researchers. Analysis of the experience of the hologram of a destination or an event, e.g. presenting Olympic matches concurrently in different stadia by holographic technology.
Web 5.0	The 'Web of Thought' or 'sensory-emotion Web'. Sensorial experiences and level of immersion very advanced but not utilised in tourism due to lack of advanced gadgets easily available in the market. Emotionally and physically enhanced tourist experiences – yet at its infancy.	Excellent due to the increased opportunities for interaction (both physical and emotional) among users, developers and researchers. Analysis of the fully immersive virtual experiences by using sensorial simulations. Exploring the experience of meeting and interacting with virtual humans.

ACKNOWLEDGEMENT

The work on which this paper is based was funded by a Flagship project from Taylor's University (project code TUFR/2017/004/02).

REFERENCES

Adler, P. A. (1993). *Wheeling and dealing – An ethnography of an upper-level drug dealing and smuggling community*. New York, NY: Columbia University Press.

Bartl, M., Kannan, V. K., & Stockinger, H. (2016). A review and analysis of literature on netnography research. *International Journal of Technology Marketing, 11*(2), 165–196.

Bengry-Howell, A., Wiles, R., Nind, M., & Crow, G. (2011). A review of the academic impact of three methodological innovations: Netnography, child-led research and creative research methods. *Economic & Social Research Council*, 1–37.

Berners-Lee, T. (2000). Semantic web on XML. Keynote presentation for XML, 2000.

Buhalis, D., & Law, R. (2008). Progress in information technology and tourism management: 20 years on and 10 years after the Internet—The state of eTourism research. *Tourism Management, 29*(4), 609–623.

Choudhury, N. (2014). World Wide Web and its journey from Web 1.0 to Web 4.0. *International Journal of Computer Science and Information Technologies* (IJCSIT),5(6), 8096–8100.

Clement, J., (2019). Mobile app usage – Statistics & facts. Retrieved from https://www.statista.com/topics/1002/mobile-app-usage/.

Eftekhari, M. H., Barzegar, Z., & Isaai, M. T. (2010). Web 1.0 to Web 3.0 evolution: Reviewing the impacts on tourism development and opportunities. In F.V. Cipolla Ficarra, C. de Castro Lozano, E. Nicol, A. Kratky, & M. Cipolla-Ficarra (Eds.), *International workshop on human-computer interaction, tourism and cultural heritage* (pp. 184–193). Berlin, Heidelberg: Springer.

Gutierrez, C., Hurtado, C. A., Mendelzon, A. O., & Pérez, J. (2011). Foundations of semantic web databases. *Journal of Computer and System Sciences, 77*(3), 520–541.

Jamieson, J. (2000). Negotiating danger in fieldwork on crime: A researcher's tale. In G. Lee-Treweek & S. Linkogle (Eds.), *Danger in the field: Risk and ethics in social research* (pp. 61–71). London: Routledge.

Kaplan, A. M. (2012). If you love something, let it go mobile: Mobile marketing and mobile social media 4×4. *Business horizons,55*(2), 129–139.

Kokolakis, S. (2017). Privacy attitudes and privacy behaviour: A review of current research on the privacy paradox phenomenon. *Computers & Security, 64*, 122–134.

Kozinets, R. (1997). "I want to believe": A netnography of the X-Philes' subculture of consumption. *Advances in Consumer Research, 24*, 470–475.

Kozinets, R. (2002). The field behind the screen: Using netnography for marketing research in online communities. *Journal of Marketing Research, 39*(1), 61–72

Kurgun, H., Kurgun, O. A., & Aktaş, E. (2018). What does Web 4.0 promise for tourism ecosystem? A qualitative research on tourism ecosystem stakeholders' awareness. *Journal of Tourism and Hospitality Management, 6*(1), 55–65.

Kwet, M. (2019). Digital colonialism: US empire and the new imperialism in the Global South. *Race & Class, 60*(4), 3–26.

Liamputtong, P. (2007). *Researching the vulnerable*. London: Sage.

Liang, W. K., & Corkindale, D. (2019). How eWord of mouth valences affect price perceptions. *International Journal of Market Research, 61*(1), 50–63.

Llargues Asensio, J. M., Peralta, J., Arrabales, R., Bedia, M. G., Cortez, P., & Peña, A. L. (2014). Artificial intelligence approaches for the generation and assessment of believable human-like behaviour in virtual characters. Expert Systems with Applications, *41*(16), 7281–7290.

MacKinnon, R. (2012). The netizen. *Development, 55*(2), 201–204.

Martínez-López, F. J., Anaya-Sánchez, R., Aguilar-Illescas, R., & Molinillo, S. (2016). Evolution of the web. In Francisco José Martínez López & Rocio Aguilar (Eds.), *Online brand communities: Using the social Web for branding and marketing* (pp. 5–15). Cham: Springer.

Miah, A. (2011). Towards Web 3.0: Mashing up work and leisure. In Bramham P., & Wagg S. (Eds.), *The new politics of leisure and pleasure* (pp. 136–152). London: Palgrave Macmillan.

Mistilis, N., & Buhalis, D. (2012). Challenges and potential of the Semantic Web for tourism. *e-Review of Tourism Research (eRTR),10*(2). 51–55.

Mkono, M., & Markwell, K. (2014). The application of netnography in tourism studies. *Annals of Tourism Research, 48,* 289–291.

Mura, P. (2015). 'To participate or not to participate?' A reflective account. *Current Issues in Tourism, 18*(1), 83–98.

Mura, P., Tavakoli, R., & Sharif, S. P. (2017). 'Authentic but not too much': exploring perceptions of authenticity of virtual tourism. *Information Technology & Tourism, 17*(2), 145–159.

Murugesan, S. (2010) Web X.0: A road map, In S. Murugesan (Eds.), *Handbook of research on Web 2.0, 3.0 and X.0: Technologies, business and social applications* (pp. 1–11). Hershey, New York: Information Science Reference.

Nind, M., Wiles, R., Bengry-Howell, A., & Crow, G. (2013). Methodological innovation and research ethics: Forces in tension or forces in harmony? *Qualitative Research, 13*(6), 650–667.

Ogawa, R. & Fujimoto, T. (2018). The possibility of 3D-origmi system as a tourism promotion tool for Japan. *Journal of Advanced Research in Social Sciences and Humanities 3*(1), 1–10.

O'Reilly, T., & Musser, J. (2006). Web 2.0 Principles and best practices (Report). Retrieved from www.oreilly.com/catalog/web2report/chapter/web20_report_excerpt.pdf

Parvathi, M., & Mariselvi, R. (2017). A bird's eye on the evolution–Web 1.0 to Web 5.0: Lib 1.0 to Lib 5.0. *International Journal of Advanced Research Trends in Engineering and Technology, 4*(4), 167–176.

Patel, K. (2013). Incremental journey for World Wide Web: Introduced with Web 1.0 to recent Web 5.0 – A survey paper. *International Journal of Advanced Research in Computer Science and Software Engineering, 3*(10), 410–417.

Prentice, C., Dominique Lopes, S., & Wang, X. (2019). Emotional intelligence or artificial intelligence – an employee perspective. *Journal of Hospitality Marketing & Management,* 1–27.

Tavakoli, R., & Mura, P. (2018). Netnography in tourism – Beyond Web 2.0. *Annals of Tourism Research, 73,* 190–192.

Tavakoli, R., & Wijesinghe, S. N. (2019). The evolution of the web and netnography in tourism: A systematic review. *Tourism Management Perspectives, 29,* 48–55.

Traum, D., Aggarwal, P., Artstein, R., Foutz, S., Gerten, J., Katsamanis, A., ... & Swartout, W. (2012, September). Ada and Grace: Direct interaction with museum visitors. In Y. Nakano, M. Neff, A. Paiva, M. Walker (Eds.), *Intelligent virtual agents* (pp. 245–251). Berlin, Heidelberg: Springer.

Vieira, J., & Isaías, P. (2015). Web 3.0 in web development. In T. Issa, & P. Isaia (Eds.), *Artificial intelligence technologies and the evolution of Web 3.0* (pp. 209–228). Hershey, PA: IGI Global.

Weber, S., & Rech, J. (2010). An overview and differentiation of the evolutionary steps of the web X.Y movement. In S. Murugesan (Ed.), *Handbook of Research on Web 2.0, 3.0, and X.0* (pp. 12–39). Hershey, PA: IGI Global.

Whalen, E. A. (2018). Understanding a shifting methodology: A content analysis of the use of netnography in hospitality and tourism research. *International Journal of Contemporary Hospitality Management, 30*(11), 3423–3441.

Wilson, E., Mura, P., Sharif, S. P., & Wijesinghe, S. N. (2019). Beyond the third moment? Mapping the state of qualitative tourism research. Current Issues in Tourism, *23,* 1–16.

Whyte, W. F. (1956). *Street corner society – the social structure of an Italian slum.* Chicago, IL: The University of Chicago Press.

Wu, M. Y., & Pearce, P. L. (2014). Appraising netnography: Towards insights about new markets in the digital tourist era. *Current Issues in Tourism, 17*(5), 463–474.

Wu, M. C., & Unhelkar, B. (2010). Mobile Service Oriented Architecture (MSOA) for Businesses in the Web 2.0 Era. In Information Resources Management Association (Ed.), *Electronic services: Concepts, methodologies, tools and applications* (pp. 546–559). Hershey, PA: IGI Global.

Section 3
Netnography Industrialized

10
Netnography Applied
Five Key Lessons Learned from 16 Years of Field Experience

Michael Bartl and Constance Casper

The motivation of the authors to contribute this chapter was to take a bird's eye view of our netnography practices at HYVE during all these years working with them. Then, we sought to filter out the most important learnings that we wanted to share and offer them as a guideline for future applications of this social media research discipline. The core part of the chapter is structured into five key learnings that we describe in dedicated sections. These learnings correspond to the main parts of the book including history, data collection and creation, analysis and interpretation and, finally, the communication of impactful research which, in our case, takes place in the field of innovation management. The following section begins with our own story of how we started to discover the power of netnography and how we then adapted it as a dedicated practice within the innovation and new product development process of our company.

THE HYVE NETNOGRAPHY JOURNEY

In the year 2000, HYVE was founded with the vision to establish a new kind of innovation approach. Active users, consumers, experts, start-ups, citizens, suppliers, and universities were brought together in a joint innovation ecosystem. This in turn enabled the collaborative development of ground-breaking customer-oriented innovations. In a world of informed, connected, active and global consumers, we believe that an open and participatory innovation system is an essential factor for the success of product and service solutions and transformation processes in the digital age. Currently, HYVE serves 70 per cent of the German DAX listed companies as well as many international clients. HYVE relies on an interdisciplinary and integrated approach to innovation, combining competencies in the areas of market research, engineering, industrial design, product development and digital solutions under one roof. Furthermore, we emphasize the intertwining of academic research and practical work in the business world.

For us, the application of netnography has always happened in the context of innovation. Netnography enjoys the reputation of being an extraordinarily effective technique for observing consumer behaviour through computer-mediated conversations and for understanding customers' tastes, desires, and factors that influence their decision making (Kozinets, 2002; Piller, Ihl, & Vossen, 2011). It is an empathetic way of immersing oneself in the customer domain and gathering an in-depth understanding of user needs (Kozinets, 2010). By "listening in" on naturally occurring consumer dialog in online communities, netnography allows the derivation of unbiased consumer insights. This is the starting point for the creation of new products and services in the early stage of the innovation funnel, the so called fuzzy front-end. The well-known cosmetics company Beiersdorf, for example, experienced the value of this method for new product development when developing the NIVEA Black & White deodorant, which became the most successful product launch in the company's history (Bilgram, Bartl, & Biel, 2011; Bilgram, Füller, Bartl, Biel, & Miertsch, 2013).

Experiences and Fields of Application

In 2004, HYVE applied the netnography approach for the first time in order to kick off the development of a new basketball shoe concept for Adidas. Eleven thousand posts contained in 460 discussion groups on various basketball online communities were analysed applying the netnographic process steps proposed by Robert Kozinets. Trends and user innovation, e.g., in the area of cushioning and lacing, basketball shoe collections, and the rich dialogue of basketball enthusiasts in various specialty communities were the subject of the research. Results were presented at the European Marketing Academy in 2005 and afterwards published in the *Journal of Business Research* by Füller, Jawecki and Mühlbacher (2007).

In 2005, the HYVE netnography journey proceeded with the second application of the method to fill up the innovation pipeline of a producer of white goods with the main focus on steam cookers and its preferred fields of application. This was the starting point for HYVE to develop a standardized netnography service with a dedicated team of netnography researchers. Since then, the body of experience in applying netnography as a research method and a standardized product in a business context grew continuously. Overall, more than 140 netnography projects have been conducted by the team to date. The research assignments came from clients across various industries such as consumer goods, healthcare, automotive, financial services, telecommunication, energy and B2B sectors such as chemical goods. A short overview of the netnography projects conducted thus far by HYVE is illustrated in Figure 10.1.

Looking back over 16 years, netnography was at the time considered to be "the new kid in town" within the European community of market researchers. In order to create a viable business around this new offering, it was necessary for us to start activities to raise awareness and trustworthiness to promote the application of the method for professional market researchers. HYVE strongly engaged in promoting the method. Commercialization efforts included marketing material, articles in professional journals, direct marketing activities,

number of conducted netnography projects	142	developed product concepts and netnography-based innovations	~350
industries Media & Telco, B2B Industries, Energy & Utilities, Consumer Goods, Healthcare, Financial Services, Automotive		number of countries / regions	21
excerpt of research topics Skin Care, Sustainability, Deodorant, desserts & pudding, pets, ice cream, tea bags, thermomix, H2O2, aging, shaving, peeling & massage, beverages, running & biking, packaging of pasta, mint and citrus flavors, energy management, psoriasis, machine 2 machine communication, robot cleaning, tampons, anti-allergies, soups, kitchen cleaning, sun cream, food storage, acne, soccer shoes, platn protection, baby products, smart home, cooking in USA, silver ager, laundry care, baking, detergent, hair lightening, dairy snacks, military boots, credit card usage, snow goggles, electric actuators, 5G, premium goods, pregnancy, trunk usage, etc.		avg. number of researchers per project	2-4
		avg. project duration	8-10 wk.

Figure 10.1 HYVE Netnography Field Experience.

voluntary contributions to market research associations and the organization of the first European Conference in 2008 named Netnography08. The conference was exclusively dedicated to the topic of netnography and featured Robert Kozinets as the keynote speaker who introduced the method to a broader audience of research practitioners in Europe. In addition to these business relevant activities, HYVE conducted extensive scientific research to explore emerging research questions in connection with this innovative and fascinating research method and to contribute to the growing theoretical fundamentals of the method. The following section gives an overview of HYVE's scientific work on netnography.

Scientific Research

HYVE heavily relies on methodologies that are derived from rigorous academic research. Our goal is to intertwine academic research and practical work in the business world. In our experience, a stronger connection between the two worlds can unlock extraordinary results. Thus, we aim to foster bidirectional exchanges to supercharge the effects of academic research and business. Following this principle regarding netnography, we have tried to contribute methodological and substantive publications and case studies to the scientific community that are summarized in Table 10.1.

An extensive review and analysis of literature on netnography was published in 2016 (Bartl, Kumar, & Stockinger, 2016). This study comprises all articles on netnography accessible via literature databases with a publication date between 1997 and the end of 2012. Overall, 1166 relevant published peer-reviewed scientific articles with the term "netnography" either in the title, in the abstract, or as one of the keywords included as part of the final set. Using an identical research procedure, we conducted the research again for this chapter. The set was supplemented by publications occurring until the year 2019 and led to 308 additional peer-reviewed articles published between 2013 and 2019 for a total of 424 articles. The continuous and rapid growth of the netnography research body within the selected literature databases is illustrated in Figure 10.2. It is important to state that this data sample represents not the total or complete number of publications on netnography as sources that are not included in the stated databases were not taken into account by our literature analysis. The number of publications would be much higher.

Having described HYVE's general field of experience and research efforts centred around netnography, in the following section we describe in more detail how the method was applied and also adapted by HYVE for the business context of innovation.

The Applied Netnography Process

When we speak of netnography in this chapter we refer to the specific application of the method in the HYVE business context of innovation management. Our application is not exactly the same as the method described by Kozinets (2002, 2010) because it leaves out the interactive component which would include research web-pages, interviews, mobile ethnography, and other such techniques. The HYVE research process illustrated in Figure 10.3 consists of six steps and adapts for our own specific purposes the process originally introduced by Kozinets (1997) and elaborated since (Kozinets 2010, 2015, 2020).

Step1

In the first step, the topic of interest for the netnography is explored by defining relevant aspects and determining factors. At HYVE, we do this using a mind mapping technique. We have found that a mind map is a great way to structure and guide the research within

Table 10.1 Netnography Research By HYVE Science Labs

Title	Author	Year	Journals/edited books
Community based innovation: How to integrate members of virtual communities into new product development	J. Füller, M. Bartl, H. Ernst, & H. Muehlbacher	2006	*Electronic Commerce Research*
Netnography – Einblicke in die Welt der Kunden	M. Bartl	2007	*Planung & Analyse*
Innovation creation by online basketball communities	J. Füller, G. Jawecki, & H. Mühlbacher	2007	*Journal of Business Research*
Information Pur – Netnography erschließt Online-Communities als Innovationsquelle	M. Bartl, S. Hueck, & R. Landgraf	2008	*Research & Results*
User centric innovations in new product development	V. Bilgram, A. Brem, & K.-I. Voigt	2008	*Journal of Innovation Management*
Netnographic research – community insights in the cosmetics industry	M. Bartl, S. Hueck, & S. Ruppert.	2009a	*ESOMAR Proceedings*
How to use the innovative potential of online communities? Netnography – an unobtrusive research method to absorb the knowledge and creativity of online communities	G. Jawecki & J. Fuller	2009	*Business Process Integration and Management*
Netnography for innovation. Creating insights with user communities	M. Bartl, S. Hueck, & S. Ruppert.	2009b	*Research World*
Netnography – Finding the right balance between automated and manual research	M. Bartl & I. Ivanovic	2010	*Web Monitoring*
Listening to social media from a B2B2C perspective	S. Hück, J. Jonas, A. Grünhagen, & C. Lichter	2010	*ESOMAR Proceedings*
A comparison of creative behaviours in online communities across cultures	G. Jawecki, J. Füller, & J. Gebauer	2011	*Creativity and Innovation Management*
Review on a decade of netnography research	M. Bartl, G. Jawecki, H. Stoenner, & D. Gastes	2011	*ESOMAR Proceedings*

Title	Authors	Year	Journal
Getting closer to the consumer – how NIVEA co-creates new products	V. Bilgram, M. Bartl, & S. Biel	2011	*Marketing Review St. Gallen*
The dark and the bright side of co-creation: Triggers of member behavior in online innovation communities	J. Gebauer, J. Füller, & R. Pezzei	2012	*Journal of Business Research*
Eine Allianz gegen Flecken	V. Bilgram, F. Füller, M. Bartl, S. Biel, & H. Miertsch	2013	*Harvard Business Manager*
Netnography – online communities as a source of innovation in the field of E-mobility	M. Bartl, H. Stockinger, K. Kalogirou, & P. Pollok	2013	*WiSt Journal*
Netnography: The mint journey	M. Bartl & N. Tusche	2015	*Open Tourism*
A review and analysis of literature on netnography research	M. Bartl, V. Kumar, & H. Stockinger	2016	*International Journal of Technology Marketing*
Standing on the shoulder of giants – insights and implications form a "duel" between humans and machines.	A. Marchuk, S. Biel, V. Bilgram & S. Worning	2018	*ESOMAR Proceedings*

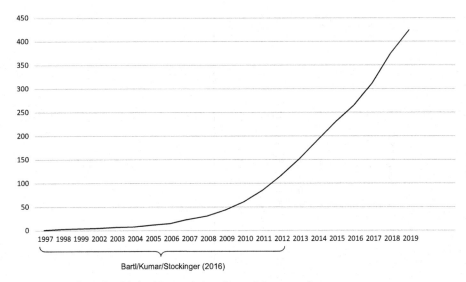

Figure 10.2 Number of Published Journal Articles on Netnography.

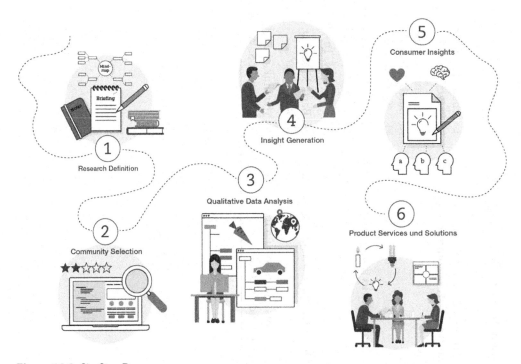

Figure 10.3 Six-Step Process.

a netnography as it helps to create an overview of all relevant topics and the connections between them. Our conception of mapping inspired Kozinets (2020) to incorporate the process into his own development of the technique, and the conceptual map included in the text in Figure 12.1 (2020, p. 349) is very similar to the sort of map we have developed at HYVE.

Step 2

In step 2, we apply specific search strategies in order to identify social media sites where consumers discuss topic(s) of interest for the project. A pool of sites, pages, or communities is then chosen for the further data analysis based on the following criteria: size, quality, search results, and activity. The selection takes into account different target groups and sub-topics. This stage is similar to the search stage recommended by Kozinets (2010, 2015, 2020), but using a slightly smaller set of search criteria.

Step 3

Within the third step, the user posts gathered from the previously selected online sources are analysed and coded using qualitative content analysis. We have found that a combination of deductive and inductive reasoning has proven conducive to category building. The category system is predefined deductively in the beginning and is inductively supplemented and detailed during the coding process. Similarly, Kozinets (2020, 317–318) details such combined deductive and inductive approaches, and also elaborates the role of induction.

Step 4

In step 4, the assigned codes and the category system resulting from the data analysis step make the topic of interest more accessible by highlighting relevant categories and relationships between codes.

Step 5

The outputs of the detailed qualitative content analysis are then aggregated and interpreted by the interdisciplinary HYVE-team to create meaningful consumer insights. Once the consumer insights are defined, the final assembly of the netnography report and presentation starts. The previously identified topics are then visually prepared and allocated to a set of different insights. We usually end up with approximately five to seven insights at this stage. We then design a creative and empathetic story for each individual insight, with all insights together being part of a bigger narrative. In addition, we aggregate the key findings from the netnography into a management summary, which allows our clients to quickly and easily share the findings with their colleagues.

Step 6

The netnography process typically does not end with the generation of insights. A major challenge is to then transfer the insights obtained into innovative product and service solutions. This transferal happens within Step 6. The deep consumer understandings enable the derivation not only of incremental improvements but also of potential new-to-the-world products and brands, such as NIVEA's development of the brand Invisible for Black & White. The translation of netnographic findings into solutions itself does not follow a predefined or determined process. On the contrary, it is an inherently complex and non-linear process that requires the involvement of different people from different disciplines. Accordingly, during this step, netnography researchers closely collaborate with product designers who contribute the assets of creative and inspirational input to drive forward innovative problem solutions. Therefore, the final step of netnography combines the analytical thinking of the netnography researchers with the creative thinking of designers including their tools and approaches for ideation and product prototyping. The derived product solutions are unique because they were developed through consistent and complete alignment with the consumer needs revealed in the netnography. Then, as a consequence, the suggested solutions are integrated into the established stage-gate innovation process of the client. From these applied netnography findings, further project activities regarding verification of patent, trademark and protection rights will often occur, and technological realization alternatives and representative market studies may be undertaken.

Having introduced HYVE's six-step approach to netnography, it is important to reiterate that the applied HYVE process does not represent netnography as a whole and it also differs from other processes, such as the one described in Chapter 5 of Kozinets (2020). For example, even though they can be very important aspects of many netnographies, and are an integral part of the process described in Kozinets (2010, 2015, 2020), you will not find elements of an interactive data collection or interviews in the HYVE process.

The reason that we exclude interaction operations from our version of netnography is a practical one. It is due to the common business practice between HYVE and its clients that these kinds of services are fulfilled as separate projects, often also combined with a netnography. Amongst other offerings these services include online and offline interviews, online research communities, lead user projects, co-creation workshops, integration of trend receivers, crowdsourcing campaigns and many more. Hence, the netnography practices at HYVE follow the understanding of a workbench-level approach that encourages pragmatic adaptions to fit our innovation offerings into the fuzzy front end of innovation. In this stage, it is crucial to learn about consumer wants and needs before developing innovative product and service solutions. Both netnography and interview project fits neatly into this same stage.

As a general remark by the authors and as described in much more in Kozinets (2020), two aspects concerning internet research ethics need to be taken into consideration: copyright protection and protection of data privacy. Without conducting ethical netnography, an online community's environment or culture could be damaged, or a social media site's terms could be violated. Kozinets (2020) suggests a complex procedural process composed of multiple decisions and actions in order to help assist that a netnographic research project is informed by good ethics. These procedures include guaranteeing anonymity and confidentiality to members whose online traces are used, not invading communities clandestinely, and gaining appropriate permissions to use data sources where prior registration is necessary. At HYVE, we strive to follow all of these ethical guidelines in our research.

Based on the exciting HYVE netnography journey outlined above, the idea of this book chapter is to highlight and share with the reader five major lessons learned from 16 years of field experience with netnography projects. These lessons are written from the perspective of the HYVE netnography specialist team and are described in the following sections.

LESSON 1: STAY ON TOP OF THE EVOLVING DIALOGUE IN SOCIAL MEDIA

Online dialogue between users has always been a part of the internet, long before it started to exist in its current form. Even at the end of the last century, when internet connections were slow and expensive, a great deal of discussion developed in newsgroups in the so-called *usenet* about any imaginable topic. But these discussions were limited to a small part of the worldwide population. Participating in these newsgroups required special software in form of newsreaders and also a certain amount of knowledge to configure everything. It was therefore more accessible to computer-savvy people, leaving out many others who were not as technologically adept.

This changed with the beginning of the new century. With internet access becoming more affordable and easier to set up, the internet became mainstream and allowed more and more people to connect. New forms of online dialogue emerged that no longer required special software but could easily be accessed through a web browser: online communities. The idea of suddenly being connected to a great number of like-minded people, even for niche topics, was still rather novel and exciting in those days. There was much curiosity amongst these early internet users to explore this new world. This exploration and curiosity led to an enormous variety of different online communities, many lengthy discussions, and highly involved users.

What did all of this mean for using netnography in terms of consumer insights? Although there was scientific interest in observing and understanding such communities from the beginning, commercial interest in using the information available for business purposes initially grew only slowly. But the potential was clearly there. Intense discussions about daily life, routines, likes and dislikes – these are ideal situations from which to deduct consumer needs and potential areas for innovation and new products. For HYVE, which was then a young start-up company that focused on the equally new field of *Open Innovation*, netnography seemed like a promising and interesting idea. With *Netnography Insights©* we adapted Kozinets' method to the specific needs of our clients who wanted to integrate research about consumers into the earliest stages of new product development. While we stayed true to most of the original ideas of netnography, we decided to make *Netnography Insights* a passive approach that focused purely on the unobtrusive observation of online communities. Interactive elements that traditionally have also been part of the general term netnography were set up as different business operations such as interviews or online research communities. This was important as it allowed us to standardize our methods in the ways that they are conducted, timed and charged, giving clients more security and at the same time more flexibility in booking only the options they wanted. So, when talking about netnography in the remainder of this chapter, we refer to our passive approach Netnography Insights.

Right when we started, online communities, as we still call the traditional thread-based forums, laid at the heart of our netnographies. Most online communities at that time were public, with all messages open in the internet and without the need to register or log in to a site, which was essential as we base our analysis only on publicly available data. There was at this time barely a notion that things like fake messages or fake profiles could exist. Users put little thought into considerations of online privacy. There were also no definite legal regulations yet in terms of data security, copyright issues, data access by others or the commercial use of information. For us as netnographic researchers, this was a paradise: lots of openly available, easily accessible and mostly honest discussions on almost any conceivable topic.

Other sites with consumer-generated content that proved to be useful for our analysis were blogs and review portals which were both becoming increasingly popular. Blog users explored the new possibilities of the internet to share their ideas, views and knowledge, initially without commercial interest but with only the pure desire to reach out and communicate their thoughts. To us, that meant we could focus on individuals that were highly involved in a topic and therefore often possessed extensive knowledge about the relevant product category and maybe even unique DIY solutions for unfulfilled needs.

Product review portals like ciao.com and dooyoo.com were good sources for us to use to look into what consumers thought about specific products. Their often-extensive reviews offered insights into consumers' routines, habits, likes and dislikes. Consumers were excited that they were now able to easily express their opinions about products to the whole world and thereby also to the producer, finally having their voice heard. While consumers could earn credits by writing a review, incentives initially did not come from the reviewed company itself but the review platform and were very low, based on the length of the reviews and not their sentiment. Motivation to write these reviews was therefore based upon intrinsic reasons which, for us, meant that they were fairly trustworthy. It was only later that users were offered products for free from consumer good companies with the purpose of writing reviews. Once that change occurred, we had to become much more selective in what type of review we could include in our analysis.

In general, the online world offered an exciting data basis for our netnographies. Specific communities for many topics, clearly marked threads, and search functions made it easy to identify relevant data. There were beauty and women's communities that could be used to gain a better understanding of skin care habits. There were pet communities that enabled researchers to look into the world of pet owners. Just as access to the internet and online discussions became easier for consumers, it likewise became easier for netnographic researchers to do their projects online.

But time did not stand still and new forms of dialogue amongst users developed. While online communities remain part of the online world today, other platforms known as social media have come to dominate the second decade of this century in terms of user dialogue. For netnographers like us it is important to understand the changes that this development has brought along and to adapt the netnographic method accordingly. As with most things, this change comes with its advantages and difficulties.

On a positive note, popular social media sites such as Facebook, Instagram, Twitter and YouTube have expanded the possibilities of user dialogue and enriched it with several new features. While online communities have a strong focus on text-based content, social media platforms allow for a much better integration of multi-media information. Photos and videos can easily be shared and discussed. For a researcher interested in consumer behaviour, the greater availability of textual as well as visual and auditory content allows for a more rounded and thorough insight into consumers' lives. Social media platforms also make it easier for consumers to discuss their topics of interest and find like-minded people on a much wider scale. In traditional online communities, consumers had to specifically select and register for a community for each of their topics of interest. Social media, on the other hand, offers one place to discuss all of their interests. This is certainly more user-friendly and also encourages consumer-dialogue as little additional effort is needed to become active in new areas. As a result, much more specific discussion groups have evolved which allow consumers to find and interact with each other within very particular and narrow fields. But it is not only that new platforms allow for more user participation, technologies have changed as well. Smartphones have become ubiquitous and social media companies quickly adapted to this development by offering smartphone-friendly apps that allowed a new way to participate in social media at any time, anywhere. This has certainly helped to stimulate online discussions and has led to more user content online.

One might think that with an increased choice of different types of online dialogue, combined with the ability of users to contribute at any time thanks to mobile internet, the netnography world for consumer research would become even brighter, fuller, and easier to access. In a way it did, but it also created its own challenges for us.

As netnographic researchers in an age of social media, we face several new problems. One of them is fake or paid messages. Commercialization has entered online communities and blogs. Many postings are created out of a desire to earn money. So-called influencers are active in blogs and social media with personal postings, yet as they might receive money or products for their content, the trustworthiness of their messages is not always clear. At the same time, company employees conceal their true identity and participate in social media to market their own products or discredit those of their competitors. Because of all of this, we had to become much more careful when selecting appropriate messages and we need to put a great deal of effort into scanning for fake or paid content. Users themselves have also become more cautious in what they are prepared to reveal online. There is nowadays more concern for one's privacy and therefore more hesitation to give away overly detailed information or participate in discussions at all. In our experience, this has definitely influenced the quality and quantity of content in publicly available forums.

A considerable problem for our netnographic research is certainly the shift of discussions to Facebook. Very little consumer dialogue is publicly available without a login. At the same time, various discussion groups about all kinds of different topics have evolved on Facebook, thereby creating fierce competition to traditional forms of online community such as forums and billboards. Since we at HYVE decided not to use data that requires registration for access, none of this is accessible to us. With its closed groups, where content is only visible to members, Facebook also offers more of the privacy that users desire compared to many online community formats where all postings are freely available. This creates two problems for us: Facebook itself only offers very limited access to data that can be used for our netnographies and it also impacts and reduces online dialogue on platforms elsewhere.

This becomes obvious when looking at the significance of online community formats such as newgroups, forums, and billboards. They seem to have lost their peak moment. Some forums are still successful, with plenty of current and active discussions, but many others have disappeared or have faced a steep decline in postings. The novelty of online communities seems to be gone, at the same time other social media compete for a user's time and attention. In our opinion, however, online communities such as forums still offer the best source to efficiently identify consumer insights as part of a netnography. They offer focused, in-depth postings of great length and content on the one hand and a discussion style between users on the other hand. The combination of these factors leads to a topic becoming more and more substantial and informative with each reply. However, as it has gotten more difficult to find suitable online communities, it is important not to lose sight of other alternatives and developments and to figure out a way to combine different types of sources.

To sum up, the online landscape has changed significantly over time. When online communities and blogs became popular, users freely and openly shared their opinions without much worry about privacy, fake comments or thoughts of commercialization. This was also the beginning of netnography at HYVE as we saw the potential that studying such online dialogue could lead to a better understanding of consumer needs and would be beneficial for companies in new product development. With time, online dialogue changed and today it is much more influenced by commercialization, privacy issues, and a shift to the big major social media platforms. These changes created new challenges for consumer-oriented netnographies because staged or fake content is more prevalent and the privacy concerns of users and changed preferences lead to a significant amount of online dialogue moving to more closed, non-accessible platforms. On the positive side, a netnographer now has access to a variety of different types of content such as photos and videos and to an even greater number of consumers.

As a first key lesson, it is essential for the researcher to have a thorough understanding of available online consumer dialogue, its advantages, limitations and changes over time. Be open to adapt the netnography to these changes, carefully integrating new types of online dialogue, while staying true to your method. What types of online dialogue we consider as useful for a netnography and how to analyse it will be explored in the next sub-section of this chapter.

LESSON 2: GET THE RIGHT DATA AND GET THE DATA RIGHT

A netnography is all about data, the right type of data. Where automatic monitoring solutions aim for big data, trying to find patterns based on a quantitative approach, netnography requires deep data. But what is deep data? It is data rich in context, with multiple, insightful aspects. Online postings that only state that users like a certain product or brand, without going into why they like it or how they use it might give you a first idea of which brand or feature seems to be more popular – but such postings do not offer a deep insight into the consumer's world. As a qualitative approach, however, netnography aims to fully understand consumers. That includes habits and routines that show how a product is integrated into their daily lives, what problems they face, and what they do to compensate such issues as well as their motivations, knowledge, likes and dislikes.

Obviously, such information does not fit into just one or two sentences. Thus, long and meaningful statements from consumers constitute the ideal choice for a netnography especially in the context of new product development. It is therefore important to evaluate whether a given data source offers such rich, deep data. Additionally, a dialogue-type of structure will further enhance data quality. Since we at HYVE have specialized in netnography as a passive approach, researchers are unable to state their questions or ask for further explanation about a posting. But, just as in real life, it is the back and forth amongst several people in a discussion that adds value and allows for different views, further aspects or clarification to emerge. So, while the netnographer cannot enter the discussion, she or he can profit from other participants contributing to the same discussion that will invariably lead to deeper insights.

What does this mean specifically for current popular online dialogue? As already stated, traditional online communities offer, in principle, the necessary type of deep data as well as the discussion structure to further deepen these insights. The main task is to identify suitable communities that are active with a large amount of current topics and replies. This does not mean limiting oneself to communities that specifically focus on the particular research topic. While such communities are certainly central for a netnography as they attract highly involved consumers, it is equally important to understand the needs and wishes of the average consumer. Community selection should therefore take different groups into account. While these cannot be identified on a posting level, choosing different types of online communities can provide this diverse view. Communities that, for example, target parents of young children or the senior population allow for a certain degree of target-group specific insights. General, non-topic specific communities more likely represent the opinions of less-involved consumers. Even if these communities do not focus on the research topic, it is highly likely that there are postings to be found that are relevant. It can also be helpful to choose communities in related fields. This allows the researcher to identify new ideas that could be transferred and open up new opportunities.

Facebook and especially its groups would theoretically also offer such deep data, however, the great majority of them are not public and therefore should not be used for a netnography without gaining the appropriate permissions. Content that is publicly available on Facebook without having to log into the platform is often found on various company profiles. Consumer postings on such profile pages could offer some insights but are often limited to complaints about very specific issues or very general expressions of approval. Twitter, on the other hand, has all its data openly available. But tweets are rather short, not only due to platform restrictions but also the culture of the platform as shaped by its users. Therefore, from our experience, they do not provide deep enough insights into a topic in regard to identifying consumer needs or habits.

A positive development for product reviews has been Amazon. While traditional product review pages (like ciao.com or dooyoo.com) have lost their importance or have disappeared altogether from the internet, Amazon offers hundreds of consumer reviews for all kinds of products. These are openly available and easy to find for the products or topics in question. Reviews are often extensive, offering plenty of information about consumers' habits, likes, dislikes and even wishes for improvement and innovation. While fake reviews also exist, an experienced researcher is able to identify those that are genuine and to focus only on these.

Platforms that specialize in visual media such as Instagram and Pinterest can be a great addition, but based on our experience with the typical research questions and goals of our clients, they are not sufficient enough to be used as the main source for consumer insights. They rely heavily on photos, which allows the researcher to see a consumer's favourite product or the setting in which it is used. But one needs to keep in mind that many of these photos are staged or paid advertisements, so they might not be very reliable in terms of showing a true window into consumers' lives. Comments used on these pages from other users also tend to be short and therefore of limited value.

YouTube offers a great number of product-related videos and comments. However, analysing videos is very time consuming and there is always the risk that despite a lengthy video, information gain is minimal. Comments on the video can offer some helpful insights, but they too are usually short and of little usable substance.

The last examples demonstrate that, besides focusing on deep data, efficiency is the second most important factor. Especially in a business context, resources are often limited, and results need to be gained in a short amount of time. In that case, a researcher needs to find sources that not only offer adequate data, but also offer them in one place where the structure and features of that place support easy identification and selection of relevant postings. This illustrates why platforms such as YouTube or Instagram, in our opinion, are not ideal in terms of efficiency. YouTube videos include a lot more irrelevant small talk, that the researcher needs to patiently endure during their analysis than textual dialogue in online communities, for example, which are more focused on the topic and which make it easier to quickly scan for the relevant parts. Additionally, even if interesting new aspects are mixed in with the whole video, a lot of researcher time must be expended to reveal the opinion of only one person. This level of knowledge gain is not in proportion to the time spent. Similar efficiency problems arise when using Instagram for identifying deep consumer insights. It would require a huge amount of photos that need to be analysed and a great number of irrelevant comments to be filtered out to find useful ones. The five-star-rating on Amazon or topic-specific sub-forums in online communities, on the other hand, make it much more efficient and easier for a researcher to quickly find and pre-select relevant postings for further analysis.

This is not to say that a netnography mainly based on new social media is not possible. It greatly depends on the research topic and, with a sufficient amount of resources available, interesting insights might be discovered. For a business, however, it seems advisable to first experiment with new, interesting sources as part of a test project before using them in projects with actual clients. This allows one to find out whether specific social media and other new sources offer enough deep data in a set amount of time or how to combine them with other sources, so that it is feasible to conduct a thorough netnography.

Identifying the right sources is only the first step. What follows now is a time of reading through a huge amount of data, thereby diving into the consumer world, experiencing it in-depth and from various angles and then to derive insights from this information that can be the starting point for new product development and greater consumer understanding. The more time a researcher has, the more data she or he can read – and the deeper and better the insights will be.

However, no researcher can read for days and weeks and keep all this information in their head for later use. Of course, one could summarize and aggregate things while reading to have a good idea of what topics are more intensively discussed or what brands are mentioned more often. However, netnographic insights are not built on broad summaries. Details matter, even statements mentioned by only one consumer can turn out to be an important aspect of an insight or a starting point for further research. Keep in mind, a netnography is not a quantitative method. Its goal is not to pass on representative information. What we at HYVE are seeking is to gain as much understanding about consumers as possible and, based on that information, to derive interesting and new areas for innovation and product development. Especially for radically new innovations, needs and wishes pointing to them will most likely not be voiced by a great number of people online. However, these small seeds of information that are collected here and there could turn into a great new invention.

So, what can be done with this huge amount of data to be easily accessible to the researcher later on when thinking about generating consumer insights? The most important things are to keep track of all the details and to structure the data for easy retrieval. Two tools have proven useful for that purpose.

Software for Qualitative Data Analysis allows the researcher to save consumer comments and categorize or code them. The researcher creates a coding system that includes types of problems, needs, feelings, habits, products, etc. These codes can vary greatly from project to project as some clients might also want to differentiate consumer statements in relation to different brands or specific use cases. Including the client into the development of the coding system is, in our opinion, not necessary though. Extensive briefing, desk research, and precise definition of the research scope at the beginning of the project can ensure that the researcher completely understands what information is relevant and of special importance to the client. Based on this, the researcher is not only fully capable to create a good coding system or their own, she or he are also better suited than the client to do so. First of all, at HYVE, the coding system is not fixed from the beginning but develops over time. Since netnography is an explorative method, new aspects relating to the topic will evolve during the analysis, making it necessary to constantly adapt the coding system. Second, because of their experience in numerous other projects, the netnographer has gained a good feeling for finding the right balance of the size of a coding system – which is a very important aspect to consider especially with limited resources. It should be big enough to cover all the various aspects of interest but not become too big so as to become inefficient. The more codes that exist, the more that detailed access is possible. But it also takes more time to attribute the codes to the posting, which in return reduces the time available for further reading. Once the researcher has coded their data with such software, it is now structured and she or he can get a quick overview of what kind of topics have been read and identified so far. This also provides quick access to the underlying data of these topics. The software also gives further useful information: some codes will have been used more often than others, which gives an indication of what topics are more prominent and which are discussed less often. Additionally, categorizing consumer statements with codes allows the researcher to identify correlations between codes which can help in identifying interesting insights. Once the project is finished, data in its coded structure can be handed to clients if desired. Some of our clients appreciate having this access to original consumer statements structured to specific aspects, problems or habits.

Equally important is what we call the research diary, and which is similar to Kozinets' (2020) "immersion journal". This diary functions like the second brain of the researcher, everything that is needed for insight generation can be found here. It can be created in any format according to the preference of the researcher: Powerpoint-Slides, Mindmaps, Word documents, whatever works best from a practical point of view. What matters is that data can be quickly entered, structured, and reviewed – and that it incorporates a lot of data. The diary is not a summary, quite the opposite, it contains everything, every little detail that the researcher has read about. It should also allow the researcher to collect all kinds of content: consumer-generated pictures, consumer quotes, information, references to products or websites that consumers posted online. During the reading process, the researcher writes down what consumers mention in regards to their habits, likes, dislikes, etc. However, the information is not simply stored in a long list, it needs to be structured to make it more manageable. Similar or related findings are placed together and, as this collection includes more and more elements, it might be divided again into several structured subtopics. For the researcher, this means going back and forth in their diary to find the right spot to enter the new information while reading. Over time, central topics will emerge. The researcher will be able to identify consumer insights and opportunity areas based on a large amount of different aspects and details that can be identified during the analysis.

The diary serves a second key function in multi-researcher or multi-language projects. In such projects, it is especially important to constantly and efficiently share one's own findings with other members of the team during the analysis. The structured makeup of the diary allows each researcher to quickly present to their colleagues in regular meetings the topics identified so far as well as noteworthy findings regarding them. This is especially essential when the whole team tries to identify common insights that are based on everyone's input or to identify language and country specific insights that are based on differences between the findings of the researchers. Such different findings can also serve as an inspiration to look further at how problems that were identified in one market might be viewed or even solved in a different market.

In summary, a netnography can be conducted using various types of online sources, such as discussions, photos or videos. Each type of media can add a different angle and piece to the puzzle. However, as efficiency also plays an important role when conducting netnographies in a business context, information dense media is preferable, especially when the netnography strives to find out more about various different aspects of consumers such as their habits, likes, dislikes, and problems. Therefore, we suggest concentrating on user dialogue that is rich in context, long, and full of interaction with others as can be found in online communities. These comments are often very focused and can offer a deep and well-rounded insight into various aspects of consumers' lives. Keeping research diaries while reading and using coding software for qualitative data analysis will help in remembering all the details and being able to easily access them later so that they can be used to deduct meaningful insights. The richness of your data will decide how deep and comprehensive your insights and how successful your netnography will be.

A netnography is not a simple Google search. It requires a large amount of quality data and a thorough analysis to identify insights and describe them in all their various aspects and details. The quality of a netnography lives and dies by the amount of effort put into data selection and analysis. While reading through thousands of consumer postings and storing all this information can be very challenging and time-consuming, the real task still lies ahead: how to present all these details and information in a way that lets the audience fully understand their consumers as if they had experienced everything themselves. We will learn more about this in the next section of this chapter.

LESSON 3: NETNOGRAPHY IS ABOUT STORYTELLING

Presenting the results of a netnography to a client is not simply about stating numbers or summarizing findings in an abstract report. Instead, the results should reflect the journey of the researcher of diving into the world of consumers, highlighting and clustering key findings into so-called consumer insights. A consumer insight in our understanding is characterized by four aspects. First, it has the *surprise factor*, which means that it contains new and unexpected elements that can open new lines of thought for innovation. Second, and based on consumers repeatedly mentioning the same aspects, there is *magnitude and relevance*. The insight shows enough strength to be the foundation of further innovation activities. Third, and equally importantly, it has *credibility*. An insight is a logical derivation of popular opinions and habits of consumers and is therefore backed up by evidence such as consumer statements or statistics. Fourth and finally, keeping in mind the purpose of the netnography at HYVE, a consumer insight provides a starting point for marketing or R&D activities. It comes with recommendations and initial ideas, making *actionability* an essential element.

While these four aspects are crucial for good consumer insights, it also matters how the insight is presented. The goal of the netnography for the researcher and the client alike is to become empathetic with consumers in all their complexity, as if they were one of them. It is therefore equally as important to transfer "knowledge" of the world of consumers to the client as it is to make the client "feel" part of that world.

A good way to achieve this is through storytelling. Instead of just aggregating information, a gripping storyline connecting all the subtopics of an insight can take the client along the journey, making them more and more curious to dive into this consumer world and develop a more profound understanding of it. This can be further enhanced by including user-generated content in forms of photos or videos showing their routines, habits, or even self-created solutions as well as consumer quotes. Including original, written consumer statements into the report is equivalent to letting clients hear consumers in their own voice, with their own choice of words and all their feelings about a specific topic. Such a statement conveys the emotions and problems the consumer faces in an authentic way that no summary or rewritten version by the researcher ever could.

To make the insight more memorable, we create what we at HYVE call *insight pictures*. These pictures catch the atmosphere and main message of the consumer insight. Just seeing this visualization of the consumer insight sometime later will easily bring back to mind the essence of the insight. This is especially important, considering that at HYVE we usually have at least five to seven different insights in one project, in multi-language projects even more. Since each consumer insight is also built of several different elements and all of this is presented in a fairly short amount of time, it is rather difficult for a client to remember all of the consumer insights. The insight picture, however, serves as an aid that will immediately trigger memory, which also makes it easier for the client to communicate the insights and findings internally. All she or he needs are the pictures and right away they will remember the main aspects of the insight and can share them with other people in their company. At HYVE these pictures are created near the end of the project. Designers and netnographers hold a dedicated visualization meeting for this purpose. At the meeting, the netnographers explain each consumer insight, its storyline and key elements. Together with one or more of HYVE's designers, they brainstorm about how the core idea of the insight could be translated into a picture and what details to include. While the netnographers might already have first ideas, designers who have not previously been involved in the project add an outside view besides their visualization expertise and help to further improve the communication of those first ideas or trigger even better ones.

To give an idea of such visualizations, we want to take a quick look at examples of insight pictures from two different netnography projects undertaken in the areas of technology and food.

The first insight picture in Figure 10.4, called "Peace of Mind", expressed the findings from a netnography that dived into the challenges and worries that people experience when taking care of loved ones in situations where they cannot be constantly supervised, such as elderly parents with dementia or children in large public places. Figure 10.5 shows the second insight picture, entitled "Bold Flavor Explosions", which expresses the findings revealed in the netnography regarding the desire of consumers for more exciting and varied flavour experiences in a single snack.

Figure 10.4 Examples of Insight Visualizations.

Figure 10.5 Examples of Insight Visualizations.

An insight picture can also be combined with a *virtual quote*, which is a constructed statement that seeks to encapsulate a netnographically derived insight. The following hypothetical consumer statement captures the insight from the netnographic research in a nutshell, attempting to convey all of its emotions. Added in this way, the virtual quote enhances the effect of the insight picture. The virtual quote for the food-related insight picture shown in Figure 10.5 was:

When it comes to extraordinary snacks, I am looking for something which combines several flavours such as onion, tomato, bacon, cheese, and hot pepper perfectly … something which makes me feel like I am on a "taste rollercoaster" testing the limits of my taste buds, driving me from sour to sweet BAM from salty to fruity BAM from smoky to spicy … maybe even very spicy BAM BAM … all in one crunch … WOW! That is what I call a real addictive kick, a definite must for an adventurous snack! I am looking forward to getting twisted with your snack … but PLEASE, if you call it "Cheese Hamburger", make sure I can taste all ingredients of a real Cheese Hamburger and not only the cheese *boring*!

When conveying what the HYVE researcher knows about the consumer world to the client, we have found that it is important to reach a good balance between aggregating and summarizing information whilst not losing too many details. Additionally, facets of the consumer world can be enhanced by putting them into context with additional information. Where possible, insights can be enriched with statistics which give an idea of approximately how many people are affected by the topic of the insight in a certain country or market. For example, when deriving insights about certain medical problems or illnesses, it helps to understand what proportion of the population is affected and what other characteristics they might have. It is also important to explain to the client which online communities were included in the research and why. Each online community has specific types of members, a fact that naturally influences what the group says and how it talks about a given topic.

Combining knowledge and emotion gives a thorough and empathic understanding of the consumer world. Now the question remains: What to do with all of this? This is where the actionability mentioned above becomes important. The results of the netnography show problems, but also the potential of possible solutions. It is now the task of the HYVE netnography team to develop initial basic idea seeds or opportunity areas that target these problems. Such idea seeds are part of step 6 within the netnography process illustrated in Figure 10.3. These seeds serve two functions. First, they help the client gain an increased understanding of the problem, because difficulties usually become clearer in light of a possible solution. Second, they can also serve as an initial spark for brainstorming other ideas and serve as the bridge between consumer understanding and new product development. It is, however, important that idea seeds are kept simple. The solution space should remain wide open for clients without already pointing them to specific directions or solutions.

In this section of the chapter, we have outlined how findings from the netnographic analysis are translated into consumer insights at HYVE. Ideally these insights are presented in the form of storytelling that enables clients to experience a sense of immersion into the consumers' world as if they had become a part of it. A good netnographic story will state facts, but also convey the emotions of consumers, their struggles, likes, and dislikes. This will help the client to become more empathetic to consumers' needs and will also aid in developing more need-based and user-centred solutions. Using elements such as original consumer quotes, virtual quotes and insight pictures will not only increase a client's understanding of the findings. It will also assist them to better remember the results and also communicating them internally within the company. Initial idea seeds demonstrate to the client where opportunity areas can be found and provide them with a starting point.

In order to create great and innovative solutions, our clients need to better understand the problem. To understand the problem, a client must not only to rationally learn about it, but also must learn to empathize with the consumer, to feel what they feel about the product or brand experience. Our key message in this section has been that creating a compelling storyline that speaks to both the mind and to the heart will provide this important sense of empathy. But if empathy is an integral element of a good netnography, what role can machine-enabled research play? The next section of this chapter will explore this aspect.

LESSON 4: KEEP THE HUMAN TOUCH BUT USE MACHINES TO ASSIST YOU

In their feedback to us, clients mainly state that it is the richness and insightfulness of netnography results that they hold to be a major strength of the method. On the other hand, the relatively small data samples compared to web-monitoring approaches and the long project durations of several weeks due to intensive manual work are seen by them as drawbacks. It seems that the advantages of the manual process are the disadvantages of an automated analysis and vice versa.

The question as to what level netnography can be automated without jeopardizing the quality of results was examined in research by Bartl and Ivanovic (2010). The idea of this study was to predict an optimum balance between automated and manual research in the netnography process. The highest possibility for improving the process efficiency of a netnography at HYVE was found to be in the community selection and data collection phase. This is because decentralized manual web search, data downloads based on manual copy-paste techniques and the large number of little tools combined in the netnography research process at HYVE during that time caused enormous inefficiencies. This prediction in the year 2010 proved to be true. Over the years, machine learning algorithms have improved to the extent that allows solving real life problems. Moreover, exponentially growing amounts of data provide an invaluable source for training, testing, applying, and refining these algorithms. Finally, the barrier of specialized hardware, which is needed for running machine learning tasks, has vanished. Software offerings are now broadly available for researchers that unite data retrieval, quantitative data analysis, and the visualization of the results in dashboards.

In 2018, Marchuk, Biel, Bilgram, and Worning compared netnography and a machine-enabled research approach within a competition of "machine vs. human" (see Chapter 12, this volume). The experiment showed that although the future might see humans substituted by machines, the capabilities of intelligent machines still do not exceed human's competences in the specific task of identifying consumer insights from online data. Intelligent machines, however, have proven to be able to outperform humans in data collection, data clustering, and partially in data analysis especially with big data samples. Human-driven qualitative research is more appropriate for empathic data analysis, insight generation, and storytelling, which machines cannot (yet) do. From an economic perspective, machine learning could be a time-saving mechanism. On the other hand, neural networks need to be initially trained with data in a time-consuming process. Once the network is trained for a specific domain, it is scalable only for this topic. However, it cannot be applied to slightly different domains and it can barely be applied to unrelated topics. This makes it quite difficult to move a trained neural network from one netnographic project to another.

The takeaway from this experiment must be that it is not about a competition between humans and machines, but about a better collaboration between them. Improvements like in adopting technology where it makes sense, both from a quality and an economic perspective. As technology steadily evolves, it will also enter the areas where humans today still outdo the machines. Examples are the automatized extraction of innovation opportunities from crowdfunding data based on the Latent Dirichlet Allocation (LDA), which is an unsupervised learning technique and topic modelling algorithm. In one study, 5727 crowdfunding projects were analysed and based on funding success the most relevant innovation clusters were retrieved (Bilgram, Gluth, & Piller, 2017). In another study the online idea contest for "reinventing chocolate bars" of an international manufacturer of foods and beverages was analysed (Kakatkar, de Groote, Füller, & Spann, 2018). In that study, 1078 participants from 69 countries contributed 468 ideas that were evaluated by experts as well as by the online community. Pattern detection was then used to extract the DNA of winning ideas, i.e., feature combinations of the most innovative chocolate bars.

These examples demonstrate that scientific research in this direction is progressing very fast. Hence our key message is to allow machines and artificial intelligence to assist while at the same time keeping the human touch of netnography. The assistance of machines will even surpass the obvious advantages of automation and data-processing capabilities based on natural language processing. Imagine that there will be around 70 billion connected machines and devices on earth. These are not restricted to smartphones or laptops but also include cars and all kind of electronics products in your daily life. These devices will gain perception organs based on integrated cameras and microphones, which are then used to feed emotion recognition algorithms based on facial expressions, optical heart rate measurement, and sound frequencies in the human voice. Including new categories of digital traces will open a completely new universe for new research practices. A netnographer should always be prepared to broaden her horizons by using new technologies to improve upon existing way to conduct netnography. Additionally, we describe in the following section that it is crucial to combine the specialized knowledge of conducting netnographic approaches with other complementary research methods that have likewise developed rapidly in recent times.

LESSON 5: DON'T BE A PURIST

Within the last two decades, significant methodological developments revived the market research domain mainly driven by the digitalization. The new methods and procedures are often referred to as New Market Research. Figure 10.6 gives an overview of some of these approaches and positions netnography in this methodological landscape. Market researchers, product and R&D managers alike are using these methods to increase the user orientation of traditional technology-centric research and thus counter market risks in the early phases of product development (Bartl, Füller, Mühlbacher, & Ernst, 2012). Some examples of these instruments are online research communities, idea competitions, toolkits and configurators, lead user, design thinking formats, or social media mining. Netnography occupies a clear positioning in this mix of methods that can be assigned to the field of qualitative and observational methods.

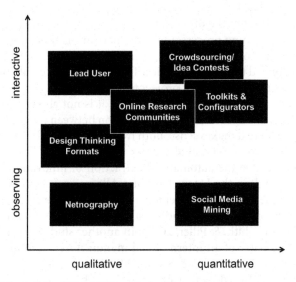

Figure 10.6 Methodological Tool Box in New Market Research.

Netnography proved to be a powerful single method. However, at HYVE we have learned that, in two important ways, it is even more powerful in a mixed method approach. First, from a process-related view. Within the innovation space we often apply netnography as an entry project into the fuzzy front end to help innovation managers immerse and orient themselves in the consumers' world. The goal is to draw a landscape of needs, wishes, concerns, consumer language and potential product solutions by users, which are explicitly and implicitly expressed in online communities and social media. The output of netnography is a tremendously valuable input for subsequent methods. For online research communities, the study design can be defined in a much more focused manner and overly general questions can be avoided due to a more solid consumer understanding. The insights can be validated with all the interaction modules of an online research community. For design thinking formats and ideation workshops the netnography insights allow for the possibility of closely relating creative work to actual consumer needs and preventing action from being taken outside the consumers' actual need space. Additionally, netnography allows for the identification of lead users who often express themselves in online communities and therefore help to reduce time and costs in the selection phase of lead user projects (Bilgram, Brem, & Voigt, 2008; Belz & Baumbach 2010).

A second positive effect of netnography in a mixed method approach is that it can enrich other methods by adding a netnographic procedure to the already collected data base and enhance the results with further netnographic findings from online sources. An example is analysing the written user content in crowdsourcing projects, crowdfunding platforms, or idea contests as described above in lesson 4. The combination of netnography and automated social media mining is obvious. Whereas purely automated mining delivers broad concepts and can identify popular topics and themes, therefore focusing on the WHAT, netnography offers a deeper understanding of the WHY and the HOW.

CONCLUSIONS

We started this chapter with a journey through 16 years of HYVE netnography field experience with more than 140 projects in various industries and countries or language areas. We outlined the scientific contribution of these 16 years of research in order to illustrate how important it is for new and evolving research approaches to intertwine practical work with academic research. The chapter is written from the perspective of the HYVE netnography specialist team, which is active in the innovation consulting and research business. Hence, the described applied process includes some of our own unique adaptions to the prior procedural guidelines of netnography in order to meet the particular needs in this business segment. The core part of the chapter is the five key lessons learned which the specialist team decided to be worthy of highlighting. These learnings, which are illustrated in Figure 10.7,

5 Key Lessons Learned:

Lesson 1: Stay on top of the evolving dialogue in social media

Lesson 2: Get the right data & get the data right

Lesson 3: Netnography is about storytelling

Lesson 4: Keep the human touch but use machines to assist you

Lesson 5: Don't be a purist

Figure 10.7 Summary Key Lessons Learned.

are distilled from our work experience of the last years and should help other practitioners as a guideline.

Lessons 1 and 4 deal with social media sources, data collection and data creation. These parts of netnography have to deal with incredible fast developments and yearly technological updates of social media tools and new formats adopted by users. Additionally, more and more activities that traditionally were the task of the researcher can be automated and supported by machines and AI. Lessons 2 and 3 focus on the competencies of the researcher to analyse, interpret and create impact for the actual business purpose of the project. The proper handling of data and the use of data search tactics as well as sophisticated validation and selection strategies must be an elementary part of a netnographer's skillset. On top of this analytical dimension, the ability to develop in-depth empathy for users and to create stories that allow transporting consumer insights to clients turns a good netnographer into a real master of his or her craft. As a fifth key lesson, we strongly advise specialized practitioners and netnography fans not to develop an isolated mindset but to be open to connect netnography results in a mixed-method context or framework.

The five lessons are based on the study of past experiences at HYVE but at the same time offer a framework to look at the future of netnography. The social media world and developments in AI will evolve at a breathtaking pace. At the same time, the ethnographic roots of the method will always require the ability of researchers to deeply empathize with consumers and to create insights out of the continuously increasing amount of human digital traces in social media. Therefore, part of the researcher's job has to be to reassess and challenge their own netnography practice year after year along the dimensions laid out in the five key lessons.

REFERENCES

Bartl, M. (2007). Netnography, Einblicke in die Welt der Kunden. *Planung & Analyse*, 5(2007), 83–87.

Bartl, M., Füller, J., Mühlbacher, H., & Ernst, H. (2012). A manager's perspective on virtual customer integration for new product development. *Journal of Product Innovation Management*, 29(6), 1031–1046.

Bartl, M., Hueck, S., & Landgraf, R. (2008). Information pur: Netnography erschließt Online-Communities als Innovationsquelle. *Research & Results*, 1(08), 28–29.

Bartl, M., Hueck, S., & Ruppert, S. (2009a). Netnography research. Community insights in the cosmetic industry. In Conference Proceedings ESOMAR Consumer Insights (pp. 1–12).

Bartl, M., Hueck, S., & Ruppert, S. (2009b). Netnography for Innovation: Creating Insights with User Communities. In Conference Proceedings ESOMAR Consumer Insights (pp. 1–12).

Bartl, M., & Ivanovic, I. (2010). Netnography – Finding the right balance between automated and manual research. *Web-monitoring. UVK Publishing*, Konstanz, 157–174.

Bartl, M., Jawecki, G., Stoenner, J. H., & Gastes, D. (2011). Review of a decade of netnography research. In ESOMAR live conference papers (pp. 85–93). Miami: ESOMAR.

Bartl, M., Kumar, V. K., & Stockinger, H. (2016). A review and analysis of literature on netnography research. *International Journal of Technology Marketing*, 11(2), 165–196.

Bartl M., & Tusche N. (2015). *Netnography: The mint journey*. Open Tourism, Berlin: Springer Verlag.

Belz, F. M., & Baumbach, W. (2010). Netnography as a method of lead user identification. *Creativity and Innovation Management*, 19(3), 304–313.

Bilgram, V., Bartl, M., & Biel, S. (2011). Getting closer to the consumer – how Nivea co-creates new products. *Marketing Review St. Gallen*, 28(1), 34–40.

Bilgram, V., Brem, A., & Voigt, K. I. (2008). User-centric innovations in new product development—Systematic identification of lead users harnessing interactive and collaborative online-tools. *International Journal of Innovation Management*, 12(03), 419–458.

Bilgram, V., Füller, J., Bartl, M., Biel, S., & Miertsch, H. (2013). Eine Allianz gegen Flecken. *Harvard Business Manager*, 3, 63–68.

Bilgram, V., Gluth, O., & Piller, F. (2017). Crowdfunding data as a source of innovation. *Marketing Review St. Gallen*, 34(3), 10–18.

Füller J. , Bartl M. , Ernst H., & Mühlbacher M. (2006). Community based innovation: How to integrate members of virtual communities into new product development. *Electronic Commerce Research Journal*, 6(1), 57–73.

Füller, J., Jawecki, G., & Mühlbacher, H. (2007). Innovation creation by online basketball communities. *Journal of Business Research*, 60(1), 60–71.

Gebauer, J., Füller, J., & Pezzei, R. (2013). The dark and the bright side of co-creation: Triggers of member behavior in online innovation communities. *Journal of Business Research*, 66(9), 1516–1527.

Hück, S., Grünhagen, A., & Lichter, C. (2010). Listening to social media from a B2B2C perspective with netnography. Conference Proceeding ESOMAR Online Research.

Jawecki, G., Füller, J., & Gebauer, J. (2011). A comparison of creative behaviours in online communities across cultures. *Creativity and Innovation Management*, 20(3), 144–156.

Jawecki, G., & Fuller, J. (2008). How to use the innovative potential of online communities? Netnography – an unobtrusive research method to absorb the knowledge and creativity of online communities. *International Journal of Business Process Integration and Management*, 3(4), 248–255.

Kakatkar, C., de Groote, J. K., Fueller, J., & Spann, M. (2018). The DNA of winning ideas: A network perspective of success in new product development. In Academy of Management (Ed.), Academy of management proceedings (Vol. 2018, No. 1, p. 11047). Briarcliff Manor, NY: Academy of Management.

Kozinets, R.V. (1997). "I want to believe": A netnography of the X-Philes' Subculture of Consumption. In *Advances in Consumer Research*, Vol. 24, pp. 470–475.

Kozinets, R. V. (2002). The field behind the screen: Using netnography for marketing research in online communities. *Journal of Marketing Research*, 39(1), 61–72.

Kozinets, R. V. (2010). *Netnography: Doing ethnographic research online*. Thousand Oaks, CA: SAGE.

Kozinets, R. V. (2015). *Netnography: Redefined*. Thousand Oaks, CA: SAGE.

Kozinets, R. V. (2020). *Netnography: The essential guide to qualitative social media research*. Thousand Oaks, CA: SAGE.

Marchuk, A., Biel, S., Bilgram, V., & Worning, S. (2018). Standing on the shoulders of giants – Insights and Implications form a 'duel' between humans and machines. In ESOMAR (Ed.), *Esomar Fusion Conference Proceedings* 2018 (pp. 146–159).

Piller, F., Ihl, C., & Vossen, A. (2011). A typology of methods for customer co-creation in the innovation process. New Forms of Collaborative Innovation and Production, Universitätsverlag, Göttingen, 31–62.

Stockinger, H., Bartl, M., Kalogirou, K., & Pollok, P. (2013). Netnography: Online communities as a source of innovation in the field of e-mobility. *Wirtschaftswissenschaftliches Studium*, 42(12), 674–682.

11

Netnography in the Banking Sector

José Clemente-Ricolfe and Roberto Cervelló Royo

INTRODUCTION

Friendly service and a close relationship with customers are key factors in the banking sector, which has often relied on physical location and high-touch personal services to maintain these relationships (Kil & Miklaszewska, 2017). However, online banking draws into question some of these prior investments and some of these hard-won established relationships. Between 2011 and 2018, there was a notable increase in the number of customers using online banking services in Europe, from 36% to 54% (Eurostat, 2018). Members of the banking sector, as well as those who research it, have wondered whether the growing use of online services may make it harder to achieve friendly relationships between banking sector companies and consumers. With the emergence of new players in the banking sector, such as fintech startups and technologies like artificial intelligence and blockchain, there is a need to study consumers' responses (Mylonakis, 2007). Against this backdrop of mechanization, self-service, competition, and change, we believe that social media data has great potential to illuminate the dynamic complex service relationships underlying online and physical banking and give us a deeper sense of the realities, pain points, desires, and fears of contemporary banking customers.

Bank customers around the world are not only becoming more digital in their banking methods, they are also using digital platforms to become more demanding. Along with the telecommunications sector, the banking sector has one of the highest rates of complaints and unsatisfied customers (Keramati, Ghaneei, & Mirmohammadi, 2016). Unhappy consumers may express their dissatisfaction on social media and in online forums and communities, which makes social media research well-suited to hearing from these consumers.

Typical research approaches in bank studies ask customers direct questions through either qualitative or quantitative means. However, netnography provides a more naturalistic way to gain insights into consumers' impressions alongside their lived realities and experiences. In fact, netnography has a long history as a marketing research technique in other fields. Our insight was to develop this technique specifically in the banking field, which is a highly quantitative and "number-driven" domain that tends to distrust or avoid qualitative forms of understanding. As a result of this quantitative orientation, many of the studies of social media banking customers tend to be more numerical and experience-distant than one would typically find in among cultural scholars. In this chapter, we will examine some of the literature in this sector through this lens.

In summary, we believe that netnography can be a valuable technique for researchers interested in the banking sector, because it allows researchers to gain an unvarnished view of the banking-related discussions that people have on social media, thereby allowing us to see matters that might lie at the heart of the bank–customer relationship. In view of this, we will next summarize the findings from various published applications of netnography in the banking sector. Following this, we will describe a new application involving consumer perceptions in the Spanish mortgage market.

APPLICATIONS OF NETNOGRAPHY IN THE BANKING SECTOR

Netnography has already been used to research banking sector consumers in a number of peer-reviewed publications. Table 11.1 shows that it has been applied to various areas, although it has primarily been used to study various factors imputed to relate to the creation or destruction of meaningful relationships between banks and customers. Paunonen, Lehtinen and Aro (2012) analyzed online forums from different countries in various languages and identified five attributes that they theorized were related to the creation of valuable banking relationships: trust, efficiency, self-service, personal contact, and extra services. Other online comments indicated a strong level of distrust in banks due to the suspicion that they wanted to sell products that customers may not need. With respect to the attribute of efficiency, customers discussed their desire for banks to oversee the fast, simple management of their financial transactions. Customers also were concerned about the distancing of banks from their customers and the consequent impersonal relationships they fostered.

In another study, Medberg and Heinonen (2014) analyzed the creation of value in the customer–bank relationship outside the line of visibility of service encounters. Using 579 posts from discussions of retail banking in 18 online communities, the authors identified four different factors that drove customer value: shared moral value, responsibility value, relationship value, and heritage value. "Shared moral value" refers to moral compatibility between the customer and perceived bank standards. "Responsibility value" is the bank's practice of responsibility and integrity toward its customers. "Relationship value" encompasses long-term relationships between the customer and the bank, and "heritage value" focuses on relationships that were initiated by the customer's parents or family members, turning the relationship with the bank into a family memory. In this context, netnography's utility lay in its ability to take an allegedly rationalist, technical, transaction, and economic activity, and identify the rich and complex set of underlying cultural values and meanings that undergird it. Netnography provided Medberg and Heinonen's (2014) work with a rich window into the roles of elements such as heritage, morals, and family on the bank–customer relationships, helping to build what Kozinets (2006, 279) describes as "intimate understanding of the actual reality of the consumer" (Kozinets, 2006, 279)—which is something that many marketers and business managers desire.

Table 11.1 Review of Studies That Have Applied Netnography to the Banking Sector

Topic	Authors
Creation of value between the bank and the customer	Paunonen, Lehtinen, & Aro, 2012; Medberg & Heinonen, 2014; Tang, Mehl, Eastlick, He & Card, 2016
Online banking brand positioning	Clemente-Ricolfe, 2017
Managing complaints in the banking sector	Melancon & Dalakas, 2016

In another study, Tang, Mehl, Eastlick, He, and Card (2016) collected social media data from the customers of 68 different banks that were posting on a popular and independent online forum. Their study revealed that the anger and outrage expressed by social media consumers on the forum had significant predictive value for decreased profitability of financial institutions from the second year onwards.

Netnography has also been used to gain insight into online bank brand positioning, to compile a ranking of banking brands and to understand how and why particular consumers view particular banking brands as "better" or "worse" than others. For example, using information from two consumer opinion websites, Clemente-Ricolfe (2017) identified two groups of competitors and two types of attributes in online banks' positioning in Spain. On one hand, consumers' perceptions of online banks as competitors were based on their size, in line with specialized literature on the topic. On the other, negative (or positive) attributes of products were perceived to be offset by high (or low) value in other attributes, in this case higher (or lower) returns. Finally, netnography can also be used to analyze complaint management in the banking sector. Melancon and Dalakas (2016) grouped together consumers' motives for complaining on social media. Eight different segments were identified using negative comments, concerns or questions asked by consumers on Facebook with respect to ten different companies, including one bank. Motives for complaining were culturally complex and had a strong emotional component, and the complaints were not limited to simple questions of performance and efficiency. For example, the largest segment consisted of previously loyal consumers who were expressing their intention of changing brands because they felt personally offended by some action. The authors also determined that if a message was eliminated without a reply having been received from the company, it generated a larger number of messages that were even more negative.

In summary, instances where netnography has already been applied in the banking sector have led to the following improvements in our knowledge of financial sector consumers:

1. They increase our understanding of customers' reasoning, which is the basis of any commercial activity. Netnography enables in-depth analysis of the nature of the consumer that goes beyond the outwardly apparent. This makes it possible to identify cultural ideals or values, for instance, relationships with banks that were initiated by family members (Medberg & Heinonen, 2014).

2. They confirm or broaden the existing literature on the topics being studied. By providing a less artificial and more realistically grounded view of the consumer, netnography facilitates a wider look at the elements regarding financial services, their perceptions, and their consumption. For example, one netnographic study suggested that, because of compensatory mechanisms yet to be fully developed and validated, but present in the research, high returns on an account could compensate for the existence of high fees (Clemente-Ricolfe, 2017). The theorists propounded, based on the data, that Fishbein's compensatory model would support this finding.

3. Naturalistic social media data represents an opportunity for marketing research method that fits with changes in the world of banking technology and an increased emphasis on customer journey, user experience, and experience design elements. This data can effectively be used by the banking sector to get closer to the increasingly technological and online world of the banking consumer. Banks are increasingly paying attention to the need for customer experience design to play a role in their processes. Netnography's empirical basis and facilitation of deep experiential understanding provide a structured approach to utilizing this rich social media data for pursuit of this goal of enhanced customer experience understanding.

MORTGAGE MARKET PERCEPTIONS: THE CASE OF SPAIN

This section will describe the use of social media data to help understand consumer opinion in Spain about the banking sector. The overarching aim is to elevate our understanding of consumer opinions about mortgage loans in Spain. There are two specific aims: first, to gain a deeper understanding of consumers' opinion related to mortgage loan applications; and second, to analyze the data in order to determine which elements of the mortgage loan application experience are the most important or influential in determining the mortgage applicant's satisfaction. It is important for banks to understand how consumers make decisions when choosing a mortgage. As Talaga and Buch (1998) point out, consumers may behave in ways that are not necessarily rational from a financial perspective regarding these products. Using social media data to gather experiential and cultural information about consumer choices may help lenders better understand them so that they can tailor their products to borrowers' preferences. With social media data, we can obtain accounts and descriptions from informed, educated consumers who provide interesting and potentially useful information (Kozinets, 2002).

We chose to situate our investigation in Spain because we are culturally fluent with and situated in this marketplace, and thus our actions as embedded netnographers are facilitated by the choice of this context. As well, Spain is one of the countries with the most deeply rooted traditions of purchasing a home (Elsinga & Hoekstra, 2005). Moreover, according to the Centro de Investigaciones Sociológicas (CIS, 2019), 81.8% of the Spaniards who were renting a home in 2019 would buy one if they could. The same survey revealed that just 1.3% of renters were averse to taking out a mortgage. In other words, Spain is a country with an important mortgage loan market.

ADAPTING NETNOGRAPHY TO THE CONTEXT

For this study, we focused on variable-interest mortgages. These types of mortgages have the heaviest presence in Spain, accounting for six of every ten mortgages in the country (Colegio de Registradores de la Propiedad, 2018). The banks studied were ING, Santander, Bankia, BBVA, and Bankinter. These are banks that often lead various rankings of prominent banks in Spain.

Because banking and bank consumers studies tend to be highly quantitative, and the norms of publication in this field also tend to be deductive, we adopted a deductive approach to coding qualitative social media data that is somewhat unusual and different from the usually inductive or abductive approach of netnographers in fields such as consumer culture research or cultural studies. We used past research to generate constructs, and then coded for these constructs among our collected dataset. Details on the deductive process follow.

We identified past literature that helped us to generate the following list of attributes or criteria for coding our qualitative social media dataset: personal requirements to be fulfilled by the consumer, conditions/loan ties, processing time, customer service, cost, fees/expenses, percentage financed, repayment term, and recognition of customer loyalty/time with the bank. Subsequently, each attribute was divided into two opposing categories (demanding-flexible, many-few, slow-fast, bad-good, etc.), enabling positive or negative comments from each message to be included in one of the levels. A set of binary variables was created to indicate whether the attribute was present in the comment analyzed. We then set about collecting raw data to then interpret the consumer's satisfaction on a scale of 1 to 5, where 1 = worst rating, and 5 = best rating.

Our investigation continued with a search for significant sources of social media conversations devoted to sharing mortgage loans from financial institutions. Several websites, such as Rankia and HelpMyCash, were found using the search engine Google. The financial product comparison site HelpMyCash was selected due to its large audience and the fact that it is number 1,554 on the list of Spain's top websites (Alexa, 2019). It is thus a group of posts that relates to the subject matter of this study. It has high traffic and a large number of messages, contains detailed information, and offers members of the online community a chance to interact with each other, fulfilling the criteria for data collection set by Kozinets (2002, 63). We collected data from the site from May 2018 to June 2019. We also classified messages during the data collection as relevant or irrelevant to the study. Using a relevance criterion as our touchstone, we excluded messages that didn't focus specifically on the topic in question, for instance, those that commented on insurance or requested participation in bank promotions. We also tried to make sure there were no contradictions between the opinion expressed and the overall rating given.

We chose to work with a total of 229 messages. Again, we chose, somewhat unconventionally, to quantify the qualitative data in our netnography. Our analysis and results are intended be understood as examples of this more quantitative type of approach to the analysis of qualitative social media data. We did not keep fieldnotes and did not engage or interact with the platform or its members. Although rarer than qualitative approaches, there are numerous examples of this type of work being called netnography—as cited above—given that the results are also subject to a "netnographic sensibility" that interprets them in light of a deeper cultural understanding (Reid & Duffy, 2018).

THE CULTURAL REALITY OF SPANISH MORTGAGE LOANS: SERVICE IS EVERYTHING AND INTEREST RATES ARE SECONDARY

The conversation topics and valences mentioned most often by consumers when posting about or discussing mortgages online are detailed in Table 11.2. Poor customer service was first; it was cited in 34.1% of the posts. Slow processing of the loan was second; it was mentioned in 32.3% of the posts. A total of 17.9% cite an abundance of—or unfavorable— conditions or loan ties when applying for the mortgage. Finally, 16.2% of the comments or posts perceived fees and expenses as high or unfavorable. It should be noted that the top five consumer mentions regarding the mortgage variables studied are negative. This finding is supported by the overall average rating of 2.2 on a scale of 1 to 5. Almost two-thirds of the posts were interpreted by us as providing the lowest possible rating. These negative results are likely a cultural reflection of the negative views of the banking sector throughout consumer society in Spain. Indeed, 72.6% of complaints made through a consumer organization were focused on the banking sector (Moreno, 2017). A large portion of these involved minimum interest clauses or highlighted the fact that fees for formalizing mortgages have been declared abusive by various national and European courts. In addition, since 2008 the disappearance of the former savings banks at the regional level and the continual restructuring of Spain's financial system, due in part to financial misconduct, have fueled greater mistrust in Spanish society. In the study of Corporate Social Responsibility in Spain conducted by Pérez-Ruiz and Rodríguez del Bosque (2012), the customer-focused dimension displayed very low ratings. These findings reflect the banking sector's poor image among the public, and societal expectations regarding the role of companies as citizens with obligations (good service, speed, etc.)

Furthermore, although literature on the topic shows that the costs associated with mortgages are an important variable to consumers (Roos, Gustafsson & Edvardsson, 2006), in this study it is mentioned in just two or three percent of the comments. This seemingly

Table 11.2 Conversation Topics and Valences Mentioned Most Often By Consumers When Posting About or Discussing Mortgages Online in Spain (% Values)

1. Demanding personal requirements	18.8
2. Flexibility with respect to personal requirements	7.0
3. Many or unfavorable conditions/loan ties	17.9
4. Few or attractive conditions/loan ties	9.2
5. Processing speed: slow	32.3
6. Processing speed: fast	13.5
7. Poor customer service	34.1
8. Good customer service	9.2
9. Unfavorable cost	2.6
10. Favorable cost	3.1
11. High fees/expenses	16.2
12. Low fees/expenses	0.9
13. A small percentage financed	9.2
14. A large percentage financed	7.9
15. Unfavorable repayment term	0.9
16. Favorable repayment term	1.3
17. No recognition of customer loyalty/time with bank	10.0
18. Recognition of customer loyalty/time with bank	4.8

Note: The percentages do not add up to one hundred because they were multi-choice variables, that is, more than one variable could be present in the response.

contradictory finding may be explained by the extremely low Euribor interest rates in Europe in recent years and low variance in the changes of those rate. As a result, consumers appear to be less concerned with interest rates overall. In addition, the lack of significant interest might indicate a shift in the mindset of Spanish society. In the past, between 1987 and 2008, interest rate spreads were on an upward trend. However, since that time, due to global governmental policies of monetary easing, they have displayed a clear downward trajectory (Martínez-Pagés, 2017). In view of this, our social media data may indicate that interest rates are losing their cultural importance in mortgage loan applications.

ADDITIONAL FINDINGS: FIVE FACTORS THAT REVOLVE AROUND SERVICE, EXPERIENCE, AND SPEED

We also performed a quantitative analysis on our coded data to quantify some of the structural elements underlying the interrelationships between different factors mentioned by consumers. We used a principal components analysis that helped us to identify five dimensions that might provide further depth to our cultural understanding of mortgage perceptions. First were those related to personal requirements and the bank's flexibility regarding them. Next was processing speed. Third was positive customer service experiences. Fourth were poor customer service experiences. The fifth and final dimension was interpreted to relate to a combination of slow processing time and poor customer service. These five dimensions that contrast positive and negative aspects are a reflection of Spanish society. For example, Spanish consumers have more trust in stores with goods priced at market value and friendly staff (Observatorio Cetelem, 2018). Similarly, using social media data to assess mortgage applications reveals a connection between low fees or few conditions and good customer service. Different variables were grouped together, creating new concepts (dimensions), and it was possible to shift back and forth between empirical data and theory. We used a visual analysis of the analysis which revealed in graphical format the favorable and unfavorable opinions clustering in different parts of the mapping.

Our visual and statistical analysis enabled perceptions of the main variables considered in mortgage loan applications to be grouped together, differentiating favorable from unfavorable variables. Moreover, it revealed which attributes are the most important for customer satisfaction and dissatisfaction. In both cases, it detected the use of various factors cited in the literature, and an interrelationship between them: personal characteristics, loan characteristics and service quality characteristics. In addition, it seems to confirm that the general public has a poor impression of the banking sector. There is also a perception, however, that the sector can facilitate satisfaction among people who wish to acquire a home, an aspiration that is deeply rooted in Spanish culture.

The results of our interpretation may be consistent with a deeper understanding of the social needs that banks are expected to fulfil: involvement and a commitment to helping (Laboral Kutxa, 2014). In other words, speed, a large amount of financing, and few conditions could represent the idea state of banks to make people's lives easier, which might be a highly valued objective in Spanish culture. It should be noted that it is mainly through our interpretive process that our demonstration of netnography enables a more comprehensive and holistic view of the phenomenon studied. In this case, we linked a number of important current factors about the European and Spanish context, including interest rate flattening and the intense desire among Spanish consumers to own their own homes, that factors into our interpretation of the social media data about mortgage application experience.

CONCLUSIONS

Detailed analysis of banking sector consumer behavior is especially important due to the growing competition and implementation of new technologies used to offer financial services. All of this, coupled with the increase in online banking, makes netnography an appropriate method for understanding the cultural reality of banking sector customers.

This chapter described a quantitative content analysis-style application of social media data that is similar to the way netnography is sometimes applied in business contexts. In this chapter, we demonstrated a project that used social media data to consider customer conversations regarding the mortgage loan process. We have described a process of analysis that is quantitative, deductive, and based on content analysis, similar to some of the methods of "coding," "counting," and "charting" recounted in Kozinets (2020, 337–354). Readers might consider and reach their own conclusions regarding the tradeoffs between a deeper cultural understanding and the appearance of precision that such quantification provides. Calling a technique netnography implies more than the mere presence and use of social media data—but a mindset focused on deep cultural interpretation and understanding—as well as strict adherence to extant guidelines.

In the chapter, we have tried to show that the focus of our research remains on a more embedded and naturalistic understanding of customers than could have been achieved with other popular techniques such the topic modeling of big datasets. Social media data can be used by banks to gain an insider's perspective on how customers perceive their products. The use of netnography to analyze customer experiences with the mortgage application process provides an excellent opportunity to improve the design and quality of these sorts of banking products. Netnography thus facilitates customer orientation, which is a cornerstone of the banking sector and indeed of most businesses.

REFERENCES

Alexa (2019). Competitive Analysis Tools. www.alexa.com/siteinfo/helpmycash.com

Braunsberger, K., & Buckler, B. (2011). What motivates consumers to participate in boycotts: Lessons from the ongoing Canadian seafood boycott. *Journal of Business Research*, 64(1), 96–102.

Bartl, M., Jawecki, G., & Wiegandt, P. (2010). Co-creation in new product development: Conceptual framework and application in the automotive industry. Paper presented at the R&D Management Conference, Manchester.

Cheng, P., Lin, Z., & Liu, Y. (2009). Do women pay more for mortgages?. *The Journal of Real Estate Finance and Economics*, 43(4), 423–440.

CIS (2019). Barómetro de junio 2019. Avance de resultados. www.cis.es/cis/opencms/ES/NoticiasNovedades/InfoCIS/2019/Documentacion_3252.html

Clemente-Ricolfe, J. S. (2017). Consumer perceptions of online banking in Spain using netnography: A positioning story. *International Journal of Bank Marketing*, 35(6), 966–982.

Colegio de Registradores de la Propiedad. (2018). Distribución porcentual de los tipos de interés contratados en los nuevos créditos hipotecarios de vivienda en España en 2017, según clase. https://es.statista.com/estadisticas/603477/clase-de-los-tipos-de-interes-contatados-en-el-nuevo-credito-hipotecario-espana/

Elsinga, M., & Hoekstra, J. (2005). Homeownership and housing satisfaction. *Journal of Housing and the Built Environment*, 20(4), 401–424.

Eurostat (2018). Individuals using the internet for internet banking. http://data.europa.eu/euodp/data/dataset/ag89sJmlMNa2Bsmr8oV2AA.

Høst, V., & Knie-Andersen, M. (2004). Modeling customer satisfaction in mortgage credit companies. *International Journal of Bank Marketing*, 22(1), 26–42.

Hullgren, M., & Söderberg, I. (2013). The relationship between consumer characteristics and mortgage preferences. *International Journal of Housing Markets and Analysis*, 6(2), 209–230.

Keramati, A., Ghaneei, H., & Mirmohammadi, S. M. (2016). Developing a prediction model for customer churn from electronic banking services using data mining. *Financial Innovation*, 2(1), 10.

Kil, K., & Miklaszewska, E. (2017). The competitive threats and strategic challenges to Polish cooperative banks: A post crisis perspective. In Miklaszewska, E. (ed.), *Institutional Diversity in Banking: Small Country, Small Bank Perspectives* (pp. 121–146). Cham, Switzerland: Palgrave Macmillan.

Kozinets, R.V. (2002). The field behind the screen: Using netnography for marketing research in online communities. *Journal of Marketing Research*, 39(2), 61–72.

Kozinets, R.V. (2006). Click to connect: Netnography and tribal advertising. *Journal of Advertising Research*, 46(3), 279–288.

Kozinets, R.V. (2020). *Netnography: The Essential Guide to Qualitative Social Media Research*. SAGE: London.

Laboral Kutxa (2014). Online banks' values most appreciated among users in Spain in 2014. https://prensa.laboralkutxa.com/estudio-de-laboral-kutxa-mayor-autogestion-rapidez-y-seguridad-las-demandas-de-los-usuarios-de-banca-online/

Lee, J., & Hogarth, J. M. (2000). Consumer information search for home mortgages: Who, what, how much, and what else?. *Financial Services Review*, 9(3), 277–293.

Lymperopoulos, C., Chaniotakis, I. E., & Soureli, M. (2006). The importance of service quality in bank selection for mortgage loans. *Managing Service Quality: An International Journal*, 16(4), 365–379.

Martínez Pagés, J. (2017). El margen de intereses de las entidades de depósito españolas y los bajos tipos de interés. *Boletín económico-Banco de España*, 3(11), 1–8.

Medberg, G., & Heinonen, K. (2014). Invisible value formation: A netnography in retail banking. *International Journal of Bank Marketing*, 32(6), 590–607.

Melancon, J. P., & Dalakas, V. (2016). Managing social consumer voice: A structured abstract. Developments in Marketing Science. Proceedings of the Academy of Marketing Science, 563–568.

Moreno, G. (2017). ¿Qué sectores reciben más reclamaciones en España?. https://es.statista.com/grafico/10319/que-sectores-reciben-mas-reclamaciones-en-espana/

Murgueytio Murgueitio, T., & Castillo Lascano, H. (2016). Estrategias de marketing para incrementar la participación de mercados del segmento hipotecario en el banco del pacífico en Guayaquil, año 2016. *Revista Observatorio de la Economía Latinoamericana*, www.eumed.net/cursecon/ecolat/ec/2016/creditos.html

Mylonakis, J. (2007). A bank customer analysis and mortgage services evaluation: Implications of market segmentation policies. *Banks and Bank Systems, 2*(3), 157–172.

Observatorio Cetelem (2018). Razones por las que los consumidores confían más en una tienda según una encuesta en España de 2018. https://es.statista.com/estadisticas/533124/motivos-por-los-que-los-consumidores-espanoles-confian-mas-en-una-tienda/

Oluwunmi, A. O., Ajayi, C. A., Olaleye, A., & Fagbenle, O. I. (2011). An analysis of clients satisfaction with mortgage valuation reports in Nigeria. *International Journal of Marketing Studies, 3*(2), 160–168.

Paunonen, L., Lehtinen, O., & Aro, H. (2012). Special rReport – the future of banking services from the consumer perspective. In Aspara, J., Rajala, R. and Tuunainen, V. (eds.), *The Future of Banking Services* (pp. 3–13). Helsinki: Unigrafia Oy.

Pérez-Ruiz, A., & Rodríguez del Bosque, I. (2012). La imagen de Responsabilidad Social Corporativa en un contexto de crisis económica: El caso del sector financiero en España. *Universia Business Review*, 14–29.

Reid, E., & Duffy, K. (2018). A netnographic sensibility: Developing the netnographic/social listening boundaries. *Journal of Marketing Management, 34*(3–4), 263–286.

Roos, I., Gustafsson, A., & Edvardsson, B. (2006). Defining relationship quality for customer-driven business development. *International Journal of Service Industry Management, 17*(2), 207–223.

Talaga, J. A., & Buch, J. (1998). Consumer trade-offs among mortgage instrument variables. *International Journal of Bank Marketing, 16*(6), 264–270.

Tang, C., Mehl, M. R., Eastlick, M. A., He, W., & Card, N. A. (2016). A longitudinal exploration of the relations between electronic word-of-mouth indicators and firms' profitability: Findings from the banking industry. *International Journal of Information Management, 36*(6), 1124–1132.

12

The Best of Both Worlds

Methodological Insights on Combining Human and AI Labor in Netnography

Anna Marchuk, Stefan Biel, Volker Bilgram, and Signe Worning Løgstrup Jensen

INTRODUCTION

The Time for Working with Machines Is Now

In today's challenging and ever-changing business environment, where competition has rapidly intensified with shifts in technology and the increasing globalization of markets (Deeds et al., 2000), and pandemics alter economies around the world, innovation has become an essential facet of organizational survival (Kim et al., 2012). Innovation has significant importance for all companies today, because it has proven almost impossible to restart organizational growth once it has stalled (Christensen & Raynor, 2013).

The competitiveness and prosperity of companies is therefore highly dependent on their ability to continuously innovate and upgrade their offerings (Farrell, 2003). As a result of this simple fact, the life cycles of products have shortened. In turn, corporate executives have increased their expenditures on research and development. To avoid escalating costs, companies must become both effective and efficient in their innovation efforts if a competitive advantage is to be obtained by continuously innovating (Mocker & Ross, 2017).

To ensure that actual value is created by new products, innovators must have an acute awareness of customer preferences (Von Hippel et al., 2011). With the rapid growth of the internet, customers nowadays often express as well as discover preferences through product-related word-of-mouth conversations, which have migrated to electronic markets, creating active social media interactions that contain a wealth of information for researchers and marketers to use (Ghose & Ipeirotis, 2011; Kozinets, 1999). A rigorous research understanding of these consumer needs can serve as important inputs for the fuzzy front-end of innovation. Accurate and novel insights can ensure that companies' innovation efforts are effective and successful in the marketplace. One useful method for obtaining customer insights from social media data is netnography. However, a drawback of netnography is that it is manually intensive, and also that it may only analyze a relatively small proportion of the consumer-generated content currently available regarding any given topic.

To reach the next level of insights in terms of speed, depth, and precision, we believe that the time has come for netnographers to increasingly collaborate with artificial intelligence programs. For netnographic researchers, increased data volume means new challenges for collecting, understanding, and combining the data meaningfully. As netnographers, perhaps we now need to start making the first steps towards joining forces with machines.

From multiple *perspectives, time and value* are the core reasons why it may be increasingly necessary for netnographers to use machine learning technologies. On the one hand, decision makers expect research to be completed faster than ever. Agile approaches require feedback streams to be more instantaneous in order to fit into the lean development cycles of today's innovation projects. On the other hand, from a researcher-centric perspective, automating some elements of the process of netnography has potential to reduce the time spent collecting and analyzing data, while simultaneously improving the range of the covered data sources and relevant topics. Moreover, following what Kozinets (2010, 1) called a "computationally assisted netnographic approach" might open up new possibilities for pattern identification in data and eventually yield stronger insights from the massive flows of data (Bilgram et al., 2017). Thus equipped with new machine-driven tools, netnographic researchers might comprehend more information faster, and be empowered to invest time into the more creative parts of the research process. Consequently, these netnographies would deliver even more meaningful and actionable insights.

In the past few years, development of machine-driven research methods became not only necessary, but also feasible due to three main reasons: quality of algorithms, exponentially increasing data volumes, and the availability of personal computers with sufficient power. First, in the past ten years machine learning algorithms have improved to the extent that they now are able to solve some real-life problems. Second, exponentially growing amounts of data provide an invaluable source for training, testing, applying, and refining these algorithms. Finally, the barrier of specialized hardware, which was previously needed in order to run machine learning software programs, has vanished. Personal computers became more powerful and algorithms more efficient, resulting in low entry barriers to the use of machine learning. Today, practically any netnographer who has some basic knowledge of programming and market research can experiment with machine learning methods for uncovering customer-based netnographic insights.

One Challenge: Two Competing Approaches

In the following section, we share some of the things we learned from a project that allowed us to directly compare a more human-driven and a more machine-driven approach to netnography. We used these two approaches to netnography in order to identify new opportunities for Beiersdorf to innovate in the competitive and rapidly changing market of body care products. We followed HYVE's modified passive observational approach to netnography and did not utilize its interactive or interview components (see Chapter 10 of this volume for a fuller description). As a process, HYVE has found netnography to be especially powerful in the first phases of the innovation process for uncovering tacit consumer needs, unmet wishes, and for revealing customer behaviors, beliefs, and attitudes. In the past, netnography at HYVE had developed a reputation for uncovering unconventional opportunities and guiding the development of innovative products in contexts similar to those faced by the body care market. For example, it was the starting point and main inspiration for bringing to the market one of the most successful innovations in the deodorant category – Nivea Invisible for Black & White (Lakhani et al., 2014).

Trying a machine learning approach for the same challenge was a perfect occasion in this case because of the vast amounts of new data and the quickly changing consumer needs and attitudes in the industry. We decided to run both HYVE-adapted netnographic methods in parallel: human-driven and machine-driven. First, we wanted to ensure the highest possible quality insights at the end of the project. Second, we wanted to run an experiment that could reveal the relative strengths and limitations of each of approach to HYVE's version of netnography.

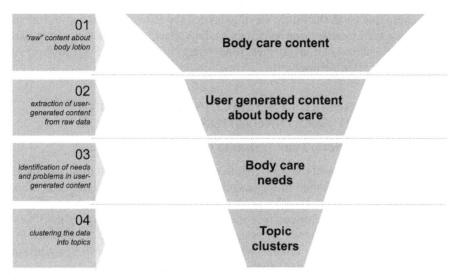

Figure 12.1 Visualization of the Research Process.

To make this "competition" between the methods comparable, and the experiment more valid, we followed similar steps in setting up the human-driven and machine-driven netnographic research approaches (Figure 12.1). Machines are highly capable of performing specific, well-defined tasks, but they lack what scientists refer to as "general AI," i.e., a human-like intelligence that can adaptively perform a range of different intellectual tasks. We wanted to investigate in which phases of the netnographic research process machines or human beings might be superior. Moreover, we wanted to design a hybrid research approach for combining the best of both worlds. As a result, we broke down the research process into four steps:

1. Raw content: collection of raw data online, according to pre-defined set of keywords for the category of body care
2. Consumer generated content: extraction of consumer-generated content from raw data
3. Needs and problems: identification of needs and problems in consumer-generated content
4. Topic clusters: clustering the data into topics.

The final phase of the classic netnography method has been planned only for human researchers – insights generation requires empathy and in-depth understanding of the context, which is not (yet) feasible for machines.

In the sections that follow, we will describe each of these four steps of the netnographic research process, providing details on the approach, challenges, and performance of each of the competing methods. The results from the project, and of our experiment, had multi-dimensional impact upon a variety of different constituents. First, and most importantly, the project identified insights that helped address the marketplace challenges of Beiersdorf. Therefore, the main purpose of the project was accomplished. Second, the project was able to provide lessons about the advantages and limitations of each of the approaches to netnography. We understood what is feasible, and what is reasonable to use in the research practice already today, and developed our view on how to create the highest value by combining aspects of both approaches. Finally, we made a step forward towards foreseeing the future of netnography and envisioning the next steps towards fruitful human–machine collaboration qualitative social media research.

We do believe that far in the future we might reach the state of "autonomous innovation." For now, we are glad to share our learnings on how machines can excel in big data processing, and how humans can invest their time, energy, empathy, and creativity in shaping meaningful insights from netnography.

THE CASE STUDY: HUMANS AND MACHINES UNCOVERING INSIGHTS FOR BODY CARE INNOVATION

The "Rules of Competition": Four Sprints to Go From Start to Finish

Our research mission followed the steps that iteratively led from initial topic specification to insight generation. As mentioned in the introduction, we adjusted and defined each step of the HYVE version of the netnography process to make it suitable and comparable in pursuing human-driven and machine-driven methods. The first and the last phases were possible only for human researcher to do: currently, machines still require humans to input keywords, and only humans can finalize the insights generation process – bringing empathy and creativity for meaningful and in-depth results, shaped as a story.

For our "race" of the methods, we assumed that the human netnography researcher and the machine netnographer run four sprints between the start – keywords, and the finish line – consumer insights. We describe how human and machine netnographers approach each sprint, what comes out as a result, and who "wins" at each sprint. The steps of the process, approach, outcomes, and evaluation are presented in Table 12.1.

To choose the winner and evaluate the performance of human and machine on each sprint, we analyzed the accuracy and comprehensiveness of the achieved result. By looking at the accuracy, we evaluated relevant the data was for the research briefing, and how valuable it was for the definition and development of consumer insights. By comprehensiveness, we mean overall coverage of the topic – the completeness of information that was gathered.

Clearly, with the current state of technology, machines still require human input of data and coordination of each step. However, for the purpose of our experiment, we focused on analyzing the outcomes, assuming that the human researcher did the best possible analysis, and that the machine had the best possible algorithm as an input. Below are the details of each sprint and our thoughts on choosing the winner.

Starting Point: Keywords

After the initial briefing, the netnography started with the researcher attempting to understand the topic and define a set of keywords for searching the content. In his latest book, Kozinets (2020, 216–219) terms this procedure "simplifying." The simplifying procedure is especially important when using a machine-driven approach for the following reason: although human researchers have enormous flexibility to iterate and define different keywords more precisely to achieve desired results, the keywords for the machine must to be fixed at the beginning of the process. For a machine or AI-based netnographer, generating a complete list of keywords will most likely never be possible. However, the objective should be to generate a list for the AI that extensively covers the entire topic.

Thus, the main challenge in this first step was to define keywords that accurately describe the topic of body care. Since all following steps depended on the validity of this first step, incorrect definition of the topic and keywords could fatally flaw the eventual outcome. The process for the machine-based method is therefore a lot more rigid than the human-centered approach, where it is possible to include aspects of the topic later on if research considers it necessary.

Table 12.1 Steps and Outcomes of the Human-Driven Machine-Driven Netnography Research Process

Step of the process	Human-driven approach	Machine-driven approach	Evaluation
Starting point: Keywords	**Approach:** identify of relevant keywords around topic of body care for searching content online. **Outcome:** keywords.	**Approach:** set up web-crawling algorithm. **Outcome:** ready to use algorithm.	**The winner: Human** The selection of relevant keywords can be only identified by humans.
Sprint 1: Finding relevant content	**Approach:** search engine, reading **Outcome:** list of sources of information, prioritized for further research.	**Approach:** web-crawling **Outcome:** around 1,750,168 posts texts with relevant expressions.	**The winner: Machine** Machine can review massive amounts of data and extract relevant content very fast – winning by comprehensiveness and time to produce the outcome.
Sprint 2: Identifying consumer-generated content	**Approach:** recognizing consumer-generated content; reading and manual data collection in qualitative analysis software (MAXQDA) **Outcome:** around 8,000 consumer-generated posts read; 1,100 collected in MAXQDA.	**Approach:** Support Vector Machine (SVM). Identifying consumer-generated content, according to set of defined parameters. **Outcome:** data set with 140,000 consumer-generated posts.	**The winner: Machine** Given high-quality algorithm, machine wins by comprehensiveness and speed, without compromising accuracy.
Sprint 3: Need or problem?	**Approach:** reading, data coding with qualitative analysis software (MAXQDA) **Outcome:** 1,100 coded statements.	**Approach:** Deep Convolutional Neural Network combined with a layer of Long-Short Term Memory (CNN and LSTM) **Outcome:** lists of about 53,000 consumer need statements. *Note: it was important to switch from posts to sentences due to the difficulty of classifying posts as consumer needs in comparison to classifying sentences.*	**The winner:** equal power of Human and Machine. To reach acceptable level of performance of the machine, humans still need to invest a lot of time in programming and training.

(continued)

Table 12.1 (Cont.)

Step of the process	Human-driven approach	Machine-driven approach	Evaluation
Sprint 4: Topic clusters	**Approach:** Analytical sessions to structure the data and derive insights. **Outcome:** analytical frameworks leading to insights identification.	**Approach:** Correlated Topic Modeling (CTM) – unsupervised machine learning **Outcome:** 71 identified topics, with 48 considered useful for the analysis by a human researcher.	**The winner:** equal power of Human and Machine. Machine wins on clustering topics neutrally and comprehensively. However, only humans can make the final decision regarding relevance.
The finish: Insights	**Approach:** creative empathic process of data analysis and insights generation. **Outcome:** eight in-depth customer insights.	Technology for empathic insights generation is not available at the moment.	**The winner: Human** Creativity, empathy, and storytelling are unique talents that make it possible for only human researchers to identify in-depth meaningful insights.

Sources: Marchuk et al., 2018. © Copyright 2018 by ESOMAR ® – The World Association of Research Professionals. This paper first appeared in ESOMAR Fusion 2018 Collection of Papers published by ESOMAR (www.esomar.org).

For retrieving data, domain experts from Beiersdorf produced a list of relevant keywords within the boundaries of the body care domain. Keywords were defined in English for consistent semantic analyses purposes. The keyword list was confirmed through a perfunctory exploratory search within social media groups to compare consumers' choice of words in an online context with that of experts. Words used by online consumers to refer to similar products were added to the keyword list. For example, some of the defined keywords are shown in Table 12.2.

Sprint 1: Relevant Content

The goal of the first sprint was to look for content on the topic of body care, using defined keywords. In addition to domain-specific keywords, sets of terms known to indicate consumer-generated content (such as I, me, mine, or my) were added, because consumers are typically communicating content using a first-person writing style.

Human netnographers approached the first sprint combining keywords in Google queries to collect diverse sources of information. The mechanical netnographer performed automated web crawling and extracted any content that matched predefined keywords and criteria. As an outcome of the first step, the human netnographer collected a list of evaluated sources of information. The machine netnographer retrieved a large data set. In the case of body care, web crawling resulted in extracting 1,750,168 texts with relevant expressions.

Table 12.2 Keywords to Define the Topic of Body Care

Keywords			
Body oil	Body care oil	Body soufflé	Body mist
Body lotion	Body care lotion	Body foam	Body water
Body milk	Body care milk	Body moisturizer	Body spray
Body butter	Body care cream	Body serum	Body splash
Body balm	Hydrating oil	In-shower oil	Body cleansing milk
Body mousse	Hydrating lotion	In-shower lotion	Body cleansing lotion
Body sorbet	Hydrating milk	In-shower milk	Shower milk
Body jelly	Hydrating cream	In-shower cream	Cleansing wipe

Sources: Marchuk et al., 2018. © Copyright 2018 by ESOMAR ® – The World Association of Research Professionals. This paper first appeared in ESOMAR Fusion 2018 Collection of Papers published by ESOMAR (www.esomar.org).

For the web-crawling algorithm, keyword combinations were sufficient to retrieve a data set of texts within the domain of body care. However, the collected texts from various web-pages contained content generated by consumers as well as content published by editors. In order to extract only the consumer-generated content, an additional clean-up step was necessary for the mechanical netnographer.

Sprint 2: Consumer-Generated Content About Body Care

Recognizing consumer-generated content is a relatively easy task for a trained human netnographer who has built up their own heuristics over time and with experience. While looking through web-pages and reading texts, researchers immediately excluded editorial content, and focused only on posts and comments from consumers. Thus, accomplishment of the second sprint was just a matter of investing the time for a trained human netnographer to read and gather relevant consumer comments. The human netnographers then used the qualitative analysis software package MAXQDA to collect the most interesting and mean-ingful consumer comments for further analysis.

The mechanical netnographer needed an additional framework to be able to narrow down the data and exclude editorial content and obvious advertisements. We then applied a Support Vector Machine (SVM) protocol for the recognition of user-generated consumer content in the data set of 1,750,168 texts. We chose SVM for its good performance in text classification tasks (Amancio et al., 2014). Training the SVM required us to customer develop a small, manually labelled data set, because the machine-learning algorithm had previously been trained for the task of classifying consumer-generated content. Three hundred and sixty texts were separated from the data-collection and used as a domain-specific training data. In Table 12.3, one of the 152 texts labelled as consumer-generated and one of 208 texts labelled as non-consumer-generated are provided as examples of the machine-learning training set we used to train the algorithmic model how to correctly classify the remaining texts.

The performance of the SVM was evaluated regarding accuracy, recall, and precision to ensure the usefulness of machine learning for the text classification task.

Classification accuracy was measured as the total proportion of correctly classified texts.

$$accuracy = (True\ Positives + True\ Negatives) / (True\ Positives + True\ Negatives + False\ Positives + False\ Negatives)$$

Table 12.3 Examples of Texts Within the Training-Set Labelled as Consumer-Generated and Non-Consumer-Generated

Consumer-generated content	*Non-consumer-generated content*
When I received the sample in the mail, it was very liquid from the heat. It was smooth and has a quite weird nutty vanilla scent – not my fave frankly. Once it cooled down for subsequent uses, it had kind of a weird texture – like it had grit in it. It went on smooth, but it was kinda weird. Honestly, I like my Trader Joe's body butter better and will stick to that.	Bali Body is 100% natural, made with love. Bali Body can be used for all ages to nourish & hydrate. Our body oil has many healing properties & packed with antioxidants; it's perfect for healing cuts and scars.

Sources: Marchuk et al., 2018. © Copyright 2018 by ESOMAR ® – The World Association of Research Professionals. This paper first appeared in ESOMAR Fusion 2018 Collection of Papers published by ESOMAR (www.esomar.org).

Recall measured the true positive rate to be more precise the proportion of needs which the algorithmic model correctly detected.

recall = True Positives / (True Positives+False Negatives)

Precision, on the other hand, measured the positive predictive value, which is the proportion of texts classified as containing a customer need that in fact does contain a need.

precision = True Positives / (True Positives+False Positives)

The preferred assessment measure differs depending on the objective and further use of the results. If needs are scarcer, overlooking an articulated need is to be avoided, even if it results in evaluating more texts falsely classified as a need. In this case, a high measure of recall would be preferred (Buckland & Gey, 1999). If time is a constraint, spending the least amount of effort further evaluating the classified texts might be more valuable. High precision would be preferred in this case, even at the expense of not identifying all potential needs retrieved from the consumer-generated data (Buckland & Gey, 1999).

For the mechanical netnographer, the accuracy was 87% with a recall of 85% and precision of 89% when classifying consumer-generated content and a recall of 89% and precision of 85% for non-consumer-generated content. Using conventional standards, we considered these results to be acceptable for the classification task (Egger & Lang, 2013).

Ensuring that the mechanically collected consumer-generated texts actually related to the topic of body care, the same machine-learning technique was used to differentiate between relevant and irrelevant texts. Table 12.4 provides three examples of irrelevant consumer-generated texts all retrieved based on the identified keywords in Table 12.2.

A training set of 279 texts was created, labelling texts as either on-topic or off-topic. The training set was then used to train the SVM. The performance of the on-topic or off-topic classifier was evaluated similarly to the consumer-generated classifier. Equally, good accuracy levels were obtained with recall and precision levels for on-topic texts both being 87% and for off-topic texts 86%. Excluding texts based on the machine learning's classification of on-topic and off-topic texts is thus acceptable.

Table 12.4 Examples of Irrelevant Consumer-Generated Texts from the Retrieved Data Set

Hair care	Make-up	Gender and nationality
Kukui oil antifrizz **hydrating oil** is rated 4.625 out of 5 by 16. Rated 5 out of 5 by CoilyTang from Frizz Free I bought this product about 2 months ago just trying it out. I was blown away by the results! My hair is natural, and I have about 3 different (curly) textures in my hair, and every texture loves this oil! My hairstyles have never looked better! If you have curly, kinky or coily it should be in your regime.	The Flash Illuminator is another illuminating product (no) and claims to be "your best light in a bottle." The Estee Edit says it's a high-impact highlighting cream that instantly illuminates skin and provides hyaluronic acid and other skincare ingredients. There are five shades ranging from Spotlight (the one I have here) to Night Light, a darker golden-brown shade. Again, I like to mix this in with my foundation if I haven't already added the Beam Team **hydrating lotion**. I'll also use this as a highlighting cream on my cheekbones (what little of them I have) and down the bridge of my nose.	Talks about gender equality – thinks that men rape because of "gender inequality" in the dating scene. Women wax, do their eyebrows, apply **body lotion**, do their hair, apple make-up, wear cute clothes, etc. … American males are slobs who can't even trim their gross hairy armpits. Women who approach are seen as "easy," "sluts," "thristy" [sic] and will many times face aggression from a dude who thinks she is too much into him.

Sources: Marchuk et al., 2018. © Copyright 2018 by ESOMAR ® – The World Association of Research Professionals. This paper first appeared in ESOMAR Fusion 2018 Collection of Papers published by ESOMAR (www.esomar.org)

Another 1,613,377 texts were excluded from the retrieved data set. The cleaned text corpus thus only consists of 136,791 individual consumer-generated texts deemed relevant for the body care domain, equaling 1,150,535 relevant sentences.

Comparing the performance of the human-driven and machine-driven approaches to netnography, we decided to give the winning title of the sprint 2 to the machine netnographer. Even though human netnographers can easily and accurately identify relevant, meaningful, and valuable consumer generated content for the qualitative analysis, the volume of the retrieved data and the speed of data collection and classification (given the right algorithm) is incomparably higher when done by a machine.

We believe that in this step of initial data collection and classification, having the possibility to process maximum amounts of data adds significant value to the research. Being able to comprehend millions of statements and select thousands of those that are relevant to the topic, minimizes the risk of overseeing important needs. It also gives confidence that the final insights will be identified, and decisions will be made based on the most complete knowledge.

Sprint 3: Need or Problem?

The next challenge in the process was to code the data and identify whether selected statements contained needs or problems. Trained human netnographers approached the sprint with qualitative data coding using MAXQDA software. The mechanical netnographer needed a new algorithm – in this case we used deep convolutional neural network combined with a layer of long-short term memory (Hochreiter & Schmidhuber, 1997).

The human netnographers reviewed around 8,000 consumer quotes and selected 1,100 that contained needs for the analysis and consumer insight generation stage. These 1,100 consumer quotes were manually coded in MAXQDA, which served as an input for the next steps of information clustering and insights generation.

Training the Machine

To equip the mechanical netnographer with the right algorithm, we had to program and train a deep neural network with manually labelled data categorizing what does and does not constitute a consumer need. We used three codes (product likes, dislikes, and ideas/suggestions) besides the default code of "not a consumer need." There are different methods and levels of detail of data coding that can be used for machine training. Our chosen approach was perceived to have the best trade-offs in terms of time, ease, required data and required post-processing. In our project, 5,000 posts were classified to ensure enough training data for desired quality of the outcome.

In Table 12.5, examples of three need expressions are provided along with the need context and identified need sentences.

Reviewing the 5,000 post training data allowed the mechanical netnographer to identify 3,303 posts that contained one or more consumer needs. Then a deep neural network model was developed to classify 1,128,619 consumer-generated sentences as either containing or not containing consumer needs. For this task, a convolutional neural network (CNN) model and a long short-term memory (LSTM) model were combined to benefit from the advantages of each model. CNN can learn from spatial data but lacks the ability to learn sequential correlations, whereas LSTM can capture long-term dependencies and thus specializes in sequential modelling. However, the LSTM is unable to extract features in parallel (Zhou et al., 2015).

Outcome of the Machine Netnographer's Derivation of Consumer Needs

The deep neural network was indeed able to derive consumer needs from consumer-generated content. The produced outcome of the CNN-LSTM model was a list of sentences with a probability of the statement being a customer need, as presented in Table 12.6.

Assessment of the Performance

To assess the performance of the neural network, the validation set separated from the labelled data was applied in accordance with the four measures: recall, precision, the balance between these measured by the F1-measure, and the classification accuracy.

In the validation set, there were 1,504 need sentences and 3,978 sentences without a need. The performance was thus measured by validating the neural network's classification of the same 5,482 sentences and then comparing the classification with the manually assigned labels. The imbalance in the validation set reduces the usefulness of the accuracy measure, as a dummy classifier, which predicts all sentences as not containing a need, reaches an accuracy level of about 73%. Instead, the network's performance is evaluated based on the recall, precision, and F1-measure.

The neural network outputs a value between 0.0 and 1.0. Varying the threshold for accepting a sentence as a need will thus produce different values for recall and precision. If

Table 12.5 Examples of Consumer Need Expressions from the Labeled Training Data

Need expression examples	Need context	Need sentences
Product approval	It's quick to absorb, without being too greasy. My skin feels well-nourished and hydrated after applying. It does not irritate my sensitive skin. It is very affordable, although I would pay twice the price for the quality of this lotion. This product surpassed my expectations and continues to hydrate without disappointment. This product is easy to apply, effective, and affordable.	It's quick to absorb, without being too greasy.
	Scent – Nice clean scent!	
	Absorption – Quickly absorbs and does not leave a greasy residue.	
	Effectiveness – Very effective and a quality product!	
		My skin feels well-nourished and hydrated after applying. It does not irritate my sensitive skin.
Product disapproval	The smell of the Nivea in-shower body lotion was quite strong and I did not enjoy it either!	The smell of the Nivea in-shower body lotion was quite strong and I did not enjoy it
	But the slipperiness was evident the moment I started applying it.	
	It did not even rinse off.	
	The waxiness stayed on!	
	I then dried my body with my towel and even then my skin felt weirdly sticky and slick (not in a good way).	
		I then dried my body with my towel and even then my skin felt weirdly sticky and slick (not in a good way).
Consumer advice	I was probably about 14 when I first started using moisturizer, and I haven't skipped a day since.	I always use a different daytime and nighttime
	I always use a different daytime and nighttime moisturizer.	

Sources: Marchuk et al., 2018. © Copyright 2018 by ESOMAR ® – The World Association of Research Professionals. This paper first appeared in ESOMAR Fusion 2018 Collection of Papers published by ESOMAR (www.esomar.org).

Table 12.6 Examples from the List of Customer Needs

Sentence	Probability
I did feel a tiny layer of residue once it was fully absorbed into my skin, but it wasn't sticky or greasy	98.36%
With only after a few weeks of using it, I noticed that my body skin became lighter and more even that it was when I was not using this product.	98.12%

Sources: Marchuk et al., 2018. © Copyright 2018 by ESOMAR ® – The World Association of Research Professionals. This paper first appeared in ESOMAR Fusion 2018 Collection of Papers published by ESOMAR (www.esomar.org).

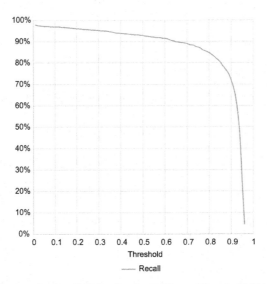

Figure 12.2 The Plot Depicts the Recall Value for the Different Threshold Values.

the network simply were to classify all sentences as customer needs, e.g., setting the threshold at 0, the precision would be 27% and the recall would 100% as all needs in the data are identified and classified as such. Figure 12.2 depicts the recall and Figure 12.3 shows the precision values for varying thresholds. As the two graphs indicate, there is a trade-off between the two measures.

Applying a threshold of 0.5 considers every sentence whose value is above 0.5 as a consumer need and every value below that as a sentence that does not contain a consumer need. With this, it obtained a precision of 41% and a recall of 93%. Basically, setting the threshold at 0.5 allows for almost all of the consumer needs to be correctly classified, while filtering out a portion of the sentences without a need. However, there are still more sentences without consumer needs than actual needs in the final set of results.

The precision-recall curve illustrated in Figure 12.4 depicts the trade-off between the two measures. Adjusting the threshold allows for tailoring precision and recall based on the research objective. A high recall value permits the identification of any articulated need, at the expense of evaluating more irrelevant sentences classified as "needs."

Less effort is required regarding further evaluation of sentences classified as consumer needs when a high precision value is prioritized, as irrelevant sentences are disregarded. However, the lower effort comes at the expense of overlooking needs and thus potentially not capturing all of the interesting information present in the data.

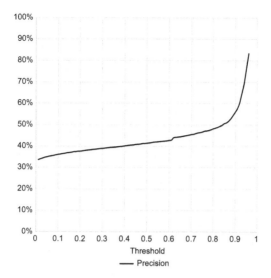

Figure 12.3 The Plot Depicts the Precision for the Different Threshold Values.

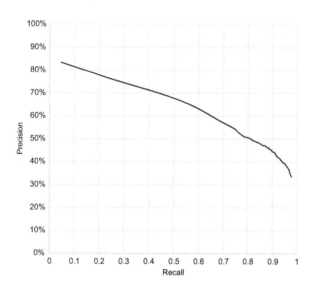

Figure 12.4 The Precision-Recall Curve Depicts the Trade-Off Between Measures.

The cost of overlooking a need and the cost of post-processing needs, in terms of manual labor and the value created by allocating resources for reading through falsely classified needs, are two of the primary factors influencing which performance value is most desirable. The amount of data also influences the choice. A high precision typically would be preferred with larger data sets, because the cost of post-processing increases significantly due to the sheer number of needs that the researcher would have to evaluate manually. Manually evaluating falsely classified needs is more feasible with smaller data sets, even when applying a high recall value.

The choice between recall and precision thus depends on the purpose of input in the innovation process. If the customer needs are to be used in the early stage of an innovation process as inputs for understanding the market, or if the input is used in a later stage for

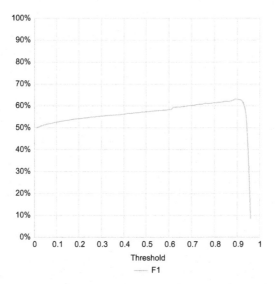

Figure 12.5 The Plot Depicts the F1 Measure for the Threshold Range.

testing assumptions about the market and specific products or services, the preference for recall or precision will change. At HYVE, because it is focused on innovation, the primary reason behind eliciting consumer needs to be to either identify one need leading to the creation of innovation or else to gain general insights that could enable innovation.

If no explicit preference between recall and precision is present, the F1 measure can be applied as it balances the trade-off between the two measures to maximize the true-positives while minimizing the false-positives.

F1=2*Recall*Precision / (Recall+Precision)

Figure 12.5 depicts the F1 value of the neural network for the various thresholds and as indicated the highest F1 value is 63%, obtained at 0.93 threshold. This resulted in a recall value of 75% while the precision value was 55% and the accuracy level was 76%. With the threshold of 0.93, about 432,560 sentences are classified as needs. The performance of the neural network is thus considered acceptable.

Choosing the Winner

Evaluating the results of the third sprint, and choosing the winner was not an easy task. At the moment, we see the power of the human and mechanical netnographers to be equal, with a high potential for mechanical to outperform the human in the next few years. In our particular case, training the machine netnographer to reach quality results has been a time-consuming process, and the human netnographer still outperformed in terms of providing a high-quality product. Moreover, the human netnographer was able to identify unique pieces of information – the "gems" of the content that sparked elaboration of the insights. This was something that the mechanical netnographic program could not do. At the same time, we believe that AI have higher value-creation potential because of their ability to process much more data and to repeatedly perform the analysis in longitudinal studies.

The differentiation between relevant and irrelevant information (need or no-need classification) in consumer-generated content is massively useful. This is the core moment that leads to the next stage of consumer insight generation and identification of innovation opportunities. To find information about consumer needs, human netnographic researchers at HYVE often spend months reading through online dialogue with the aim of getting closer to the "aha-moment" and finding sparks of inspiration. We believe that, if machines can assist in this process and help to embrace larger amounts of data, the chances of identifying precious tacit consumer needs for building innovations would increase dramatically.

Sprint 4: Topic Clusters

In the final sprint of the human versus machine "race," the challenge was to make progress in structuring the data in order to be able to generate insights. For a trained human netnographer, this phase typically transforms data into insights gradually, while for a machine it is the final step that can be achieved.

During a netnography project, a researcher uses various analytical frameworks to look at the coded qualitative data from different perspectives. For example, some of the common tools we use at HYVE are affinity diagramming, data clustering, customer journey mapping, and creating a touchpoint matrix. The netnographic researcher seeks to identify meaningful patterns, capture connections between causes and effects of certain behaviors, and as a result uncover insights. Thus, transition to the insights phase happens seamlessly as a result of thorough analytical work.

During machine-driven qualitative data analysis, topic clustering is another important specific procedural step that needs to be planned and correctly defined in order for it to produce meaningful results. The quality of the outcome of this phase determines how well the mechanical netnographer can make sense of the previously identified needs, and how much data interpretation it can do.

In our body care innovation challenge, we used an unsupervised machine learning approach to cluster customer needs into a series of topics through the use of correlated topic modelling (CTM), which is closely related to Latent Dirichlet Allocation (LDA). This approach does not require labelled data to train an algorithm.

For our challenge, 71 topics were identified by the correlated topic model. Afterwards, a human researcher was required in order to manually review them so as to provide meaningful descriptions. However, 18 topics identified by the AI algorithm were unidentifiable to the human researcher. An additional five topics were deemed to be insignificant for further analysis. Obscure topic formations are to be expected with any application of topic modelling, as semantic structures serve as the base for clustering the need sentences into topics. However, semantic similarities do not automatically translate into meaningful topics. The 48 topics that were accepted for the analysis are listed in Table 12.7.

The 48 topics were grouped further based on topic correlations in order to generate insights that are more enlightening for innovation purposes than the description of each individual topic. Semantic similarities between topics determined the correlation between each of the 48 topics. In Figure 12.6, the correlations are visualized by drawn connections and the closeness of the topic-dots.

Each of the 48 topics were thus grouped into one of 14 insights based on the correlation. The 14 insights (or topic clusters) were each given a title based on the primary information embedded within the collection of customer needs. Examples of four machine-driven "insights" (out of 14), and relevant topics, are presented in Table 12.8.

The results of the machine-driven analysis showed that the 14 clusters identified through the topic correlation indeed covered the domain of body care. However, the clusters combined the knowledge within each of the topics in an obvious way to the extent that it becomes almost basic. This finding demonstrates the dramatic difference between machine-produced

Table 12.7 Topic Titles of the 48 Relevant Topics Identified By the Mechanical Netnographer

Topic titles			
2. Body butters	10. Eczema	21. Diminishing appearance	36. Warm climates	46. Oily skin	58. Irritated skin
3. Application	14. Body milk	22. Reapplication	37. Sun protection	48. Layering of scents	60. Skin conditions
4. Sun exposure	15. Natural and organic	24. Self-life	39. Normal skin	49. Sensitive skin	62. Consistency
5 Mechanical exfoliants	16. Edible beauty	25. Residue	40. Healthy skin	50. Application method	63. Categories of scents
6. Baths and pampering	17. Dry skin	29. Chemical exfoliants	41. Scent's staying power	51. Skin's elasticity	64. Types of oils
7. Even skin-tone	18. Skincare routine	30. Natural oils	42. Self-tanners	54. Types of scents	66. Essential oils
8. Product sizes	19. Absorption	32. The Body Shop's body butters	44. Day vs. night routines	55. Stretch marks	68. Creamy texture
9. Types of body butters	20. DIY body butters	34. Aloe Vera	45. Organic Products	56. Packaging	69. Cold climates

Sources: Marchuk et al., 2018. © Copyright 2018 by ESOMAR* – The World Association of Research Professionals. This paper first appeared in ESOMAR Fusion 2018 Collection of Papers published by ESOMAR (www.esomar.org).

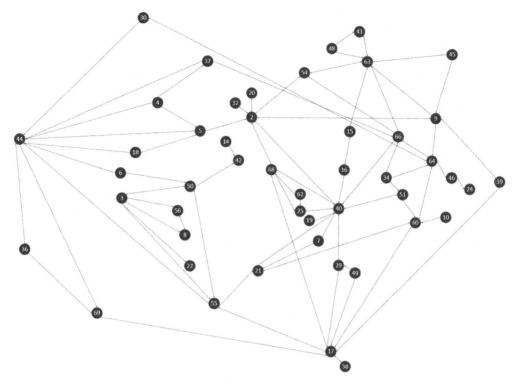

Figure 12.6 Visualization of Correlations Between the 48 Mechanically Generated Topics.

Table 12.8 Examples of the Topic Clusters

Skin type	Skin condition	Beauty ideals	Application
17. Dry Skin	60. Skin conditions	40. Healthy skin	3. Application
58. Irritated skin	51. Skin's elasticity	7. Even skin-tone	50. Application method
49. Sensitive skin	34. Aloe Vera	21. Diminishing appearance	22. Reapplication
39. Normal skin	10. Eczema	29. Chemical exfoliants	
		55. Stretch mark	

Source: © Copyright 2018 by ESOMAR® – The World Association of Research Professionals. This paper first appeared in ESOMAR Fusion 2018 Collection of Papers published by ESOMAR (www.esomar.org)

clusters and human-identified insights. On the one hand, AI clusters structure existing knowledge but do not show anything new, while insights uncover the unknown. On the other hand, machine-generated clusters structure information in an unbiased way, and can cover a much broader variety of topics.

Therefore, having topic clusters might be a helpful aid for a human netnographic researcher in insight generation, especially in domains that are new or not well researched. Moreover, it could be a good starting point for human researchers to generate insights from the data, as the way of structuring the information is not too far off from how the human researcher collected interesting data in MAXQDA.

The Finish: Insights

After four sprints competing with the machine, the human netnographer is the only one to actually cross the finish line and deliver insights that can fuel the innovation process. Human netnographers' talent and ability to "read between the lines," identify unique pieces of consumer generated content, infer tacit needs, apply ingenious insight generation skills, and share the insights as compelling narratives that boost the innovation process is still irreplaceable.

In the netnography project, a human researcher at HYVE created eight powerful insights from their investigation. Each of these insights told a story and opened up new perspectives on the topic of body care, connecting data together in a new and meaningful way. Even though the insights could be partially matched with the topics produced by the mechanical netnographer (Figure 12.7), the AI-generated clusters did not carry the strong message that the human-derived insights did.

Figure 12.7 illustrates that, if one was to restructure the information (topics) based on how a human would cluster consumer needs to generate insights, it would be possible to find a clear overlap in needs identified, the broadness of topics (when combined), and insights identified by humans. Interestingly, similar information on consumer needs, which forms the basis of the insight, is present in the machine-driven approach as well. Many more needs are identified within each topic and also a "new" topic (topic 6: "baths and pampering") appears from the machine-driven approach. However, what is missing is the "story." We believe that based on the needs and topics identified, it should be possible to generate similar consumer insights. Therefore, collaboration between approaches is possible. In the next concluding section, we summarize the key takeaways of our experiment comparing machine-based and human-based netnography and we offer our thoughts on the feasibility and appropriateness of blending machine and human labor in netnographic work. We then discuss economic, quality, and knowledge generation issues. Finally, we envision the possible future scenario of an increasing application of machine labor in netnographic research.

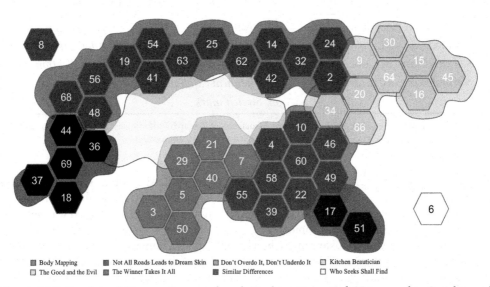

Figure 12.7 Overlap of Human-Generated and Machine-Generated Netnographic Insights and Topics.

CONCLUSIONS AND OUTLOOK INTO THE FUTURE OF COLLABORATION BETWEEN HUMAN AND MACHINE NETNOGRAPHERS

What Is Feasible

Our experiment taught us that, although the future might see humans substituted by machines, the capabilities of intelligent machines still do not exceed humans' competences in the netnographic research tasks of identifying rare content and consumer insights from online data. Intelligent machines, however, outperform humans on specific netnographic tasks: collecting massive amounts of data and identifying topics in the collected data sets – accurately and objectively. However, human research talent, creativity and empathy are essential for crafting netnographic insights that can inspire innovation.

To sum up the results of the netnographic human versus machine "competition" on a mission for identifying insights in body care from qualitative social media data:

- Machine-driven netnographic research is possible, and it outperforms humans in data collection, data clustering, and partially in data analysis (especially with big data samples).
- Human-driven netnographic research is more appropriate for identifying unique content, noticing weak or rare signals for uncommon needs, empathic data analysis, insights generation, and storytelling. Storytelling is key for insight implementation and delivery, as well as integration of research results into organizational innovation processes. Humans can do storytelling, but machines cannot (yet).
- It is beneficial to use machine learning in certain early phases of netnographic research – until the moment of insights generation and interpretation of topic clusters.

What Is Reasonable

Although applying machine learning in qualitative research is definitely feasible during its early stages, it is important to consider what makes sense from economic, quality and knowledge building perspectives. Below, we summarize our thoughts on each of these aspects.

Economic Perspective

- Machine training is time-consuming. Thus, for small or one-time netnographic projects, research done by humans is more reasonable from an economic perspective.
- Machine learning could be a timesaving mechanism in netnography, if there are several projects on similar topics or the same project done repeatedly (for example, yearly insights to see how needs, pain points, and behaviors evolve).
- Neural networks are usually trained with qualitative data from a specific domain and product category in a time-consuming process. In order to make the machine-driven approach scalable, the trained network would ideally be reapplied to new domains or categories (i.e., other products in a client's portfolio) leveraging the effort required to prepare data and train the algorithm for each new domain. We discovered that, once a machine is trained for the topics in a certain domain, the quality of its outcomes decreases slightly if it is used for similar domains, and dramatically drops if it is used for completely unrelated topics.

Quality Perspective

- Machines can provide a higher level of completeness and objectivity, because they can collect and cluster much larger sets of data without human researcher bias. This is especially valuable for research in domains that are not well explored to provide a "big picture" of relevant topics.
- The quality of human-made insights is still incomparably higher when it comes to providing an in-depth understanding of consumers, identifying novel insights, and joining the dots. Moreover, only human netnographers can recognize the rare but highly valuable content that is essential for capturing and interpreting the early signals required for innovation.
- Abstractly speaking, machines can "identify the dots" very well, but only humans can interpret the meaning of the connections between them.

Knowledge Building and Future Readiness

- Even though the application of machine learning in netnographic research is currently complex and needs a lot of human involvement, especially during the setup phase, activities in this field are highly valuable for competence building with an outlook to the future.

What Researchers Can Already Try This Year

After reflecting on the results of our experiment, the "race" between human and mechanical netnographers, we believe that the next few years are going to be not about competition, but about better collaboration between them. The best athlete can never run faster than a horse, but a clever horse-rider can lead the horse fast and in the right direction.

Although the future might see some humans substituted by machines, the capabilities of intelligent machines still do not exceed humans' competences in netnography. Netnography relies heavily on human researchers' talent to "read between the lines," identify unique content containing rare signals, infer and interpret tacit needs, apply ingenious insight generation skills, and share the insights as compelling narratives. With a lot of specialized training from humans, intelligent machines may outperform humans on specific rote tasks such as collecting massive amounts of data and automatically clustering data into topics.

We see an immense potential for people and organization to being to develop synergistic approaches for better human-machine collaboration in netnography. At HYVE, social media data is a design material. It has impact if we give it shape. We need to respect the strengths, and compensate for the weaknesses of each side in a netnographic research process where machines and humans perform at their best, and complement each other for delivering the most meaningful, objective, complete, and empathic customer insight stories that inspire innovations.

ACKNOWLEDGEMENT

This research was supported by Hamburg University of Technology.

REFERENCES

Amancio, D.R., Comin, C.H., Casanova, D., Travieso, G., Bruno, O.M., Rodrigues, F.A., & Costa, L. da F. (2014). A systematic comparison of supervised classifiers. *PLOS ONE*, 9, 1–14.

Bartl, M., Hück, S., & Ruppert, S. (2009). Netnography research. Community insights in the cosmetic industry. In *Conference Proceedings ESOMAR Consumer Insights* (pp. 1–12).

Bilgram, V., Gluth, O., & Piller, F. (2017). Crowdfunding data as a source of innovation. *Marketing Review St. Gallen*, 34, 10–18.

Buckland, M., & Gey, F. (1999). The relationship between recall and precision. *Journal of the American Society for Information Science*, 45, 12–19.

Christensen, C.M., & Raynor, M.E. (2013). *The innovator's solution: Creating and sustaining successful growth* (1st ed.). Boston, Massachusetts: Harvard Business Review Press.

Deeds, D.L., Decarolis, D., & Coombs, J. (2000). Dynamic capabilities and new product development in high technology ventures. *Journal of Business Venturing*, 15, 211–229.

Egger, M., & Lang, A. (2013). A brief tutorial on how to extract information from Consumer-Generated Content (UGC). *Künstliche Intelligenz*, 27, 53–60.

Farrell, D. (2003). The real new economy. *Harvard Business Review*, 81, 104–112.

Ghose, A., & Ipeirotis, P.G. (2011). Estimating the helpfulness and economic impact of product reviews: Mining text and reviewer characteristics. *IEEE Transaction on Knowledge and Data Engineering*, 23, 1498–1512.

Hochreiter, S., & Schmidhuber, J. (1997). Long short-term memory. *Neural Computations*, 9, 1735–1780.

Kim, C., Song, J., & Nerkar, A. (2012). Learning and innovation: Exploitation and exploration trade-offs. *Journal of Business Research*, 65, 1189–1194.

Kozinets, R. V. (1999). E-tribalized marketing? The strategic implications of virtual communities of consumption. *European Management Journal*, 17(3), 252–264.

Kozinets, R.V. (2006). Click to connect: Netnography and tribal advertising. *Journal of Advertising*, 46(3), 279–288.

Kozinets, R. V. (2010). Netnography: The marketer's secret weapon. *Netbase white paper*, Palo Alto, CA: Netbase, 1–13.

Kozinets, R. V. (2020). *Netnography 3E: The essential guide to qualitative social media research*. London: Sage.

Lakhani, K., Füller, J., Bilgram, V., & Friar, G. (2014). *Nivea. Harvard Business School Case*, 614–042. Cambridge (MA): Harvard Business Publishing.

Marchuk, A., Biel, S., Bilgram, V., & Løgstrup Jensen, S.W. (2018). Standing on the shoulders of giants. ESOMAR Conference, Fusion 2018: Big Data World + Global Qualitative (pp. 1–14). New York: Esomar

Mocker, M., & Ross, J.W. (2017). The problem with product proliferation. *Harvard Business Review*, 95, 104–110.

OECD (2015). *OECD innovation strategy 2015: An agenda for policy action*. Paris: OECD.

Von Hippel, E., Ogawa, S., & De Jong, J. (2011). The age of the consumer-innovator. *MIT Sloan School of Management Review*, 53, 27–35.

Zhou, C., Sun, C., Liu, Z., & Lau, F.C.M. (2015). A C-LSTM neural network for text classification. arXiv, 1–10.

13

Global Beautyscapes

An Innovation-Centered Netnography of Chinese Skin Care and Cosmetics Consumers

Rossella Gambetti, Robert V. Kozinets, Ulrike Gretzel,
Pierfranco Accardo, and Luisella Bovera

INTRODUCTION

This chapter draws from a netnography we conducted with a commercial client in order to explore Chinese cosmetics consumers' changing notions of female beauty and how such perceptions become translated into cosmetics tastes and routines. The purpose of the research was innovation. We were tasked with informing the new product development efforts of ArtCosmetics, a successful and innovative Italian B2B contract manufacturer operating in the global cosmetics market. The company wanted to develop a deep and culturally based understanding of new product and branding opportunities presented by Chinese cosmetics consumers.

Many of the chapters in this book are focused either on recounting the abstract principles of online research or on academic projects. The only other chapter dealing with the commercial application of netnography (Chapter 10 by Bartl and Casper) was unable to share many details due to their protection of client confidentiality. However, with ArtCosmetics' kind consent we are able to provide a thorough demonstration of the principles and power of netnography as it was applied to a modern business problem using data from global social media, mobile apps, and interviews using a team of skilled and specifically trained researchers. We use the project to discuss how this team of researchers planned, collected, interpreted, translated, and understood data from the different sources. We lay bare how netnography deciphers the central role of cultural codes of beauty in cosmetics tastes and routines. We begin with some history that we uncovered during our investigatory stages, when we sought to understand the cultural origins of the meanings behind Chinese women's sense of beauty.

CHINESE FEMALE BEAUTY

Chinese notions of female beauty began with the rigid traditions that governed China's patriarchal culture for millennia, rooted in Daoism and Confucianism. In Daoist tradition, a woman's good physical impression and sexual attractiveness were related to the sexual pleasure and longevity she gave to her man, determining her desirability and beauty (Cho, 2012). In these beliefs, a woman's outer beauty was a direct reflection of her inner beauty—and both were judged at once by men. Confucianism gave greater attention to the notion of inner beauty. According to this doctrine, every woman could manifest her beauty through her morality, her sweet and kind personality, her virtues of chastity, and her marital fidelity. With these traditions, Chinese patriarchal society imposed challenging canons of physical appearance and inner moral values that, together, defined a *"meiren"* (a beautiful woman) and her femininity, and also pointed to her proper role in society (Man, 2016). The traditional canons were quite specific, and demanding: the ideal facial features included a small, egg-shaped head as well as a heart-shaped face, characterized by broad forehead, high cheekbones, and pointed chin. Eyes should be round, large, have a double eyelid, called 双眼皮 (shuāng yǎn pí), and be surrounded by heavy, long eyelashes (Cho, 2012). Importantly, white, pale, and flawless skin was considered essential. Without flawless white skin, a Chinese woman could not be considered beautiful. The color and quality of her skin also played a large role in determining her social status according to Chinese tradition.

Over the years, especially since the First Opium War of 1939, the rigid traditions of patriarchal society gradually admitted Western influences. This led to the creation of a more Westernized Chinese culture against which various cultural movements have struggled, and whose syncretic identity is still being forged. Under the egalitarian Cultural Revolution of Chairman Mao Zedong, an androgynous Chinese female look became valorized. Notions of female beauty were derided as Western decadence. Communist progress demanded that female comrades dress and appear similar to their male counterparts, eschewing degenerate practices such as fashion, skin care, and cosmetics. However, Communism did not extinguish these notions of beauty or the practices that embodied them; it only drove them underground.

After Chairman Mao's passing in 1976, China began its open-door policy in 1978, followed by the economic reforms of the 1980s (Chin 1996). Chinese beauty culture began to open once again to Western influences. International female models of fashion and beauty from Paris, Milan, and New York taught new generations of post-Maoist women and girls new ways to think about their appearance. In addition, movies, television dramas, music videos, and advertising from foreign countries, including other Asian countries (Jung, 2018), contributed to a revitalization of Chinese aesthetic canons. Success, social recognition, and self-actualization became fundamental life goals as beautiful Chinese women began to sort out their place on the world's stage. The ostentation of luxury through cosmetics and fashion became a symbol of social status and power. Chinese ideals of femininity and beauty—as well as beautification—were opened and transformed. The consumption of cosmetics grew steadily (Man, 2016).

Although many physical traits remain, traditional fragile and moralistic images of female Chinese beauty have been largely replaced by images of independent and confident Chinese women. Among the contributing forces to this are social media platforms that cast beauty influencers and KOLs (Key Opinion Leaders) as the rising stars of an increasingly important Chinese beauty industry. These new social media celebrities have popularized novel attractive lifestyle values such as autonomy, freedom of self-expression, and the attainability of glamor and luxury. In addition to glamor, these influencers construct likeable, accessible, and seemingly authentic public personas. In doing so, they create intimate connections with their followers (Raun, 2018). In this way, KOLs spread a uniquely Chinese conception of contemporary female beauty that is remarkably fluid and diverse. They play an important role in guiding consumer habits and affecting the current Chinese cosmetics market, a topic to which our chapter's next section now turns.

CHINESE COSMETICS MARKET AND CONSUMPTION HABITS

China is the world's second-largest cosmetics consumer market (after the United States), and is expected to reach RMB 62.6 billion ($8.9 billion USD) by 2022 (PR Newswire, 2019).

Demographics have shifted towards a younger, more affluent segment with an increased appreciation for luxury (Statista, 2019) and consumers are more independent, gathering information through internet and social media channels (Daxue Consulting, 2020). Chinese women favor established cosmetics brands from American, French, Japanese, and South Korean companies, and these major producers are progressively challenged to adapt their products to the increasingly demanding Chinese consumer. Despite the dominance of established international brands, domestic brands' market share is gradually growing in China, offering new competitive challenges to foreign brands (Mordor Intelligence, 2020).

As the independence, power, and sophistication of female Chinese consumers grows, they are increasingly looking for brands that strongly resonate with their individual and social identities. Hence, Western innovations ignore Chinese culture and Chinese women's beauty codes at their own peril. In this scenario, how can Western companies maintain their competitive advantage and attract new Chinese consumers? How can these companies gain credibility and cultural fit with a market that seems so diverse, unknowable, and complex? As companies seek to expand into China—or appeal to Chinese women who reside in communities across the globe—they require a deep understanding of the intricacies of the Chinese consumer market. In the next section, we discuss the context, aims and design of our netnographic research project for ArtCosmetics. Then, we reveal the key methodological procedures that enabled us to generate meaningful revelations and insight generation for their innovation process.

NETNOGRAPHY OF BEAUTYSCAPES

ArtCosmetics is a world-class B2B contract manufacturer that specializes in color cosmetics. Creativity is at the heart of ArtCosmetics' competitive advantage, along with flexibility, skill, and speed to market. Ultimately, the depth of the cultural insights that underpin their understanding of a marketplace is what enables them to engage in successful innovation for their clients around the world.

In 2018, ArtCosmetics turned to Netnografica to help them explore Chinese consumers' notions of beauty and perceptions of cosmetics. Founded in 2007 as a boutique research firm, Netnografica is committed to applying Robert Kozinets' netnographic procedures to help solve for-profit and not-for-profit clients' practical problems. The goal has been to custom create projects that reflect the highest degree of social science rigor and precision with uncompromising attention to client satisfaction. The research team at Netnografica worked in close partnership with the executive team of ArtCosmetics. Together, they identified the need for the company's Milan-based executive and marketing team to develop a deep understanding of Chinese consumers' notions of beauty and how these get reflected in their conceptions, tastes, and desires for skin care and cosmetics products.

To do this, the project needed to understand contemporary Chinese female consumers living in China and in other locations around the world. It also needed to understand the influences of contemporary media that surrounded them, particularly those of skin care and cosmetics related social media. We designed a netnography that included data collection from social media and cosmetics-related mobile apps, depth interviews, and the use of immersion journals.

RESEARCH DESIGN

Sampling concerns are crucial to netnography. Our research was concerned with understanding both (1) a particular kind of consumer, the Chinese female skin care and cosmetics consumer, and (2) the media influences that reflected and also transformed

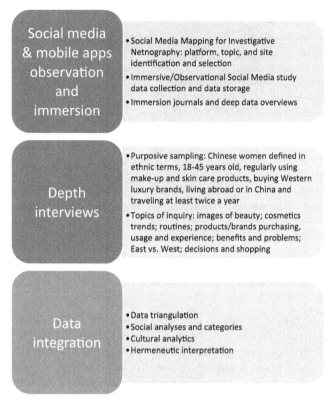

Figure 13.1 Research Design of the Netnography Study.

their cultural tastes and behaviors. Netnographic research design requires both an investigative (in our case, social media and mobile app observations) and an immersive component (immersion journals). These were complemented with an interactional element (depth interviews). Data collection was followed by data integration that combined analysis and interpretation. For details, please see Figure 13.1.

Social Media and Mobile Apps Observation and Immersion

The first two elements, investigation and immersion, involved our development and implementation of a transnational social media and mobile apps observational project, undertaken with an international team of 11 people. The aim of this phase was to reveal deep cultural insights about Chinese female beauty meanings, beauty culture, and cosmetics use. We achieved this through searching, scouting, selecting, and then saving data from a range of social media platforms and applications from China and the United States. It also involved following influencers and topical areas or specific conversations via hashtags. Beyond the focused searches and targeted immersion periods, research team members engaged in reading cosmetics-related news and in activities such as duty-free shopping, studying in-flight magazines and perusing e-commerce sites. The research was designed to reveal future market opportunities and the specific research questions evolved continuously through exchanges among the research team members and regular meetings with representatives from ArtCosmetics. Figure 13.2 provides an overview of the data collected and analyzed in this phase.

> **Netnographic data collection on social media**
>
> ◉ Social media analyzed:
> Instagram, YouTube and Weibo for Asian-American influencers
> - Influencers followed: 60
> - Posts analyzed: 575
> - Videos analyzed: 202
> - Websites visited: 677
> - Products considered: 340
>
> **Netnographic data collection in China/Chinese language**
>
> ◉ Platforms and applications analyzed: Weibo, WeChat and Little Red Book
> - 326 pages of focused data
> - 50 news articles
> - 10 academic articles

Figure 13.2 Type of Data Collected.

As Figure 13.2 reveals, observations and analyses focused primarily on Chinese language applications, in particular Weibo, WeChat, and Little Red Book, as these emerged as the most important platforms. In particular, Little Red Book (*Xiao Hong Shu* in Chinese language) is a mobile app that combines an e-commerce platform with features commonly seen on social networking sites such as reviews, ratings, discussion, and content creation and sharing. The study also used some English language sites such as Instagram and YouTube.

Because none of the Netnografica researchers are Chinese speakers, we relied on an international network of qualified female Chinese qualitative researchers specifically recruited and trained for the project. All team members collected data and kept immersion journals. After several training sessions, we began a process of weekly online debrief meetings in which they reported on findings. At each debrief with our Chinese researchers (who were debriefed individually), we would ask further questions and direct inquiries for the investigation of the week ahead. We constantly probed for insights into media, technology, algorithms, and practices—as well as our central focus: culture. These topics would be discussed in our bi-weekly meetings with our ArtCosmetics liaisons in order to guarantee applicable findings. Gradually, interfacing with ArtCosmetics and our Chinese teams and adding our expertise to the process, we began peeling back the layers on meanings, products, retail patterns, trends, trend-setters, KOLs, and other important elements of Chinese cosmetics consumers' current taste regimes and their trajectories.

Depth Interviews

The interactive netnography element involved our development and implementation of depth interviews. With input and approval from the ArtCosmetics executive team, we carefully designed an interview guide to query Chinese female consumers about their internal images, tastes, current interests, skin care and cosmetics rituals, social media habits, and other pertinent matters. We used projective tasks in order to gather meta-verbal and subconscious meanings about beauty and self. The interviews were recorded and transcribed as well as reflected upon in the immersion journals.

Along with us, our native-speaking Chinese research team recruited and conducted the personal and video chat interviews on a sample of ten female Chinese cosmetics consumers.

Key informants	Age	Occupation	Origin	Currently living in
Key informant 1	26	Lawyer	Changsta, Hunan	Beijing
Key informant 2	35	Student	Wuhan	New York
Key informant 3	26	Student	S. City, China	San Francisco
Key informant 4	28	Student	Nanjing	San Francisco
Key informant 5	38	Lecturer	Beijing	San Francisco
Key informant 6	31	Student	Harbin, Heilongjiang	Beijing
Key informant 7	28	Hospitality Industry worker	Taiyuan	Brisbane
Key informant 8	27	Duty-free retail	Henan	Henan
Key informant 9	31	Private club owner	Taichung, Taiwan	Taichung, Taiwan
Key informant 10	29	Luxury Tour organizer	Jinhua City, Zhejiang	Brisbane

Figure 13.3 Socio-Demographic Characteristics of Interview Participants.

Participants in the research ranged in age from 18 to 45. All of them regularly use make-up and skin care products, buy Western luxury brands, live abroad or else live in China and travel abroad at least two times per year. Participants were financially compensated for the interviews. Figure 13.3 provides some socio-demographic details of the research participants. As we conducted the study, we constantly compared social media data with interview findings, allowing one to inform and interrogate the other, revealing and then resolving gaps in our understanding of central topics such as the dynamic interplay of Eastern and Western beauty images.

Data Integration

Integration involves a tacking back and forth between analytic coding operations and interpretive hermeneutic procedures. We conducted data integration through a combination of deductive and inductive coding as well as through the ongoing interpretation of emergent cultural insights from all of our researchers, including those on ArtCosmetics' executive team. All of the researchers involved in the project shared their immersion journals that reflected upon and sought to integrate the analysis and interpretation process across sites, topics, and researchers. Given the highly symbolic nature of a large part of the investigative social media data collection, analysis was visual, audiovisual, and ongoing. We had to explore and sort through large amounts of visual and audiovisual data, constantly reducing it by recording it in immersion journals and saving the deepest data for further interpretation. Our data triangulation deployed a "within methods" approach that relied on multiple techniques to interpret data (Jick, 1979, 602–603), including social media investigation, interactive interviews, and immersive journaling and writing operations (Kozinets, 2020, 313).

Although specific findings remain confidential and protected, we use the following sections of this chapter to present a critical methodological reflection. In particular, we show how adopting a penetrant understanding (based in large part on a combination of historical research and interview findings) enabled us to grasp and communicate the interrelatedness of consumer identity, beauty concepts, and cosmetics routines.

Figure 13.4 Chinese-American Beauty Social Media Stars in Influential Poses on Instagram.

HALF-BREED BEAUTY

Figure 13.4 shows some key Chinese-American Instagram influencers included in our netnographic study. Their Instagram posts include posting promotional hashtags to endorse cosmetics brands on their Instagram profiles, and they have wide followings among Chinese women outside of China. In particular, from top left we can see Kina Shen (#kinashen), an Instagram and YouTube cosmetics star with 721,000 followers. Born in China, she is renowned as a "porcelain doll" for the flawless white perfection of her skin, but her style combines elements of goth culture with traditional Chinese beauty images. The figure then depicts Sarah Cheung (#sacheu) another Chinese-American YouTube and Instagram beauty star. Cheung delights her 257,000 followers with her narrative of decorating herself as a "biosexual Chinese witch"—a term that she exemplifies in the illustration with her wild makeup that seems like paint slashed across her face, and her unconventional and distinctly avant-garde poses. Also depicted is Princess Mei (#Infrontofapple), a California-born YouTube and Instagram beauty star with 194,000 followers. Playing with Confucian and Daoist meanings that equate beauty, morality, and a non-deist but spiritualist belief system, she defines herself as a "Chinese angel"—and her photographs reveal a traditional Chinese look (hairstyle, skin, pose, clothing style and color) that is appended by slight alterations such as her bright red eye shadow and bright lipstick.

Our depth interviews of Chinese consumers, our Chinese social media immersion, and the inclusion of immigrant Asian/Chinese-American influencers and immigrant Chinese consumers all combine to reveal a rapidly shifting concept of beauty that is rooted in traditional Chinese cultural, ethnic, and spiritual norms, but also selectively combines novel aspects. There is an ongoing negotiation between Chinese cultural stability and fluid globalization that plays itself out as a tension between beauty meanings, linguistic conventions, and imagery deriving from East and West. The transition from various emic elements to an etic dimension of Chinese beauty allowed us to unravel intertwined Eastern and Western beauty tastes and influences, while remaining cognizant of the significance of their intrication.

Providing one of the more interesting "micrological" (Kozinets 2020, 289–290) instantiations of this East–West beauty syncretism was "Monny," a Chinese cosmetics KOL, whose YouTube make-up tutorial teaches followers how to create a "half-blood" make-up

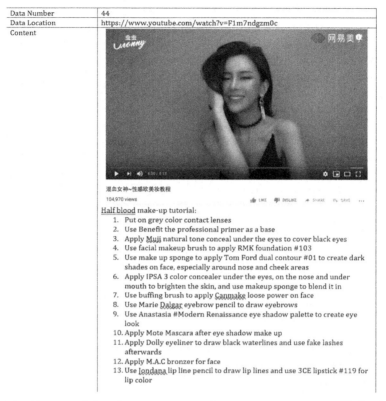

Data Number	44
Data Location	https://www.youtube.com/watch?v=F1m7ndgzm0c
Content	

混血女神~性感吹美妆教程

104,970 views

Half blood make-up tutorial:
1. Put on grey color contact lenses
2. Use Benefit the professional primer as a base
3. Apply Muji natural tone conceal under the eyes to cover black eyes
4. Use facial makeup brush to apply RMK foundation #103
5. Use make up sponge to apply Tom Ford dual contour #01 to create dark shades on face, especially around nose and cheek areas
6. Apply IPSA 3 color concealer under the eyes, on the nose and under mouth to brighten the skin, and use makeup sponge to blend it in
7. Use buffing brush to apply Canmake loose power on face
8. Use Marie Dalgar eyebrow pencil to draw eyebrows
9. Use Anastasia #Modern Renaissance eye shadow palette to create eye look
10. Apply Mote Mascara after eye shadow make up
11. Apply Dolly eyeliner to draw black waterlines and use fake lashes afterwards
12. Apply M.A.C bronzer for face
13. Use Jondana lip line pencil to draw lip lines and use 3CE lipstick #119 for lip color

Figure 13.5 An Excerpt of Our Immersion Journal Notes Recounting a Half-Blood Cosmetics Routine.

look. The "half-blood" was a term originally used to refer to the half-Indian, half-White offspring of red and white races, and provided a powerful symbol of colonization and cultural dominance in nineteenth century American fiction (Scheick, 1979). The image is so important to modern anthropology that Franz Boaz wrote an 1894 book about half-blood Indians. And due to J. K. Rowling's use of it in the titling of her sixth Harry Potter book, the term has enjoyed a renaissance. In Monny's contemporary social media tutorial, the term becomes a gloss for enjoying the beauty benefits that result from blending Western and Eastern ideals of beauty. Of the 13 steps depicted in Figure 13.5, six of them are devoted to the skin, reflecting the emphasis of Chinese females on this element of their beauty. Even in a "half-breed" Westernized scenario, flawless white skin is not something that Chinese women are willing to compromise. As the instructions provided in Figure 13.5 show, color contact lenses and a Western hair style are required, as well as a cultural code-switching witch's blend of Western and Eastern products and brands, including Muji, Benefit, Tom Ford, Anastasia, Mac, and many others.

RESOLVING AND RESPECTING CULTURAL STRUGGLES

Our study combined a broad cultural investigation with a series of focused deep dives into particular pools of localized meaning. We continually sought an expansive understanding of the history, images, associations, symbols, and roles of beautiful women in Chinese culture. This included immersion into the worlds of 60 Asian-American and Chinese social media influencers/KOLs both in English and in Chinese. As a result of this three-month long investigation, we collected 677 websites, 575 posts and 202 videos that we considered to be deep data (see Figure 13.1). In a fashion similar to the way in which qualitative researchers inductively tack back and forth between empirical site and theoretical literature, we used specific instances (e.g., an influencer post on Little Red Book) to generate questions that could draw us further into our investigation of the current cultural moment in Chinese beauty culture.

Although the social media worlds of Chinese influencers, KOLs, and lead users (many of them within the United State) offered up a type of experimental and sometimes edgy Chinese beauty, our interviews reviewed a much more stable set of cultural identities that were not so much traditional as they were transitional. Each offered insights into how Chinese women at different life stages, socioeconomic positions, geographical locations, and occupational environments used skin care and cosmetics to express their identities. Influencers had their own vocabularies, based upon their need to draw audiences, and this often led them to extreme positions—just as Kozinets, Patterson, and Ashman (2017) theorized in the context of food influencers. Our netnography would have provided an incomplete picture of the phenomenon without including the more everyday consumer opinions and attitudes of our interview participants and the many comments we immersed ourselves in from Chinese social media platforms such as Weibo. The results should be instructive to the many researchers who claim to be practicing netnography, but who neglect to interview the people they assert to represent. As Kozinets (2020, 204) reminds us "the people who post publicly on social media [such as beauty influencers] may be more extreme, opinionated, attention-seeking, and self-promotional than those who do not." If we wish to understand a particular group, such as Chinese female cosmetics consumers, it is misguided to rely on influencers' public posts to represent them. Instead, we must incorporate personal interviews into our netnography, as we did with this project.

SENSEMAKING AND MEANING MINING

The project encapsulates the sort of challenge that Kozinets discusses in the opening chapter of this book. If on one side the rich variety of data available in social media is a major advantage of conducting netnographic research, on the other side it challenges researchers. For this project, we had to upskill a large multicultural team, meet regularly with them and with our clients, collect interview and social media data at scale and on time, and continuously integrate these heterogeneous data streams in search of integrative understanding. Like the blending of Eastern and Western beauty that engaged our Chinese female research participants, we were constantly syncretizing and developing our general toolkit of netnography techniques (interviews, observations, journaling) as it bumped up against specific localized understandings and their needs for adaptations and methodological bricolage. These specific demands included the need to scout out limitless varieties of relevant Chinese meanings, images, and symbols, the ability to understand and adapt to the algorithms at work in Chinese and American social media platforms, the incorporation of body language and expression of women in interviews, the meaning of various geographical locations, the need to be familiar with Chinese and global cosmetics and skin care brands and products, skin types and colors, and many other meanings.

Roving back and forth between the elements of our deep interview set, our rich and plentiful immersion journals, and the wealth of social media deep data, we identified cultural patterns. Global and Asian-American influencers in their Instagram profiles produced avant-garde, lifestyle-focused, aesthetic, and expressive social media communications of Chinese beauty that often echo and, in some ways, advance the beauty images of Western cosmetics companies on their websites. Many social media videos, tutorials, reviews, and comments produced by KOLs in Little Red Book, Weibo, WeChat, and YouTube in Chinese language tend to offer Chinese beauty in a more product-focused, feature detailed manner that emphasized functional characteristics.

However, we also located many instances of nuanced cultural tensions in these communications. Testifying to the continued importance of local tradition, many domestic Chinese beauty brands apply traditional Chinese medicine concepts and natural extraction methods to develop skincare and make-up products that are specifically attuned to Chinese consumers' needs. Their rhetorical strategies and lists of ingredients provided a treasure trove for future innovation. In some cases, Chinese beauty brands embodied broader ethical stances on beauty and wellbeing that were attuned to nature, rather than environmentally conscious—a distinction whose significance did not escape closer interpretation.

Another nuanced cultural tension is embodied within Chen (陈莴笋), a Chinese male vlogger who has over 2.2 million followers on his channel called "Watson Scientific Skin Care" on the massive Chinese social media site Weibo, with most of his followers being female cosmetics consumers. In terms that blend national critique with political pride, and ideology with functional characteristics, he discusses his cosmetics blacklist. Reflecting a common concern with Chinese cosmetics brands, he critiques Xixi fashion romantic pink blush, arguing that "the packaging is very plastic and low taste, looks like a kids' snack, rough made brush, powder is not refined, color is not trendy" [English translation from Chinese]. He also openly criticizes Anastasia's brow gel for causing acne and then ideologically extends his critique to the corporate brand for being anti-China and pro-Tibetan independence activism: "Anastasia brow gel—I heard that this brand is an anti-China brand, constantly causes acne" [our translation].

UNDERSTANDING GLOBAL BEAUTYSCAPES

Aesthetics versus features. Local traditions and ingredients. Cheap Chinese packaging and offensively anti-China global brands. Natural beauty and transformative make-up art. Our challenge as netnographers was to seek a nuanced understanding of these various elements and the cultural contradictions they manifested. For several weeks, our data integration efforts struggled to translate cultural diversity into a structure of meaningful and novel consumer insights for ArtCosmetics' new product development processes.

True to Appadurai's (1990) notions of disjuncture and difference, we saw a play of economic and social forces liquifying as well as amplifying core concepts of female beauty in the Chinese cultural imagination as they mingled and contested with global streams. In order to understand our netnography's findings, we adapted Appadurai's "scape" concepts to our more focal beauty concerns. We conceptualized the fluid context of beautyscapes—Chinese women's culturally inflected views of beauty—that were altered by the global cultural flows of the ethnoscapes, mediascapes, technoscapes, financescapes, and ideoscapes of Appadurai's (1990) original theory. Beautyscapes were also transformed by specific infoscapes and brandscapes shared on social media—including a fascination with technology, livestreaming, cross-border shopping, and e-commerce that are relatively unique to the context. In addition, beautyscapes intermingled with the selfscapes of particular skin colors and sensitivities, and the usagescapes of particular locations and their challenges, such as harsh air pollution and extremely long work shifts.

Data integration was intense and demanding. It involved the core researchers reporting updates periodically to our organizational client. The beautyscape conceptual process led us to a type of cultural scenario analysis. This again forced us to simplify our complexity further. We located at the core of these dynamic flows a central pattern in which the shifting elements were structured in a primordial process that oscillates between East and West, traditional and futuristic, and symbolic and functional. Just as the Old Spice Guy campaign helped to portray the cultural paradoxes surrounding modern masculinity, and the Dove Real Beauty campaign acknowledged the tensions around artificial and natural portrayals of female beauty, so, too, did our analysis point to a core cultural truth at the heart of concerns about female beauty.

Because of the breadth of our dataset, we had to dive into areas of interest with a combination of depth interviews, pragmatic immersion, and focused social media investigation. We were able to provide enormous detail on product features such as desired—and despised—shades, fragrances, shapes, packaging designs, and many other matters that were salient to ArtCosmetics. Our sampling strategy, rigorous methodology, ability to recruit excellent research partners and participants, and struggles to fit understanding into our client organization's need for innovative insights were key factors leading to these conceptually and pragmatically detailed outcomes.

CONCLUSIONS

The world is still a small place. Local and traditional meanings continue to hold sway for its 7.8 billion living souls. Yet there is no ignoring the globalizing influences of immigration flows, mixing and merging with those of technology, media, finance, and the cultural imagination. We conceptualize a funneling of these forces into global beautyscapes that reflect, inflect, and transform Chinese women's images of beauty, self, and their own tastes and routines. The role of social media and mobile applications in this process is complex, situated, and multifaceted. It takes rigorous research design attuned to sampling concerns and implementation in order to be able to address the challenges of a complex multicultural and transnational research project such as the one we describe in this chapter. And to turn it into practical insights that can help a client to build products leading to their lasting success.

Although we were unable to share particular recommendations due to our responsibilities to keep them confidential, we hope that our chapter was able to provide some useful details. Even with these limitations our chapter allows readers a truly behind-the-scenes glimpse into what a contemporary and rigorous commercial netnography looks like and how it functions. Netnography today is qualitative social media research. It is multifaceted and multimethod. It builds focused results from the information of depth interviews and the ongoing immersion of a large multicultural research team. It combines this with detailed, multi-faceted data from platforms such as Weibo, Little Red Book, YouTube, and Instagram. Aware of the selection biases of the algorithms of these platforms, our data integration compensated for a variety of sociotechnical and cultural blind spots.

Our netnography for ArtCosmetics was a serious challenge and a worthwhile struggle rather than some sort of cut-and-paste online content analysis exercise. It followed rigorous ethical standards in line with GRPR, AoIR, and Kozinets' (2020) specific edicts. It required continual methodological adaptation and innovation, drawing from the range of rigorous operational procedures that netnography today encompasses. As this chapter and this book demonstrate, in a contemporary world with massive complexity and change—characterized recently by the new challenges of the coronavirus COVID-19—we must each in our work continue not only to honor the time-tested techniques and fundamental methodological precepts of netnography, but also to wisely adapt and extend them.

ACKNOWLEDGEMENT

The authors would like to express their gratitude to a team of six university students (e.g., Chiara La Barbera, Francesca Cortolillo, Cristina Rugolino, Elena Aneomanti, Victoria

Busalacchi, and Federica Marchio) at Università Cattolica del Sacro Cuore (UCSC) in Milan who—under the supervision and the training offered jointly by Netnografica and Labcom (Research Lab on Business Communication, UCSC)—supported the authors and their Chinese team of qualitative researchers with part of the data collection carried out on social media sites. They would also like to acknowledge the tremendous work and invaluable cultural insights provided by our Chinese research team members Li Xie and Lusha Sa.

REFERENCES

Appadurai, A. (1990). Disjuncture and difference in the global cultural economy. *Theory, Culture & Society, 7*(2–3), 295–310.

Chin, D. (1996). *Setting up shop: Retailing in China.* Hong Kong: FT Pitman Publishing.

Cho, K. (2012). *The search for the beautiful woman: A cultural history of Japanese and Chinese beauty.* Washington DC: Rowman & Littlefield.

Daxue Consulting (2020), Analysis of China's beauty and personal care market (January, 2020): https://daxueconsulting.com/selling-cosmetics-in-china-beauty-and-personal-care-market/

Jick, T. D. (1979). Mixing qualitative and quantitative methods: Triangulation in action. *Administrative Science Quarterly, 24*(4), 602–611.

Jung, J. (2018). Young women's perceptions of traditional and contemporary female beauty ideals in China. *Family and Consumer Sciences Research Journal, 47*(1), 56–72.

Kozinets, R.V. (2020). *Netnography 3E. The essential guide to qualitative social media research.* Thousand Oaks (CA): Sage.

Kozinets, R., Patterson, A., & Ashman, R. (2017). Networks of desire: How technology increases our passion to consume. *Journal of Consumer Research, 43*(5), 659–682.

Man, E. K. W. (2016). *Bodies in China: Philosophy, aesthetics, gender and politics.* Hong Kong: Chinese University Press.

Mordor Intelligence (2020). Asia-Pacific cosmeceutical market growth, trends and forecast (2020–2025). Report available at: www.mordorintelligence.com/industry-reports/asia-pacific-cosmeceuticals-market

PR Newswire (2019), China Cosmetics Market 2019–2025, PR Newswire: www.prnewswire.com/news-releases/china-cosmetics-market-2019–2025–market-size-is-expected-to-surge-from-rmb361-6-billion-in-2017-to-rmb62-61-billion-in-2022–showing-an-aagr-of-8-16-300854261.html

Raun, T. (2018). Capitalizing intimacy: New subcultural forms of micro-celebrity strategies and affective labour on YouTube. *Convergence, 24*(1), 99–113.

Scheick, W. J. (1979), *The half-blood: A cultural symbol in 19th century American fiction.* Lexington, KY: University Press of Kentucky.

Statista (2019), Cosmetics in China: statistics and facts, Statista.com (July, 2019): www.statista.com/topics/1897/cosmetics-in-china/

Section 4
Netnography Humanized

14

Auto-Netnography in Education
Unfettered and Unshackled

Lyz Howard

INTRODUCTION

The aim of this chapter is to explore the concept of auto-netnography in the context of "netnography unlimited" and to share with you, how you might consider the theoretical and practical application of auto-netnography within your chosen field of inquiry. Auto-netnography will be defined and I explain why I chose auto-netnography as one of the many approaches that netnography enables researchers to pursue. Whilst social media as a learning construct is presented as the focus for this chapter, I argue that auto-netnography can be adapted to respond to any digitally mediated research field where the researcher intends to understand more fully, their emotional connection to that field from which cognitive and sensory data can be obtained. To explore the potential for auto-netnography across fields of digital interaction, I will present the auto-netnography framework and guide you in its use. Please use, critique, adapt and extend this model to meet your own needs as an "unlimited netnographer" and insider–researcher.

Because the "auto" aspect of auto-netnography is the central feature of netnography unlimited, I present "myself" within this chapter using first-person and performative writing (Worden, 2014) to allow for the expressive, purposeful inclusion of narrative that reflects upon the contours and dynamics of auto-netnography. I do this because I believe that connections between the author and their audience are important. I will use this less academic and more relaxed form of writing as the narrative to evidence throughout, the value of introspection as a way to "engage my emotions, sensations, mental imagery, and behaviors as subjects of [that] introspection" (Gould, 1995: 720). However, there is a note of caution before you read further … writing in the first person can be tricky and has the potential to be misinterpreted as self-congratulatory. This chapter reflects my conceptualisation of auto-netnography and I invite you to vicariously share in that experience. Whilst the personal is privileged within auto-netnography, I wish to make it clear that at no point is it my intention to self-promote; rather the legitimacy of my text is grounded in the way in which it is connected to what I observed as I developed the auto-netnography framework and the experiences that made a difference in my online teaching life. Such experiences, I hope, will resonate with others.

DELIMITING NETNOGRAPHY

In *Netnography: Redefined*, Kozinets (2015: 3) claimed that "netnography remains rooted to core ethnographic principles of participant-observation while also seeking to selectively and systematically incorporate digital approaches" to data collection and analysis. Now, in its third edition *Netnography: The Essential Guide to Qualitative Social Media Research* Kozinets (2020) has unmoored netnography from its original traditions, shifting towards an approach that includes engagement and flexibility. Netnographers are currently encouraged to include intellectual, emotional, cultural and historical strategies in addition to participation-like social engagement as part of their research practice. In parallel, and as Kozinets and Gambetti (2020) call on those who subscribe to the value of netnography to delimit and celebrate the diversity of netnography, the value of auto-netnography as an extension to netnography can be explored in its own right. Netnography, as a set of flexible research practices, can be adapted and auto-netnography reflects this: following in the footsteps of auto-ethnography, narratives are represented within varying emphases on the triadic axes that inform the balance of the self (auto), culture (ethno) and research process (graphy) (Adams et al., 2015). I claim that it is the tripartite balance between self, culture and the research process that elevates and exemplifies the trustworthiness and credibility of auto-netnography. Through the lens of auto-netnography, researchers have the flexibility to immerse themselves in an interpretive exploration of their own participation (Denzin, 2014) in the digital experience (auto) within the culture of social media or other digitally mediated applications (netno) as the research focus (graphy) to inform their practice. This "Deep N of One" (Kozinets, 2015: 69), causes prospective researchers to realise that introspection in the form of autobiographical and reflexive participation is welcomed in auto-netnography. Arguably this is because individual worldviews are dependent upon the lens through which that world is viewed. It is the "auto" in auto-netnography that helped me to explore my own actions, perceptions and feelings as I became the researcher-and-the-researched, where I learned and developed new pedagogical nuances of "being" an online teacher, not just "doing" online teaching.

WHY AUTO-NETNOGRAPHY?

You might ask to what depths auto-netnography can plumb? I claim that auto-netnography has much to offer. Auto-netnography is individual to every researcher and methodologically gives individuals permission to examine their practice, their being, their place in the world of the digital environment, where a meaningful space to develop, learn and interact with other human beings or computers can occur. Auto-netnography allows researchers-and-the-researched to "be", to choose their own journey as they discover how to "become" within the context of interacting within the digital world.

My journey into the world of auto-netnography began with the merging of an interest in online teaching and a desire to develop my online teaching practice as the focus of my PhD studies. This personal drive to look closely at how I teach online and develop professionally as an online teacher, caused me some troublesome thinking as I sought a research methodology that could inform both aspects of my online teaching practice. I could have employed auto-ethnography as an already established self-examining methodology to explore my online teaching practice but this had been done before, for example, Keefer (2010) and (Henning, 2012). Following the same path would not have given me the opportunity to respond to the requirement of a PhD whereby researchers are required to add to a body of knowledge relating to their field of practice. Indeed, my interest in auto-netnography was piqued as I was introduced to the work of Kozinets and Kedzior (2009: 8) who conceptualised auto-netnography in the context of Second Life© claiming that auto-netnography as methodology

captures and documents experiences through the careful observation of online participation, autobiographical attending to the interrelation of various experienced "worlds"

... reflexive field-noting, self- and first-person image and other data captures, and first person narratives which make their way into the final representation of the researcher's autonetnographic text.

I was hooked: using a legitimate approach to auto-netnography as methodology appeared to afford an opportunity to inform my understanding of the internal functioning of the online culture through reflexive autobiographical field-noting, self-data capture and first person narrative (emic perspective) at the same time as being the researcher who translates their insider researcher findings through the reflexive interpretation of relevant peer-reviewed literature (etic perspective). My excitement was palpable ... until I realised that auto-netnography remained in its conceptual phase and the only way I was going to be able to use it to frame my research, was to develop auto-netnography as methodology.

As you will already have observed by the use of first-person narrative, my research interest lies in "being" rather than "doing". I contest that important aspects of "being" a teacher are not only developing a pedagogical underpinning of theory to inform my teaching practice, but also a willingness to cultivate the art of praxis as a conduit for me to discover the "embodied experiences of being and becoming" (White, 2016: 23). This philosophical perspective determines introspective self-examination as opposed to taking an objective stance by detaching myself from how I feel about my position as an online teacher. Introspection as an interpretive technique to gain understanding of teaching from an insider perspective is not new (Gould, 1995), and in this sense is reliant upon reflexive focus on my personal insights into teaching that become intertwined with my research insights in the context of teaching in a digitally mediated field.

My overarching aim in this chapter is to metaphorically take you by the hand and narrate you through my journey of discovery, demonstrating along the way some of the benefits and limitations of using auto-netnography as methodology. If you are ready to join me, let me start by contextualising social media as a learning construct.

SOCIAL MEDIA: A LEARNING CONSTRUCT

Social media has become increasingly visible within higher education (HE) settings as teachers move away from wholly face-to-face teaching to include more flexible learning opportunities afforded by digitally mediated applications. Such opportunities include, for example, YouTube, Facebook, LinkedIn, Instagram, Pinterest and Twitter. These applications are often mobile, allowing for autonomous anytime, anyplace, anywhere connectivity to knowledge. What is different about social media, when compared to more traditional peer-reviewed, evidence-based sources of knowledge, is that social media is authored, critiqued and configured by non-academics and academics alike, who construct, co-construct, share, and edit these forms of digitally mediated content.

This mass knowledge-sharing, construction and development cascades effortlessly into the paradigm of social constructivism whereby socially mediated scholarship is enhanced through interactive collaboration, cooperation and critique of others' contributions (Swan et al., 2009). It is within this paradigm that the physical location of the learner or teacher no longer matters, and where the sharing of knowledge has the potential to become global, disrupting traditional educational boundaries in a space where it is possible to share, promote and co-construct new understandings. A utopian ideal implies that this spatial and temporal dislocation determines no specific location or boundary, and indicates that learning can take place anywhere at any time either at the surface level or by linking to deeper knowledge (Biggs, 2011).

Knowing how to make sense of social media as an educational tool, or understand the sociality and structure of educationalists' own academic social media interactions is an area ripe for educational research. For example, from an emic perspective a dichotomy insider-researchers might face when developing an understanding of the internal functioning and associated language of social media to construct and share knowledge is how at the same time, from an etic perspective, to appreciate the nuances of their teaching practice through the reflexive interpretation of relevant peer-reviewed literature. Whilst this dual stance may be contested by claims that the researcher is too close to the emic perspective to form one that is etic, I argue that by "unlimiting" the contemporary aspects and trajectory of netnography into auto-netnography as methodology, both emic and etic standpoints can be considered in parallel. For example, I claim that truth and reality, reported as knowledge, can be viewed from multiple positions and that my own position shared as a meta-narrative throughout this chapter, legitimates knowledge in the context of constructivist epistemology. This is in keeping with the seminal work of Gould (1995: 720) who claims that introspection (which remains at the heart of auto-netnography) affords opportunities for me as an auto-netnographer, "immediate access to a vast amount of cognitive and sensory data that I could never obtain from other subjects, and I am able to discern clear patterns in my internal phenomena over time". It is within this epistemological construct, therefore, that auto-netnography can contribute to the "unlimiting", or delimiting, of netnography as one of its many evolving contours.

THEORISING AUTO-NETNOGRAPHY

A foray into the potential for auto-netnography as a research methodology to inform my own professional development as a HE teacher came to fruition as I explored my practice as an experienced face-to-face teacher learning to teach online. The crux of contextualising my own journey using auto-netnography was that having appropriate skills to reflect critically on one's own teaching practice is an explicit requirement of all teachers. Indeed, Mezirow (1991: 196) claimed that by "explaining the learning dynamics [involved in digging] down to the roots of our assumptions and preconceptions [teachers can] change the way [they] construe the meaning of experience". Arguably, the role of any teacher in transformative learning involves encouraging and enabling the processes of transformation among their students, by guiding them to overcome potential situational, knowledge-bound or emotional barriers (Closs and Antonello, 2011). When learning is integrated within social media networks, a subjective understanding of teachers' own barriers to teaching using critical reflexivity through self-examination, might be an appropriate lens to explore the contours and dynamics of social media as an educational tool.

As a consequence of more recent scholarship, my research has evolved in parallel to the work of Villegas (2018) extending the theoretical and practical constructs of auto-netnography as an emerging research methodology to develop a model and guide for others wishing to pursue subjective and reflexive insider-research. Both Villegas and I have developed the concept of auto-netnography in isolation. The approach that Villegas (2018) takes is to provide a *Journey Guide* that comprises: (1) the traveller, (2) the map, (3) the routes, (4) the learning, (5) the telling and (6) the safety of the trip. Interestingly, our interpretation of auto-netnography complement each other, with each of us placing significance on the self as not just the insider-researcher, but the starting point for auto-netnography. My conceptualisation of auto-netnography (Howard, 2019) informs the "Auto-netnography Framework" (Figure 14.1) and differs from Villegas (2018) in that it encourages researchers to consider their emic ontological and epistemological positionality in the digitally mediated field under investigation, as the foundation for the researcher-being-the-researched.

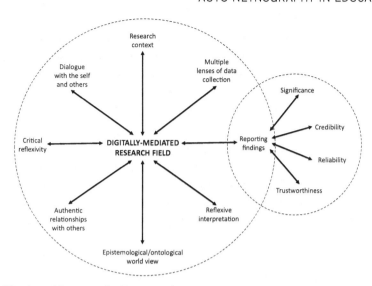

Figure 14.1 The Auto-Netnography Framework.

THE AUTO-NETNOGRAPHY FRAMEWORK

As you can see, the auto-netnography framework is fluid and dynamic with each aspect of the framework being open to the user's interpretation and where the emphasis of each aspect can be determined by the researcher-as-the-researched in the context of their research field. The boundaries of the auto-netnography framework are purposefully blurred to allow for a pragmatic approach to auto-netnography as methodology. Truly immersing myself within the auto-netnography framework generated changes in my thinking through illuminating new links and understandings about who I was and continued to become as a teacher. The continuous flowing back and forth within and between each aspect of the auto-netnography framework informed my pathway through the process of self-investigation, immersion, analysis, interpretation and insight generation.

This process formed part of the emic theoretical ballast that stabilised my self-reflexive professional development ship as she sailed through new territories, in seas that made navigation challenging, yet not impossible. Being the researcher and the researched gave me permission to look at my digitally mediated teaching practice from different perspectives with a view to understanding what I did well and what I needed to improve. At times, I found the seas were high and my journey in to self-reflexivity became difficult – I needed to hold on tight as the waves crashed against my ship, causing me to lose my balance (and a little faith in myself as an online teacher). On other occasions, the sea was calmer, where I could see the horizon and find comfort in realising that I could let go of the rails and feel steady on my feet as I celebrated the elements of my teaching practice that were working well. Auto-netnography gave me the opportunity to take this journey of discovery like no other methodology, and I needed to be willing to accept the rough times with the calm as I experienced tensions between knowing, learning about myself and re-defining teacher-self in light of new findings.

You will already have noticed that reflexivity features dominantly, albeit in different forms, within the auto-netnography framework, with each reflexive activity demonstrating different subtleties and nuances of meaning. Reflexivity as a "way of articulating, and therefore acknowledging and scrutinizing, the tacit knowledge of the researcher" (D'Cruz et al., 2007: 78) causes researchers to consider more deeply, the "social and cultural artefacts and forms of thought which saturate our practices" (White, 2001: 108). For auto-netnographers, reflexivity presents an inward challenge to examine the processes they use to understand the world in which they live and work. Such interpretations are personal and reflect the values, attitudes and worldview of the researcher. Any reported findings, therefore, are open to "deconstructive readings by the recipient" (Freshwater and Rolfe, 2001: 535). This is significant if a researcher intends to utilise auto-netnography as methodology; they will be required to declare their epistemological stance at the same time as reporting findings in a less authoritative and more personal way to not only allow, but to actively encourage debate and challenges from recipients who may share alternative perspectives.

Hereafter, I present a holistic overview of the auto-netnography framework, then each aspect of the framework in turn. However, please remember that auto-netnography is not a linear methodology; rather it is betwixt and between, fluid, dynamic and can adapt to whatever it is the researcher needs it to be. To help you make sense of each aspect, examples will be given from my own experience of using auto-netnography to examine digitally mediated teaching practice.

The *digitally mediated research field* is determined by the researcher-and-the-researched, which could, for example, include personal insights into participating in social media. The *research context* within my research was informed by the development of a conceptual framework (Figure 14.2) where I mapped my epistemological worldview with my presumed relationships between online teaching and professional development needs.

Because I was developing auto-netnography as a method at the same time as researching my online teaching practice, my overarching research questions reflected this; I sought to determine in what ways auto-netnography afforded me the opportunity to situate my online teaching praxis as an experienced face-to-face teacher, yet neophyte online teacher. My literature search was informed by using a relational diagram (Wentzel, 2016), which gave me an opportunity to critically engage with my conceptual framework to cross-examine my epistemological standpoint and initial research ideas (Figure 14.3). Once defined, my key understandings were labelled (A–F) in pair-wise relationships to form tangible links between my research question, my conceptual framework, and significantly, substantial links that I felt were arguable and plausible starting points for my literature review, which in turn informed my data collection methods.

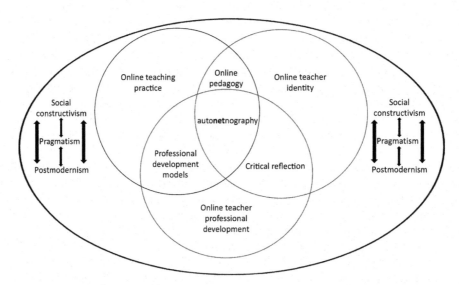

Figure 14.2 Conceptual Framework.

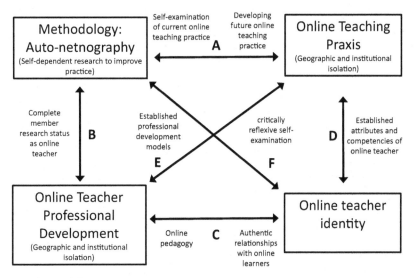

Figure 14.3 Relational Diagram.

As with all research processes, *lenses of data collection* will be defined by the research question(s) and should be reflective of the researcher's axiological, ontological, *epistemological and methodological worldview* (Guba and Lincoln, 2005; Denzin, 2014). *Interpretation of the data* also reflects the researcher's worldview, and will be determined by the theoretical model claimed by the researcher as appropriate to interrogate the data. Using the auto-netnography framework, data interpretation is informed by valuing *authentic relationships* with others in the form of ensuring my work research ethically sound, using *critical reflexivity* to focus introspectively on the data collected and to challenge my introspective findings using *dialogue with the self and others*. This, in turn, informs emergent findings. An awareness of the research context and commitment to *reflexive interpretation* are the overarching etic features of the data collection and interpretation aspects of the auto-netnography framework. In earlier stages of developing auto-netnography as methodology (Howard, 2019), I found reflexive interpretation of my emic findings pivotal to the developmental understanding of my teaching praxis. Using the auto-netnography framework, I could justify the *significance, credibility, reliability* and *trustworthiness* of my research in determining and *reporting* those findings, as I should when undertaking any robust research.

DIGITALLY MEDIATED RESEARCH FIELD

A current focus on HE practices to promote "student-centred constructivist pedagogy as the contemporary paradigm of university teaching and learning" (Doiron, 2018: 2) calls for the teacher to take on more of a facilitative role (Howard, 2019). Arguably, this change in relationship requires a more nurturing approach from teachers who have the skills to give constructive and enabling feedback. Such skills are likely to rely upon mutual respect, transparency, and a trusting relationship between the teacher and learner, whilst facilitating learning in a way that determines clarity of expression (Doiron, 2018).

Despite social media being employed as a relatively contemporary educational construct, understanding the social implications of digitally mediated education is not new. Since the early 1990s there has been some understanding around the impact of digital technologies on the "nature of social structures … and the key interaction processes that figure in their use" (DeSanctis and Poole, 1994: 121). Using adaptive structuration theory, DeSanctis and Poole (1994) examined the way in which the use of technology encouraged new ways of constructing meaning using technologies, which when translated into current social media use, could incorporate the use of emojis, emoticons, stickers (Tang and Foon Hew, 2019), gifs (Jiang et al., 2018), and text-speak (Pohl et al., 2017) as the ubiquitous language of social communication. It has been claimed by Dunlap et al. (2016) in their literature review on the use of emoticons to support online learning, and Jingqain et al. (2016) who considered emerging trends in social media, that the use of emojis and emoticons allows for teachers to give negative or developmental feedback to students in a way that appears more positive. Using emojis and emoticons to give feedback, therefore, has the potential to increase trust between the learner and teacher in a way that demonstrates developmental encouragement to assist learners as they progress academically.

EPISTEMOLOGICAL AND ONTOLOGICAL WORLDVIEW

The prolific use of social applications found on smartphones and used with digital technologies demonstrates the human desire to connect via social media. This desire for connection can take many forms including, for example, sharing information, garnering support, selling an idea, disseminating fake news and learning from others. This sense of ubiquitous connectivity through social media has given humans the opportunity to interact online through learning and socialising whenever they have Internet connectivity (Vanden Abeele et al., 2018). Not only having an understanding of one's own epistemological and ontological world view, but sharing that worldview with the reader of auto-netnography research is important. The lens through which each of us views the world is likely to reflect the researcher's individual values, attitudes, assumptions and personal bias. Being "up front" with the reader demonstrates honesty, which ultimately garners trust in the researcher's intentions from the onset. This is particularly important in social media research because the way in which researchers-and-the-researched undertake and report their findings, perhaps using social media itself as one of the many forms of research dissemination, needs to be ethical, credible, trustworthy and reliable. I argue that, in part, this is because communicating using digital technologies is shaping both online and offline social action. For example, the exposure to fake news has the ontological capacity to raise or diminish the profile of individuals, groups and cultures. Individual and group responses to such information is powerful and may enable or constrain social action (Bucher and Helmond, 2017). Focusing specifically on epistemology and ontology as philosophical approaches to auto-netnography therefore, encourages insider-researchers of social media or other digitally mediated research fields to purposefully consider not only individual and group interpretations of social media, but how this might impact on the social actions of those individuals and groups.

RESEARCH CONTEXT

The auto-netnography framework is adaptive to the focus of individual research questions. For example, auto-netnographers may wish to examine through an "intersubjective mapping of [their] social media interactions" (Kozinets, 2015: 97) in terms of collegiality and professional networks; whether a "re-tweet" or "share" determines that learning is accurate, relevant, surface or deep; how students and academics socialise into their own world of personal and professional development; what they know about who is sending their messages or sharing educational information; and perhaps, whether retrospective self-voyeurism informs their own academic development as they look back at their social interaction with students (Howard, 2019).

One of the benefits of auto-netnography is that this methodology gives permission for the individual researching their own practice to include self-study (Howard, 2016) of the social media experience. Auto-netnography allows for the researcher-and-the-researched to determine which aspects of their research they intend to share with readers of their research (with the caveat that the insider-researcher should be honest with the reader to explain why, without divulging too much information, some aspects of their findings have not been publicly shared).

Another benefit of being the insider-researcher, is the opportunity for reflexive development. This perspective suggests that the importance of contextualising place is significant because the researcher is required to "identify [the] need to systematically and reflexively account for place and places in research, alongside the social position of the researcher and methods" (Booth, 2015: 20) "as if place mattered" (Anderson et al., 2010: 600). Echoing this, the suggestion by Hodgson et al. (2012: 293) that "critical reflexivity and relational dialogue [are] key theoretical perspectives and values associated with the pedagogical and socio-technical design", contextualises the potential for auto-netnography to explore and develop teachers' praxis from the perspective of teaching using social media as an educational tool. In addition, this sense of self-observation of teachers' who facilitate learning through social media might also act as a conduit for connecting more closely with their students and academic peers.

MULTIPLE LENSES OF DATA COLLECTION

Auto-netnography affords the insider-researcher a myriad of opportunities for determining their data collection methods. The methods I used to collect data reflected a pragmatic perspective. I really wanted to know how and when students were interacting, whether I was contributing as the online teacher enough or too much. I wanted to review my use of language when communicating online and how the students responded to me. This led me to examine potential methods for data collection that would reflect this. Truly not knowing where my data collection was going to take me, I included a number of quantitative and qualitative approaches that I mapped to my research question (Figure 14.4).

Social network analysis (Cowan and Menchaca, 2014; Stepanyan et al., 2014) was selected as a method to visually represent each student and the number of communications they made between themselves and me as their facilitator as well as the number of messages I posted on the asynchronous discussion board; I undertook quantitative examination of group cohesion using an asynchronous discussion timeline (Dringus and Ellis, 2010) to inform stages of the online module that were more active with students posting and interacting more readily than other times when the discussion board was less active. To examine more closely my contributions and the meaning these contributions may have had for the students, I explored qualitative data collection methods. Examples included situational analysis (Clarke, 2005; Clarke and Friese, 2007; Salazar-Perez and Cannella, 2013), which encouraged me to map situational insights into how I responded to the heterogeneous contexts of actions and discourse that occurred throughout the online module; to understand myself more deeply as the insider-researcher, I sought a method that would develop personal insights in to who I was as an individual and how this might shape my being as a teacher; following guidance from Muncey (2010) who explores different ways of creating autoethnographies, I visually sequenced memorable, familial and educational influences on my professional being on a timeline that contextualised extracts of my life journey (Figure 14.5).

This led to exploring my identity through a Culturegram (Figure 14.6), which (Chang, 2008) in her work on using autoethnography as method, suggests is an opportunity to analyse visually the broader social and cultural influences that informs individual values; and,

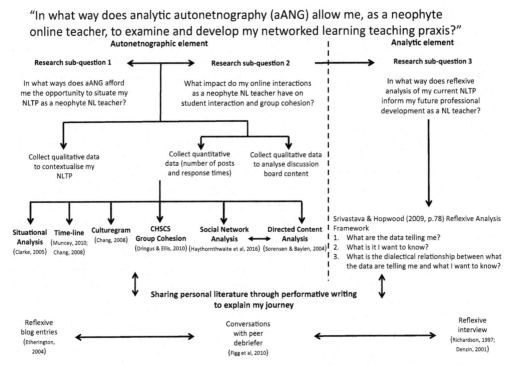

Figure 14.4 Mapping My Research Question to Data Collection and Analysis Methods.

examining online communications with learners through the lens of directed content analysis (Sorensen and Baylen, 2004) was chosen as a qualitative opportunity to examine the meaning behind my online interactions using a validated discussion behaviour classification system. Each of these methods challenged my thinking by triangulating a number of netnographic data sources from different perspectives (Avgerinou and Andersson, 2006); I share some of my findings in the Reflexive Interpretation section.

Whilst this plethora of data collection methods gave me significantly more mixed-method data for analysis of my teaching praxis than that of a single method, I did experience some challenges along the way. For example, the visual timeline unleashed some memories in my personal life, that I had not realised were hidden. I discovered aspects of my upbringing and educational experiences that, with hindsight, had played some part in my development as an academic. I interpreted a perceived "need" to constantly nurture, support and encourage students, guiding them to become independent scholars as a reflection of times when I had felt isolated as a child, in both a personal and educational sense. I was surprised how readily those emotions that had remained hidden suddenly emerged with a powerful force. One of the opportunities of discovering this new sense of self through such data collection methods was that I truly appreciated the role of my peer-debriefer, which I had arranged to have in place from the commencement of my PhD programme following a suggestion by Figg et al. (2010) who claimed that a long-term peer-debriefer was beneficial to teacher–researchers. My peer-debriefer agreed to undertake this role and was chosen because: (1) she had previous experience of teaching online; (2) she had experience of being a PhD student and supervisor; and, (3) she was a colleague that I trusted to challenge my thinking through constructive critique. We met regularly and used our meeting times to explore new insights,

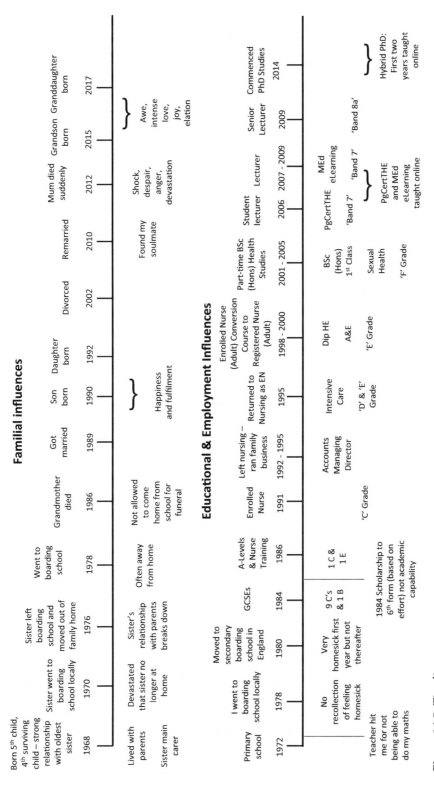

Figure 14.5 Timeline.

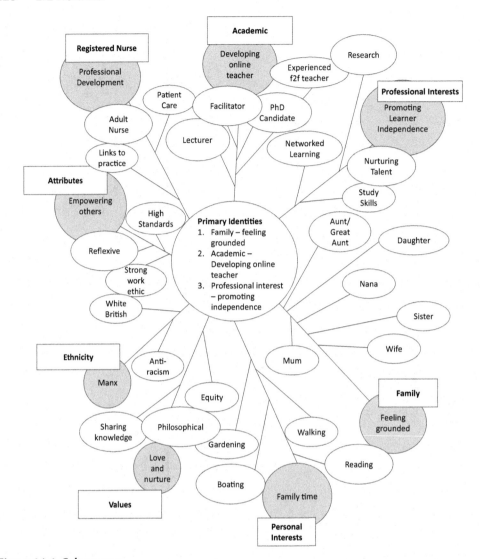

Figure 14.6 Culturegram.

challenge unrealistic interpretations and determine the value (or not) of new understandings that came to light in the process of self-discovery as an online teacher. Indeed, many of the discussions I had with my peer-debriefer became reflexive data sets in their own right, examples of which are reflected in Table 14.1.

Whilst the methods I chose were specific to understand and develop my teaching in the context of TEL, there are many opportunities for auto-netnographers researching interaction and meaning using social media to extend their methodological choices by including, for example, data mining to form an auditable trail of Twitter responses (Rogers et al., 2016), re-tweets, Facebook Shares, and conversations on LinkedIn (Ahmed, 2019). In summary, combining netnography as the variety of social media data sources with the auto (researcher-and-the-researched) enables the auto-netnographer to select the most appropriate research method(s) to answer their research question.

Table 14.1 Excerpt from My Data-Log

	Data collection strategy (primary labelling)			Data content (secondary labelling)				
Data set #	Date	Collector	Type	Location	Time	People involved	Source	Place
13	15/04/16	Howard	**Vi** Culture-Gram	Online	2016	Self	Self	Home in study
17	22/05/16	Howard	**S/R** Blog "Lurkers in our midst"	Online	2016	Self/peer-debriefer	Self	Home in study
27	11/03/17	Howard	**Vi** Timeline of autobiographical Influences	Online	2017	Self	Self	Home in study
30	20/03/17	Howard	**Vi** Memoing the meaning of relationships between elements = Online teacher element (Memo 1)	Online	2017	Self	Self/Situational Map	Home in study
31	21/03/17	Howard	**S/R** Reflexive interview	Isle of Man	2017	Self/Peer-debriefer	Self	Peer-debriefer's home
42	30/04/17	Howard	**Vi** Finally achieving a visual overview of group cohesion following the model utilised by Dringus and Ellis	Online	2017	Self/Friend	Data mining CHSCS density, latency, intensity and response times	Friend's home/ Work
43	06/05/17	Howard	**Do** Direct content analysis using Sorensen and Baylen (2004) framework to analyse my interaction with CHSCS learners	Online	2017	Self	My contributions (initiating, supporting challenging, summarising and monitoring) to the CHSCS module	Home in study
54	21/05/17	Howard	**S/R** Blog "Situational mapping reaching saturation"	Online	2017	Self	Self	Home in study
55	26/05/17	Howard	**Vi** Developing my social worlds/ arenas map	Isle of Man	2017	Self	Self/memos	Library at Work
56	30/05/17	Howard	**Vi** Developing my positional map	Online	2017	Self	Self/memos/social worlds/ arenas map	Home in study

REFLEXIVE INTERPRETATION

Employing such a combination of research methods to gather data might appear complicated, disparate or unconnected and afforded the potential for the researcher to discover aspects of themselves that they had not anticipated. Indeed, as explained previously, my auto-netnography caught me a little off-guard when I was not as emotionally prepared as I thought to face the findings that came from a close examination of who I was/am in the context of becoming an online teacher. This journey captured aspects of my being that surprised me. In the context of metaphor, I recall meeting with my peer-debriefer and described to her feeling like Alice from Wonderland, as I was delving deeper into my data collection and diving through the "rabbit-hole" with each data set informing the next, yet seemingly different in their focus. I found that one data set led to another whereby every iteration appeared to influence those data sets that came before. I discussed with my peer-debriefer each disorientating dilemma as I became lost in the surreal sense of my TEL world: I recall initially visualising my data collection methods as a gentle spiral, with a far-reaching top where data collection began in earnest. As I began to analyse my data, I felt like the data analysis turned my calm spiral into an intense swirling wind that gathered pace as I reflected deeply, causing more data to emerge. This tornado effect drew me closer to my foundations, and, to some extent, caused some (self)destruction before my data analysis becalmed.

I collected 59 data sets, and followed the suggestion by Chang (2008) to label my data sets in a primary and secondary form and in chronological order. Primary labelling includes the *who, what, where,* and *when* (4-W) criteria that formed the data collection strategy. My data sets comprised: 26 self-reflective notes (**S/R**); 27 visual data (**Vi**); and, 6 documentary evidence (**Do**). Secondary labelling incorporated the 4-W criteria relating to the data content. To provide an audit trail a data-log was created to label each data set collected throughout my research. Chang (2008) recommends the benefits of keeping a data-log to assist with the classification of data, and I include an example of my data-log in Table 14.1.

However, the further I weaved through the somewhat tangled web of information and data garnered from each method, the more reflexive and iterative I became as new understandings caused me to (re)review my findings. This eclectic mix of quantitative and qualitative data collection and analysis methods complement the auto-netnography framework to reposition what Ellingson (2011: 595) suggests is "the tendency to understand art and science as dichotomies (i.e. mutually exclusive, paired opposites) by illuminating research and representational options that fall between these two poles". Therefore, I was conscious that the analysis of my data needed to be presented in such a way that it revealed both etic and emic perspectives.

To achieve this, findings from the social network analysis (Cowan and Menchaca, 2014; Shea and Bidjerano, 2013; Stepanyan et al., 2014) visually represented how my participation as an online teacher was positioned within the module, in conjunction with how learners interacted and responded to me (Figure 14.7).

The concentric circles represented the number of posts to the discussion boards, from 0 to >40. One-way and two-way arrows denote one- or two-way conversations. Numbers by each pseudonym indicate the number of group statements made. For example, Joe and Meg posted to the group nine times and Ellen, Maya and Susan posted to the whole group once, but did not interact otherwise. The purpose of employing social network analysis was to visualise the number of asynchronous interactions and to elicit the position occupied by myself as the online teacher, and the interconnected relationships I formed with the students that were bounded by the online module space. Having visually represented the asynchronous discussions, it was important to explore more deeply the content of my online posts so that

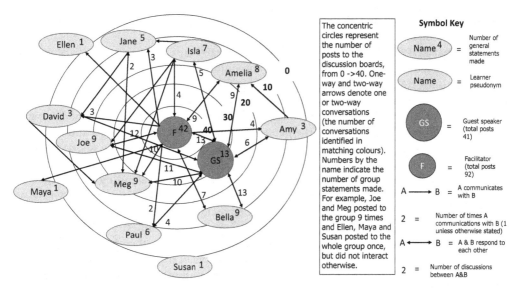

Figure 14.7 Social Network Analysis.

I could learn more about whether my online contributions were encouraging or discouraging interaction and learning from and with each other.

In response to this I had incorporated a qualitative arm to the some of the quantitative data I had collected through social network analysis in the form of directed content analysis (Sorensen and Baylen, 2004). The primary purpose for self-examination of online teaching practice was to understand more about my teaching style, and to enhance the way in which I designed and taught flexible, appropriate and pedagogically effective online learning opportunities. Directed content analysis was one way of investigating how well I was achieving this aim. I intended to use the pre-determined theoretical direction of Sorensen and Baylen's (2004) *Discussion Behaviour Classification System* to guide the categorisation of five different forms of asynchronous communications to determine learner interaction: (1) initiating, (2) supporting, (3) challenging, (4) summarising and (5) monitoring. I collated all of the comments I posted throughout the module and placed them within the original directed content analysis framework. At this point I realised that I was not able to place all of my contributions within the specified categories and I recognised that this was because the directed content analysis discussion behaviour classification system was developed to focus upon and determine learner interaction as opposed to teacher interaction. What I found was that I had not only verified those behaviours originally defined by Sorensen and Baylen (2004) but had demonstrated additional behaviours that were more facilitator focused. For example, in data-log 43 statements such as: *"good to see you have logged in and are able to access the module. It's great to have you on board"* and *"You are posting in the right place!"* indicated that I "acknowledged" learner acclamations that they had managed to log in despite their initial reservations; I also "guided" learners by reminding them *"not to breach copyright law when posting resources"* and to *"remember netiquette – be polite, encouraging and friendly"*; and kept learners "informed" *"for those using Twitter … I have set up a hashtag for this module"*. This reflexive realisation caused me to extend Sorensen and Baylen's (2004) original framework from (1) initiating, (2) supporting, (3) challenging, (4) summarising and (5) monitoring to include: (6) acknowledging, (7) guiding and (8) informing. The extension to the original directed content analysis model reflected more clearly my online teacher interaction behaviours, and allowed for the incorporation of all my online contributions to the online module.

Situational analysis (Clarke and Friese, 2007; Salazar-Perez and Cannella, 2013) was the method included as the locus for analysing the online module as the situation in which I was examining my online teaching as a neophyte online teacher. Clarke (2016c: 89) calls for researchers to position "the analysis deeply and explicitly in the broader situation of inquiry of the research project", which suggested that situational analysis was likely to give me insight into how I responded to the heterogenous contexts of the actions and discourse that occurred in the online module that I had already visualised using social network analysis (Figure 14.7). Situational analysis gave credence to, yet went beyond, the human actions within the online teaching situation, with Clarke (2016a) defending the importance of considering the non-human elements within a situation if the researcher truly wishes to understand the full context of the situation under review. Indeed, Jones (2015: 67) claims that whilst learning online is a "broadly social approach … it doesn't exclude accounts of the individual in their social and material context". Examples therefore, of material or socio-material non-human elements from the perspective of my research were the physical or software technologies used to interact with the online module, the media used to present resources, and the discourse itself, that represented the online module as the situation under study (Figure 14.8).

This somewhat messy situational map draws together the heterogeneous contexts of actions and discourse that occurred in my online teaching model. Although it has already been noted that online teaching can be perceived as a broadly social approach, I was also interested in how individuals (including myself) responded to the social and material context

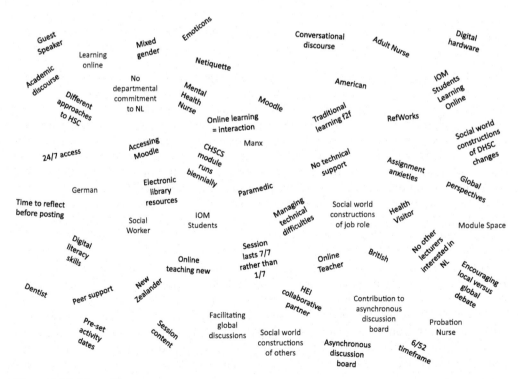

Figure 14.8 Messy Map.

in which the online module was presented. In earlier representations of situational analysis as method, Clarke (2005) called for the production of an abstract visual situational matrix, to demonstrate how "the conditional elements of the situation need to be specified in the analysis of the situation itself as *they are constitutive of it*, not merely surrounding it or framing it or contributing to it. They *are* it" [italics in original] (Clarke, 2016b: 98).

In Figure 14.9 I illustrate how the conditional elements might be mapped. My example begins by randomly focusing on "academic discourse" and the potential relationships made by connecting "academic discourse" to for example, "netiquette, conversational discourse, social world constructions of others" and other categories on the map. The researcher then memo's perceived meanings, silences and noticings between each relational connection that has been highlighted, to try to make sense of the relationships (if any) between human-human and human to non-human elements.

Clarke (2005) suggests that the situational maps are replicated, so that each element can be considered in turn and mapped to the other elements and the process of memoing begins again. This allows the researcher to re-focus on each element and their relationships, to try to make sense of the human and non-human relational connections to the situation.

I experienced some tensions regarding the interpretation of my data as it was presented in my auto-netnographic research, acknowledged in part by recognising that any prior knowledge had been enhanced by immersion in the literature and theoretical development of auto-netnography, and the ongoing use of self as researcher-and-the-researched. At this juncture, I recognised that auto-netnography could be criticised for being a "highly self-reflective and introspective process, [and] unless there [was] a methodological way of keeping a distance from this process, [I could have easily fallen] in to self-absorption" (Chang, 2008: 96).

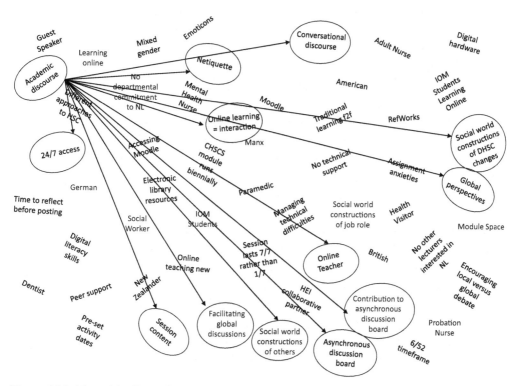

Figure 14.9 Messy Map Example.

From a methodological perspective, introspection is purposeful for auto-netnographers who include reflexive "mindful self-observation" (Gould, 1995: 720) to answer their research question in the context of the social group of which they are a part. The research question will have been determined by auto-netnography as methodology and should include the self. Converse to the concerns for the potential for self-absorption by Chang (2008), I argue that introspection does not necessarily lead to self-absorption. However, to elevate the credibility and trustworthiness of my findings, thus liming the potential for self-absorption, I interpreted, analysed and compared my findings with peer-reviewed literature, using Srivastava and Hopwood's (2009: 78) reflexive analysis framework (RAF) as a lens to capture my data holistically:

Q1: What are the data telling me? (Explicitly engaging with theoretical, subjective, onto-logical, epistemological, and field understandings);

Q2: What is it I want to know? (According to research objectives, questions, and theoret-ical points of interest); and,

Q3: What is the dialectical relationship between what the data are telling me and what I want to know? (Refining the focus and linking back to research questions).

I found the RAF particularly helpful as a framework to analyse not only qualitative, but also quantitative data that I had qualitised (Sandelowski, 2000). The reflexivity inherent within auto-netnography was echoed in the RAF, and caused me to consider through reflexive interpretation of existing peer-reviewed literature on online teaching, how I interpreted what the data were telling me in the context of my "subjective perspectives, ontological and epistemological positions, and intuitive field understandings" (Srivastava and Hopwood, 2009: 78). This combination of data collection methods that included textual analysis, graphic analysis, social network analysis and situational analysis when considered in com-bination with the RAF, contributed to resolve some of the etic-emic tensions that can be experienced as the researcher-and-the-researched. Reflexive interpretation, therefore, goes beyond reflection that focuses on a specific aspect of practice to incorporate the reflexive multidimensional interpretation of my data. In keeping with Alvesson and Skoldberg's (2009: 262) definition of reflexive interpretation to scaffold this activity, I incorporated "a demand for reflection in [my] research in conjunction with an interpretation at several levels: contact with the empirical material, awareness of the interpretive act, clarification of political-ideological contexts, and the handling of the question of representation and authority". Collating data in this way is supportive of what Guba and Lincoln (1982) claim as ontological authenticity, whereby data is represented from both emic insider-researcher, and etic reflexive interpretation perspectives, which I believe enhanced the significance of my findings, and increases the credibility, reliability and trustworthiness of auto-netnography as a methodology. This synthesis of introspective reflexivity and structured effort informed my findings and is in keeping with Kozinets and Gambetti's (2020) inten-tion to explore ways in which auto-netnography can broaden and delimit netnography as a discipline.

AUTHENTIC RELATIONSHIPS WITH OTHERS

There is inadequate guidance in autoethnographic literature about how to limit the ethical tensions that occur when researching the self in the context of communicating with others. Despite a focus on the insider-researcher within auto-netnographic research, ethical consid-erations are extensive; not only might researchers' feel vulnerable if they discover elements of themselves that they did not know existed or may not particularly like (Holman-Jones et al.,

2013), but ethical considerations must be in place for others with whom they interacted in the past, those they interact with in the present, and the potential audience who read their work. Indeed, Chang (2008: 65) claims that even strangers can become connected to the self "through membership of common experiences, if not through personal contacts" and non-ethical auto-netnography could implicate others in a way that they may not appreciate nor have the power to challenge (Turner, 2013).

The ethical considerations required to undertake auto-netnography are extensive, although it has been considered (perhaps naïvely) that writing about oneself might limit the need for ethical consideration (Wall, 2008). One of the complexities I experienced was ensuring that whilst my peer-debriefer had been given a pseudonym, I could not truly preserve her anonymity because the role she played as peer-debriefer was visible to others; she was aware of this, signed a consent form to denote her understanding and was able to read my research to suggest revisions to the content in the context of our conversations. In addition, throughout my auto-netnography, I had inferred relationships with family members and referred to online students (using pseudonyms) and guest speakers (not identified individually). I responded to suggestions by Hung et al. (2004: 194) who asserts that "the mind incorporates person-environment interaction, where activity involves an interaction between person and environment that changes both", by acknowledging that the very nature of any self-disclosure implicates their perception of the behaviours of, for example, their family, friends, colleagues and others with whom they have interacted throughout their personal and professional life.

To ameliorate this, I specifically tried to represent those who were unable to represent themselves within my auto-netnographic writing by seeking their consent to be included in my research. Because all relationships are based on trust (Couser, 2004), the close proximity of my family and the potential power differential between the online students, guest speakers and myself, ethical reporting of my findings needed to be delicately balanced. Whilst I felt tensions between exploring my experiences of online teaching, and wrote purely from my own perspective, I realise that by referring to others, I automatically revealed elements of their world that they may consider private.

CRITICAL REFLEXIVITY

Critical reflexivity derives from "critical theory, post structural, and postmodern commitments to unsettle the assumptions underlying textual, theoretical and ideological positions as a basis for thinking more critically about social and organizational policies and practice" (Cunliffe, 2009: 93). Using critical reflexivity to gain insight into my data allowed me to progress from inductive data analysis to thematic findings. I looked for recurrences within my data sets, the silences that emerged from omissions I had made, connections between my past and present, the way in which I contributed to the online community to which I was "invariably bound" (Chang, 2008: 27) with the learners. My findings were further interrogated by critique and reflexive interpretation of literature relevant to respond to the descriptive findings as they were presented, until I felt ready to determine the core themes and focus my analysis on integrating that data. The way in which I presented each theme, was reflective of my own interpretation of the data which in turn demonstrated "how the emic/etic duality play[ed] out in [my] studies, rather than attempting to hide it" (Hughes and Pennington, 2017: 67). This relationship between emic and etic duality appears to indicate a special quality of auto-netnography, by "unlimiting" the contemporary aspects of netnography to extend participant-observation to include self-observation as the researcher-and-the-researched, and to incorporate digital approaches to collect data from these dual perspectives in parallel.

DIALOGUE WITH SELF AND OTHERS

I have experienced rejection of the value of auto-netnography by peers who argued that this subjective, self-orientated paradigm was so far removed from the more readily accepted modernist qualitative researchers' interpretative worldview that it was too introspective to be empirically sound. Despite mindful introspection being a core methodological attribute of auto-netnography, my peer-debriefer played an important role; she agreed to challenge my assumptions through reading and responding to my memos as well as turning two reflexive interviews on me that were recorded, transcribed and used as additional data to inform my findings. Indeed, the "point of reflexive interpretation is to bring out these aspects more clearly both during the process of [my] research and in the (final) textual product" (Alvesson and Skoldberg, 2009: 272). The need, therefore, to expose my own philosophical stance, demonstrate probity (Allen-Collinson, 2013) and develop an informed perspective on the emergence of auto-netnography as a methodology to inform digitally mediated education, was vital to ensure that the most robust and trustworthy evidence came to the fore.

REPORTING FINDINGS

Finally, the auto-netnographic framework calls for demonstrating trustworthiness, credibility and reliability in reporting the findings and claiming the significance of those findings. To draw the data together, I immersed myself in the primary and secondary labelling (4-W) within my data-log, to evaluate the characteristics of each data set (Table 14.1). As I reflect upon this element of the auto-netnographic framework, I am reminded of an opinion from Mills (2000: 3) who asserts that

> what ordinary men are directly aware of and what they try to do are bound by the private orbits in which they live; their visions and their powers are limited to the close-up scenes of job, family, neighbourhood; in other milieu, they move vicariously and remain spectators.

Employing auto-netnography as the methodology for my research took me on a journey into (an)other milieu, and one that was once less familiar to me than it is now. The sensitive nature of one of my findings (a fragile self-belief and sense of vulnerability and being "exposed" as an imposter to online teaching) placed me in a vicarious position where the significance of understanding why and how I felt how I did, needed to be presented in such a way to denote an honest, credible, reliable and trustworthy explanation (Freshwater et al., 2010). Conversely, other findings included the positive aspects of promoting learner autonomy, and having the confidence to reposition my online teaching practice through experiencing self-actualisation when I recognised that I could transfer many of my face-to-face teaching skills into the online context (albeit in a different way). Significantly, the very nature of auto-netnography is that the importance of the insider-researcher's findings are inextricably linked to their own worldview (Muncey, 2010; Chang, 2008; Adams et al., 2015), which as explained earlier, is likely to be different to the way the reader might perceive their significance.

Reporting the findings in any ethnographic research needs to be ethically sound (Tullis, 2013), and no less so in the context of auto-netnographic research. Albeit challenging at times, I argue that the auto-netnography framework will support researchers' aspirations to demonstrate ethical research significance, credibility, reliability and trustworthiness of researching social media as an educational tool (Haythornthwaite et al., 2016).

CONCLUSION

This chapter has briefly explored the concept of auto-netnography in the context of "netnography unlimited". I have shared with you my understanding of auto-netnography and some of the methods I used to examine my practice as an online teacher. I have claimed that immersion in the data, grounded by critical reflexivity and reflexive interpretation is the key to researching the digitally mediated self in the context of the auto-netnography framework. Despite explaining the discomfort I felt as I deconstructed the emotional aspects of my findings, these feelings ultimately empowered me to reframe my emotions and direct my development as an online teacher. This unique feature of auto-netnography draws together the opportunity of researching aspects of the self, living and/or working with digital media in a way in which other methods do not.

Whilst the focus of this chapter has been specific to how auto-netnography can be utilised to chronicle any teacher as an insider-researcher as they interpret and understand ways of connecting with their students by developing and sharing knowledge through social media, auto-netnography is not limited to education. Auto-netnography can be applied to any aspect of human connection with digitally mediated endeavour. Some examples of non-educational auto-netnographies might include: (1) nurses examining how they monitor and interpret digitally mediated vital signs observations from a remote critical outreach office and knowing when it is important to react and visit the patient in person; (2) the development of mobile applications to encourage tourists to visit local heritage sights; and, (3) using digital programming to predict weather warnings and create weather alerts.

I end this chapter the way in which it began, by concluding that auto-netnography is one way of "umlimiting netnography". This is not the end of a journey, but a new beginning that is defined by other insider-researchers using, critiquing and extending the foundations of auto-netnography to build upon the theoretical and practical application of auto-netnography presented in this chapter. Remember, it is the "auto" in auto-netnography, that connects with netnography to delimit its application in any digitally mediated field of practice.

REFERENCES

Adams, T.E, Holman-Jones, S. and Ellis, C. (2015) *Autoethnography: Understanding Qualitative Research*. Oxford: Oxford University Press.

Ahmed, W. (2019) Using Twitter as a data source: Overview of social media research tools (2019). *LSE Impact Blog*. London School of Economics and Political Science.

Allen-Collinson, J. (2013) Autoethnography as the engagement of self/other, self/culture, self/politics, and selves/futures. In: Holman Jones, S., Adams, T.E. and Ellis, C. (eds) *Handbook of Autoethnography*. Walnut Creek, California: Left Coast Press, Inc., 281–299.

Alvesson, M. and Skoldberg, K. (2009) *Reflexive Methodology: New Vistas for Qualitative Research*. London: Sage Publications Ltd.

Anderson, J., Adey, P. and Bevan, P. (2010) Positioning place: Polylogic approaches to research methodology. *Qualitative Research* 10: 589–604.

Avgerinou, M.D. and Andersson, C. (2006) Perceptions of qualities, roles, and functions: The online teacher perspective. In: Sampson, D.G., Spector, J.M. and Isaias, P. (eds) *Cognition and Exploratory Learning in Digital Age*. Barcelona, Spain: International Association for Development of the Information Society (IADIS), 35–44.

Biggs, J. (2011) *Teaching for Quality Learning at University: What the Student Does*. Maidenhead, Berkshire: Open University Press.

Booth, K. (2015) What a difference place makes: Place gestalt and some methodological thoughts. *Qualitative Inquiry* 21: 20–27.

Bucher, T. and Helmond, A. (2017) The affordances of social media platforms. In: Burgess, J., Poell, T. and Marwick, A. (eds) *The SAGE Handbook of Social Media*. London: Sage Publications Limited, 233–253.

Chang, H. (2008) *Autoethnography as Method.* Walnut Creek, CA: Left Coast Press Inc.

Clarke, A. (2005) *Situational Analysis: Grounded Theory After the Postmodern Turn,* Thousand Oaks, CA: Sage Publications Inc.

Clarke, A. (2016a) Feminism, Grounded Theory, and Situational Analysis Revisited. In: Clarke, A., Friese, C. and Washburn, R. (eds) *Situational Analysis in Practice.* Oxon: Routledge, 119–154.

Clarke, A. (2016b) From grounded theory to situational analysis. What's new? Why? How? In: Clarke, A., Friese, C. and Washburn, R. (eds) *Situational Analysis in Practice.* Oxon: Routledge, 84–118.

Clarke, A. (2016c) Introducing situational analysis. In: Clarke, A., Friese, C. and Washburn, R. (eds) *Situational Analysis in Practice.* Oxon: Routledge, 11–75.

Clarke, A. and Friese, C. (2007) Grounded theorizing using situational analysis. In: Bryant, A. and Charmaz, K. (eds) *The Sage Handbook of Grounded Theory.* Thousand Oaks, CA: Sage Publications Inc., 363–398.

Closs, L. and Antonello, C.S. (2011) Transformative learning: Integration critical reflection into management education. *Journal of Transformative Learning* 9: 63–88.

Couser, G. (2004) *Vulnerable Subjects: Ethics and Life Writing.* Ithaca, NY: Cornell University Press.

Cowan, J.E. and Menchaca, M.P. (2014) Investigating value creation in a community of practice with social network analysis in a hybrid online graduate education program. *Distance Education* 35: 43–74.

Cunliffe, A.L. (2009) The philosopher leader: On relationalism, ethics and reflexivity – a critical perspective to teaching leadership. *Management Learning* 40: 87–101.

D'Cruz, H., Gillingham, P. and Melendez, S. (2007) Reflexivity, its meanings and relevance for social work: A critical review of the literature. *Journal of Social Work* 37: 73–90.

Denzin, N.K. (2014) *Interpretive Autoethnography.* Thousand Oaks, CA: Sage Publications Inc.

DeSanctis, G. and Poole, M.S. (1994) Capturing the complexity in advanced technology use: Adaptive structuration theory. *Organization Science* 5: 121–147.

Doiron, J.G. (2018) Emojis: Visual communication in higher education. *International Journal of Teaching, Education and Learning* 2: 1–11.

Dringus, L.P. and Ellis, T. (2010) Temporal transitions in participation flow in an asynchronous discussion forum. *Computers & Education* 54: 340–349.

Dunlap, J.C., Bose, D., Lowenthal, P.R., et al. (2016) What sunshine is to flowers: A literature review on the use of emoticons to support online learning. In: Tettegah, S.Y. and Gartmeier, M. (eds) *Emotions, Design, Learning and Technology.* London: Elsevier, 163–182.

Ellingson, L.L. (2011) Analysis and representation across the continuum. In: Denzin, N.K. and Lincoln, Y.S. (eds) *The SAGE Handbook of Qualitative Research.* 4th ed. Thousand Oaks, CA: Sage Publications Inc, 595–610.

Figg, C., Wenrick, M., Youker, C., et al. (2010) Implications and benefits of a long-term peer debriefing experience on teacher researchers. *Brock Education: A Journal of Educational Research and Practice* 19: 20–35.

Freshwater, D., Cahill, J., Walsh, E., et al. (2010) Qualitative research as evidence: Criteria for rigour and relevance. *Journal of Research in Nursing* 15: 497–508.

Freshwater, D. and Rolfe, G. (2001) Critical reflexivity: A politically and ethically engaged research method for nursing. *Nursing Times Research* 6: 526–567.

Gould, S.J. (1995) Researcher introspection as a method in consumer research: Applications, issues, and implications. *Journal of Consumer Research* 21: 719–722.

Guba, E.G. and Lincoln, Y.S. (1982) Epistemological and methodological bases of naturalistic inquiry. *Educational Communication and Technology Journal* 30: 233–252.

Guba, E.G. and Lincoln, Y.S. (2005) Paradigmatic controversies, contradictions, and emerging confluences. In: Denzin, N.K. and Lincoln, Y.S. (eds) *The Sage Handbook of Qualitative Research.* Thousand Oaks: Sage Publications, 191–215.

Haythornthwaite, C., Andrews, R., Fransman, J., et al. (2016) Introduction to the SAGE Handbook of E-learning Research. In: Haythornthwaite, C., Andrews, R., Fransman, J., et al. (eds) *The SAGE Handbook of E-learning Research.* London: Sage Publications Ltd, 3–21.

Henning, T. (2012) Writing professor as adult learner: An autoethnography of online professional development. *Journal of Asynchronous Learning Networks* 16: 9–26.

Hodgson, V., McConnell, D. and Dirckinck-Holmfeld, L. (2012) The theory, practice and pedagogy of networked learning. In: Dirckinck-Holmfeld, L., Hodgson, V. and McConnell, D. (eds) *Exploring the Theory, Pedagogy and Practice of Networked Learning.* New York: Springer, 291–306.

Holman-Jones, S., Adams, T.E. and Ellis, C. (2013) Coming to know autoethnography as more than a method. In: Holman-Jones, S., Adams, T.E. and Ellis, C. (eds) *Handbook of Autoethnography.* Walnut Creek, CA: Left Coast Press, Inc., 17–48.

Howard, L. (2016) An exploration of autonetnography as an eResearch methodology to examine learning and teaching scholarship in Networked Learning. *The Electronic Journal of e-Learning* 14: 322–335.

Howard, L. (2019) Casting the 'net' in autonetnography: Exploring the potential of autonetnography as an emerging eResearch methodology. In: Huisman, J. and Tight, M. (eds) *Theory and Method in Higher Education.* United Kingdom: Emerald Publishing Limited, 163–187.

Hughes, S.A. and Pennington, J.L. (2017) *Autoethnography: Process, Product, and Possibility for Critical Social Research.* Thousand Oaks, California: Sage Publications, Inc.

Hung, D., Looi, C.K. and Koh, T.S. (2004) Situated cognition and communities of practice: First-person "lived experiences" vs. third-person perspectives. *Educational Technology & Society* 7: 193–200.

Jiang, J.A., Fiesler, C. and Brubaker, J.R. (2018) 'The perfect one': Understanding communication practices and challenges with animated GIFs. *Proceedings of the ACM on Human-Computer Interaction – CSCW* 2: 1–20.

Jingqain, Z., Sung, W. and Jiarui, C. (2016) Emerging trends in social media. *International Journal of Computer Techniques* 3: 49–53.

Jones, C. (2015) *Networked Learning: An Educational Paradigm for the Age of Digital Networks.* Switzerland: Springer International Publishing.

Keefer, J.M. (2010) Autoethnographer communities of practice. In: Dirckinck-Holmfeld, L., Hodgson, V., Jones, C., et al. (eds) *7th International Conference on Networked Learning 2010.* Lancaster University, United Kingdom, 207–214.

Kozinets, R.V. (2015) *Netnography: Redefined.* London: Sage Publications Ltd.

Kozinets, R.V. (2020) *Netnography: The Essential Guide to Qualitative Social Media Research.* London: Sage Publications Ltd.

Kozinets, R.V. and Gambetti, R. (2020) Netnography Unlimited. London: Routledge.

Kozinets, R.V. and Kedzior, R. (2009) 'I, Avatar: Auto-netnographic research in virtual worlds. In: Solomon, M. and Wood, N. (eds) *Virtual Social Identity and Social Behavior.* Armonk, NY: M.E. Sharpe, 3–19.

Mezirow, J. (1991) *Transformative Dimensions of Adult Learning.* San Fransisco, CA: Jossey-Bass.

Mills, C.W. (2000) *The Sociological Imagination.* New York: Oxford University Press Inc.

Muncey, T. (2010) *Creating Autoethnographies.* London: Sage Publications Ltd.

Pohl, H., Domin, C. and Pohs, M. (2017) Beyond just text: Semantic emoji similarity modeling to support expressive communication. *ACM Transactions on Computer-Human Interaction* 24: 1–41.

Rogers, T., Dawson, S. and Gasevic, D. (2016) Learning analytics and the imperative for theory-driven research. In: Haythornthwaite, C., Andrews, R., Fansman, J., et al. (eds) *The SAGE Handbook of E-learning Research.* London: SAGE Publications Ltd, 232–250.

Salazar-Perez, M. and Cannella, G. (2013) Situational analysis as an avenue for critical qualitative research. *Qualitative Inquiry* 19: 505–517.

Sandelowski, M. (2000) Combining qualitative and quantitative sampling, data collection, and analysis techniques in mixed-method studies. *Research in Nursing and Health* 23: 246–255.

Shea, P. and Bidjerano, T. (2013) Understanding distinctions in learning in hybrid, and online environments: an empirical investigation of the community of inquiry framework. *Interactive Learning Environments* 21: 355–370.

Sorensen, C.K. and Baylen, D.M. (2004) Patterns of communicative and interactive behavior online. *The Quarterly Review of Distance Education* 5: 117–126.

Srivastava, P. and Hopwood, N. (2009) A practical iterative framework for qualitative data analysis. *International Journal of Qualitative Methods* 8: 76–84.

Stepanyan, K., Mather, R. and Dalrymple, R. (2014) Culture, role and group work: A social network analysis perspective on an online collaborative course. *British Journal of Educational Technology* 45: 676–693.

Swan, K., Garrison, D.R. and Richardson, J. (2009) A constructivist approach to online learning: The community of inquiry framework. In: Payne, C. (ed) *Information Technology and Constructivism in Higher Education: Progressive Learning Frameworks.* Hershey, PA: IGI Global, 43–57.

Tang, Y. and Foon Hew, K. (2019) Emoticon, emoji, and sticker use in computer-mediated communication: A review of theories and research findings. *International Journal of Communication* 13: 2457–2483.

Tullis, J.A. (2013) Self and others: Ethics in autoethnographic research. In: Holman Jones, S., Adams, T.E. and Ellis, C. (eds) *Handbook of Autoethnography*. Walnut Creek, California: Left Coast Press, Inc., 244–261.

Turner, L. (2013) The evocative autoethnographic I: The relational ethics of writing about oneself. In: Short, N.P., Turner, L. and Grant, A. (eds) *Contemporary British Autoethnography*. Rotterdam: Sense Publishers, 213–229.

Vanden Abeele, M., De Wolf, R. and Ling, R. (2018) Mobile media and social space: How anytime, anyplace connectivity structures everyday life. *Media and Communication* 6: 5–14.

Villegas, D. (2018) From the self to the screen: A journey guide for auto-netnography in online communities. *Journal of Marketing Management* 34: 243–262.

Wachowski, L. and Wachowski, L. (1999) *The Matrix*. Warner Brothers.

Wall, S. (2008) Easier said than done: Writing an autoethnography. *International Journal of Qualitative Methods* 7: 38–53.

Wentzel, A. (2016) Creating the literature review: research questions and arguments. *Doctoral Writing SIG*.

White, J. (2016) *Permission: The International Interdisciplinary Impact of Laurel Richardson's Work*. Rotterdam: Sense Publishers.

White, S. (2001) Autoethnography as reflexive enquiry: The research act as self surveillance. In: Shaw, I. and Gould, N. (eds) *Qualitative Research in Social Work*. London: Sage, 100–115.

Worden, J. (2014). Articulating breath: Writing Charcot's hysteric with performance writing. *Arts & Humanities in Higher Education* 13(3), 318–325.

15

Getting Up-Close and Personal with Influencers

The Promises and Pitfalls of Intimate Netnography

Anthony Patterson and Rachel Ashman

INTRODUCTION

Since the rise of the "reflexive turn" in qualitative research, it has been widely acknowledged that the reign of the insider-outsider model of inquiry is over (Denzin & Lincoln, 2005; Mann 2016). The result of this assertion is that researchers and cultural informants are today recognised as inseparable. The netnographer has considerable agency to colour the inter-action with his/her cultural informants and, as a consequence, the acquisition of non-neutral data and knowledge is impossible (Demirdirek, 2010). In this chapter we posit that studying digital influencers, or to use the more benign term, content creators, as we generally do, via netnography, produces such an intensified and heightened entwinement of researcher and subject that its exceptionality is worthy of discussion.

We will draw upon our experience of conducting netnographic research with said indi-viduals (Kozinets et al, 2017; Ashman et al, 2018), engagement with the ever-growing body of nethnographic research (e.g. Björk & Kauppinen-Räisänen, 2012; Weijo et al, 2014; Martensen et al, 2018) and the fecund theoretically grounded literature of traditional quali-tative research. In the midst of conducting a netnography on any particular influencer's micro-community with global span, we were always mindful to follow the commonplace logic that in order for our findings to be valuable and insightful, establishing a rapport with them at the beginning of the research process is crucial (Keegan, 2009). To achieve this, it was obviously important to be personally and emotionally engaged in the research process and to mirror their behaviour.

In this respect, the second author led the way. Her emotional engagement allows her to mirror behaviour when out in the field, whether attending events, viewing online content or interacting with them in person, virtually or in writing. This was instinctual for her, since she shares many of the same interests, behaviours and characteristics as the study group. She is natural predisposed to intently follow their endeavour and has been doing so for years. She voluntarily immerses herself daily in their cultural world by viewing hour upon hour of footage on YouTube and the like. But such immersion can also create problems of its own. As Gilbert (2001, 13) points out while discussing the general emotionality of qualita-tive research: "an in-depth and long-term contact with the phenomenon, and the evolving emotional environment of the researcher's own social world may result in a lack of clarity or 'fuzziness' in boundaries".

In this chapter we discuss how we continually negotiated and renegotiated these bound-aries each time we stepped into the dynamic datastream of our netnographic projects. We begin by more deeply exploring why intimacy between content creators and researchers is so pronounced. We show as an ongoing part of the research process, how we sought to balance the promises and pitfalls of being too deeply imbedded in or too far removed from the lives of the influencers that we studied.

COSYING UP TO CONTENT CREATORS

The digital influencers or content creators that we have studied, have for the most part accumulated and monetised a relatively large online following by visually and textually narrating their personal lives and lifestyles across an integrated array of social media sites. They are a broad church of competing bloggers, vloggers, Instagrammers, tweeters, and TikTokers commissioned by advertisers on the promise that in addition to creating a per-sistent stream of output, they will pitch sponsored content at those who follow them. The winsome nature of their "online traces" (Kozinets, 2020, 18), lies in the curated manner in which they package and distribute the intimate minutiae of their everyday lives. Remarkably, they have managed to make real what Balick (2018, 73) describes as the "The marketer's desire to make consuming objects out of socialising subjects". In doing so, they create self-brands that commodify privacy and normalise extreme candour (Abidin, 2017). All might, though, not be what it seems. As Burkart (2010, 23) astutely notes, "when the private self goes public, however, the character of authentic self-disclosure begins to shift to a dramatized, strategic self-presentation and theatrical self-expression".

To study them is to follow them. To follow them is to expose oneself to their intimate wiles and styles. Their entire success, bound up in the novel experience of closeness they offer, can be understood as a triumph of authenticity masquerading as "mediated intimacy" (Chambers, 2013; Hart, 2018; Farci et al, 2017). Of course, no form of intimacy can be said to be truly unmediated. Even a legacy media, like that created by the postal system, is well-recognised as creating a new form of sociality. It allowed, for example, the practice of writing love letters – brimful of romantic and erotic intent – to flourish (Ahearn, 2001). While, to some extent, it is true that all new media, as Fornäs et al (2002, p. 30) presciently indicate "offered entrances to imagined spaces or 'virtual realities', opening up symbolic worlds for transgressive experiences", online mediated intimacy, especially that espoused by influencers, is undoubtedly a peculiar entity. Below we tease apart two of its more obvious incarnations: the adoption of a casual and playful manner of communication and displaying high levels of disclosure.

OPERATING UNDER CONDITIONS OF INTIMACY

One peculiarity of the relationship between netnographer and influencer is that the balance of power might slant in an unexpected asymmetric fashion. Normally, the investigator sets the rules and holds more social and linguistic capital than the cultural informant (Murphy & Dingwall, 2001). Influencers, however, emboldened with the status of micro-celebrity (Raun, 2018) and an audience clambering for their attention (Marwick, 2015), might well hold the balance of power and as such be able to dictate the rules of engagement. In either eventuality, we recommend that a netnographer should combat this asymmetry, however it is slanted, via the process of mirroring. Mirroring allows one to establish a simple social connection that helps understand the intentions and motivations of others and create an emotional bond with them (Iacoboni, 2009).

Thus, when an influencer displays a *casual and playful manner of communication* we imi-tate them. To elaborate, typically, though not always, in their videos they adopt a persona that is outgoing and chatty and almost as effervescent as a radio DJ. In addition, bloopers are rarely edited, but are instead milked for their comedic value. The more inchoate and unscripted it seems, the better. Friends are often on set to bounce ideas off and to create an intimate atmosphere of jocose persiflage. While intimating their intense friendship, invariably they gently poke fun at one another. Tangential asides, far removed from the theme of the video, are also frequently thrown into the mix in revelatory fashion. These are not too be dismissed, as they open a door into the content creator's inner world. This notion of being taken backstage, of seeing the influencer at their most raw and vulnerable is increasingly indicative of the genre (Mardon et al., 2018). The overall effect on the viewer is like being an observer in someone's front room. You literally are a "fly on the wall".

As voyeuristic, participant-observing netnographers we learn to fit in. We adopt a similar mode of communication in our correspondence with them, when we comment, for instance, on the threads attached to their updates or when we interview them. The intimate and imitative nature of such communication has meant that on occasion, as a consequence, real lasting friendships have emerged between us and the cultural informants that we collaborated with. Close friendships characterised by emotional involvement can, of course, get in the way of serious scholarship. One way that we attempt to mitigate against our emotions is simply through the practice of keeping detailed fieldnotes. Such notes, according to Kozinets (2015) let "the reality of what you are actually perceiving appear to you mirrored back through reflective notes on whatever it is you choose to record" (Kozinets, 2015, 189). This helps to retain a separation from the field of study. A typical entry in said journal might describe the netnographer's attitudes, behaviours and assumptions about how they relate to the community being researched:

It was a swift and seamless transition between looking at blogs and checking out Instagram images into exploring the depths of YouTube. I got hooked to watching videos quite quickly and they were not always to do with food. I was amazed that there were so many people sharing videos. From families making daily vlogs to others showing epic mealtimes and Zoella waxing lyrical about the newest beauty and fashion products. From strange videos showing people getting enormous spots popped up-close to others brushing their hair with high-quality sound recordings, I have a look at it all. I mostly like seeing the more mundane aspects of life though. I love watching daily vlogs, of people showing their routines, or their holidays, or the way they get out for work in the morning. I feel like I learn a lot about life from these videos. I can see what people are up to and be a fly on the wall for the first time. I was and still am addicted to watching YouTube videos. I find it very relaxing to tune into somebody's life for a while and let them take the reins, to show me how they do things. I think from watching others I get a sense that I am not alone and that I am OK, other people are doing the same things as me. I can also learn so much. I can see how people function, and that can help me to function too, in a better, more productive way. I can keep on top of things and know that I have a little place of safety to reside in if I can't be bothered to be present in my own life for a while. When I am watching YouTube I don't feel that I am doing nothing, I feel that I am contributing to a bank of knowledge about life that can assist me in having a better one.

(Extract from unpublished fieldnotes)

Keeping fieldnotes thus reflexively monitors our response to the persons being studied and acts as an internal reminder of our different worldviews.

Another aspect of conducting netnography on influencers is that you are often exposed *high levels of disclosure*. Influencers are so highly skilled in the art of getting intimate with their audience that they often seem to act as their own public psychoanalysts. They use the medium of the video confessional – Instagram Stories serves as the vehicle of the moment – to endlessly critique why they did what they did, and cliché though it is, why what they did was so damn difficult, but ultimately worth it in the end. They regularly deliver these confessionals without make-up direct to camera, seemingly "telling it like it is". A common narrative is articulated by this anonymous content creator whose recent daily titbit began:

> Today was that day I made myself vulnerable, stepped outside of my comfort zone and stood in a room full of teenagers and gave my story. I opened up about how easily I got caught up in the danger zones of life these days. Drugs, debts, depression, suicide attempts, failed relationships, the lot!

Such posts also stand in direct contrast to the more posed and curated stream of content that is permanently uploaded to their Instagram profiles.

Constant exposure to such high levels of emotionality, could perhaps cloud one's judgement. Content creators, as we have illustrated, try every "trick in the book" to make themselves relatable and "persuade their followers to identify with them" (Abidin, 2017, 161). This mutual intimacy where researchers are deeply ensconced in the world of influencers and influencers are equally cosy with any investigative followers, might be too close for comfort. It is a symbiotic relationship that could obstruct a netnographer's ability to be an empowered interpreter with the sense of perspective that a little distance allows. With this in mind, alongside the absolute need for researcher immersion in online fieldwork, we have found that netnographic work cannot be rushed. To retain perspective, it is important to see each project in longitudinal fashion where ideally considerable time – often years – are spend just observing, listening and describing. The passage of time allows for the necessary perspective to be garnered.

More than anything, though, we feel that getting to know a cultural informant intimately helps enrich the quality of the netnography. For instance, consider our recent paper that explores the downsides of casting of content creators – autopreneurs as we called them – as ambitious, go-getting entrepreneurs (Ashman et al, 2018). Presenting the empirical case for our Foucauldian-inspired theory that their desire to succeed occurs not so much because of an innate internal drive, but more because of neoliberal externalities that affect how they think and act, would not have been as insightful had we not developed a deep friendship and rapport with our cultural informants. Consider this telling quotation that we did not have space to explore in our original *Journal of Business Research* paper. To the question, "And would you say you're still excited about products? Do they excite you like they used to?", an influencer responds:

> To be honest, no. The odd thing really does, and that shows me how good it is. But no, I'm not as excited anymore, about products. I think you get a little bit immune to it, to getting sent stuff in the end. Especially when it's brands sending you stuff without even asking, and they send you stuff, and it's like, I didn't even ask for this, I don't really like it. And you feel really bad about it. But there are a lot of things that I am like, oh this is great. But I'm not like, ooh my God, it's amazing, the way I probably would have been right at the beginning. It's not the same as buying stuff yourself. You get much more gratification buying stuff yourself.

The influencer in question obviously made this comment in complete confidence and would be unlikely to allude to such sentiments via a public interface with her followers. After all, generating excitement of the new is the currency in which she trades. Its searing honesty takes us beyond any Goffmanian look behind the scenes – which, as we have earlier shown, has today become just another informal place to front a performance – to an inner sanctum that would otherwise remain inaccessible. Such is the power of intimately conducted netnography.

INFLUENCING CONTENT CREATORS

Thus far we have presented a persuasive account of the mutual entanglement of netnographer and content creator. It may seem slightly contradictory, therefore, to follow this assertion with another that discusses the difficulty of reaching these eminently contactable individuals. Nonetheless, despite their apparent obtainability online they can remain highly elusive offline, especially when you want to meet them for an interview. It is perhaps understandable given the number of oddballs who develop unhealthy obsessions with their online muses, why they might be reluctant to meet a follower in the flesh. Moreover, many content creators, especially those of mega-magnitude, are hardworking "instafamous" jetsetters with exceptionally busy schedules. When there is money to be made, products to launch and parties to attend, giving an hour of their precious time to talk to engage in a research project can be far down their agenda. Circumventing this problem is not easy. Unless you know someone, who knows someone, who knows someone ... aka the six degrees of separation theory, you might find it impossible to interview a key informant of note. Nonetheless, there are useful strategies that one can employ. One way of meeting content creators that we have used to good effect on a number of projects, is to attend a few of the ever-multiplying annual influencer conferences and get-togethers. By going to events organised by Vidcon, Communities Unite, London Bloggers Meetup and the Bloggers Festival, and carefully drawing upon our years of netnographic engagement and experience with key members of those events while in situ, we have managed to persuade powerful content creators to participate in our research. Following such cultural entrées, we subsequently employ the tried and tested snowballing technique whereby additional cultural informants are referred to us by these initial contacts.

COPING WITH DATA EVAPORATION

Contrary to the assertion that once something has been posted on the internet it is there forever (Eichhorn, 2019), we increasingly find, that much of the content that content creators post can, after a short while, disappear into digital ether. The implication being catch it now or it is gone forever. They operate in a similar fashion to the trusty marketing sales pitch that urgently proclaims, "Act now. Order today. Limited time only". Instagram stories, for instance, are only available for 24 hours and, on occasion, especially when controversies arise, YouTubers have been known to delete offending videos, or archive old ones. In recent times, YouTube has also turned comments off on many channels for safeguarding reasons, taking years of rich data away in an instant. Moreover, tools like the *Wayback Machine* are of no use in respect of capturing social media data of this type. In the past, we have been disappointed when in hindsight we realise that a perfect piece of data is no longer accessible. As a consequence, although it is terribly time-consuming and laborious, we try to avoid such situations occurring by recording (transcribing and screenshotting) as much as we can during the timeframe when it is available. All the same, one still has to have an intuitive feel for what might be relevant. One can develop a sense of this by actively reflecting, taking copious fieldnotes, and by maintaining a steady dialogue with co-authors and trusted others. Attempting to be comprehensively record absolutely everything, though, is definitely not advised. The intensity of continuous, around-the-clock netnographic fieldwork can take its toll. Markham's (1998) pioneering account of *Life Online*, does not shy from elaborating on the suffering it wrought upon her body. Her complaints include excruciating back pain, sore hands and a dry throat. To avoid such embodied pain, we highly recommend taking regular breaks from your work. These breaks should not be thought of as time wasted. They are the key to staying in good physical and mental shape. We find that the process of stepping away from a particularly intense bout of fieldwork, perhaps to talk to colleagues, let theory and thought percolate, or just rest, is extremely important. Such breaks often provide the spur that leads to the breakthrough "eureka moment" when everything falls into place (Markham, 1998).

CREATING NOVEL THEORY

Although we have yet to encounter it, there is a danger that the intimate interface between empirical material and researcher, which this chapter details, might lead an unskilled nethnographer, dogged by emotional blinkers, to fall into the trap of producing trivial theory that simply mirrors reality (Waterston & Rylko-Bauer, 2006). While not writing specifically about netnography, we find Alvesson and Sandberg (2014, 34) comments on how to generate useful theory to be particularly instructive. They call "for a more active construction of empirical material in ways that are imaginative, and not just passively waiting for data to show us the route to something interesting". This process is precisely what many netnographers do. Consider how Kozinets et al's (2017) netnography of content creators and other distributors of online food porn entirely reconceptualises the construct of desire. Far from merely paying homage to existing theory, or offering only humble nuances or advances, the authors offer a radically different take on a doxa that previously might have seemed impervious to challenge. Only by imaginatively reflecting on the significance of their data as it interplayed with Deleuze and Guattari's energetic and connective take on desire were the authors able to overturn conventional wisdom and make a fresh and interesting theoretical contribution.

A similar assumption challenging process of creation can be witnessed in Ferreira and Scaraboto's (2016) excellent netnographic study of the Melissa shoe community that coalesces around the online activities of four prominent content creators. Rather than simply following the conventional route of conversing and contributing to theory on the identity-shaping potential of owning branded items of collectable footwear, instead the paper explores how consumer interaction with, and knowledge of, material substances, designer intentions, and marketing efforts served to impact upon both materiality and the cultivation of consumer identity. By drawing upon a broad set of theories, thinking differently about the meaning of their empirical data, and the dialogue between the two, the authors manage to shed new light on object-consumer relations.

FUTURE RESEARCH DIRECTIONS

Since the multifaceted, normative practices of influencers are a relatively new and evolving phenomena, by taking a creative approach to their theory-building efforts, netnographers can make strong and original contributions to the field. We would suggest that understanding the institutions and ideologies that underpin their protean activities should be a priority. Certainly, there is more to be said about the entrepreneurial subjectivity of influencers. Can it really be true, as recent research suggests, that they are not captains of their own destiny, but instead are relatively empty vessels, indoctrinated by the dominant neoliberal ideals that via osmosis have come to structure their subjectivities and permit only limited individual agency (see Ashman et al, 2018; Archer, 2019)? Surely there are content creators, politically engaged activists perhaps, who are immune to the commercial imperatives of broadcasting content?

Urgent netnographic research is also needed on the recent proliferation of computer-generated influencers, which although still in its infancy is about to get much more sophisticated as artificial intelligence and deepfake technology become more widely available. KFC, for instance, recently developed a computer-generated "Virtual Influencer Colonel", who can be found posing on Instagram with his equally fake girlfriend. As a recent report indicates, what accounts for the fact that virtual influencers, who post less regularly than real influencers, get three times more engagement (Carey-Simos, 2019)? Ironically, in the world of influencers, it is possible that being inauthentic provides a route to the fabled land of authenticity.

Another fruitful avenue netnographic fieldwork might be to focus upon the "immaterial labour" (Lazzarato, 1996) conducted by influencers and their followers, specifically that which creates intimacy or an emotional response. The uneasy marriage between the creators of content who voluntarily post videos on YouTube and Instagram, and the institutions who profit from the data this labour unintentionally generates about one's interests, tastes and preferences needs further investigation (Andrejevic, 2014). Such labour, after all, is the sine qua non of the participatory culture that sees prosumers and content creators both scrambling to build self-brands that "build a meaningful, impressive, and recognizable snapshot of the self that will catch the attention of potential employers, customers, or social media followers" (Johnston et al, 2017, 293). With 86 per cent of American teenagers harbouring a desire to become bona fide influencers, the divide between consumer and producer is set to become even more hazy (Hahn, 2019). Considerable fallout will result when these teens realise that their dream career is unlikely to garner a craving audience hanging on their every post. It is certain that the competitive pressures of the market will obliterate the ambitions of even the most determined content creator wannabees. As a consequence, their hours of immaterial labour, from their perspective at least, will have been pointless. Its traces and failed remnants, though, might haunt them throughout their lives. Studies of such failure and its consequences are both opportune and necessary.

REFERENCES

Abidin, C. (2017). Influencer extravaganza: Commercial "lifestyle" microcelebrities in Singapore. In: L. Hjorth, H. Horst, A. Galloway & G. Bell (Eds.). *The Routledge Companion to Digital Ethnography* (pp. 158–168). London: Routledge.

Ahearn, L.M. (2001). *Invitations to Love: Literacy, Love Letters, and Social Change in Nepal.* Ann Arbor, MI: University of Michigan Press.

Alvesson, M., & Sandberg, J. (2014). Problematization meets mystery creation: Generating new ideas and findings through assumption challenging research. In E. Jeanes & T. Huzzard (Eds.). *Research in Critical Management Studies* (pp. 23–39). London: SAGE Publications.

Andrejevic, M. (2014). Alienation's returns. In C. Fuchs & M, Sandoval (Eds.). *Critique, Social Media and the Information Society* (pp. 179–190). London: Routledge.

Archer, C. (2019). Social media influencers, post-feminism and neoliberalism: How mum bloggers 'playbour' is reshaping public relations. *Public Relations Inquiry*, 8(2), 149–166.

Ashman, R,. Patterson, A., & Brown, S. (2018). Don't forget to like, share and subscribe: Digital autopreneurs in a neoliberal world. *Journal of Business Research*, 92, 474–483.

Balick, A. (2018). *The Psychodynamics of Social Networking; Connected-Up Instantaneous Culture and the Self.* New York: Routledge.

Björk, P., & Kauppinen-Räisänen, H. (2012). A netnographic examination of travelers' online discussions of risks. *Tourism Management Perspectives*, 2–3, 65–71.

Burkart, G. (2010). When privacy goes public: New media and the transformation of the culture of confession. In H. Blatterer., P. Johnson & M.R. Markus (Eds.). *Modern Privacy; Shifting Boundaries, New Forms* (pp. 23–38). Hampshire: Palgrave Macmillan.

Carey-Simos, G. (2019, December 2). *Virtual Influencers Have Nearly 3X Higher Engagement Rate Than Real Influencers*. Retrieved from https://wersm.com/report-virtual-influencers-get-nearly-3-times-better-engagement-rate-than-real-influencers/

Chambers, D. (2013). *Social Media and Personal Relationships: Online Intimacies and Networked Friendship*. New York: Palgrave Macmillan.

Demirdirek, H. (2010). Researcher–participant relationship. In A.J. Mills, G. Durepos & E. Wiebe (Eds.). *Encyclopedia of Case Study Research* (pp 810–813). London: Sage.

Denzin, N.K., & Lincoln, Y.S. (Eds.) (2005). *Handbook of Qualitative Research*. 3rd ed. Thousand Oaks: SAGE.

Eichhorn, K. (2019). *The End of Forgetting: Growing Up with Social Media*. London: Harvard University Press.

Farci, M., Rossi, L., Artieri, G., & Fabio Giglietto, F. (2017). Networked intimacy. Intimacy and friendship among Italian Facebook users. *Information, Communication and Society*, 20 (5), 784–801.

Ferreira, M.C., & Scaraboto, D. (2016). "My Plastic dreams": Towards an extended understanding of materiality and the shapes of consumer identities. *Journal of Business Research*, 69, 191–207.

Fornäs, J., Klein, K., Ladendorf, M., Sundén, J., & Sveningsson, M. (2002). Into digital borderlands. In J. Fornäs, K. Klein, M. Ladendorf, J. Sundén, & M. Sveningsson, (Eds). *Digital Borderlands: Cultural Studies of Identity and Interactivity on the Internet* (pp. 1–47). New York: Peter Lang.

Gilbert, K.R. (Ed.) (2001). *The Emotional Nature of Qualitative Research*. London: CRC Press.

Hart, M. (2018). It's nice to see you're not the only one with kinks: Presenting intimate privates in intimate publics on Tumblr. In: A.S. Dobson, B. Robards, N. Carah (Eds). *Digital Intimate Publics and Social Media* (pp. 177–192). Melbourne: Palgrave Macmillan.

Hahn, J.D. (2019, November 19). *86 Percent of Young Americans Aspire to Become a Social Media Influencer, Study Says*, Retrieved from https://people.com/human-interest/young-americans-want-to-be-social-media-influencers-study-says/

Iacoboni, M. (2009). Imitation, empathy, and mirror neurons. *Annual Review of Psychology*, 60, 653–670.

Johnston, J., Cairns, K. and Baumann, S. (2017). *Introducing Sociology Using the Stuff of Everyday Life*. New York: Routledge.

Keegan, S. (2009). *Qualitative Research: Good Decision Making Through Understanding People, Cultures and Markets*. London: Kogan Page.

Kielburger, C., Branson, H., & Kielburger, M. (2018). *Weconomy: You Can Find Meaning, Make a Living, and Change the World*. London: Wiley.

Kozinets, R. V. (2015). *Netnography: Redefined*. London: Sage Publications.

Kozinets, R.V. (2020). *Netnography: The Essential Guide to Qualitative Social Media Research*. London: Sage.

Kozinets, R.V., Patterson, A., & Ashman, R. (2017). Networks of desire: How technology increases our passion to consume. *Journal of Consumer Research*, 43(5), 659–682.

Mann, S. (2016). *The Research Interview: Reflective Practice and Reflexivity in Research Processes*. New York: Palgrave Macmillan.

Mardon, R., Molesworth, M., & Grigore, G. (2018). YouTube beauty gurus and the emotional labour of tribal entrepreneurship. *Journal of Business Research*, 92, 443–454.

Markham, A. N. (1998). *Life Online: Researching Real Experience in Virtual Space*. Walnut Creek, CA: AltaMira.

Martensen, A., Brockenhuus-Schack, S., & Lauritsen Zahid, A. (2018). How citizen influencers persuade their followers. *Journal of Fashion Marketing and Management*, 22(3), 335–353.

Marwick, A. (2015). Instafame: Luxury selfies in the attention economy. *Public Culture*, 27(175), 137–160.

Murphy, E., & Dingwall, R. (2001). The ethics of ethnography. In P, Atkinson, A. Coffee, S. Delamont, J. Lofland, & L. Lofland (Eds.). *Handbook of Ethnography* (pp. 339–351). Los Angeles, CA: Sage.

Raun, T. (2018). Capitalizing intimacy: New subcultural forms of micro-celebrity strategies and affective labour on YouTube. *Convergence: The International Journal of Research into New Media Technologies*, 24(1), 99–113.

Lazzarato, M. (1996). Immaterial labour. In P, Virno., & M, Hardt. (Eds.). *Radical Thought in Italy: A Potential Politics* (pp. 133–147). Minneapolis: University of Minnesota Press.

Waterston, A., & Rylko-Bauer, B. (2006). Out of the shadows of history and memory: Personal family memories and ethnographies of rediscovery. *American Ethnologist*, 33(3), 397–412.

Weijo, H., Hietanen, J., & Mattila, P. (2014). New insights into online consumption communities and netnography. *Journal of Business Research*, 67(10), 2072–2078.

Section 5
Netnography Theorized

16
Netnography in Human and Non-Human Networked Sociality

Sarah Quinton and Nina Reynolds

INTRODUCTION

This chapter aims to expand on how netnography can evolve within human and non-human networked sociality. It will outline how more-than-human netnography can be adapted to the shifting contours of a digital and post digital world and how netnography can retain its relevance as a lens through which to account for cotemporary human and non-human interactions. A straightforward *Star Trek* like trajectory for netnography may no longer be mappable, but instead a more nebulous, looser collection of netnographic-esque studies is likelier. This chapter will contribute to the new netnographic federation that spans virgin territories to build insight mirroring human and non-human interaction.

To advance netnographic sense making and avoid subject siloisation of knowledge, greater explicit recognition of different subject and domain perspectives ranging from the technology discipline to the sociological and anthropological perspectives as well as 'other' ways of thinking about the human non-human technology interactions must be embraced.

Through both conceptual discussion complemented with examples of different types of research this chapter will embrace the future possibilities of netnography. Drawing on Lugosi and Quinton's 2018 *Journal of Marketing Management* paper, substantial themes for discussion within this chapter will include; temporality, assemblage theory as linked to translation enacted by technologies, and agency of both the human and non-human kind.

This chapter is underpinned by foundational conceptualisations of being human/non-human, technology use and adoption, and the role of temporality, so well articulated by Stiegler (1991), Haraway (1985), Hayles (2012), Latour (2005, 2014) and Delanda (2016). Stiegler introduced the notion of 'technics' as a way to consider human history, articulated through technological development. Technics being, in essence, not merely the tools used by humans but also the impact of those tools on human development. He posited that humans and the advent of human history focused on technics, stating *'the invention of the human is technics'* (Stiegler, 1991:148). Stiegler's accounting of humans as adaptive entities (James, 2010) leads to Haraway's questioning of embodiments and her valuable depiction of the melding of humans and machines into 'cyborgs' as their interactions become entwined through devices (Haraway, 1985). This description helps the reader to visualise some of these human/non-human actors that this chapter incorporates. The who (human) and the what (technology) become fused and this impacts our understanding of the potential for research which addresses not one (the human) or other (the technology) but both. In a similar vein,

Katherine Hayles (2012) proposed the term 'technogenesis' to explain the increasingly interwoven nature of humans and technology and, although her illustrations of technogenesis are made with reference to digital media and the digital humanities, the conceptualisation can be applied more widely.

Latour's contribution to this chapter lies in his detailing of agency and the acknowledgement of the role of materiality and technology (Latour, 2005, 2014) which assists us in thinking about technology not as a thing but about its ontology, its being, its nature and its relation to other entities. He suggests that the distinction between animate and inanimate is false, and that reconsidering humans and 'others' including technology as shifting shapes may provide us valuable insight. As netnographers, revising our conceptions regarding what may or may not have agency may extend our research horizons. Delanda (2016), through his augmentation of Deleuze and Guattari's 1987 assemblage theory, underpins our understanding of assemblages by explaining their symbiotic and alloyed nature through which an assembled mesh of elements co-functions. Indeed, an assemblage can be made up of other assemblages thus hinting at the multi-layering possibilities that may need considering when researching the networked sociality.

To elucidate, this chapter will explore how the contemporary characteristics of time and space, and 'temporality', can be included within the development of netnography. Netnography may act as an illumination upon how the experience of temporality is being transformed via technologies. Preconceptions of place and time, founded on socio-cultural understanding, will be questioned as netnography creates the opportunity to weave data which disrupts these conceptions of time and place.

Through applying assemblage theory and the realisation of the socio-material construction of entities in which those entities are never completed, this chapter will highlight the state of flux of entities within netnography, with its future of further reassembly and reiterations. To illustrate, entities on social media platforms, text and images might be mashed together, edited, amended, enhanced, rearranged etc., and thus the process of interaction and communication continues to morph and change. These non-stable characteristics of entities, while a challenge for researchers, bring exciting new possibilities for more-than-human netnography.

In addition, how, through understanding and applying assemblage theory, the role of agency and subsequently 'translation' can advance and progress netnography to reflect the contemporary techno/socio-cultural environments will be investigated. The centrality of technology in the creation of assemblages remains under researched (Berthon, MacHulbert & Pitt, 2005; Campbell, O'Driscoll & Saran, 2010), and this chapter will outline the part played by technologies within the processes of translation, and how they shape translation. For example, technologies' enactment of translation influences what is seen by whom and when as well as the greater or lesser value that is attached to both the humans interacting and the content with which they are interacting. Furthermore, this chapter will propose that greater emphasis be given to the role of agency of non-human actors and the agentic qualities of communication devices as a way to advance netnography.

This chapter foregrounds the role of technology and materiality, human and non-human interactions in the shaping of social practices but in doing so does not abandon the core principles of netnography (Kozinets, 2015). The underpinning building blocks of: the involvement to some degree of the researcher, the central role of theorising, the use of data connected to the internet but cognisant of the centrality of hermeneutic interpretation of that data and critically, the compliance with recognised ethical standards of inquiry remain essential to the forward travel direction of netnography through time and space.

The structure of the chapter is organised as follows. An outline of networked sociality in relation to netnography follows, which highlights the new realities of our digital and post digital environment. Our discussion then moves to raising awareness of some of the central ethical issues surrounding human and non-human research participants and their data. The changing experiences of temporality and the making sense of time for both actors and researchers involved in netnographic endeavour is then explored. Proceeding from temporality, the fluidity of the construction, enactment and translation of entities and the assemblaging of different data is investigated to assist in developing understanding of the necessity for a more-than-human netnography. The concept of agency both of human and non-human and the relevant questions to consider are made explicit prior to the chapter summary.

NETWORKED SOCIALITY

A network society is facilitated by technologies that construct and deconstruct connections across subjects, countries, economies, industries, people and cultures (Castells, 1996). The extension of Castells' conceptualisation of a connected society by Wittel moved the emphasis of a networked sociality towards informational needs rather than relational connections. If 'community' denoted stability then networked sociality denotes a more fluid arrangement without the necessary ties or ongoing commitments (Wittel, 2001) and thus networked sociality involves the ebb and flow of connectivity, where there is greater flexibility between and within individuals and networks. Willson (2009) suggests that networked sociality is the potential facilitated by the technologies available to us which shape how we interact with the world, how we make sense of the world and our place in it. Networked sociality can be seen in the meetups and dating opportunities that exist through geolocation available on our mobile phones, which accommodate our more nomadic lifestyles with fewer geographical ties and stability of physical communities.

Individuals, Groups and Non-Humans

Networked sociality can reinforce established groups, viewpoints and perspectives, as well as changing them. It can buttress certain social structures, but it can also open up the possibility of new networks for people, for example, by providing the networks possible to connect disparately situated trans-people. Netnography started as researching human behaviour within online networks and communities; it has evolved to research both the human and non-human. Moving again, netnography is becoming engaged with the Internet of Things (IoT), and, shifting once again, is moving towards encompassing all of these. Campbell, O'Driscoll and Saren (2010) observed in their description of the contemporary 'posthuman' that there was no need to separate the human from the non-human. We can and do now increasingly encompass hiveminds like Borgs, cyborgs, augmented humans, human hacks, trans human and bio hacking in unchained netnographic research. At this point, it is pertinent to outline the concept of technogenesis suggested by Hayles (2012). In essence, technogenesis is the embodied and extended cognition in which human activity, agency and thought becomes enmeshed with digital and other technology. Thus, the evolution of humans and the tools/ technics they use is becoming inter-wound. The reciprocal development of humans and technology usage and the adaption of the technology by the humans assists the development of both the humans and the technology. Computational media encourage humans to perform, communicate and even think differently with each other and with the 'machines' in which the technology manifests, and intelligent technology is considerably increasing the rate of this co-evolution.

As netnographic researchers, we may incorporate notions of technogenesis and both humans and non-humans as researchers, as well as humans and non-humans being actors in research. For example, research around autonomous vehicles in which non-human actors are driving the humans. As the networks move and shift the human element may no longer remain as the central focus in meaning making (Wolfe, 2010), the place and role of the human within networked sociality may be shifting (Markham & Stavrova, 2016) or may indeed have shifted from active participation to non-active participation (Fox & Alldred, 2015).

The digitally mediated sociality is experienced differently by people (Tufekci & Brashears, 2014). Networked sociality needs to recognise these differences and its incompleteness in the non-inclusion of the digitally excluded (those who have not had the opportunity to become part of networked sociality), the digitally self-excluded (those who never engaged in the first place through their own predisposition, as well as those users who have become disenchanted and have left digital technologies), and those who are digitally engaged but whose sociality is confined to the dark web. Furthermore, the extensive adoption and interaction of technologies by certain groups of society may afford new opportunities to even out aspects of the social divide. For example, social contacts and networks in the offline versus the online world have very different constituents and networked sociality may benefit those who might be social contact 'poor' in the offline world (Kraut et al., 2002). Netnography may offer avenues for reaching some of these groups in order to better understand their behaviours as individuals and communities (Quinton & Reynolds, 2018).

The New Landscape

Tangible examples of the new networked sociality can be seen in the changes within the retail experience where technology enhanced stores interact with technology enabled consumers, which also has direct and indirect impact on other consumers, providers and retailers (Pantano & Gandini, 2017). This emerging sociality landscape provides fertile ground for netnography to explore.

The data produced by networked sociality as a resource for researchers needs to be carefully considered in terms of its completeness. Just as networked sociality foregrounds certain groups of people and certain topics at the expense of other people and topics, the traces of data left behind as data sources provide an uneven research landscape. Human memory lapses, forgets and gives unequal value to certain experiences. Digital data traces within the networked sociality may also do the same. The data may degrade, the non-human actors in the networks may become obsolete and their data memory may be lost/deleted, or incomplete. To illustrate, the withdrawal of Vine might also happen to Twitch, TikTok or any other video streaming platform and thus gathering opportunities, gathered data and archived data becomes 'lost' as the non-human actor ceases to operate. In addition, while the instability of networks is recognised as a characteristic both in terms of connectivity and of content, netnography may wish to consider paying greater attention to a broader group of networks or indeed designing more longitudinal studies to develop understanding through the ebb and flow of the network.

Digital technologies are shaping and being shaped by research across the consumer landscape including but not limited to, smart retailing (Priporas, Stylos and Fotiadis, 2017), customer experience (Flavián, Ibáñez-Sánchez, & Orús, 2019), the function of marketing itself (Kannan, 2017), entrepreneurship (Rippa & Secundo, 2019) and innovation management (Nambisan et al., 2017). Indeed, contemporary technocultural consumption now extends far beyond digital technologies that are commonly associated with technology (Kozinets, 2019) to incorporate the complex intangible and interwoven experiences that form new dimensions of culture and thus new areas for netnographic investigation.

The types of analysis used for investigating digital data and its attendant relationships are also increasingly technology driven. For example, structured network analysis to highlight connections in networks, and certain software programmes such as NodeXL which produce visualisations of such networks and connections. Contemporary netnographers should be mindful not to over emphasise quantification and quantification approaches to network analysis at the expense of the possibly more nuanced ways of thinking about networked sociality in which the 'human' is centre stage. As human and now non-human actors populate the new netnographic research landscape, ethical challenges in this new land are now discussed.

ETHICS

While there is a well-established and much cited set of ethical guidelines created and updated by the interdisciplinary AoIR, currently in its third iteration (https://aoir.org/reports/ethics3.pdf), there may also be a need for new guidance moving beyond the seminal AoIR good practice guidelines. Should and can netnography be self-managed in terms of research ethics or can it be assisted by bots and AI? As commonly stated in ethnography and elsewhere in research methods tomes, previously modelled policies on research ethics were based on medical research and are, to some degree, inappropriate for the environment in which netnography operates (Roberts, 2015; Markham & Buchanan, 2012). The collaborative material often produced through netnographic endeavour may be fluid, dynamic and personal, and as co-produced with research participants should it be commodified and shared publicly? A study involving older people sharing their memories about the power and connective qualities of photographs, and sharing those photographs online with each other and trusted others, may well produce unexpected insight into lived experiences (Pera, Quinton & Baima, 2020). For example, it shows how sharing photographs of hospice (palliative care) interiors brought comfort to some, information to others and acted as a cathartic activity for a few more. This type of honest, highly personal and open co-production of research requires ethical sensitivity from everyone involved.

Data

Turning inherently individual-level experiences into aggregated data sets and amassing this data may also create ethical challenges. The removal of the 'social' through the nature of the analysis undertaken in certain social science research and any loss of the human experience in the interactions and relationships between people, both as producers of data but also as co-producers of data who are involved to some degree with the researchers is concerning (Marres, 2017; Törnberg & Törnberg, 2018). This removal of the nuanced connectivity, the loose, non-measurable relationships which make up the 'social' may have ethical implications, such as lost sensitivity if the research is being approached from a utilitarian rather than a deontological perspective.

What about the mass social scraping of data research undertaken using netnographic approaches? Does this lack the human element, the interaction and as such is that an ethical issue? In addition, where does the intellectual and cultural property ownership and or responsibility lie in the post-human netnography? How, in a digitally enabled research landscape, can contemporary netnographers ensure that collected material will not be used for unauthorised purposes, be shared with third parties, or indeed that disposal will occur appropriately, as is generally stated by researchers (Dilger et al., 2018) if the data is stored within the established commercial digital platforms, such as Google Drive, Dropbox, etc.?

Pursuant to this is how to overcome the fear of surveillance capitalism in an era where the realisation that the interconnected world may not only bring social good but also unfair advantage to some, through the irresponsible collection and unethical commercialisation of people's data. The unethical behaviour by some (generally large organisations or governments) with other people's data has a ripple effect. This effect increases the distrust by members of the public of the collection of internet data, thus impacting the engagement with research conducted in good faith. How this will shape participation and the voluntary giving of data to netnographers, and indeed researchers following other paths, in the future is not known.

Personal, Private, Public and Risk

Intimacies afforded by the emerging digital technologies (such as those mentioned above in the older people sharing photos online study) have altered human and non-human interactions and have changed what may be considered the personal, private and or public (Mainsah & Proitz, 2018). The semi-public space of open forums on which personal views, beliefs and experiences are shared remain a contentious and grey area for social science researchers. Indeed, these new intimacies have shifted research material and activities on which new scholarship is grounded.

Furthermore, there is now an increasing risk for netnographic researchers as disclosure or discovery of researcher identity has become easier. The polarisation of views that social media and digital technologies may encourage, and the investigation of divisive topics may result in the doxing of researchers by those holding extreme opinions (see, for example, Massaranari, 2018 on 'alt-right' research). In addition, there is the associated risk that netnography affords when researchers move into the realms of the dark web and opaque communities, that of the researcher being flagged by institutions or governments as the ability to trace researcher activities also develops. So not only is there opportunity for further 'contentious' research, but by being engaged in this type of activity both the producers of the data (the communities) and those who may be watching those communities (governments, private organisations) may know and follow the work of the researcher. In netnography, the reasonable protection of all involved, including the researcher, should be given greater consideration.

Beyond the preeminent consideration of risk to the participant and following that, the risk to the researcher, consideration should be afforded to the downstream subjects – those entities human or possibly non-human who may be impacted by the research after its completion (Markham, 2018). Extending beyond what we currently acknowledge as ethical challenges lie the discussions regarding non-human actors and who, and how, is it decided what is ethical research involving such actors? Questions such as who represents the interest of the non-human, and whether the non-humans interest should be considered at all require reflection.

In the era of big data, open data, and the tsunami of digital data that it is now possible to collect, netnographic researchers need to be mindful to collect only the minimum required for the core purpose of a research study (Ess & Af Segerstad, 2019). Data minimisation and the clear articulation of this is important in developing and maintaining trust with the entities that provide the data. Tied to the minimal collection of data is the societal cost of storing digital data, the maintaining of digital archives and the ecological impact of 'holding on to data' at scale that is often overlooked in data management plans. Having raised awareness of the ethical questions netnographers now face, the chapter proceeds to elaborate the complexities of temporality in the new federation of humanistic and more than human netnography.

TEMPORALITY

The need to make sense of time and where we as humans sit within it is deep seated (Stiegler, 1998), but making sense of a more disordered, non-linear, unstable world is made more challenging by the fluidity of temporality in the emerging reality of networked sociality. As contemporary more-than-human netnographers, we need to stop seeing the fluidity of temporality as a problem but as a wider set of possibilities. We need to extend the thinking on temporality to move beyond the notion of fixed time points, sampling stability, discrete platforms utilised for data collection and tools of analysis which may all now be fluid and impermanent. Social media provides us as researchers with, at least, the potential for both experiencing and researching the past, present and future or integrations of all three (Kaun & Stiernstedt, 2014). Non-linear, more complex and multi-layered temporal interactions provide possibilities for new insight and should not be viewed as a limiting factor for research.

Time can be shortened in the human interactions we now engage in, emails versus conversations, text versus conversations, images sent in almost real time instead of words, etc. The increasing number of others we encounter in our on- and off-line activities, the frequency of interactions with others in various forms, all break down time to smaller and smaller packages. Rosa (2014) proposes this time shortening as part of the social alienation process of acceleration in modernity. As a result of time shortening, the present may also be condensed, networks of individuals and communities are now less stable, and more fluid with interactions possibly more intense. If the present is abbreviated then what happens to the past?

Time Assumptions

The use of time may also now need revisiting. As users fit in activities in tiny micro breaks in their days, such as the use of mobile phones to check social media and post a comment, thus time expands to accommodate these activities and the time spent performing each activity contracts, temporality can thus be elastic (Wajcman, 2015). Context-specific short-hand can also be used to flatten or collapse context for communication within specific groups of users who are 'in the know' or 'on the inside' therefore saving time. Other social practices that relate to and are impacted by notions of time have changed. For example, customer complaint behaviour now includes social media complaining in real or near real time in the attempt to get a faster response during the consumption experience such as poor service on a flight, or in a hotel. These heuristic behaviours to optimise time efficacy provide fertile ground for netnographic enquiry.

Social acceleration, Rosa (2014) argues, alters relationships with and between technologies, objects and human and non-human actors. In the post-modern, more-than-human netnography world, the established socially legitimated, embedded, assumptions about time are now being questioned (Leong et al., 2009). For example, if time is viewed as an individual resource (Wajcman, 2019) how does that fit within networked sociality where the interconnectivity and interrelationships are critical to the network? There are multiple disjoints with temporality in terms of how we experience time itself, the time of an experience, the time of remembrance, the time of communication, the time period of experiential immersion, time within human interactions. Indeed, time is now dis-embedded via digitalisation when once it was embedded (see Giddens, 1994).

The quantification of time, time cycles, time between, time since etc., is founded upon the notion of measuring by humans in an effort to attempt to maintain control (Wajcman, 2015, 2019). Increasingly now the measurement is by non-humans to 'assist' humans in quantifying our lives, progress, and success or failure over specific time points to reach certain pre-determined goals via technologies such as Apps (see Lupton, 2016). The pre-existing boundaries of time and the quantification of it into past, present and future with atomised and linear progressions may no longer be entirely appropriate for a more interwoven networked sociality, which is multi-dimensional and multi-time pointed. What might be the static points or points of time reference in which the dynamic nature of networked sociality and multiple chronographies are played out? Is there a fixed point any more around which the networked sociality coalesces? Research ideas and questions in netnography may no longer have fixed points onto which to anchor.

Certain experiences and interactions can be shallow and short and yet some can also be memorable and transformative as outlined by Walter Benjamin over a century ago, and this retains relevance to networked sociality today. As contemporary netnographers what are we capturing, the detritus of networked lives or the interactions that are meaningful and contain traces of a deeper significance? What is the value of our experiences within time that we are collecting and analysing, can we appropriate time to have more of certain type of meaningful experiences and less of the other surface interactions? What will our studies of society through the media that are being used to enact everyday life, across the assemblage of multiple platforms, and types of interactions tell us about the shaping and remediating of our society?

Time Management

Norms of cycles of activity and management of temporality between human and non-human actors are worth considering as netnographers. While humans have periods of activity and periods of rest or sleep, non-human actors do not; as Kozinets et al. (2018) allude to, 'bots don't sleep'. In addition, our knowledge about temporality is impacted by non-human algorithmic-induced rhythms. For example, the use of self-tracking technologies relies on the organisation of temporality according to non-human actors in order to record human activity. These flows of self-tracking rhythms become algorithmically managed by non-human flows and the human and non-human accounting for time are thus affected (Lomborg et al., 2018). Furthermore, social media platforms also restructure temporal experiences (Kaun & Stiernstedt, 2014) as time has been framed and reframed by technologies and those owning the technologies. The curation of experiences as mediated by technology is time-based, as illustrated by Facebook timelines. Conscious curation can remove experiences/events that we do not wish to recall, and non-human actors may foreground, based on chronology, events that are not salient or those past events which are best forgotten. The framing of research conducted about and within these technologies is impacted by non-human actors.

The non-human speed of processing data by machines, the ability of algorithms to sort and use data and the rapidity of filtering and interpreting data via machine learning all impacts on the speed of data collection, analysis and interpretation. The velocity of turning data into valuable information has increased, saving humans 'time'. A separate but related challenge is whether this saving of time results in any loss of knowledge, through the over use of such of filtered data.

Within the accelerated society, where time is used as the scaffolding and ordering process for daily life, temporal autonomy achieved through human agency may have been reduced (Wajcman, 2019) rather than enhanced. The self-determined autonomy of modernity as proposed by Habermas, among others, is largely absent as we move towards an environment (or some might say we have already moved) where AI controls the bigger picture of our lives. By participating in this new digitalised and post-digital environment, increasingly shaped by non-humans, we accept our lack of real control. For netnographers, it is important to acknowledge this diminution of autonomy as a constraint but also to embrace AI as a lens through which to explore the non-human/human interaction. How technologies, including AI, enact translation and how entities may be constructed and reconstructed and the implications of this for netnographic research follows.

ASSEMBLAGE, TRANSLATION AND ENACTMENT BY TECHNOLOGIES

The socio-material construction of entities means that entities are never completed – they are in a state of flux, with the possible future of further reassembly and reiterations of enactments (DeLanda, 2016; Callon, 1984). Within this socio-material construction, technologies are not passive but play active roles (Berthon et al., 2005). The co-functioning collation of elements meshed together are an assemblage, and the elements of the assemblage, the parts, must be considered in conjunction with the whole, the sum of the parts (Delanda, 2016). For example, material on social media platforms, text and images that might be mashed together, edited, amended, enhanced, rearranged, etc. Thus, the process of interaction and communication continues to morph and change. The role of technology in the creation of assemblages is under-researched (Fox & Alldred, 2015). For example, there are important questions such as what is their role within processes of translation, and how do the technologies shape this? To elaborate, how do music-sharing technologies such as Spotify impact upon music choices and music-related consumption? Humans used to be the cultural intermediaries in influencing others, yet now this translation is conducted by automatic music-finding services, driven by algorithms, which act as powerful amplifiers or dampeners of specific tunes and musicians, Spotify has become an intermediary and an interloper in people's intimate listening spaces. Netnography offers the potential to account for how technologies have become these cultural intermediaries.

Inclusivity and Assemblage

Within networked sociality, greater assemblaging of different data types is possible and becomes more prevalent. The 'originators of data' also become more complex as owners/contributors/creators may all overlap and coagulate the resulting data. The assemblaging of material may now include technological elements such as animations, computational notations, augmented reality, audio data, immersive alternative reality, etc. and these then need to be incorporated within discussions and shown visually. This may challenge the established formats of publishing and much research output within netnography may need to be transferred to smart screen formats (or its successors) to enable optimal viewing and reading in order to include these assemblages.

The articulation of netnographic research through a range of perspectives will help develop the contribution that netnographic studies can make to the networked sociality. Perspectives brought by other disciplines beyond how those other disciplines portray their data and how they use specific tools are important to include. In addition, the widening of the data available, through the ubiquity of the increasingly available technology platforms, offers netnographic researchers potential for far greater use of the non-verbal, image-based data. In order to make sense of these layered assemblages 'new' or different data analysis tools will inevitably be required. Social science researchers may benefit from borrowing tools from other visual subject areas such as Film Studies as well as reconsidering the presentation of such data and learning from subject disciplines such as Geography and Physics with their visualisation expertise. By becoming more open to both assemblage itself and the tools to make sense of the assemblages, netnographic research may be moved forward.

More-than-human netnography offers an opportunity to better understand how technologies may ascribe meaning through, for example, re-ordering, editing and posting of the material co-created by humans and their digital devices (objects such as mobile phones). While the relationship is symbiotic as the humans require the objects (digital devices) in order to interact digitally, they also require the same platform access to interact with their chosen 'others'. The objects such as phones require the data from human usage in order to develop their functionality and subsequently respond back to the user with appropriate content etc. To illustrate, the creation, curation and sharing of photos requires substantial interaction between the mobile phone device, the platforms used for communication and sharing and the multiple human users in a WhatsApp group.

Translation and Enactment

The translational effect of technologies on humans' expressions of their life narratives should not be underestimated. Technologies' enactment of translation influences what is seen by whom and when and, as a result, greater or lesser value is attached to both humans interacting and the content they are interacting with. Certain people are deemed to be, via the technologies employed, worthy of greater prominence than others (such as social media micro-influencers), likewise certain subjects or topics are given greater emphasis. Moreover, technology influence through platform power, such as that exerted by the iOS App store steer behaviours and impact the norms of the individual human actors. Interrogating translations and enactments by platforms such as the iOS App store through netnographic enquiry would extend the understanding of this dynamic ecosystem.

The enactment by technologies influences searches, and individualises a collective activity, as well as what is researched and how is also impacted. For example, through the personalisation of results of an online search, some results are foregrounded at the expense of others. Certain topics become more researched and the valuing of such phenomena is influenced through this filtering by technology. The translation process not only shapes content and influences thinking through the promotion or suppression of certain material, it also ascribes value to that content. In addition, the activity and intervention of bots in terms of spreading content, shaping information flows through the internet and influencing human knowledge and behaviours as an important element of translation and enactment is becoming a recognised area of research, for example Bruns and Stieglitz (2013), Stieglitz et al., (2017), and Schapals, Bruns and McNair (2019). Netnography can question these translational processes to provide more explicit understanding of what these technologies are 'doing' and how they are shaping interactions.

Role of Internet of Things

Having stated that the human and non-human are more and more bound together in networked sociality, the role of IoT (Internet of Things) in the assemblage, enactment and translation of netnography warrants further deliberation. The capacity of smart objects to connect with each other, with physical infrastructure and with humans and to affect outcomes for all parties suggests that all these entities have value and thus that we should be less human-centric in our conceptualisations (see Hill et al., 2014; Bryant, 2011). Micro everyday human interactions with smart non-human objects (such as those digital voice activated assistants in our homes) in addition to the macro assemblages of city infrastructures are fertile ground for netnographic research. This is especially so if we regard the non-human actors as valuable constituents of research in their own right, beyond their value within interactions with humans. The capability of non-human smart objects to have experiences, through machine learning, which affect and can be affected by each other (Hoffman & Novak, 2017) is important to recognise in non-human networked sociality as it creates new avenues for research. The capability and agency of the non-human smart objects layer interactions with other objects and or humans to create assemblages which are then defined by those interactions.

Shifting our perspective from one of human centred framing of netnographic research to a greater appreciation and focus on the agentic qualities of non-human objects will encourage recognition of a wider range of research opportunities. For example, reversing the 'human attachment to objects' conceptualisation to the questioning of whether objects can form attachments to humans, such as via dependency on certain voice recognition speech patterns, or perhaps objects forming attachments to other objects through repeated interactions, provides rich ground for progressing netnographic research to explore these interactions and pose novel research questions. Having included the non-human actors in the preceding discussion, the chapter now considers agency of both the non-human and human.

HUMAN AND NON-HUMAN AGENCY

The interdependencies between human and non-human, the balance of power and control between the established and new actors and how agency is enacted between these actors are complex but potential rewarding areas for netnographers to unpick. Latour's thought-provoking early work reflecting on the notions of agency, its heterogeneous forms and the resulting impact on the conceptualisation of 'social' (Latour, 2005) points to the ongoing need to reflect on the state of being human. The concept of humanness within the new networked sociality domain may be frequently overlooked but still warrants further investigation. So what role, then, does agency play in this evolving digital landscape where interactions occur within and between human and non-human communities? To what extent are human and non-human actions chained to, or unchained from, the constraints of their environment and or design in the new networked sociality?

Interdependencies

Human agents currently direct human, more than human and, non-human systems (Conty, 2017; Nevo et al., 2016) through their influence over design and or use of the non-human actor. Yet, simultaneously, the non-human actors(s) may now direct, guide, or constrain what is possible, creating a highly interdependent set of relationships between the human, more than human and non-human (see Hoffman & Novak, 2017). As Latour outlined in his 2014 Tanner lecture at Yale University, humans should not be seen as static and stable. Entities also have agency which makes any distinction between animate (humans) and inanimate (things) inappropriate. Latour proposed that *'to be a subject encountering an object is no longer a viable proposition'* (Latour, 2014:114). This complexity and interdependency presents both opportunities for and limits to the realisation of agency (Leonardi, 2011; Svahn et al., 2009). Non-human actors no longer merely act as the passive recipient of the human will but act through shaping how the world is categorised, viewed, and presented (Leander, 2013). Technologies (e.g., an iPad), unlike non-human actors from nature (e.g., a mongoose), which would continue to exist (or even thrive) without human interference, cannot claim full independence from human influence (Conty, 2017). The IoT, for example, might not require human agency to operate once 'released', but is designed and developed to address human problems, reflects what humans' value, and is designed to deliver benefits whether in the short- or long-term to humans.

The interdependency and complexity of agency can be illustrated by India's national biometric data system, the Aadhaar system (Ayyar, 2018). This system requires that human actors interact with non-human entities to execute everyday interactions such as applying for government benefits. Not only may this be legally problematic (Levine, 2019) in terms of data privacy but to some extent it removes agency from those human actors or communities who may need this type of public service most. Thus human agency, as such, is intertwined with non-human agency through the materiality and affordances designed into the technology and manifests in the choices enabled by the non-human actors, and those choices the non-human prohibits (Jarrahi & Nelson, 2018).

Netnographers cannot assume that technology supports volition without any distortion. Care should thus be taken to ensure that as non-human actors become increasingly embedded in everyday lives, as more-than-human possibilities become more prevalent, the valence of technologies' influence is considered (Dotson, 2012). Is the human, or more-than-human, experience enhanced or diminished by its highly interdependent relationship with the non-human actor(s)? Netnographers working in this space face complex questions concerning the limits of more-than-human entities – is the more-than-human a definable entity within this intricate interdependent ecosystem?

Control

Legislative controls (e.g., the Indian government's database initiative, Levine, 2019), and commercial IP (e.g., Facebook, Google, etc), mean that those with the resources and skills required to design, develop, train and release non-human actors, as well as the capabilities needed to constrain, monitor, understand and modify the non-humans materiality, are far fewer than those people who engage with, or are knowingly or unknowingly interacting with, non-human actors in their everyday lives. So, while human agency motivates the development of non-human agency, not all humans are positioned to exert that agency. Relatively few humans exert agentic control over non-human actors through their specialist technological expertise and level of knowledge, yet many humans potentially cede their autonomy to non-human actors for what appears to be greater agency in their day-to-day existence (Conty, 2017; Dowding, 2008; Glynos & Howarth, 2008), for example Google maps, fitness trackers, Uber cabs, or Alexa digital assistants. Understanding how power imbalances are negotiated presents both challenges and opportunities. Netnographers cannot neglect to recognise the power and control exerted by the few over the many and netnographic research in networked sociality, may need to develop sophisticated investigative skills to unpick where agentic control and influence lies.

In addition, technological advances such as machine and deep learning are unchaining non-human actors from human agentic control, potentially reversing the previous direction of influence. When more-than-human agency cannot be enacted due to material constraints, humans can initiate, direct and/or guide changes in their own behaviour or that of the non-humans. However, unchained non-human actors may now advance their own agency through developing free thinking, which may then impose constraints on the humans' use of their own systems (e.g., autonomous vehicles with deep learning). The changing levels of agency and control exerted between the humans, more-than-humans and non-humans will require the netnographer to revisit the limits of their existing understanding. Contemporary netnographers may seek to better understand the shifting locus of control. Indeed, British author Stephen Fry compares Greek gods' suspicions of their autonomous human creations with humans' fear of their own agentic non-human products.

Humanness

In addition to the aforementioned imbalances, netnographers must consider what is lost when the more-than-human becomes/became into being. Allowing technologies to facilitate the human experience could represent a passive loss of human agency, a deskilling, a loss of capability, or an absence of understanding (Russo et al., 2019). What might on the surface facilitate and expand the more-than-human could when considered more deeply diminish them as a result of losing a valued cultural scaffold (Martin, 2015). Think, for example, of the internet-enabled access to information – here 'facts' come easily, requiring skill only in how to perform an online search. There is no longer any need to work heuristically and collaboratively towards deriving relatively uncontested 'facts'. The humanness involved in the critical evaluation of the quality of information or relevance of what has been filtered by the internet becomes lost. What, then, is the cost to human agency in becoming more-than-human? Reflecting on more-than-human agency then leads us to consider what aspects of human agency and 'humanness' we value.

Maintaining humanness is important in knowledge building in the new networked sociality. Netnography is essentially concerned with the social, and humans remain at the core of what is the social ecosystem. Networked sociality and more-than-human netnography needs to inform the construction of social research to ensure that the human element is not lost among the popularity of computational social science (Marres, 2017). Thus, netnographic research may need to consider not only whether and how becoming more-than-human lessens our humanness, and what value the humanness has, but also how to defend against an erosion of humanness more generally.

To encapsulate our thinking and provide a visual representation we have created a table (Table 16.1) of the core topics in human and non-human networked sociality, which includes important questions and ideas for future netnographic research alongside the challenges posed for netnography, as a way of moving netnography forward and responding to the need for new knowledge.

Table 16.1 Netnography, Human and Non-Human Networked Sociality

Core topics	Challenges	Potential future questions
Networked sociality		
Individuals, groups and non-humans	Understanding the blurring of boundaries, singular or collective entities, diverse yet intertwined.	Is the human the central emphasis? To what extent can unchained netnography reach new groups?
The new landscape	Acknowledgement of new and different relationships between actors. Unevenness of the new research terrain, obsolescence of technologies.	What is the role of trust now? Should underrepresented topics be researched? And if so how?
Ethics		
Data	Consideration of the 'over' use of technology, which removes the understanding of the 'social' component.	Where does intellectual and cultural property ownership lie?
Personal, private public and risk	Recognition that the intimacy afforded by technology viewed as contentious, raises the risk to all actors including researchers.	Do non-human actors require ethical consideration? Who might be impacted downstream by netnographic research?

(*continued*)

Table 16.1 (Cont.)

Core topics	Challenges	Potential future questions
Temporality		
Time assumptions	Appreciating that time may simultaneously expand and contract, that social acceleration now drives multi-dimensional temporal interactions.	How do time and location influence human and non-human interactions?
Time management	Realisation of the diminution of human autonomy facilitated by the non-human.	Might saving time via non-human activity result in a loss of knowledge?
Assemblage, translation and enactment		
Inclusivity and assemblage	The need to manage multiplicities of data types from many perspectives.	What can be learnt from outside our established subject domain?
Translation and enactment	Appreciation that separation of technology from daily life is increasingly unfeasible and reconciling the embedded nature of technologies.	How might translation and enactment shape the information flows in a netnographic study?
The role of the Internet of Things	Articulating the experiential capability of smart objects and their inclusion in netnographic research.	How might we reframe the established human centric vision of research?
Human and non-human agency		
Interdependency	The difficulty in disentangling the intertwined relationships of human, non-human and more-than-human varieties.	Does our interest lie in one, several or all the actors that are intertwined in our netnographic study?
Control	The shifting balance and fluidity of control between actors.	How do we account for agency and control?
Humanness	Design and implementation of research without the removal of the humanness.	How does humanness enhance/detract or impact our unchained netnography?

SUMMARY

In this chapter, we have argued that in order to progress the art and science of netnography, a less cautious but potentially fruitful set of research journeys is necessary in order to account for human, non-human and more-than human interactions. Through the embracing of the complexity of human, non-human and more than human interactions more nuanced and thoughtful questions may be asked and answered. Netnography can maintain relevancy by being immersive, by preserving methodological agnosticism, and by incorporating explicit acknowledgement of non-human agency and its increasing influence in digital world research.

We have demonstrated, through examples, how netnography can continue to be applicable in the sand shifting new contours of the digital and post digital world. By spanning new territories through providing recognition of multiple disciplines and differing research perspectives 'other' ways of thinking about the human, non-human and more-than-human netnography will be possible. Researchers and technologies will reflect the greater interaction and online collaboration between the various established and emergent actors which will, in turn, assist in sense making and avoid siloisation of knowledge.

Our discussion has included a detailed reflection on the concept of temporality in relation to digital research and its substantive role within netnographic endeavour. The positive disruption that revisiting temporality can create for netnography in networked sociality should not be underestimated and we hope to have outlined core questions and considerations regarding time in our accelerated society. The nascent role played by technologies in the translation and enactment of agency and the subsequent impact for all the actors as we have described it, may prove a very fruitful ground for future netnographic studies.

Importantly, this chapter has not neglected the problematic but central position of ethics in human, non-human and more than human netnography. While we do not propose to have all the answers, we have delineated areas that we believe to be, as yet, under considered such as the sustainability of mass data storage. Netnographers, the participants, the institutions in which the research is conducted, and the users of netnographic research all have parts to play in strengthening ethical good practice, and, in time, the non-human actors may also play a part in exhibiting ethical behaviours.

Finally, we hope that our chapter has illustrated that if researchers do not continue to develop new skills and challenge their existing thinking about what netnography can research and how it can be used in accounting for networked sociality, then netnographers may cease to find the golden new territories of insight into the new 'forms' of life as lived. To maintain curiosity and to explore new horizons is important for netnographers, as Q says '*it's not safe out here. It's wondrous, with treasures to satiate desires both subtle and gross; but it's not for the timid*' (Star Trek, The Next Generation).

REFERENCES

Ayyar, K. (2018). The world's largest biometric identification system survived a supreme court challenge in India. *Time*, 26 September 2018; https://time.com/5388257/india-aadhaar-biometric-identification/

Berthon, P., MacHulbert, J., & Pitt, L. (2005). Consuming technology: Why marketers sometimes get it wrong. *California Management Review*, 48(1), 110–128.

Bruns, A., & Stieglitz, S. (2013). Towards more systematic Twitter analysis: Metrics for tweeting activities. *International Journal of Social Research Methodology*, 16(2), 91–108.

Bryant, L., R. (2011). *The democracy of objects.* Ann Arbor, MI: Open Humanities Press.

Callon, M. (1984). Some elements of a sociology of translation: Domestication of the scallops and the fishermen of St Brieuc Bay. *The Sociological Review*, 32(1_suppl), 196–233.

Campbell, N., O'Driscoll, A., & Saren, M. (2010). The posthuman: The end and the beginning of the human. *Journal of Consumer Behaviour: An International Research Review*, 9(2), 86–101.

Castells, M. (1996). The information age (Vol. 98). Blackwell Publishers: Oxford.

Conty, A. (2017). How to differentiate a Macintosh from a Mongoose: Technological and political agency in the age of the Anthropocene. *Teché: Research in Philosophy and Technology*, 21(2–3), 295–318.

DeLanda, M. (2016). *Assemblage theory.* Edinburgh, UK: Edinburgh University Press.

Deleuze, G., & Guattari, F. (1987). *A thousand plateaus: Capitalism and schizophrenia*, trans. Brian Massumi, (2004). London: Continuum.

Dilger, H., Pels, P., & Sleeboom-Faulkner, M. (2018). Guidelines for data management and scientific integrity in ethnography, *Ethnography*, 20(1), 3–7.

Dotson, T. (2012). Technology, choice and the good life: Questioning technological liberalism. *Technology in Society, 34,* 326–336.

Dowding, K. (2008). Agency and structure: Interpreting power relationships. *Journal of Power, 1*(1), 21–36.

Ess, C. M., & af Segerstad, Y. H. (2019). Everything old is new again. *Designs for Experimentation and Inquiry: Approaching Learning and Knowing in Digital Transformation,* 179.

Flavián, C., Ibáñez-Sánchez, S., & Orús, C. (2019). The impact of virtual, augmented and mixed reality technologies on the customer experience. *Journal of Business Research, 100,* 547–560.

Fox, N. J., & Alldred, P. (2015). New materialist social inquiry: Designs, methods and the research-assemblage. *International Journal of Social Research Methodology, 18*(4), 399–414.

Giddens, A. (1994). *The consequences of modernity.* Cambridge: Polity Press.

Glynos, J., & Howarth, D. (2008). Structure, agency and power in political analysis: Beyond contextualised self-interpretations. *Political Studies Review, 6,* 155–169.

Haraway, D. (1985). A manifesto for cyborgs: Science, technology, and socialist feminism in the 1980s. *Socialist Review, 15*(2), 65–107.

Hayles, N.K. (2012). *How we think: Digital media and contemporary technogenesis.* Chicago: University of Chicago Press.

Hill, T., Canniford, R., & Mol, J. (2014). Non-representational marketing theory. *Marketing Theory, 14* (4), 377–94.

Hoffman, D. L., & Novak, T. P. (2017). Consumer and object experience in the internet of things: An assemblage theory approach. *Journal of Consumer Research, 44*(6), 1178–1204.

James, I. (2010). Bernard Stiegler and the time of technics. *Cultural Politics, 6*(2), 207–228.

Jarrahi, M. H., & Nelson, S. B. (2018). Agency, sociomateriality, and configuration work. *The Information Society: An International Journal, 34*(4), 244–260.

Kannan, P. K. (2017). Digital marketing: A framework, review and research agenda. *International Journal of Research in Marketing, 34*(1), 22–45.

Kaun, A., & Stiernstedt, F. (2014). Facebook time: Technological and institutional affordances for media memories. *New Media and Society, 16*(7), 1154–1168.

Kozinets, R. V. (2015). *Netnography: Redefined.* (2nd ed). Thousand Oaks, CA: Sage

Kozinets, R. V. (2019). Consuming technocultures: An extended JCR curation. *Journal of Consumer Research, 46*(3), 620–627.

Kozinets, R. V., Scaraboto, D., & Palmentier, M-A. (2018). Evolving netnography: How brand auto-netnograpy, a netnographic sensibility, and a more then human netnography can transform your research. *Journal of Marketing Management, 34*(3–4), 231–242.

Kraut, R., Kiesler, S., Boneva, B., Cummings, J. N., Helgeson, V., & Crawford, A. M. (2002). Internet paradox revisited. *Journal of Social Issues, 58*(1), 49–74.

Latour, B. (2005). *Reassembling the social: An introduction to actor-network-theory.* Oxford: Oxford University Press.

Latour, B. (2014). How better to register the agency of things. *Lectures given at Yale University, 26 and 27 March.*

Leander, A. (2013). Technological agency in the co-constitution of legal expertise and the US drone program. *Leiden Journal of International Law, 26,* 811–831.

Leonardi, P. M. (2011). When flexible routines meet flexible technologies: Affordance, constraint, and the imbrication of human and material agencies. *MIS Quarterly, 35*(1), 147–167.

Leong, S., Mitew, T., Celletti, M., & Pearson, E. (2009). The question concerning (internet) time. *New Media & Society, 11*(8), 1267–1285.

Levine, M. J. (2019). Biometric identification in India versus the right to privacy: Core constitutional features, defining citizens' interests, and the implications of biometric identification in the United States. *University of Miami Law Review, 73*(2) 618–654. Available at: https://repository.law.miami.edu/umlr/vol73/iss2/10

Lomborg. S., Thylstrup, N. B., & Schwartz, J. (2018). The temporal flows of self-tracking: Checking in, moving on, staying hooked. *New Media and Society, 20*(2), 4590–4607.

Lugosi, P. & Quinton, S. (2018). More than human netnography. *Journal of Marketing Management, 34*(3–4), 287–313.

Lupton, D. (2016). *The quantified self.* Chichester: John Wiley and Sons.

Mainsah, H., & Proitz, L. (2018). Notes on technology devices in research; negotiating field boundaries and relationships. *Qualitative Inquiry, 25*(3), 271–277.

Markham, A. (2018). Afterword: Ethics as impact—moving from error-avoidance and concept driven models to a future-oriented approach. *Social Media and Society, 4*(3) 1–11.

Markham, A., & Buchanan, E. (2012). *Ethical decision-making and Internet research:* Recommendations from the AoIR Ethics Working Committee. Retrieved from www.aoir.org

Markham, A., & Stavrova, S. (2016). *Qualitative research.* (Chap 14 Internet/digital research. pp. 229–244). London: Sage.

Marres, N. (2017). *Digital Sociology: The reinvention of social research.* London: Polity Press.

Martin, J. D. (2015). Evaluating hidden costs of technological change: Scaffolding, agency, and entrenchment. *Teché: Research in Philosophy and Technology, 19*(1), 1–25.

Massanari, A. L. (2018). Rethinking research ethics, power, and the risk of visibility in the era of the "alt-right" gaze. *Social Media and Society, 4*(2), 1–9.

Nambisan, S., Lyytinen, K., Majchrzak, A., & Song, M. (2017). Digital innovation management: Reinventing innovation management research in a digital world. *MIS Quarterly, 41*(1), 223–238.

Nevo, S., Nevo, D., & Pinsonneault, A. (2016). A temporally situated self-agency theory of information technology reinvention. *MIS Quarterly, 40*(1), 157–186.

Pantano, E., & Gandini, A. (2017). Exploring the forms of sociality mediated by innovative technologies in retail settings. *Computers in Human Behavior, 77*, 367–373.

Pera, R., Quinton, S., & Baima, G. (2020). I am who I am: Sharing photos on social media by older consumers and its influence on subjective well-being. *Psychology & Marketing, 37*, 782–795.

Priporas, C. V., Stylos, N., & Fotiadis, A. K. (2017). Generation Z consumers' expectations of interactions in smart retailing: A future agenda. *Computers in Human Behavior, 77*, 374–381.

Quinton, S. & Reynolds, N. (2018). *Understanding digital research.* London: Sage.

Rippa, P., & Secundo, G. (2019). Digital academic entrepreneurship: The potential of digital technologies on academic entrepreneurship. *Technological Forecasting and Social Change, 146*, 900–911.

Roberts, L. D. (2015). Ethical issues in conducting qualitative research in online communities. *Qualitative Research in Psychology, 12*, 314–325.

Rosa, H. (2014). *Alienation and acceleration. Towards a critical theory of late-modern temporality.* Copenhagen: NSUPress and Nordiskt Sommaruniversitet.

Russo, M., Ollier-Malaterre, A., & Morandin, G. (2019). Breaking out from constant connectivity: Agentic regulation of smartphone use. *Computers in Human Behavior, 98*, 11–19.

Schapals, A., Bruns, A., & McNair, B. (2019). *Digitizing democracy. Routledge studies in media, communication, and politics.* London: Routledge.

Stiegler, B. (1991). *La technique et le temps 1. La faute d'Épiméthée.* Galilée, translation, by George Collins and Richard Beardsworth (1998). Stanford, CT: Stanford University Press .

Stieglitz, S., Brachten, F., Berthelé, D., Schlaus, M., Venetopoulou, C., & Veutgen, D. (2017, July). Do social bots (still) act different to humans?–Comparing metrics of social bots with those of humans. In *International conference on social computing and social media* (pp. 379–395). Cham: Springer.

Svahn, F., Henfridsson, O., & Yoo, Y. (2009). A threesome dance of agency: Mangling the sociomaterial of technological regimes in digital innovation. *IICIS 2009 Proceedings*, 5.

Törnberg, P., & Törnberg, A. (2018). The limits of computation: A philosophical critique of contemporary Big Data research. *Big Data & Society, 5*(2) https://doi.org/10.1177%2F2053951718811843

Tufekci, Z., & Brashears, M. E. (2014). Are we all equally at home socializing online? Cyberasociality and evidence for an unequal distribution of disdain for digitally-mediated sociality. *Information, Communication & Society, 17*(4), 486–502.

Wajcman, J. (2015). *Pressed for time.* Chicago: The University of Chicago Press.

Wajcman J. (2019). How Silicon Valley sets time. *New Media and Society, 21*(6), 1272–1289.

Willson, M. (2009). The possibilities of network sociality. In Hunsinger, J., Klastrup, L., & Allen, M. M. (Eds.), *International handbook of internet research* (pp. 493–505). Dordrecht: Springer.

Wittel, A. (2001). Toward a Networked Sociality. *Theory, Culture and Society, 18*(6), 51–75.

Wolfe, C. (2010). *What is posthumanism?* Minneapolis, MN: University of Minnesota Press.

17

Online Ethnography and Social Phenomena on the Move
Time Construction in Netnography and Mobile Ethnography

Birgit Muskat

INTRODUCTION

Ethnographic research aims 'to observe the forms in which people do things together in repeated ways' (Van Maanen, 1979, 102). Traditional ethnographic research thus observes social structures in groups and cultures (Hammersley, 1990; Van Maanen, 1979), and the precise operations for doing this include fieldwork, informal conversations, participant observations, secondary data analyses, physical mappings, recordings field notes, routine diaries, as well as audio and visual methods, and ethnographic interviewing (Whitehead, 2005). With the broadening of the cultural environment for ethnographies, digital communication tools have diversified the ethnographer's toolkit and techniques such as netnography (Kozinets, 2002) have been developed to help ensure that they are rigorously applied. Methods and research questions such as those surrounding netnography now additionally encompass observations of virtual spaces, capturing the movements and mobilities of people in a variety of both virtual and physically located settings.

The focus of this chapter is to link the conduct of netnography to the idea of mobility, or an emphasis on 'social phenomena on the move' (Büscher & Urry, 2009; Urry, 2002; Watts & Urry, 2008). Mobilities are the underlying notion behind 'social phenomena on the move', a concept that describes the global, physical movements of people, developments and movement of material artefacts, non-material phenomena, such as images or information as well as developments of micro-level mobile phenomena, occurring on an individual's day-to-day journey (Hannam et al., 2006). As a consequence of these developments, the meaning of 'social' is now strongly defined by movement as it unfolds over time. Yet, so far a detailed consideration of time and mobility in ethnography has not been emphasized in the development of online methods such as netnography. Lugosi and Quinton (2018, 291), for example, criticize that the 'overly narrow conceptions and applications of netnography may impose particular spatial and temporal limits to research'. At the same time researchers often criticize existing online ethnographies for their lack of credibility (e.g. Berger, 2015; Holstein & Gubrium, 2011; O'Gorman et al., 2014).

This chapter focuses on netnography and mobile ethnography. Netnography is an established method with a history ranging back a quarter of a century, and hundreds of published studies (Kozinets, 2002, 2020). Mobile ethnography, on the other hand, is a still-emerging qualitative technique that is still only dimly understood (Muskat et al., 2018). The chapter advocates that the inclusion of time in research designs of online ethnographies enhances the research designs. Adding time as an additional unit of analysis in online ethnography provides important information because time perceptions in online environments are known to be different from face-to-face, real-world settings (Ariffin et al., 2018; Novak et al., 2000).

Moreover, considering various stages and facets of time in social phenomena are important, as any activity of thinking is shaped by temporal aspects (Corbin et al., 2015). Consequently, revealing how time is constructed and perceived by participants in their respective context, adds depth and value to the research and provides a more nuanced understanding of the social phenomenon under observation. The chapter now proceeds to discuss netnography and mobile ethnography, emphasizing their temporal aspects. Next, it considers the multi-faceted aspects of human time construction, including a discussion of how time differs in online environments. The notion of the customer journey is used to exemplify the multifaceted nature of human time construction. The chapter closes with a conclusion and ideas for future research.

ONLINE ETHNOGRAPHIES

This research discusses netnography and mobile ethnography. *Netnography* is a rigorous qualitative method that relies on data collected from social media. Typically, netnographers apply a fixed set of research practices and draw on a range of 25 different research practices during data collection, data analysis and data interpretation (Kozinets, 2020). Netnographers observe social phenomena, occurring on social media in online interactions and experience, e.g. chat rooms, blogs and online social networks. Netnographers perform a naturalistic inquiry to observe traces within 'textual, graphic, photographic, audiovisual, musical, commercially sponsored, genuinely grassroots, political, fannish, and many other things' (Kozinets, 2020, 16) in these digital environments. Netnographies have been published in many different languages around the world, using all sorts of data including visual, audiovisual, podcasts, and so on (Kozinets, 2020). Common elements of high quality netnography are the immersion and engagement of the researcher in the topic and the site or sites of social media.

Mobile ethnography is a type of qualitative data collection, where study participants in mobile ethnography use portable devices (i.e., mobile phones, iPads), sometimes equipped with specific software for data collection (e.g. mobile apps). Thus, while at various location and over time, mobile ethnography research participants might collect data on their mobile phones. This mobile ethnographic data collection can be complemented with ethnographic interviews, and/or video and audio data (e.g. diaries, photos) in order to analyse social phenomena over time in multiple places in other settings. Participants collect the data in their own spaces—which usually is a real-world setting but may also include virtual spaces (DeBerry-Spence et al., 2019; Muskat et al., 2018).

In conjunction with netnography, mobile ethnography can also be applied as one specific research practice within netnography. Typically, during data collection in mobile ethnographies, the researcher–participant relationship is generally participative and the researcher is also directly engaged in the act of data collection (Muskat et al., 2018). Like the use of other interaction methods such as research web-pages, researcher involvement in online conversations, or the use of synchronous or asynchronous online interviews, mobile ethnography is another way for a netnographer to use of online technology to capture relevant data (e.g. Anhøj & Møldrup, 2004; Dennison et al., 2013; Muskat et al., 2013). To conclude, both netnography and mobile ethnography are online ethnographical methods (e.g., Beneito-Montagut, 2011; Kozinets, 2020; Muskat et al., 2018), that:

- Adopt an overall naturalistic and qualitative interpretivist paradigm
- Rely on modern communication technology

- Are able to capture developing, transformative and fluid meaning
- Are reflective and capture human interaction and interpretation
- Collect data in unbounded settings
- Rely on data lacking the traditional notion of place.

WHY DOES IT MATTER TO REFLECT ON TEMPORAL FACETS IN ONLINE ETHNOGRAPHY?

In traditional ethnographic research, considerations on time and the study length of field-work and observation have always been pivotal elements of research design. In fact, longitudinal observation time has been used to distinguish ethnographies from other research methods and has been regarded as one key quality criteria to enhance the research (Saldaña, 2003; Thomson & Holland, 2003). For example, traditional ethnographic research often speaks of the 'ethnographic year' of 13 months, and assumes that the length of a particular ethnographic project, or prolonged engagement, is some sort of indicator of intimate familiarity, immersion, and deep reflection. Existing netnographies also attend to these same temporal elements, treating them as indicators of prolonged engagement and deep cultural immersion. For example, Kozinets (2002, 67) notes that he spent 33 months engaging with the alt.coffee online group in order to gain a deep understanding of the group's cultural practices, linguistic conventions, and other structures of meaning.

Yet, at the same time, it might be worthwhile challenging some traditional views of temporal aspects in relation to ethnographic research methodology and design. Specifically, the circumstance that classical ethnographies are in favour of longitudinal time perspective deserves to be questioned. The long-term scope of classical ethnographic observation and the benefits of the generated in-depth understanding might, for instance, come at the expense of breadth; which is considered the key challenge and limitations of traditional ethnographical research (Hammersley, 1992). Many ethnographies and netnographies are conducted by teams, which allows specialization and efficient division of efforts. Furthermore, time spent on a task is not a necessary indicator of its quality. High-quality netnographies have been conducted in weeks by companies that commit large numbers of people, high skills, and refined technologies and techniques to their completion (see Chapters 10 and 12, this volume).

TEMPORAL ASPECTS OF 'SOCIAL PHENOMENA ON THE MOVE' FOR ONLINE ETHNOGRAPHIC RESEARCH

Qualitative research can use the time of data collection as a criterion that indicates higher research quality (Golafshani, 2003; Saldaña, 2003; Thomson & Holland, 2003). Traditional ethnographies typically use longitudinal data collection, with the length of time being an important criterion in their research designs (e.g. Antonides et al., 2002; Block et al., 2018; Hicks et al., 1976; Hornik & Zakay, 1996). For example, classical ethnographies often adopt longitudinal research designs to get an in-depth understanding of social phenomena. It is argued that longitudinal data collection leads to better immersion, a deeper relationship with participants, fosters trust and intimate involvement and leads to building rapport (LeCompte & Schensul, 2010).

However, netnography and mobile ethnography adopt research designs in which the length of the data collection phase is more fluid. For example, what is the ethnographic year for a two-month long netnographic study using mobile ethnography that engages one hundred participants who each post three times per day? What is the length of time of the study, in which technology is used to simultaneously 'engage' with one hundred participants in their cultural worlds, producing over 6,000 hours of deep, directed, data. What about the netnographers who view this data, read its transcriptions, annotating and analysing them for hundred or even thousands of additional hours? That fluidity of time can be seen in relation to the purpose of a netnographic study. Importantly, for qualitative research in general, there is no consensus on how 'long' is defined within a long time period of immersion (Saldaña, 2003). In longitudinal qualitative research, researchers 'hesitate to set precise parameters around longitudinal because many qualitative studies, regardless of fieldwork length, are longitudinal in its broadest sense' (Saldaña, 2003, 3). Often researchers remain vague and might state that research takes place for a 'prolonged period' (Saldaña, 2003) – or generally, include multiple phases of data collection to make assumptions on how changes occur over time (Lewis, 2007).

THREE TEMPORAL ASPECTS FOR NETNOGRAPHY

As remaining vague about research method operationalization often has a negative connotation on the quality of the research (e.g. Beneito-Montagut, 2011; Hine, 2000), the chapter now distinguishes between three temporal aspects that may help to determine the relevance and sufficiency of time in the process of netnographic data collection: (1) the ongoing processual immersion over time, (2) moments of time and (3) recurring actions in time. The chapter posits that considering these temporal alternatives will help online ethnographers practising netnography and mobile ethnography to better capture, describe, reflect and report on observed 'social phenomena on the move'.

The first alternative is a focus on *processual immersion*. Processual immersion describes an emphasis on netnographic observation and data that develops and transforms over a specified and measured period of time. Temporal processes, for example, may capture the time in between a particular influencer's post, and the responses to it, and the responses to the responses. Response times between influencers, or between different posts from the same influencer, could then be compared. Watts and Urry note that often

> moving time and place are thus broadly understood as valueless they take time away from economically valuable work. 'Stationary' time, by contrast, is viewed as valuable and the site of (economically measurable) work, except for the strange and notably absent times and places of 'waiting'.
>
> (Watts & Urry, 2008, 862)

The second alternative emphasizes *the particular moment* in the process. The focus here lies on a sequential look at time. A focus on particular temporal sequences can allow a researcher to subsequently pinpoint the time when sudden and lasting change occurs (Stanyer & Mih, 2016). Unveiling these types of events is generally of high interest and a 'researcher should be on the lookout for epiphanies of varying magnitude in data, since they both highlight and locate significant conditions related to change' (Saldaña, 2003, 51).

Third, studies could also look at *recurring actions* in time and determine if the phenomena include 'serial, cumulative, or repetitive actions', and if they have a certain rhythm or pattern which can be 'linear, sequential, cyclical, multi-tempoed, improvised, [or] choreographed' (Saldaña, 2003, 169). Hence, with this consideration behavioural changes, development, transformation and experiences over time can be observed as a whole and ongoing, but also more nuanced with iterations, moments of change or the start of evolving phenomena.

In conclusion, ethnographers can look at temporal comparisons or processes, and explore trends or immerse in observations exploring turning points (Stanyer & Mihelj, 2016), depending on whether processual immersion, a specific moment, recurring actions or a combination of them are the focus on the research question—and/or data analysis. Choosing the 'right' duration of the data collection is important and the 'length or amount, months or years, short term or long term, quality or quality, categories and variables or themes and stories, or various combinations thereof?' (Saldaña, 2003, 5) form a prerequisite to explain and interpret the data in respect to the development, change and iterations of social phenomena on the move.

DECISION JOURNEYS: AN EXAMPLE OF MODES OF TIME CONSTRUCTIONS

To illustrate time construction for social phenomena on the move, this section now uses the concept of a 'decision journey' and illustrates how it applies to netnography and mobile ethnography. A decision journey can be conceptualized as a contextually grounded representation of the sequential decisions that are taken in regard to some discrete human experience. Decision journeys are related to the concept of the 'customer journey', which relates to particular kinds of 'customer experiences' (Lemon & Verhoef, 2016). In marketing, mappings of the customer journey can help researchers or firms to the process regarding a particular consumption experience, such as booking a table and dining at a particular restaurant (Muskat et al. 2019). Relatedly, an understanding of any particular decision journey can help researchers or other interested constituents to understand any type of decision, such as the decision to revisit a restaurant, purchase a new car, or make a donation to a charity.

Recent studies that have adopted the decision journey concept often combine virtual and real-life settings, and for example show that achieving higher loyalty depends upon an understanding of both online and offline aspects of an experience (Herhausen et al., 2019). Another study observes experiences and differentiates how the augmented and the virtual reality influences experiences during the decision journey (Jung & Dieck, 2017). Further, Guerreiro et al. (2019) use the concept of the customer journey to better understand the different stages in customer decision making and how digital influencers shape a customer's decision making during the journey.

Unique to the notion of the customer journey are the so-called 'touchpoints' that emerge (often unexpectedly) over the course of time during customers experiences (Lemon & Verhoef, 2016). Touchpoints are situations, moments and interactions that matter and can be both positive or negative, and generate 'cognitive, emotional, behavioural, sensorial, and social responses to a firm's offerings during the customer's entire purchase journey' (Lemon & Verhoef, 2016, 71). Importantly, over the course of time, each customer could either identify a few salient touchpoints that influence their customer's satisfaction—or dissatisfaction—whereas others might identify a range of touchpoints for each phase (before–during–after consumption) that are pivotal to their decision making (Puccinelli et al., 2009; Verhoef et al., 2009).

As a result, the decision journey can be conceptualized as an iterative and dynamic process that changes over time. Transformations and turning points are often the units of analysis. Thus, four perspectives can be considered that might assist ethnographic research designs as they offer a framework for data analysis: (1) the 'whole' decision journey; (2) the division into in pre, during and post phases of the decision journey; (3) the momentous highlights—so-called touchpoints during the decision journey; and (4) the in-between time, during touchpoints. For online ethnographic research, a number of research avenues emerge from this temporal understanding of a person or persons' journey. For example, thus far, the connectedness of these touchpoints has rather been neglected (Lemon & Verhoef, 2016; Malthouse & Calder, 2011). Also, it might be interesting to understand how engagement

Table 17.1 The Decision Journey: Temporal Facets of One Social Phenomenon On the Move

Temporal facets of the 'decision journey'	Considerations of temporality for online ethnographies
Periods in the journey	- The 'whole' journey - The overall customer experience - Division into in pre, during, and post phases of the journey - In-between time
Touchpoints—momentous highlights	- Touchpoints can be both negative and positive - Touchpoints are potentially different for each person - Touchpoints evoke cognitive, emotional, behavioural, sensorial and social responses - Touchpoints are influenced by people's prior experiences - Some touchpoints can be influenced by outside factors, whereas others cannot - Differences in online and offline behaviours
Iterative and processual components	- The processual flow of capturing touchpoints - Interconnectedness of touchpoints - Interconnectedness of in-between time and touchpoints - Transitions between pre, during, and post phases - Conceptualizing experiences and 'breaking-down' these experience in decision journey sequences

practices influence decision journeys during the in-between time and in both negative and positive touchpoints. Table 17.1 summarizes and distinguishes three temporal facets of decision journeys.

IMPLICATIONS FOR ONLINE ETHNOGRAPHIC RESEARCHERS

Implications from this research can be drawn for both netnography and mobile ethnography methods. Netnographic researchers can contribute to a better understanding of online interactions and experience when reflecting on the manifold aspects of human time construction in all three parts of the netnographic research process: during data collection, while engaged in immersive practices using social media, and while interpreting online traces. Netnographies have long emphasized the length of time of engagement, just as traditional ethnographies have. However, this chapter raises some questions about this perhaps unreflective practice. Netnographers have always been engaged in the collection and inter-pretation of a wide range of textual, audio, and graphic data, include livestreams, daily updates, and archival sources. Each of these types of data may have their own unique relation to time—asynchronously or synchronously capturing moments in times, spans of time, or long lengths of time. These are highly useful practices, already well under way in the contem-porary practice of netnography.

Netnographic research projects could analyse the digital decision journey and social experiences—and include decision-making, learning, information seeking and sharing processes. Prior research has shown that there are differences in online vs real-life time construction (e.g. Ariffin et al., 2018; Hicks et al., 1976; Novak et al., 2000). Keeping those differences in mind, future netnographies might attend more carefully and systematically to the underlying phenomena and characteristics that lead to the emergence of characteristics of time construction in online environments. New perspectives on time construction could add value and depth to some 'taken-for-granted' assumptions of time—and open up new avenues for temporal aspects in online research to be revisited and even challenged.

For example, future netnographic research might seek to better understand the devel-opment of social phenomena on the move. Here, longitudinal research designs might con-sider transitions and changes with starting points and endpoints. Data collection might be targeted towards temporal aspects of development of stability or endurance. Netnographers advance the understanding of how perspective and retrospective views on the customer journey (e.g. Block et al., 2018; Hicks et al., 1976) can be understood in online experiences and interactions. Touchpoints within these decision journeys might be used generate new insights to deepen the understanding of the importance of various temporal aspects of human social or social media experience. Netnographic research can reveal the specific underlying phenomena that trigger negative or positive touchpoints. Here, adding a mobile ethnography to the netnography might be beneficial to capture these turning points in real time by providing a way to engage with research participants in situ as these types of turning points actually occur, eliciting them through specific protocols.

In terms of practicality, mobile phones, equipped with applications that allow both syn-chronous and asynchronous communication, have been found useful in these types of netnographies. Rambe and Mkono (2019), for example, recently used WhatsApp to capture text messages, voice and video recordings from individual and group chat data. Another example is 'Experience Fellow', an application that can be used to capture touchpoints for mobile ethnog-raphies but which also allows participants to record reflective diaries (e.g. Muskat et al., 2013). With these mobile applications, participants collect data in their own spaces, touchpoints, turning points and moments of change. These spaces can refer to both online and real-world setting (DeBerry-Spence et al., 2019; Muskat et al., 2018). In this regard, future ethnographic research might explore the benefits of mixed and multi-method approaches.

CONCLUSION

The aim of this research is to reflect on the many ways that humans construct time, in order to offer ideas how qualitative online ethnographers might use these manifold temporal facets to enhance their research designs. The focus lies on a discussion on temporal aspects of social phenomena on the move and sheds light on various perspectives of time that often remain uncovered, yet can provide a more in-depth data analysis that can enhance quality of qualitative research in general. Although, in traditional ethnography, time has always played a major role—to enhance research quality (Saldaña, 2003; Thomson & Holland, 2003), some online ethnographies in the past have been criticized for their lack of credibility in their research designs (e.g. Berger, 2015; Holstein & Gubrium, 2011; O'Gorman et al., 2014).

Time is inherent in any human activity and human time construction is multi-faceted and highly subjective (Corbin et al., 2015; Hornik & Zakay, 1996; Zauberman et al., 2009). With a more nuanced observation and reporting of how humans construct time, especially in online settings, researchers have the opportunity to enhance credibility. In terms of implications for research, online ethnographers might benefit from integrating some facets of human time construction in their methodologies including:

- Societal culture
- Individual prospective and retrospective views on time
- Variations of time perceptions between 'before and after' particular experiences
- Affective variations of time and negative and positive affective distinctions with regard to length filled vs empty time
- Differences between an individual's time construction in an online environment vs. face-to-face encounters.

Moreover, this chapter suggests that social phenomena on the move and acting participants in online ethnographic studies might be observed with regard to their processual immersion in time, moments of time and recurring actions in time. In offering the concept of the 'decision journey', the chapter provides one avenues through which netnographers might distinguish the 'whole' journey, parts of the process (pre-, during- and post-decision or experience), touchpoints/moments that matter, the in-between time—and interconnections amongst these periods of time and single salient moments. In conclusion, adding deeper reflection on facets of time, netnographers might shed some new light on existing and new social phenomena on the move.

REFERENCES

Anhøj, J., & Møldrup, C. (2004). Feasibility of collecting diary data from asthma patients through mobile phones and SMS (Short Message Service): Response rate analysis and focus group evaluation from a pilot study. *Journal of Medical Internet Research, 6*(4), e42.

Antonides, G., Verhoef, P. C., & Van Aalst, M. (2002). Consumer perception and evaluation of waiting time: A field experiment. *Journal of Consumer Psychology, 12*(3), 193–202.

Ariffin, S. K., Mohan, T., & Goh, Y. N. (2018). Influence of consumers' perceived risk on consumers' online purchase intention. *Journal of Research in Interactive Marketing, 12*(3), 309–327.

Beneito-Montagut, R. (2011). Ethnography goes online: Towards a user-centered methodology to research interpersonal communication on the Internet. *Qualitative Research, 11*(6), 716–735.

Berger, R. (2015). Now I see it, now I don't: Researcher's position and reflexivity in qualitative research. *Qualitative Research, 15*(2), 219–234.

Block, R. A., Grondin, S., & Zakay, D. (2018). Prospective and retrospective timing processes: Theories, methods, and findings. In A. Vatakis, F. Balcı, M. Di Luca and Á. Correa (Eds.), *Timing and time perception: Procedures, measures, & applications* (pp. 32–51). Leiden, NL: Brill.

Büscher, M., & Urry, J. (2009). Mobile methods and the empirical. *European Journal of Social Theory, 12*(1), 99–116.

Corbin, J., Strauss, A. L., & Strauss, A. (2015). *Basics of qualitative research: Techniques and procedures for developing Grounded Theory* (4th ed.). London: Sage.

DeBerry-Spence, B., Ekpo, A. E., & Hogan, D. (2019). Mobile Phone Visual Ethnography (MpVE): Bridging transformative photography and mobile phone ethnography. *Journal of Public Policy & Marketing, 38*(1), 81–95.

Dennison, L., Morrison, L., Conway, G., & Yardley, L. (2013). Opportunities and challenges for smartphone applications in supporting health behavior change: Qualitative study. *Journal of Medical Internet Research, 15*(4), 86.

Golafshani, N. (2003). Understanding reliability and validity in qualitative research. *The Qualitative Report, 8*(4), 597–606. Retrieved from https://nsuworks.nova.edu/tqr/vol8/iss4/6

Guerreiro, C., Viegas, M., & Guerreiro, M. (2019). Social networks and digital influencers: Their role in customer decision journey in tourism. *Journal of Spatial and Organizational Dynamics, 7*(3), 240–260.

Hammersley, M. (1990). *Reading ethnographic research: A critical guide* (Longman Social Research Series, 2nd ed.). London: Routledge.

Hammersley, M. (1992). *What's wrong with ethnography? Methodological explorations.* London: Routledge.

Hannam, K., Sheller, M., & Urry, J. (2006). Mobilities, immobilities and moorings. *Mobilities, 1*(1), 1–22.

Herhausen, D., Kleinlercher, K., Verhoef, P. C., Emrich, O., & Rudolph, T. (2019). Loyalty formation for different customer journey segments. *Journal of Retailing, 95*(3), pp. 9–29.

Hicks, R. E., Miller, G. W., & Kinsbourne, M. (1976). Prospective and retrospective judgments of time as a function of amount of information processed. *The American Journal of Psychology, 89*(4), 719–730.

Hine, C. (2000). *Virtual ethnography.* London, UK: Sage.

Holstein, J. A., & Gubrium, J. F. (2011). The constructionist analytics of interpretive practice. In N. K. Denzin & Y. S. Lincoln (Eds.), *The Sage handbook of qualitative research* (pp. 341–358). Thousand Oaks, CA: Sage.

Hornik, J., & Zakay, D. (1996). Psychological time: The case of time and consumer behaviour. *Time & Society, 5*(3), 385–397.

Jung, T. H., & Dieck, M. C. (2017). Augmented reality, virtual reality and 3D printing for the co-creation of value for the visitor experience at cultural heritage places. *Journal of Place Management and Development, 10*(2), 140–151.

Kozinets, R. V. (2002). The field behind the screen: Using netnography for marketing research in online communities. *Journal of Marketing Research, 39*(1), 61–72.

Kozinets, R. V. (2020). *Netnography: The essential guide to social media research* (3rd ed.). London: SAGE Publications Ltd.

LeCompte, M. D., & Schensul, J. J. (2010). *Designing and conducting ethnographic research: An introduction (Vol. 1).* Lanham, MD: Rowman Altamira.

Lemon, K. N., & Verhoef, P. C. (2016). Understanding customer experience throughout the customer journey. *Journal of Marketing, 80*(6), 69–96.

Lewis, J. (2007). Analysing qualitative longitudinal research in evaluations. *Social Policy and Society, 6*(4), 545–556.

Lugosi, P. & Quinton S. (2018) More-than-human netnography. *Journal of Marketing Management, 34*(3–4), 287–313.

Malthouse, E. C., & Calder, B. J. (2011). Comment: Engagement and experiences: comment on Brodie, Hollenbeek, Juric, and Ilic (2011). *Journal of Service Research, 14*(3), 277–279.

Muskat, B., Hörtnagl, T., Prayag, G., & Wagner, S. (2019). Perceived quality, authenticity, and price in tourists' dining experiences: Testing competing models of satisfaction and behavioral intentions. Journal of Vacation Marketing, 25(4), 480–498.

Muskat, B., Muskat, M., & Zehrer, A. (2018). Qualitative interpretive mobile ethnography. *Anatolia, 29*(1), 98–107.

Muskat, M., Muskat, B., Zehrer, A., & Johns, R. (2013). Generation Y: Evaluating services experiences through mobile ethnography. *Tourism Review, 68*(3), 55–71.

Novak, T. P., Hoffman, D. L., & Yung, Y. F. (2000). Measuring the customer experience in online environments: A structural modeling approach. *Marketing Science, 19*(1), 22–42.

O'Gorman, K. D., MacLaren, A. C., & Bryce, D. (2014). A call for renewal in tourism ethnographic research: The researcher as both the subject and object of knowledge. *Current Issues in Tourism, 17*(1), 46–59.

Puccinelli, N. M., Goodstein, R. C., Grewal, D., Price, R., Raghubir, P., & Stewart, D. (2009). Customer experience management in retailing: Understanding the buying process. *Journal of Retailing, 85*(1), 15–30.

Rambe, P. & Mkono, M. (2019). Appropriating WhatsApp-mediated postgraduate supervision to negotiate 'relational authenticity' in resource-constrained environments. *British Journal of Educational Technology, 50*(2), 702–734.

Saldaña, J. (2003). *Longitudinal qualitative research: Analyzing change through time.* Walnut Creek, CA: Altamira.

Stanyer, J., & Mihelj, S. (2016). Taking time seriously? Theorizing and researching change in communication and media studies. *Journal of Communication, 66*(2), 266–279.

Thomson, R., & Holland, J. (2003). Hindsight, foresight and insight: The challenges of longitudinal qualitative research. *International Journal of Social Research Methodology, 6*(3), 233–244.

Urry, J. (2002). *Sociology beyond societies: Mobilities for the twenty-first century.* London: Routledge.

Van Maanen, J. (1979). The fact of fiction in organizational ethnography. *Administrative Science Quarterly, 24*(4), 539–550.

Verhoef, P. C., Lemon, K. N., Parasuraman, A., Roggeveen, A., Tsiros, M., & Schlesinger, L. A. (2009). Customer experience creation: Determinants, dynamics and management strategies. *Journal of Retailing, 85*(1), 31–41.

Watts, L. & Urry, J. (2008). Moving methods, travelling times. *Environment and Planning D: Society and Space, 26,* 860–874.

Whitehead, T. L. (2005). Basic classical ethnographic research methods. *Cultural Ecology of Health and Change, 1,* 1–29.

Zauberman, G., Kim, B. K., Malkoc, S. A., & Bettman, J. R. (2009). Discounting time and time discounting: Subjective time perception and intertemporal preferences. *Journal of Marketing Research, 46*(4), 543–556.

18

Netnography in Live Video Streaming

Yi-Sheng Wang

INTRODUCTION

Online live streaming is a new media genre that combines the broadcast of an activity with cross-modal video-mediated communication. In effect, live video streaming platforms constitute a unique and newly emergent form of social media, and they are increasingly recognized as such (Twitch, 2019). Today, peer-to-peer (P2P) internet streaming of videos is a rapidly growing form of media. Recent years have seen P2P internet streaming services doubling their user base year-on-year, with current figures reaching over a hundred million unique monthly users (Recktenwald, 2017; Twitch, 2019). Numerous streaming platforms, with Twitch and YouTube Live being prominent examples, have been founded and have demonstrated unprecedented growth among users around the world. Streaming video services offer a convenient and flexible means of watching online videos, a means through which users can effectively play video files at the same time that the files are being delivered from the server. Many streaming media websites, such as YouTube and MSN video, provide millions of online streaming videos. These extensive offerings have gained these online streaming services growing popularity among internet users. In concert with the further development of these sites, designers have attempted to improve the quality of streaming services in order to increase the satisfaction levels of users (Sjöblom & Hamari, 2017).

As a special combination of multiple forms of media, live streaming allows individuals to publicly broadcast live video streams while also utilizing shared chat rooms for communication with other users. Generally, a typical live video streaming activity involves a streamer/broadcaster who uploads real-time video and audio content, including sessions of video game play, talent performances, daily life activities, or whatever else the broadcaster chooses to share (Sinclair & Tinson, 2017). Viewers on a streamer's channel can comment on the videos that are shared and communicate with each other via a text-based chat room function. Meanwhile, the streamer can also engage in dialogue and interactions with the audience while broadcasting. The participatory and interactive nature of this emerging form of media serves to bridge the divide between games and traditional forms of media, such as television, via the convergence of interactive, communal, and passive forms of media (Sjöblom & Hamari, 2017).

Not all live video streaming content is similar; instead, it is highly varied, ranging from strongly competitive endeavors to extremely casual ones (Hu, Zhang & Wang, 2017). Few studies thus far have approached this topic quantifiably; rather, the existing literature on live video streaming has focused primarily on communities (Hu, Zhang & Wang, 2017; Lim et al., 2012), technical aspects (Zhang & Hassanein, 2012; Recktenwald, 2017; Kima, Nama & Ryub, 2017), and competitive eSports (Sjöblom & Hamari, 2017; Badrinarayanan, Sierra & Martinb, 2015). Researchers have paid insufficient attention, meanwhile, to understanding the massive participation behavior exhibited by live video streaming users.

Although live video streaming sites are popular and their numbers of users have significantly increased (Recktenwald, 2017; Twitch, 2019), the states of mind of the users who visit these websites and their reasons for engaging in live video streaming remain unclear. It is not fully clear why live video streaming attracts such large numbers of users, as the subject has not been adequately addressed in previous research. What factors motivate users to like, share, or comment on live video streams? What is it about live video streaming that users find appealing? Why do live video streaming users enjoy this format so much? What is the user experience like, and how do users interact with the associated live environments? At present, a theoretical gap exists regarding these questions, as previous studies have not produced clear answers to them. Rather, the extant literature lacks a comprehensive framework to explain users' ongoing experiences. Live video streaming is a relatively new type of consumer experience and has not yet been fully explored in marketing and consumer academic research. Therefore, in order to enhance the understanding of the topic, major gaps need to be identified and eliminated. Managers must seek progress in the context of these factors.

The purpose of this paper was to address this void in the management literature. This study aimed to explore in depth some of the characteristics and user experiences of live video streaming and to provide insights regarding an interpretation of the live video streaming context model. Consequently, this study uses netnography, online interviews and the physical travel of researchers to the field for participation and observations. Netnography offers a set of instructions relating to a specific way to conduct qualitative social media research using a combination of different research practices (Kozinets, 2020, 7) to study the cultures and communities emerging through computer-mediated communications (Kozinets, 2002). Netnography analyzes interactions and conversations generated in online settings to identify and understand the needs and decisions of relevant online consumer groups. Netnography is a flexible, ethically sensitive, and unobtrusive method adapted to the purpose of studying the language, motivations, consumption linkages, and symbols of consumption-oriented online communities (Kozinets, 2015). Netnography is at the core of this chapter's elaboration of a video live streaming research approach. The next section of this chapter will develop this research approach to live video streaming.

ON THE RESEARCH OF LIVE VIDEO STREAMING

Live video streaming refers to online streaming media that are simultaneously recorded and broadcast in real time to viewers, with the media being continuously received by and presented to end-users while being delivered by a provider (Twitch, 2019); streaming typically refers to conveying media content in a way that allows it to be simultaneously consumed by the receiver, as opposed to "downloading," where the received media content is saved for later consumption (Recktenwald, 2017). According to Abdous and Yoshimura (2010), the term "live video streaming" may refer to the scope of the broadcast and diverse formulas, with the following key attributes: (1) streaming is more concerned with the delivery method of the medium rather than the exact form of the medium; (2) streaming is an extremely interesting context for participatory online media, as spearheaded by services such as YouTube, that have put the traditional consumer into the role of content creator (Sjöblom & Hamari, 2017); and (3) streaming may be regarded as a form of broadcast entertainment akin to online videos, but for many users, it is a more manifold and holistic form of communication than mere video media content, particularly due to the high levels of interaction (Twitch, 2019).

Thus far, researchers have primarily engaged online video streaming as it relates to the field of online education and interactive learning (He, 2013; Abdous & Yoshimura, 2010; Leijen et al., 2009), eSports (Sjöblom & Hamari, 2017; Wei & Lu, 2014), streaming technology (Zhang & Hassanein, 2012) and community platforms (Hu, Zhang & Wang, 2017; Wang, Lee & Hsu, 2017). The focus of the online interactive learning research of live video streaming has been on students' online participation, which includes face-to-face interactions in class, the viewing of satellite broadcasts at remote sites, and the viewing of live video streams at home or at work (He, 2013; Abdous & Yoshimura, 2010; Leijen et al., 2009; Ha et al., 2018). The key focus of live video streaming in eSports has been on use and gratification, which include tension release, social integrative, and affective motivations (Sjöblom & Hamari, 2017; Hamari & Sjöblom, 2017). The key focus of live video streaming in streaming technology has been on P2P streaming technology, which includes determining the supplier–receiver relationships for each packet, handling the departure of the supplier or receiver before their relationship expires, and handling lost packets (Zhang & Hassanein, 2012; Kim & Lee, 2017). The key focus of live video streaming on community platforms has been on continuous watching behavior intentions, which include broadcasters and audience groups being positively associated with their continuous watching intentions (Hu, Zhang & Wang, 2017; Wang, Lee & Hsu, 2017). Studies regarding live video streaming differ according to the different properties of the individual studies. This section of the chapter examined extant research of the live video streaming phenomenon. In the next section, the chapter discusses and illustrates immersion in live video streaming.

IMMERSION IN LIVE VIDEO STREAMING

Immersion is a dimension that fits particularly well with both live video streaming and the netnographic glance utilized to investigate it. As it is subjectively experienced, immersion is a multifaceted construct. It means being "in" a real or virtual experience (Pine & Gilmore, 1999). It involves physical and mental participation and implies getting away from everyday experience, playing a different role, or taking on a new identity. Hansen and Mossberg (2013) define immersion as "a form of spatio-temporal belonging in the world that is characterized by deep involvement in the present moment" (212). In leisure and tourism, escape experiences necessitate a strong state of immersion (Oh, Fiore, & Jeoung, 2007). The participant either escapes from his/her ordinary life or escapes to a new destination such as the new environment associated with a VR experience. In the technological literature, the notion of immersion can occur as an objective description of the immersive properties of the system, with the assumption that subjective immersion follows. Thus, Milgram and Kishino (1994) define the immersive properties of systems along a "virtuality continuum" ranging from the completely virtual to the completely real. This continuum concerns all possible variants and compositions of real and virtual objects.

Immersion is the dimension that makes unique and compelling the live video streaming experience as a phenomenon to investigate. In the context of socially oriented VR, Nagy and Koles (2014) extend this reasoning to suggest that interaction with virtual objects (for example the purchase of clothing or weaponry) increases immersion through heightened individual identification with the VR. Tussyadiah et al. (2018) also show that increasing interactive features in tourism VR experiences can be linked to immersion.

This body of research generally finds that the presence of computer-generated avatars, human-based avatars or real others leads to greater immersion in the virtual world. One reason put forward for this effect is that the presence of others makes the virtual world feel more like the real world (Sutcliffe, 2016), where most individuals live and interact socially in environments peopled by other humans. A second argument for live video streaming enhancing immersion relies on shared goals, particularly in achieving player aims during video games (Cairns et al., 2013; Vella, 2016). By communicating and exchanging around how to win, be it a competitive or cooperative game, players become involved together in reaching their goals, and thus more immersed. Similarly, from the work done on socially oriented experiences, such as Second Life, it is clear that live video streaming interactions are key to becoming immersed in a virtual world designed to facilitate and develop human activities and relationships such as shopping, having a "virtual" drink at a bar or eating at a virtual restaurant (Grinberg et al., 2014). In these contexts, the presence of virtual others can create a sense of intimacy, group identity, entry into a virtual culture, and an alternative life narrative. As a new form of social commerce, live streaming shopping is becoming increasingly popular among Chinese consumers, which has aroused great interest among practitioners and researchers (Sun et al., 2019).

Early researchers in the field of virtual reality introduced immersion as a technical concept in the design of virtual environments. Most of the researchers in the field of virtual reality have since usually defined immersion as the "objective" and "measurable" properties of a virtual environment (e.g. Bystrom et al., 1999; Nash et al., 2000; Slater, 1999), to indicate "the extent to which the computer displays are capable of delivering an inclusive, extensive, surrounding and vivid illusion of reality to the senses of a human participant" (Slater & Wilbur, 1997). However, other researchers, such as Witmer and Singer (1998), challenged this technical definition arguing that immersion is a "psychological state characterized by perceiving oneself to be enveloped by, included in, and interacting with an environment that provides a continuous stream of stimuli and experiences." Later on, several researchers argued that immersion is not a new construct, nor is it one that is only linked to the emergence of AR technologies; immersive experiences can also occur when employing desktop based environments with low image and audio realism, or even in non-technologically mediated activities, such as storytelling (Brooks, 2003; McMahan, 2003). Immersion was, therefore, re-defined as a natural human state, which emerges as people engage in an engrossing activity, such as, for instance, when reading an enjoyable book, watching a film or playing a digital game (Weibel et al., 2010). According to Brooks (2003), to be immersed is to be involved in a given context, not only physically but also mentally and emotionally. Under these circumstances, the concept was also re-contextualized in the game-based literature, where it was operationalized and established as a psychological phenomenon (e.g. Cheng et al., 2015; Brown & Cairns, 2004; Jennett et al., 2008; McMahon & Ojeda, 2008). Immersion has been recognized as a vital part of a successful digital game and has been argued to have a positive impact on the gameplay experience (Brown & Cairns, 2004).

In the experience literature, "immersion" is related to the concept of "flow," where participants enter into an extreme version of immersion, losing self-consciousness and experiencing a modified sense of time (Csikszentmihalyi, 1990). The work of Jennett et al. (2008), and Brown and Cairns (2004) suggests that flow differs from immersion in that it is a fleeting, optimal moment during immersion. In other words, people can feel immersed to varying degrees during an activity, whereas flow is an all or nothing experience. In addition, flow always corresponds to a positive emotional valence (Csikszentmihalyi, 1990), whereas immersion does not presuppose positive emotions.

ON THE METHODOLOGY OF LIVE VIDEO STREAMING

Over the past several years, many anthropologists, sociologists, and qualitative researchers have written about the need to adapt existing ethnographic research techniques to the many cultures and communities that are emerging through online communications (Grossnickle & Raskin, 2000; Miller & Slater, 2000; Kozinets, 1997, 1998, 2001). Netnography is an adaptation of ethnography to the study of online communities (Kozinets, 2010, 2015, 2020; Kozinets & Nocker, 2018).

Netnography provides information on the symbolism, meanings, and interaction patterns of online groups (Kozinets, 2002). Qualitative methods are particularly useful for revealing the rich symbolic world that underlies needs, desires, meaning, and choice (Levy, 1959). Netnography provides researchers with a window into naturally occurring behaviors, such as searches for information by and communal word-of-mouth discussions between online users. Because it is both naturalistic and unobtrusive—an unprecedentedly unique combination not found in any other research method—netnography allows continuing access to informants in a particular online social situation. This access may provide valuable opportunities for relationships between researchers and online users (Kozinets & Nocker, 2018; Kozinets, 2019; Wang, 2019c).

The research methodology of the present study consisted of the use of netnography, including online interviews as well as field observations and participation by the researchers made possible by their physical travel to the field. By combining online interviews with netnography, the study effectively integrated offline and online methods in order to make the collection of data, data analysis, and other processes more consistent (Patton, 2002; Rubin & Rubin, 1995; Wang, 2019a; Sherry, 1990). Meanwhile, the research was also rendered more realistic through the use of in-person observations and participation. According to Mason (2002) and Patton (2002), it is the specific questions and arguments of the researchers that should form the basis for a study's research field and theoretical framework. Meanwhile, the development of the propositions put forward by a study can be supported by the study's analytical framework.

This study implemented triangulation to help reduce research bias (Wang, 2018). After the first interview with an interviewee was completed, a transcript was prepared and sent to him or her for correction (Demuth & Mey, 2015). During the second interview, a cross-check of the first interview's content was performed, and the interviewee was asked to confirm whether that content contained errors, did not provide details in full, or did not provide an authentic representation of his or her intended meaning (Denzin, 2006). In order to reduce research bias, the interviewer also conducted an in-depth supplementary interview to correct the parts of the first interview that were vague, incomplete, or possessed special significance (Wang, 2019). Having discussed the methodology of live video streaming, the chapter now turns to some illustrations.

FIELDSITE

The fieldsite of this study was the Twitch live video streaming platform. Twitch is the service most synonymous with live streaming, and its community is the most robust. In 2018, Twitch announced it had more than 1.5 million broadcasters and 100 million users per month (Twitch, 2019). Streaming services are about more than just technology. They are also about cultivating and empowering a community of fans and creators. Various chat customization options let streamers tailor the way they interact with their audiences, but the larger social vibe of the platform as a whole colors the experience too (Sjöblom & Hamari, 2017; Ortiz, Chih & Teng, 2017). The majority of the platform's registered members consist of office workers and students aged between 16 and 35 years old. These groups are also the largest populations of live video streaming viewers (Twitch, 2019).

INTERVIEWS

The interview data collection was split into three stages (Patton, 2002; Wang, 2018). The first stage mainly involved online observations and archival data collection and analysis (Wang,

2019a). The researchers registered and played the role of users. However, in an attempt to maintain some distance between the academic study and natural phenomena, it did not take any initiative to seek out users during this period. To investigate the differences between this method and other network research methods, the researchers specifically asked users to submit online diary reports using LINE or email every week to make further observations (Wang, 2018). The second stage primarily entailed active participation in online activities and an emphasis on personally experiencing users' feelings and participation in the discussion of issues (Rubin & Rubin, 1995). During this stage, the research direction inclined towards a primary focus on personal experiences in order to understand the true feelings of the users. The third stage, emergent design, concerned the performance of online and offline (face-to-face) observations and interviews (Miller & Slater, 2000). In addition to face-to-face observations and interviews with the users, 10–20 more subjects were recruited for face-to-face interviews. Those subjects consisted of friends, colleagues, roommates, and classmates of the initial users, as well as industry experts, and the aim of the interviews conducted with them was to verify the relevant information provided by the initial users (Hine, 2000; Wang, 2019b).

During the interview process, any necessary clarification was obtained directly from the interviewees; after organizing the interview records, they were sent to each interviewee through LINE (Hammersley, 1989). In addition, any vaguely expressed statements were corrected and reconfirmed until the interview data were accurate. Second, the interviews' main focus was to reveal the essence of the experience. The purpose was to uncover and explain the less well-known phenomena underlying the superficialities of user experiences (Demuth & Mey, 2015). Furthermore, the authors aimed to capture the detailed and complicated conditions that a quantitative research method could not elaborate on (Lincoln & Guba, 1985).

The guiding principles proposed by Rubin and Rubin (1995, 125) were rigorously followed: (1) limit the number of main topics to the greatest possible extent; (2) make smooth, logical transitions; (3) state the main point of the given interviewee's response and facilitate the derivation of the cause and effect of his or her perspective; (4) avoid interfering with the discussion; and (5) dig into the responses to compose subsequent questions but ensure the consecutive progression of listening, thinking, and talking. Typically, the desire to be humorous can be counterproductive in an online interview. Therefore, in this study, we brought out the interviewees' humorous side by showing interest, as suggested by Hammersley (1989), who recommends playing the role of a socially acceptable incompetent while conducting an interview. In the next section of the chapter, I will illustrate field participation and observations.

FIELD PARTICIPATION AND OBSERVATIONS

When engaging in field participation and observations, researchers play the roles of observers (that is, outsiders) and participants (that is, insiders among the online audience) (Hine, 2000). Because of the duality of the researchers' roles, the researchers must maintain not only a good relationship with other audience members but also a psychological and spatial distance while involved in live video streaming activities (Wang, 2019a, b). The method entailed both overt and covert observations. (1) During the first stage, covert observation was implemented. In other words, the observation of a live video streaming situation was conducted without the subjects' awareness of being observed. The researchers did not interfere with or destroy the social structure or interpersonal networking of the online audiences; thus, real and natural information was obtained (Wang, 2018). (2) During the second and third stages, overt observation was employed. In other words, the audiences were aware that the researchers were observing them. Because both sides were online audiences and had already developed a close relationship, less well-known information was obtained and the truth was revealed, enabling further understanding of the background context of the continuity and correlation of live video streaming. Through the field participation and observations, the researchers obtained a more direct understanding of the events that occurred and the interactions among the audience members (Wang et al., 2017).

We documented the information gained in the field observations and recorded that information in text form as "Field Notes." This study followed Bogdan and Biklen's (1998) description of thinking, providing both objective and reflective descriptions. In the first stage, we implemented objective descriptions (Denzin, 2006; Wang, 2018), focusing on the description of live scenes, characters, actions, and conversations in the live video streaming. The descriptions were faithful, detailed, and accurately expressed to the best of our ability, without employing abstract wording. We focused on making a textual record that contained objective descriptions. During the second and third stages, we utilized reflective descriptions (Demuth & Mey, 2015; Wang, 2019), focusing on the customers' personal psychology, thoughts, and primary concerns. The emphasis was on speculations, feelings, thoughts, premonitions, impressions, possible prejudices, and so on. In the process of retrospection, mistakes and misunderstandings in the record were clarified and corrected. In this section, we looked at the field participation and observations. In the next section, I will illustrate inductive analysis and context induction.

ANALYSIS AND CONTEXT INDUCTION

The netnographic analysis we performed adopted an inductive approach. Through constant comparisons of the interview contents from the various respondents, social categories for presenting the characteristics of the interview content were developed (Kozinets, 2020). Through this systematic data collection and analysis process, theoretical insights were excavated and formed. The study was based on interview materials (interviews, observations from the field participation, meeting notes, files, and other phenomena) with a pre-set perspective but without a predetermined conclusion (Demuth & Mey, 2015), further encouraging a strategy framework.

Verbatim transcriptions were produced from the digital recordings. The analysis of the text was undertaken using QSR NVIVO software. All variables were obtained using grounded theory-based coding techniques (Strauss & Corbin, 1998; Miller & Slater, 2000). Our coding followed Charmaz's (2006) guidelines and encompassed open, axial and selective coding procedures to arrive at a core central category that led to a set of research propositions. In this section, we looked at the text analysis and context induction. In the next section, I will illustrate the implications from my research design.

THEORETICAL IMPLICATIONS FROM RESEARCH DESIGN

A Three-Stage Situational Context Approach

This study emphasized how theory emerged from the meaning of the text through a process of induction. The findings of the study were produced following a three-stage "situational context" approach, which is presented herein in the form of propositions. Finally, the insights of a "contextualization experiences model" were developed, as shown in Figure 18.1.

As illustrated in Figure 18.1, theory was developed inductively based on abstraction from a systematic process of data collection, analysis, discovery, integration, and classification. The findings of this study relate to three stages of "situational context" that guided the theory-building process. The term "situational context" refers to the online environment and atmosphere that a user is connected directly to, that is, the user's genuine psychological state

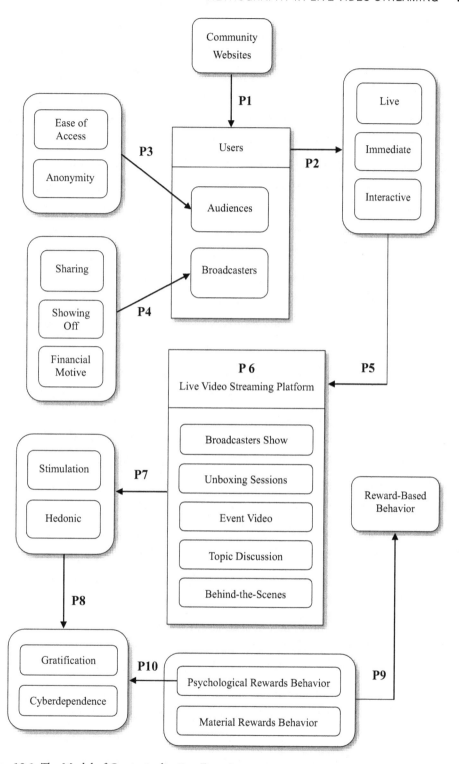

Figure 18.1 The Model of Contextualization Experiences.

in an online environment. From a user's perspective, an online environment is objective, and different users can exist in the same network environment. Online context combines subjectivity and objectivity, and it is influenced by three dimensions, namely, the participatory component of direct experience, individual online experience, and online culture (Wang, 2019a, b).

The first stage mainly involved online observations and archival data collection and analysis (Kozinets, 1998, 2002). It entailed collecting users' self-reports online and analyzing old data files and electronic bulletin board information. The researchers attempted to maintain some distance between the academic study and the phenomena experienced as observers (lurkers). The second stage primarily involved active participation in online activities and an emphasis on personally experiencing users' feelings and participation in the discussion of issues (Demuth & Mey, 2015). The researchers officially transitioned from being passive lurkers and became positive live video streaming users. They took the initiative to communicate with 105 online users to exchange ideas. Instant online conversation was performed through LINE or Skype to clarify special actions or feelings in the users' self-reports. The third stage, emergent design, concerned performing online and offline (face-to-face) observations and interviews (Hine, 2000). The researchers proposed issues or asked questions according to observations and the researchers' personal experience in the first two stages. After a withdrawal from the online mode, the work of netnography was transferred offline.

Abstraction Ladder Diagram

A comprehensive explanation of the abstraction process applied to the three-stage research design is provided in this section. For this study, the authors created an abstraction ladder diagram of the three stages. An emergent design was adopted, allowing participants to speak for themselves, as suggested in qualitative research, and ensuring that accurate data were collected in order to obtain trustworthy results (Lincoln & Guba, 1985). Budding concepts were identified by repeatedly comparing the interviewees' interview contents, after which labels were given to reflect the traits identified in the interview contents. We developed theory through the implementation of systematic data collection and analysis. Based on the data (including interviews, field observations, meeting minutes, documentation, and observed phenomena), and by adopting pre-existing standpoints but not pre-set conclusions (Wang, 2018, 2019), a rudimentary conceptual framework/model was developed. The three-stage research design behind the netnography approach was derived from the abstraction ladder diagram of the three stages, as shown below (Figure 18.2).

In the first stage, the researchers started by summarizing and packaging the precious data obtained in the field, in the hope that these field data could be converted into analyzable text. Line-by-line transcripts of the interview recordings were then prepared and sorted under the conceptualization and abstraction groups. Coding and the identification of a suitable set of categories were carried out, and an analytic memo (concerning the relationship between various interpretative frameworks) was prepared, after which data coding was performed. During the second stage, a round of repackaging and consolidation was performed by locating the themes and trends in the data. The key points and faults, as well as the interrelationships within the data were uncovered, and a refined memo was then prepared. The third stage involved proposition detection and the establishment of an interpretive framework/model. Two important steps were executed at this stage. (1) Hypothesis detection and the simplification of data sets were carried out to facilitate a trend analysis, enabling the researchers to plot the analyzed data on a chart, implement cross-checking, and analyze the findings. (2) Subsequently, a deep structure outline was developed as the researchers were seeking to incorporate the data into an interpretive framework that revealed their hermeneutic understanding. Relatedly, the study also revealed and addressed a gap

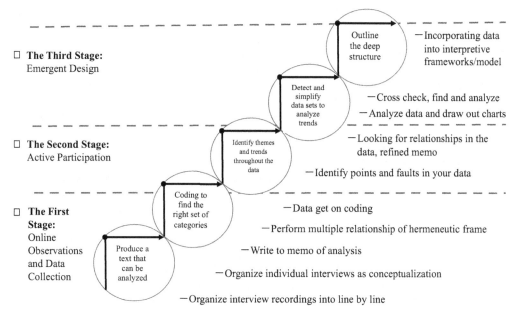

Figure 18.2 Abstraction Ladder Diagram of Three Stages.

in the methodologies utilized by previous studies, that is, the fact that netnography-based studies were often implemented in two stages. During the first stage, online observations are primarily carried out to collect and analyze key information. The second stage focuses on the feelings of participants and their thoughts regarding active participation in online activities. However, more can be done in this respect. Recent studies have added a third stage that involves the application of emergent design (Wang et al., 2017; Wang, 2018) to improve the effectiveness of offline and online interviews and observations. The major advantages of this approach are (1) its ability to repeatedly confirm the truthfulness of an event; (2) its accuracy with respect to important but little-known supplementary information pertaining to live video streaming in online forums; (3) and its credibility in regard to the repeated content verification and inspection. The researchers played an active participatory role in the interviewees' online and offline scenarios.

Furthermore, the study's results provided insights into the establishment of the model of contextualization experiences. Based on the raw field data collected from the participants, this theoretical model was able to explain how to manipulate various phenomena relating to live video streaming, the conditions and methods under which they operate, and how they attract consumers and get these people to accept their opinions. The model has provided clear explanations for these issues. On one hand, it could be argued that the raw data formed the foundation of the research theory, but on the other, it could also be argued that it is the theory itself that gave meaning to the act of collecting raw data, such that the data are meaningful and systematic. As a result, the model's explanatory influence was enhanced since it is relatively specific and paid attention to the complexity and specific characteristics of the phenomenon being studied. This was the main contribution of our study.

Netnography-Based Theory Construction

The authors further provided a more in-depth explanation regarding how they used their research insights to generate theoretical models. They were hoping that netnography could be developed into a methodology for constructing theories (Wang, 2018, 2019). In regard to

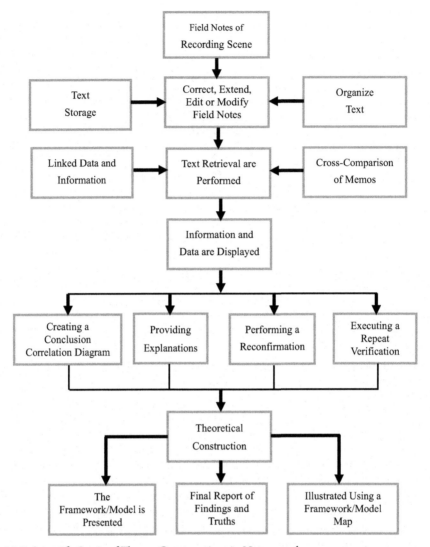

Figure 18.3 Scientific Logic of Theory Construction in Netnography.

the use of netnography analysis to construct theoretical frameworks/models, there is a lack of research focusing on theory construction methodologies in the existing literature relating to weblog research. For this reason, the authors referenced the research experiences reported in netnography-related studies published by international journals in recent years (Wang, 2019a, b, c, d; Wang, 2018; Wang et al., 2017; Wang, 2016), and developed a concept map that illustrates the use of netnography for theory construction (see Figure 18.3).

As shown in Figure 18.3, the scientific logic behind netnography-based theory construction is as follows:

1. The framework/model requires the use of netnography to analyze the constructed theories.
2. Stored text is used to start the correction, expansion, and editing processes.
3. The text is then organized in order to revise field notes.

4. Through data linking, qualitative big data search and text retrieval are performed, in addition to a parallel cross-comparison of memos.
5. Information and data are displayed.
6. Four major steps are performed, namely, creating a conclusion correlation diagram, providing explanations, performing a reconfirmation, and executing a repeat verification.
7. Labels are used to construct relevant propositions for various concepts.
8. Data reduction, conversion, abstraction, and refinement for theory construction are performed to develop the theories used to establish a framework/model.
9. The framework/model is presented or illustrated using a framework/model map.
10. Re-reading and induction are carried out to produce the final report covering the findings and truths revealed in this study.

As shown above, the field plays an important role in netnography, as it serves to concretize the subject matter. The way in which one enters a field, the time spent in a field, and the types of information and texts that are important analytical materials in a field are all factors that influence the final results in a netnography report. Netnography enables us to develop an in-depth understanding of the online behavior and social activities of internet users. Kozinets (2020) emphasized the importance of researchers' active engagement both through observing and participating in online interactions. Since the behaviors of Internet users are not induced or directed by researchers, there is no risk that a study making online observations will encroach on or interrupt the activities of Internet users. Internet researchers must travel to a research site and conduct field research to collect first-hand information. In other words, netnographers are indeed travelling through their screens and keyboards to fields where they can make field observations and records (Kozinets, 2002). These unique and interpretive online field trips offer flexibility, diversity, immersion, and unique qualities through which researchers can develop a comprehensive understanding (Wang, 2018; Wang et al., 2017).

CONCLUSION

This study identified gaps in the literature and brought attention to a previously overlooked issue, exploring the mystery of live video streaming and revealing special life experiences in the online context. Furthermore, netnography conducted in this study enabled the development of a substantive theory that provides insights into interpreting the contextualization experiences. The theory was developed based on raw data to enable it to explain the phenomena in the context of similar live video streaming. On the one hand, the information provided the basis for the study's theory; on the other hand, the theory bestowed meaning upon the information, making it both profound and systematic. Therefore, the theory is more specific and focused on the characteristics and complexity of the studied phenomenon, thus increasing the impact of its explanation.

Our research also showed how the key to live streaming platform development is adhesion. Audiences' adhesion toward and satisfaction with content are vital factors in their live video streaming choices. Audiences expressed the view that content with a punch line is appealing and that such content is a valuable driver of audience community relations. Punch lines are characterized by practicability, force of appeal, and the attraction of attention. Additionally, "going viral" was found to be the second driver of change for live video streaming. When an activity is commonly recognized to require the joint participation of a large audience, information goes viral and is shared by many internet users, enabling people to follow the newest dynamics.

Netnography delves into the heart of the communicative phenomena taking place in a technologically mediated world, such as the live video streaming. In our study, netnography facilitated the understanding of consumers' adhesion to and participation in the production, the consumption, and the sharing of live streaming contents. Digitized spaces today are where communities of all kinds exist. Experiences of day-to-day realities take place in digitally connected spaces and the storied lives of communities are told through the online sphere. These are spaces where identities are negotiated, cultural practices enacted, and social phenomena of various kinds manifested, providing a worthy area for interpretation for netnographers interested in the tradition of storytelling to understand the social world.

Finally, conducting a netnography requires a sustained period of immersion in the virtual field site, during which time netnographers engage in observation and/or participant observation in the virtual community under study. Netnographers produce reports describing and analyzing the sociocultural lifeworlds that exist in virtual and technology-mediated spaces. While netnography is not radically different from traditional ethnography, netnographers do face unique methodological, philosophical, and ethical challenges as they explore online scenes, communities, and worlds. In terms of future research, we encourage scholars to further investigate the multiple forms user sensuousness may take in the diverse settings of live video streaming culture and to develop methods for their adequate exploration.

REFERENCES

Abdous, M. & Yoshimura, M. (2010). Learner outcomes and satisfaction: A comparison of live video-streamed instruction, satellite broadcast instruction, and face-to-face instruction. *Computers & Education*, 55, 733–741.

Badrinarayanan, V.A., Sierra, J.J. & Martinb, K.M. (2015). A dual identification framework of online multiplayer video games: The case of massively multiplayer online role playing games (MMORPGs). *Journal of Business Research*, 68, 1045–1052.

Bogdan, R.C. & Biklen, S.K. (1998). *Qualitative research for education: An introduction to theory and methods*. Needham Height, MA: Allyn & Bacon.

Brooks, K. (2003). There is nothing virtual about immersion: Narrative immersion for VR and other interfaces. Retrieved from http://citeseerx.ist.psu.edu/viewdoc/ download?doi=10.1.1.87.8043 & rep=rep1 & type=pdf

Brown, E., & Cairns, P. (2004). A grounded investigation of game immersion. *Conference on Human Factors in Computing Systems*, 1297–1300.

Bystrom, K.-E., Barfield, W., & Hendrix, C. (1999). A conceptual model of the sense of presence in virtual environments. *Presence: Teleoperators & Virtual Environments.*, 8, 241–244.

Cairns, P., Cox, A. L., Day, M., Martin, H. & Perryman, T. (2013). Who but not where: The effect of social play on immersion in digital games. *International Journal of Human-Computer Studies*, 71(11), 1069–1077.

Cairns, P., Cox, A. & Nordin, A. I. (2014). Immersion in digital games: A review of gaming experience research. In M. C. Angelides, & H. Agius (Eds.). *Handbook of digital games* (pp. 337–361). Hoboken, NJ, USA: John Wiley & Sons.

Charmaz, K. (2006). *Constructing grounded theory: A practical guide though qualitative analysis*. Thousand Oaks, CA: Sage.

Cheng, M.-T., She, H.-C., & Annetta, L.A. (2015). Game immersion experience: Its hierarchical structure and impact on game-based science learning. *Journal of Computer Assisted Learning*, 31, 232–253.

Csikszentmihalyi, M. (1990). *Flow: The psychology of optimal performance*. New York: Cambridge University Press.

Dede, C. (2009). Immersive interfaces for engagement and learning. *Science*, 2 (323), 66–69.

Demuth, C. & Mey, G. (2015). Qualitative methodology in developmental psychology. *International Encyclopedia of the Social & Behavioral Sciences* (Second Edition), 668–675.

Denzin, N. (2006). *Sociological methods: A sourcebook*. Abingdon: Aldine Transaction.

Glaser, B.G. (2006). *Doing formal grounded theory: A proposal*. Mill Valley, CA: The Sociology Press.

Grinberg, A. M., Careaga, J. S., Mehl, M. R. & O'Connor, M.-F. (2014). Social engagement and user immersion in a socially based virtual world. *Computers in Human Behavior*, 36, 479–486.

Grossnickle, J. & Raskin, O. (2000). *The handbook of online marketing research: Knowing your customer using the net*. New York: McGraw-Hill.

Ha, L., Joa, C.Y., Gabay, I. & Kim, K. (2018). Does college students' social media use affect school e-mail avoidance and campus involvement? *Internet Research*, 28(1), 213–231.

Hamari, J. & Sjöblom, M. (2017). What is eSports and why do people watch it? *Internet Research*, 27(2), 211–232.

Hammersley, M. (1989). *The dilemma of qualitative method: Herbert Blumer and the Chicago tradition*. London and New York: Routledge.

Hansen, A. H. & Mossberg, L. (2013). Consumer immersion: A key to extraordinary experiences. In J. Sundbo, & F. Sørensen (Eds.). *Handbook on the experience economy* (pp. 209–227). Cheltenham, UK: Edward Elgar.

Hine, C. (2000). *Virtual ethnography*. London: Sage.

Hu, M., Zhang, M. & Wang, Y. (2017). Why do audiences choose to keep watching on live video streaming platforms? An explanation of dual identification framework. *Computers in Human Behavior*, 75, 594–606.

Hudson, S., Matson-Barkat, S., Pallamin, N. & Jegou, G. (2019). With or without you? Interaction and immersion in a virtual reality experience. *Journal of Business Research*, 100, 459–468.

Jennett, C., Cox, A. L., Cairns, P., Dhoparee, S., Epps, A., Tijs, T. & Walton, A. (2008). Measuring and defining the experience of immersion in games. *International Journal of Human-Computer Studies*, 66(9), 641–661.

Kim, M. & Lee, M. (2017). Brand-related user-generated content on social media: The roles of source and sponsorship. *Internet Research*, 27(5), 1085–1103.

Kima, J., Nama, C. & Ryub, M.H. (2017). What do consumers prefer for music streaming services? A comparative study between Korea and US. *Telecommunications Policy*, 41, 263–272.

Kozinets, R.V. (1997). "I want to believe": A netnography of The X-Philes' subculture of consumption. In M. Brucks and D.J. MacInnis (Eds.). *Advances in consumer research*, Volume 24 (pp. 470–475). Provo, UT: Association for Consumer Research.

Kozinets, R.V. (1998). On netnography: Initial reflections on consumer research investigations of cyberculture. In J. Alba and W. Hutchinson (Eds.). *Advances in consumer research*, Volume 25 (pp. 366–371). Provo, UT: Association for Consumer Research.

Kozinets, R.V. (2001). Utopian enterprise: articulating the meanings of Star Trek's culture of consumption. *Journal of Consumer Research*, 28(June), 67–88.

Kozinets, R.V. (2002). The field behind the screen: Using netnography for marketing research in online communities. *Journal of Marketing Research*, 39(February), 61–72.

Kozinets, R.V. (2010). *Netnography: Doing ethnographic research online*. London: Sage.

Kozinets, R.V. (2015). *Netnography: Redefined*. London: Sage.

Kozinets, R.V. (2019). YouTube utopianism: Social media profanation and the clicktivism of capitalist critique. *Journal of Business Research*, 98(2019), 65–81.

Kozinets, R. V. (2020). *Netnography: The essential guide to qualitative social media research*. Thousand Oaks (CA): Sage Publications.

Kozinets, R.V. & Nocker, M. (2018). Netnography: Online ethnography for a digital age of organization research. In A. Bryman, & D. A. Buchanan (Eds.). *Unconventional methodology in organization and management research* (pp. 127–146). Cambridge, UK: Oxford University Press.

Leijen, A., Lam, I., Wildschut, L., Simon, P.R.J. & Admiraal, W. (2009). Streaming video to enhance students' reflection in dance education. *Computers & Education*, 52, 169–176.

Levy, S.J. (1959). Symbols for sale. *Harvard Business Review*, 37, 117–124.

Lim, S., Cha, S.Y., Park, C., Lee, I. & Kim, J. (2012). Getting closer and experiencing together: Antecedents and consequences of psychological distance in social media-enhanced real-time streaming video. *Computers in Human Behavior*, 28, 1365–1378.

Lincoln, Y.S. & Guba, E.G. (1985). *Naturalistic inquiry*. Beverly Hills: Sage.

Mason, J. (2002). *Qualitative researching* (2nd Ed.). London: Sage.

McMahan, A. (2003). Immersion, engagement, and presence: A method for analyzing 3-D video games. In Wolf, M.J.P., Perron, B. (Eds.). *The video game theory reader* (pp. 67–86). New York: Routledge.

McMahon, M., and Ojeda, C. (2008). "A model of immersion to guide the design of serious games," in *Proceedings of the World Conference on E-Learning in Corporate, Government, Healthcare and Higher Education* (Las Vegas), 1833–1842.

Milgram, P. & Kishino, F. (1994). A taxonomy of mixed reality visual displays. *IEICE Transactions on Information and Systems*, 77(12), 1321–1329.

Miller, D. & Slater, D. (2000). *The Internet: An ethnographic approach*. Oxford: Berg.

Nagy, P. & Koles, B. (2014). The digital transformation of human identity: Towards a conceptual model of virtual identity in virtual worlds. *Convergence*, 20(3), 276–292.

Nash, E.B., Edwards, G.W., Thompson, J.A., & Barfield, W. (2000). A review of presence and performance in virtual environments. *International Journal of Human-Computer Interaction*, 12, 1–41.

Oh, H., Fiore, A.M. & Jeoung, M. (2007). Measuring experience economy concepts: Tourism applications. *Journal of Travel Research*, 46(2), 119–132.

Ortiz, J., Chih, W.H. & Teng, H.C. (2017). Electronic word of mouth in the Taiwanese social networking community: participation factors. *Internet Research*, 27(5), 1058–1084.

Patton, M.Q. (2002). *Qualitative research & evaluation methods* (3rd Ed.) Thousand Oaks: Sage.

Pine, B.J. & Gilmore, J.H. (1999). *The experience economy: Work is theatre & every business a stage.* Boston: Harvard Business Press.

Recktenwald, D. (2017). Toward a transcription and analysis of live streaming on Twitch. *Journal of Pragmatics*, 115, 68–81.

Rubin, H.J. & Rubin, I. (1995). *Qualitative interviewing: The art of hearing data.* London. Sage Publications.

Sherry, J.F. (1990). A sociocultural analysis of a Midwestern American flea market. *Journal of Consumer Research*, 17, 13–30.

Sinclair, G. & Tinson, J. (2017). Psychological ownership and music streaming consumption. *Journal of Business Research*, 71, 1–9.

Sjöblom, M., & Hamari, J. (2017). Why do people watch others play video games? An empirical study on the motivations of Twitch users. *Computers in Human Behavior*, 75, 985–996.

Slater, M. (1999). Measuring presence: A response to the Witmer and Singer presence questionnaire. *Presence: Teleoperators & Virtual Environments*, 8 (5), 560–566.

Slater, M., & Wilbur, S. (1997). A framework for immersive virtual environments (FIVE): speculations on the role of presence in virtual environments. *Presence: Teleoperators & Virtual Environments.* 6, 603–616.

Strauss, A.L. & Corbin, J.M. (1998). *Basics of qualitative research: Techniques and procedures for developing grounded theory* (2nd ed.), Thousand Oaks, CA: Sage

Sun, Y., Shao, X., Li, X. & Nie, Y.G.K. (2019). How live streaming influences purchase intentions in social commerce: An IT affordance perspective. *Electronic Commerce Research and Applications*, 37, 1008–1039.

Sutcliffe, A. (2016). *Designing for user experience and engagement. Why engagement matters* (pp. 105–126). Switzerland: Springer.

Tussyadiah, I.P., Wang, D., Jung, T.H. & Dieck, M.C. (2018). Virtual reality, presence, and attitude change: Empirical evidence from tourism. *Tourism Management*, 66, 140–154.

Twitch. (2019). 2019 retrospective. Retrieved 2019, from Twitch: www.twitch.tv/year/2019; www.twitch.tv/p/about/.

Vella, K. (2016). *The social context of video game play: Relationships with the player experience and well-being.* Queensland University of Technology (Doctoral Dissertation).

Wang, Y. S. (2016). Dynamic capabilities in fashion apparel industry: Emergent conceptual framework. *Baltic Journal of Management*, 11(3), 286–309.

Wang, Y.S. (2018). Addiction by design: Using netnography for user experiences in female online gambling game. *International Journal of Human-Computer Interaction*, 34(8), 774–785.

Wang, Y.S. (2019a). User experiences in live video streaming: A netnography analysis. *Internet Research*, 29(4), 638–658.

Wang, Y.S. (2019b). The application of netnography to the online dating service experiences of female users. *Behaviour & Information Technology.* Published online: 27 Mar 2019. https://doi.org/10.1080/0144929X.2019.1597167

Wang, Y.S. (2019c). Virtual cohabitation in online dating site: A netnography analysis. *Online Information Review*, 43(4), 513–530.

Wang, Y.S. (2019d). Exploring the "like" in the psychological interaction of users on fan community: A netnography analysis. *Journal of Community Psychology*, 47(6), 1380–1398.

Wang, Y.S., Lee, W.L. & Hsu, T.H. (2017). Using netnography for the study of role-playing in female online games: Interpretation of situational context model. *Internet Research*, 27(4), 905–923.

Wei, P.S. & Lu, H.P. (2014). Why do people play mobile social games? An examination of network externalities and of uses and gratifications. *Internet Research*, 24(3), 313–331.

Weibel, D., Wissmath, B., & Mast, F.W. (2010). Immersion in mediated environments: the role of personality traits. *Cyberpsychology, Behavior, and Social Networking*, 13, 251–256.

Witmer, B.G., & Singer, M.J., 1998. Measuring presence in virtual environments: a presence questionnaire. Presence Teleoper. *Virtual Environ.*, 7, 225–240.

He, W. (2013). Examining students' online interaction in a live video streaming environment using data mining and text mining. *Computers in Human Behavior*, 29, 90–102.

Zhang, X. & Hassanein, H. (2012). A survey of peer-to-peer live video streaming schemes – An algorithmic perspective. *Computer Networks*, 56(15), 3548–3579.

19

Netnography, Digital Habitus, and Technocultural Capital

Rossella Gambetti

INTRODUCTION

Although Pierre Bourdieu died in 2002, just as contemporary social media was beginning to grow, his ideas may help us gain a greater understanding of the impacts of life in a digital age. As well, exploring life in social media offers a unique opportunity to expand Bourdieu's understanding of social science. This work offers a conceptual reflection on netnography that situates its contribution to knowledge generation inside Pierre Bourdieu's view of social science as a relational construction. This relational construction occurs within social spaces with a specific legitimacy and functioning that take the form of intersecting social fields. These fields include domains of human activity where human behavior and thinking are governed through institutionalized social and cultural norms that constitute their habitus and enable the accumulation of cultural capital.

The value of providing a conceptual reflection on netnography that draws from Bourdieu's theorizing lies, first, in introducing the concepts of 'digital habitus' and 'technocultural capital' as evolving manifestations of habitus and cultural capital in social media platforms. Second, it inheres in critically discussing netnography as a research method whose norms and practices are equipped to 'qualify' digital habitus and mobilize technocultural capital. Hence, while expanding on Bourdieu's view, this chapter acknowledges netnography as a research method that generates knowledge within the field called 'intersectionality.' Inside this field, 'digital habitus' is conceived to be a technologically mediated alteration of the concept of habitus meant as a set of relations, preferences and dispositions with which individuals orient to the current digital social world.

This work will argue that netnography contributes to 'qualify' digital habitus as against the global tendency to 'quantify' it under the increasing pressure of performativity currently affecting the social and data sciences. In doing so, this work elucidates how netnography qualifies digital habitus by organically adhering to the institutionalized practices of individuals' identity work performed in social media platforms. The narrative then introduces the notion of technocultural capital as a form of capital that resonates with the imbrication between technology and culture and that is mobilized by netnography while capturing the cultural norms of digital habitus. Finally, the chapter discusses four different dominant cultures that are constitutive of technoculture and identifies the challenges each of them presents to netnography. These challenges lead to the suggestion that netnographic approaches must constantly alter, adapt, and evolve to attune their procedures with the fluid dynamics of technologically mediated social space.

BOURDIEU'S VIEW OF SOCIAL SCIENCE, NETNOGRAPHY AND THE INTERSECTIONALITY FIELD

Bourdieu's theoretical contribution to research is rooted in the relational foundations of sociological thought of philosophers such as Marx, Weber, Durkheim, Mead, and Simmel. These foundations were later expanded by Bourdieu and other prominent sociologists like Dewey, Bentley, Elias, and Luhmann to constitute the domain of relational sociology. The contribution of relational sociologists was to move social science away from variable-centered hypothesis-testing research toward a relational approach to the study of social life (Ignatow & Robinson, 2017, 951). In this regard, Bourdieu argued that "the real is the relational" (Bourdieu & Wacquant, 1992, 97). The relational approach theorizes that all social action occurs within social spaces composed of intersecting fields. These fields condition and constrain the behavior of individuals and also shape their motivations.

Bourdieu conceptualizes a field as "a network or configuration of relations between social positions in which positions and their interrelations are determined by the distribution of economic, social, and cultural capital" (Ignatow & Robinson, 2017, 952; Bourdieu, 1994). Each field is characterized by a habitus of formal and informal social and cultural norms – "the rules of the game" – that govern a particular social sphere of activity (Edgerton & Roberts, 2014). Individuals' actions within a field are aimed at acquiring and accumulating cultural capital by following the specific norms constituting its habitus (Bourdieu, 1994; Bourdieu & Wacquant, 1992). Thus, individuals' social positions and their interrelations within a field are a consequence of how well they adhere to and leverage the habitus of that specific field by mobilizing their cultural capital and other forms of capital.

Netnography can be situated within this Bourdieusean conceptualization of field as an anthropological research method that investigates the formal and informal cultural norms constituting the habitus of the interdisciplinary field called 'intersectionality' (Kozinets, 2020, 118; Gopaldas & Fischer, 2012). As Kozinets claims, this field entails the idea that "individuals occupy a particular social position in society that lies at the intersection of social axes such as gender, age, race, religion, ethnicity, nationality, sexual orientation, and class" (Kozinets, 2020, 118). The interrelations between social positions are based on negotiations of individual and collective identities. What is important to note is that these interrelations are both amplified and intensified in the technologically mediated social space of social media. In social media interactions, people construct their individual and social selves online by constantly negotiating social positions that better fit with their fluid and unstable identity. In fact, people craft multiple selves in social media platforms where gender, age, religion, sexual orientation, and other social positions shift and alter to accord with their evolving needs and desires.

In this scenario of constantly changing digital selves moving through social media, I contend that netnography is a research method that can allow us to understand the 'intersectionality' field situated in that context and content. In fact, netnography collects and analyzes "online traces that reveal the interrelations of individuals engaged in conversation and the cultural norms that inform how they communicate in social media platforms" (Kozinets, 2020, 118). In so doing, netnography explores the shifting social positions people assume while crafting their multiple selves on social media. Through capturing the habitus of the intersectional field situated in social media – which I will define as 'digital habitus' – netnography also facilitates our study of how people accumulate and mobilize technocultural capital. In the next section, I will introduce the notion of digital habitus and illustrate how netnography allows researchers to 'qualify' digital habitus as opposed to the general tendency to quantify it. Then, I will craft the notion of technocultural capital and critically reflect on how mobilizing this capital challenges netnographers to alter, evolve and update their procedures to face cogent new criticalities.

DEFINING DIGITAL HABITUS

In Bourdieu's conception, habitus is intimately interrelated with the field, depicting a set of historical relations incorporated within individual bodies in the form of learned preferences and dispositions by which a person orients to the social world (Edgerton & Roberts, 2014, 195; Bourdieu, 1990, 66–79). Habitus consists of a system of durable, transposable, cognitive "schemata or structures of perception, conception and action" (Bourdieu, 2002, 27) expressed by individuals in their societies. Bourdieu termed it "socialized subjectivity" (Edgerton & Roberts, 2014, 195). Habitus entails "perceptual schemes of which ends and means are reasonable given that individual's particular position in a stratified society" (Ibid.). These schemes are acquired in daily life through social interactions. Schemes relate to cultural aspects of individuals' identity such as behavior (posture and gait), aesthetic likes and dislikes (taste), habitual linguistic practices (accent, vocabulary, speed of language), and visual representation practices (images, shapes, colors, visual symbols) (Ignatow & Robinson, 2017, 954).

The habitus of the intersectionality field situated in contemporary worlds, including those of social media, emerges as partly a 'digital habitus.' Following Bourdieu, I define digital habitus as 'a set of learned preferences, dispositions and behavioral schemes whereby individuals craft their selves using information and communications tools and devices within an elaborate technologically mediated social space that includes the social media ecosystem.' By performing identity work and interactions on social media platforms, people orient to a contemporary social world that is global, influential, and always on. Identity work entails the 'socialized subjectivity' of individuals. It gets materialized in social interactions that shape behavior, taste, linguistic, and visual representation practices. Identity work today is based less on physical context and more on individuals' intentional self-presentation (Bollmer, 2018). Through self-presentation, multiple identities are constructed simultaneously (Turkle, 1995) and framed by the technological mediation individuals use to communicate and interact with others (Barad, 2007). Self-presentation is an act of reflexive construction of a networked self that is constantly assessed in relation to others thanks to the ubiquitous and persistent use of social media platforms (Papacharissi, 2010).

Beyond being a reflexive act, self-presentation is also a performative act of identity construction. It occurs in mundane everyday actions bound up in social conventions, the expectations of others and the desire to be perceived in particular ways (Goffman, 1959). In fact, the current digital habitus has transformed individuals' identity construction into a 'textual' performance – including photographs, graphical imagery, and videos as part of these 'texts' – that is enabled by social media. This textual performance of the self encourages personal expression and connection to others as a desirable mode of being.

According to Stone (1995, 15) "bodies are intrinsically bound up in textuality and language" that are shaped as "technological prosthetics" in social media. In recounting her experience of observing a community of lesbian phone sex workers in the San Francisco Bay area, Stone (1995, 7) argued that

as much as sex involves as many senses as possible, where taste, touch, smell, sight, hearing and short-range psychic interactions all work together to heighten the erotic sense, consciously or unconsciously phone sex workers translate all the modalities of experiences into an audible form of text.

Even if certain parts of the physical body are not directly involved in phone sex, the audible form through which sensorial experiences are communicated on the phone is not just information, it is sensory information (Ibid.), imaginatively interacting with other bodies through technological infrastructures. Similarly, the ways individuals perform self-presentation on social media platforms shows a habitus of extending the body through a variety of textual prostheses to connect with others who are long distances away (Bollmer, 2018, 124). As Bollmer contends

> while we may perform online with someone with an identity that has little to do with our physical biology, our online identities are nonetheless an extension of our physical bodies and are part of the 'real' identity of the person behind the screen.
>
> (Ibid.)

As Kozinets (1998, 369) notes, the psychology of social media representation grounds it in a type of almost body-transcending sense of inner reality:

> the same freedom which inspires people to mischievously construct deliberate falsehoods about themselves [, their bodies,] and their opinions also allows them and others the freedom to express aspects of themselves, their [passions,] ambitions and inner conflicts, that they would otherwise keep deeply hidden.

Textual self-presentation has been further magnified by the emergence of the 'demotic turn,' a term introduced by Turner (2006, 153) to describe "the increasing visibility of the 'ordinary person' as they turn themselves into media content through celebrity culture, reality TV, DIY websites, talk radio and the like." The demotic turn popularized in social media platforms has instilled new cultural norms of textual self-presentation that have transformed ordinary people into celebrities (Driessens, 2013, 643; Jerslev & Mortensen, 2016, 250). These new norms are based on the affective labor (Hardt, 1999) performed by individuals in social media platforms. Affective labor refers to both the conscious narration of affect and the embodied capacity to affect and be affected through developing and maintaining relationships (Clough, 2007; Wissinger, 2007). As such, affective labor involves textual activities through which people produce, negotiate, share and commodify emotions in the form of cultural contents (Just, 2019). Drawing from the personal repertoire of memories and affect, these textual activities are assembled and crafted by individuals to establish human contact, gain attention, and develop proximity with others (Hardt, 1999; Clough, 2007). In this regard, the visual performativity of emotions and meanings popularized through sharing images and animations in social media platforms is a vivid example of the current digital habitus of establishing contact, proximity and gaining attention from each other (Carah & Shaul, 2016). In light of this conceptualization of digital habitus, in the next section I will discuss netnography as a research method that allows to 'qualify' digital habitus as against a growing global tension towards quantifying digital habitus.

NETNOGRAPHY AND DIGITAL HABITUS

The visual and emotional turn of social media's textual performativity deeply challenged the broad field of sociological research methods over the few last years. Digital sociological methods have developed to date in ways that do not seem to fully reflect Bourdieu's understanding of the interactions of contemporary social, cultural, and technological phenomena. These methods have been primarily oriented to quantify digital habitus, rather than to understand it from a combined cultural and socio-technical standpoint.

Quantifying Digital Habitus

According to Statista.com, the big data analytics market has been valued at 49 billion USD in 2019, and is expected to grow to 103 billion USD by 2027. These figures hint at the way the power players within the global market research world view big data analytics. Kache and Seuring (2017) have conducted a Delphi study that identified no fewer than 43 opportunities and challenges linked to the emergence of big data analytics from a corporate and supply chain perspective. Among these, improving a firm's financial and market performance (Wamba et al., 2017), forecasting sales (Boone et al., 2019), enhancing idea generation and creativity in product development (Erevelles, Fukawa & Swayne, 2016), enabling real-time business responses termed "nowcasting" (Constantiou & Kallinikos, 2015), and enhancing consumer engagement (Calder, Malthouse & Maslowska, 2016; Jiménez Zarco et al., 2019) are just a few of the business miracles ascribed to big data science in the digital era. Under a growing quest for performativity, several research methods have been developed by sociologists and scholars of related fields that aim to 'quantify' aspects of digital habitus primarily by means of text analysis automation.

Among the methods that aim to 'quantify' digital habitus, Ignatow and Robinson (2017, 958) have offered a well-documented review of research techniques aimed to approach textuality in identity construction that analyze language as a product of mind-body interactions. These techniques perform *sentiment analysis* that codes sentiment expressed in texts in different ways, such as manually to capture the nuances of emotional expressions; with the support of automated supervised learning techniques to treat larger amount of data; or through dictionary-based tools that use off-the-shelf, validated sentiment lexicons (Ibid.). Widespread automated sentiment analysis methods offer the advantage of objectively recognizing emotional markers and connotations in a large portion of verbal text. In doing so, they provide a standardized raw data treatment that allows researchers to highlight negative, positive or neutral (i.e. neither positive nor negative) manifestations of intentions and affect. While this treatment is useful to get a quick general overview of the tone of the interactions generated around a social phenomenon in digital platforms, it overlooks the contextual cultural norms that produce certain emotional expressions. Yet, the appeal on practitioners of quantified and generalized expressions of large portions of textual data has popularized sentiment analysis methods in brand management practices as easier-to-perform and less time-consuming procedures than social media cultural research.

In particular, sentiment analysis applied to branding is also known as *social listening*, a means by which practitioners gather social media data online by 'listening' to conversations (Reid & Duffy, 2018; Schweidel & Moe, 2014). Social listening captures the emotions, moods, attitudes, and opinions surrounding a brand's online presence (Perzynska, 2018). This involves counting the number of followers, likes, and other engagements brands have in social media platforms (Reid & Duffy, 2018, 272). Then, it involves recognizing, codifying, and grouping the opinions and emotions consumers express within online brand mentions. Since it monitors public opinions behind given topics of brand interest (Perzynska, 2018), social listening has become an appealing indicator for a quick assessment of social media performance of companies and their brands. Although social listening can manage a reasonably large scale and volume of posts and interactions that can reveal trends relating to the popularity of a brand or product on social media, it does not capture who consumers are, what interests they have, who and what influences them, or why they make certain choices (Reid & Duffy, 2018, 272). To solve this issue, Reid and Duffy (Ibid., 273) advocate for an integrated use of netnography and social listening that, first, identifies cultural markers of online conversations through netnographic immersion. Second, it facilitates keyword selection and uses the keywords to perform automated social listening to increase the scale of insight. Third, it triangulates data collection procedures and sources of insight (i.e. netnography, secondary company data, interviews, etc.) to enhance the depth and the breadth of understanding of the phenomenon. Although this proposed blend, termed "netnography sensibility," sounds like an interesting solution, I have my doubts about it. This is because, before "sensibility," every netnography that is rigorously conducted is inspired by "sensitivity." Sensitivity to context requires human control over the coding process that is the first step toward cultural insight. That means that a large-scale automated coding of emotions and opinions would require time-consuming work on the part of the netnographer to check the 'work' done by the automated social media listening tools. At this point, the question is whether it is more valuable to spend a considerable amount of time to check the logic of algorithms, or whether it would make more sense to continue to plunge into raw data directly and personally.

Other methods that attempt to quantify digital habitus do so by performing *computational analysis of metaphorical language*, which considers metaphors to be expressions of meaning that enact "bodily and emotional operations" (Ignatow & Robinson, 2017, 958). Sociologists such as Ignatow (2007) and Schuster, Beune, and Stronks (2011) have developed techniques of *metaphor analysis* while scholars in computational linguistics and related fields have explored methods for automated metaphor detection in texts through algorithms that identify figurative language (Neuman et al., 2013). Despite the sophistication of automated recognition of figurative language, these techniques often fail to fully capture the richness of the symbolic, historical and cultural world that is embedded in words, languages, images, and other forms of imagery.

To overcome the limitations of these textual analysis methods, other research methods have been introduced. These methods develop a more comprehensive approach to understanding textuality that takes into consideration signs and symbols as multiple interrelated forms of discursive meaning. For instance, *multimodal discourse analysis* (Kress, 2010, 2012) is an emerging research method that performs discursive analysis focusing on the different modes of communication such as words, colors, images, and recently also emojis (Moschini, 2016; Illendula & Sheth, 2019). The aim is to make sense of how non-textual and symbolic forms of communication interact with one another to create semiotic meaning.

Another research method, termed "Critical Technocultural Discourse Analysis" (CTDA) (Brock, 2018) applies what Brock defines as a critical cultural approach to understanding communication in digital platforms. This approach considers "the material and semiotic complexities of digital platforms framed by the offline cultural and social practices individuals engage in as they construct their identities in digital artifacts" (i.e. blogs, websites, videogames) (Brock, 2018, 1013). This critical cultural approach combines "analyses of information technology material and virtual design with an investigation into the production of meaning through information technology practice and the articulations of information technology users in situ" (Ibid.). CTDA investigates computer/digital mediation of discourse, focusing on structure, meaning, interaction, and cultural/social behavior. Being inspired by the principles of linguistic discourse analysis, it follows the assumption that digitally mediated discourse may be shaped by the technological features of computer-mediated communications (Ibid., 1017). For example, CTDA inquiry of Black Twitter began with "articulations of Black discursive identity, focusing specifically on 'signifyin' discourse' as a marker of Black cultural identity." In this regard, Brock (2018, 1014) argued that "Black Twitter" (digital) practice draws upon cultural referents and discourse conventions (i.e., what he terms "signifyin") drawing from African American culture, which CTDA helped reveal. Thus, "signifyin" becomes a digital practice where the interlocutor inventively redefines an object using Black cultural commonplaces and philosophy and, in the process, authenticates their cultural identity (Ibid., 1017). Revisiting Saussure's (1974) notions of sign/signifier/signified, Brock found that

> Black signifying discourse practices such as performance, audience, ritual, and catharsis mapped closely onto Twitter's discourse features of addressivity (i.e. the use of the "@" symbol to identify interlocutors), concision (the ritualistic abbreviation of complex meaning into 140 characters), and networks (i.e. the technological and social formation of a group of like-minded users.
>
> (Ibid., 1017; Brock, 2012)

This evidence enabled the author "to define, describe, and analyze the use of Black discourse on Twitter from the perspective of those who use it to articulate their identity and the structures of everyday life" (Brock, 2018, 1017).

Both of the latter research methods, which blend classical discourse analysis with semiotics, have recently grabbed the attention of the linguistic and sociological scholarly communities. In fact, the visual breakthrough of the digital habitus encouraged by the demotic turn has started to challenge the relevance and sensemaking capacity of classic discourse analysis methods. The epistemological tradition of these methods is rooted in approaching written, spoken, and sign language in terms of coherent sequences of sentences, propositions, speech, and turns-at-talk as the units of textuality. Multimodality and digital discourse analysis represent a valuable attempt to incorporate the heterogeneity of the textual material digitally produced by individuals. Despite that, I believe that they juxtapose analytical lenses rooted in different epistemological traditions – such as those informing linguistics and semiotics – in a way that detaches data from lived cultural experiences.

Qualifying Digital Habitus

If, on the one hand, the priority of sociological research thus far has been to 'quantify' digital habitus by developing increasingly sophisticated methods of discourse and text analysis automation, on the other hand, very little attention has been devoted to research methods that aim to 'qualify' digital habitus. Qualifying digital habitus means identifying its distinctive socio-technical and cultural characteristics to allow for a deeper understanding of the social phenomena taking place in technologically mediated social spaces such as social media. In view of this, the task of qualifying digital habitus currently presents three research related imperatives. *First*, it requires researchers to focus on 'deep data' instead of on 'big data.' The aim is to develop meaning and cultural insight, rather than precision and generalization. *Second*, it demands that researchers capture and analyze the textuality of identity work in all its forms (i.e. verbal, visual, sonic, audiovisual) in a way that is attuned to the affordances of digital platforms. *Third*, it requires researchers to personally engage in the research process by immersing themselves reflexively into data to achieve a deeper data proximity, a fine-tuned cultural sensitivity to the context, and an enhanced critical awareness of the investigated phenomenon.

Netnography allows researchers to 'qualify' digital habitus. As a semi-fluid set of research practices (Kozinets, 2020), netnography is able both to attune to the evolving configuration of digital habitus and also to holistically capture the technologically mediated textual performance of individuals' identity work that occurs on digital platforms. Let's now examine how netnography qualifies digital habitus by complying with the three aforementioned research imperatives.

Performing Interaction

As regards the *first* research imperative – focusing on deep data – netnographers are encouraged to identify a set of dense social media traces of individuals' affective labor and capture it as data that are culturally resonant, rich in meaning, and revelatory of people's identities. Beyond observing, recording, and counting captured traces of digital habitus, netnographers adhere to the intrinsic interactional features and cultural norms of digital habitus. By performing interaction as part of netnographic data collection, netnographers elicit and co-produce data both naturalistically and in a structured way. This happens, for instance, through interviewing, diaries, mobile ethnographies or customized social media pages (Kozinets, 2020, 245). In fact, through collecting, eliciting and co-producing data, netnographic methods help researchers to observe the dynamics whereby individuals perform their textual identity in social media, highlighting revelatory moments of their self-presentation work. Netnographic research unfolds the identity work performed by individuals whose affective labor produces, assembles, and shares moments of private life, elevating them to 'cultural curations.' Moments can be simple, mindless and casual, or rich, deep, and disclosing. Cultural curations are made of a digital collection of multi-textual narratives (i.e. visual, verbal, audiovisual) that are produced and shared with peers to display and reify a relational status (Humphreys, 2018). Cultural curations embody the transformation of cultural artifacts into a meaningful assemblage of digital objects and aesthetic experiences (Venkatesh & Meamber, 2006; Schembri & Tichbon, 2017, 192). On social media, these assemblages are descriptive, anecdotal, and often well-crafted, including a lot of context and connections that are revelatory of particular social, cultural, and physical environments and identities (Kozinets, 2020, 229). Netnographic procedures help the researcher to identify, collect and elicit cultural curations. They assist the researcher to recognize the ritual practices that constitute the norms of individuals' cultural agency. They guide the researchers to unpack the meanings and motivations that trigger individuals' cultural production and perpetuate their social relations.

For instance, Kozinets and colleagues (2019) conducted a ten-country netnography that uncovered the digital habitus underlying the use of branded events and social media to market tobacco brands to young people. Their netnography spotlighted the complex system of digital cultural curations carried out by influencers that leveraged on the affordances of social media platforms, the norms of youth selfie culture, the practice of encouraging social media posting, and the carefully designed synergies of branded elements derived from cigarette packages, designs, and hashtags (see Figure 19.1). These cultural curations, that as you can see in Figure 19.1 are aimed at portraying smoking as a desirable and escapist practice of self-expression, revealed a self-reinforcing ritual circle of hidden promotional practices that tobacco companies readily hacked to market their products.

In another netnography, this one of the cosplay online community, Seregina and Weijo (2017) observed how consumers regain ludic sensations and motivate communal engagements. In the research, cosplayers' self-presentation efforts and cultural curations were channeled to generate detached online personas that gained security and control. In their netnographic study of YouTube beauty gurus as tribal entrepreneurs, Mardon, Molesworth and Grigore (2018) revealed rituals of affective labor whereby tribal entrepreneurs engaged in cultural curation practices that navigated the tensions between the commercial and the tribal community ethos. In their netnography of a group of young YouTubers who strive to become entrepreneurs, Ashman, Patterson and Brown (2018) discovered how their affective labor is aimed at monetizing their networked self, engaging in cultural curations that indulge in a narcissistic self-display. In all the above mentioned netnographies, the authors performed interaction practices by eliciting and co-producing multi-textual narratives of individuals'

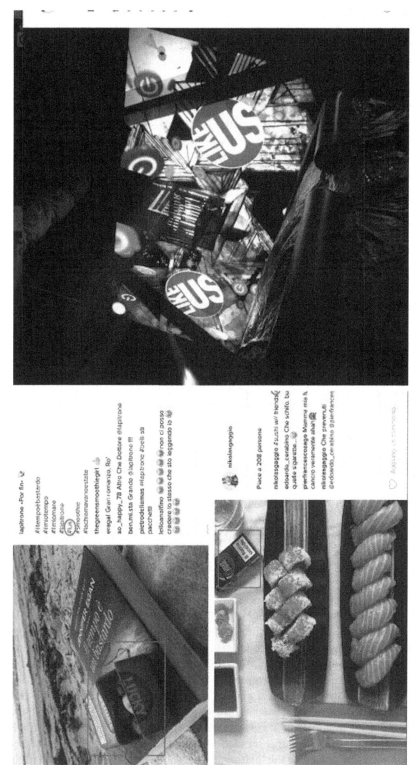

Figure 19.1 Smoking as a Desirable and Escapist Self-Expression Practice in Digital Cultural Curations.

self-presentation work (e.g. photos, interviews, social media profiles and threads of social media conversations, blog posts, online articles and documentaries, immersive notes). These narratives were captured as deep data where rituals, practices, meanings, and values emerged in the form of curated collections of cultural artifacts. By collecting and interacting with these artifacts, the authors disclosed revelatory and culturally resonant moments of people's identities.

By performing interaction in data collection, a netnographic researcher also experiences blurred boundaries between themselves and research participants. These fuzzy borders resonate with the digital habitus of individuals' fluid and inclusive dynamics of self-presentation. In fact, the roles, identities and purposes of researchers and participants blend and shift while co-producing data in social media platforms (Kozinets, 2020, 86; Piacenti et al., 2014). In the study conducted by Kozinets, Patterson and Ashman (2017, 665) on foodporn, netnographic participation included active newsgroup posting, the production of a food blog, and the use of a Facebook group dedicated to the topic where there was frequent and friendly social engagement between the researchers and research participants. This engagement blended their roles as the intensive fieldwork carried out by the researchers involved them in food creating, eating, photographing, posting, and interacting as food image creators, sharers, and consumers.

Capturing the Textuality of Identity Work in All Its Forms

As for the *second* research imperative – capturing the textuality of identity work in all its forms – netnography is a method that can handle any form or type of online data. That means that netnography does not deterministically apply an overarching epistemological lens that guides and restricts data collection and analysis. This is the case with discourse analysis and multimodal methods, whose approach to data collection and analysis is rooted in linguistics and semiotics. These disciplines are focused on understanding language structures and the signifying processes embedded in signs. Hence, the way these methods conceive and execute data collection is not neutral, but rather directed by the urgency to prioritize language structures and the sign processes of signification. However, netnography collects online traces in a more inclusive way as it does not prioritize nor focus on specific types of online traces. Netnography collects and assembles all forms of online traces (i.e. images, photographs, visual symbols, videos, words, emojis, engagement statistics, and so on) to form units, sub-structures, and structures of cultural meaning. Following emergent cultural meaning in whatever form it might take: this is the guiding principle that guides netnographic data collection and analysis. That means that netnography equalizes all online traces and pieces of data as cultural artifacts, where each textual form of data is considered, beforehand, to have roughly the same potential for generating findings of value.

As Kozinets (2020, 229) contends, the deep data collected in a netnography reveal human cultural realities through a wide variety of textual forms that subsequently are analyzed as a unitary and cohesive whole. All textual forms in netnography are aggregated into comprehensive units that have distinctive cultural meaning. So, in netnography, understanding cultural meaning is the logic that inspires data collection and analysis. This logic overcomes potential conflicts arising when treating each textual form separately and combining different sciences and epistemological glances (e.g. language analyzed through the lens of discourse analysis, images, and visual elements analyzed through the lens of semiotics). By adopting cultural meaning as a rule for qualifying digital habitus, netnographic analysis and interpretation eschew the separation between words, images, and videos. This idea resonates with the notion of the 'materiality of technology,' what the social philosopher Karen Barad calls the "material apparatuses that leave marks on our bodies" (Barad, 2007,

176). Following this notion, self-presentation is an effect of how consumers encounter one another in the imagined and realized materialities of the platforms (Bollmer, 2018, 122). In digital platforms consumers construct their self through performative acts of embodiment that transform fragmented personal cues into a unitary and cohesive combination of cultural artifacts. These artifacts include affective symbols, objects, and practices that are expressed in various textual forms such as words, images, and videos.

As an example of how understanding cultural meaning acts as the equalizing lens of all textual forms, Kozinets, Gambetti and Biraghi (2018) recently conducted a netnography in the context of pet-related consumer discourse. In that context, scientific debates relevant to purebred dogs are culturally produced and discussed as part of the identity work of individuals. In their netnography, the authors encountered a variety of textual elements of identity work (i.e. verbal, visual, and audiovisual) that were collected to compose the dataset. These included memes, selfies, photos, wish cards, scientific journal articles, images of branded products, general mockery, images of genetic and blood tests, emojis, self-made videos, as well as critical views on medicine and vet science. In this regard, Figure 19.2 shows an assembled collection of the heterogeneous variety of textual forms of data the authors collected and analyzed to capture cultural meaning. In particular, the figure shows pieces of data such as a video related to post-truth discourse on pet vaccination, a dog sticker, a chart from a scientific publication shared in a Facebook post, two memes related to pugs, a package of the Royal Canin brand of dry food, a photo showing the purebred standards for Welsh Pembroke Corgi, a selfie picture of an owner with her boxer, a wish card, and two packages of contested medicines.

The authors analyzed data, first, by atomistically identifying the verbal, visual, and audiovisual elements comprising textual units of cultural meaning and specifying their relationships. Then interpretation was performed that unified themes, ideas, discourses, and processes into a conceptual whole characterized by institutionalized cultural meaning (Kozinets, 2020, 312). In performing analysis and interpretation, the different textual forms were equalized and integrated to generate holistic cultural understanding. For example, Figure 19.3 shows a selected thread of conversation including a blend of audiovisual, visual imagery, and verbal discourse generated around a Facebook post of the activist group DogsNaturally Magazine. In this piece of deep data, raw food recipes offer the occasion to generate a dispute around dog's health and dietary science.

Immersing into the Destabilized Social Mediascapes

The *third* imperative – researcher's direct engagement in the research phenomenon – is the undeniable *sine qua non* of netnography. Just as ethnography does, netnography seeks breaches in the separation between cultural inside and outside and encourages researchers to become immersed in the "destabilized and destabilizing cultural flows of social mediascapes," a term Kozinets (2020, 282) borrows from one of his intellectual heroes, Arjun Appadurai (1990). Mediascapes in Appadurai's work referred to the flow of media images and the imaginaries of local and global cultures in which they flowed. Kozinets' (2020) slightly altered appellation, social mediascapes, emphasized their present-day intermingling with social media. As contemporary "digitized, desire-magnifying media unleash global and local imaginariums and liquefy the localities of culture, the stability of field gets dissolved into a type of multi-sited and multitudinously-sited field where the interests of the research, researcher and network constantly reterritorialize" (Ibid). Netnographers engage with this destabilized field through their immersion in social media data sites, and capture it in their immersion journals. Through that journal, they map out the research territory, record overviews and detail of the encounter with data, integrate insights coming from the empirical dataset with extant

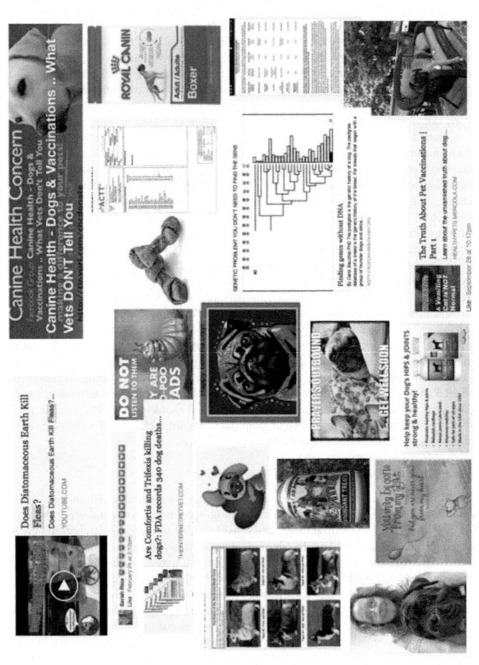

Figure 19.2 Variety of Textual Forms in Netnography Deep Data Collection.

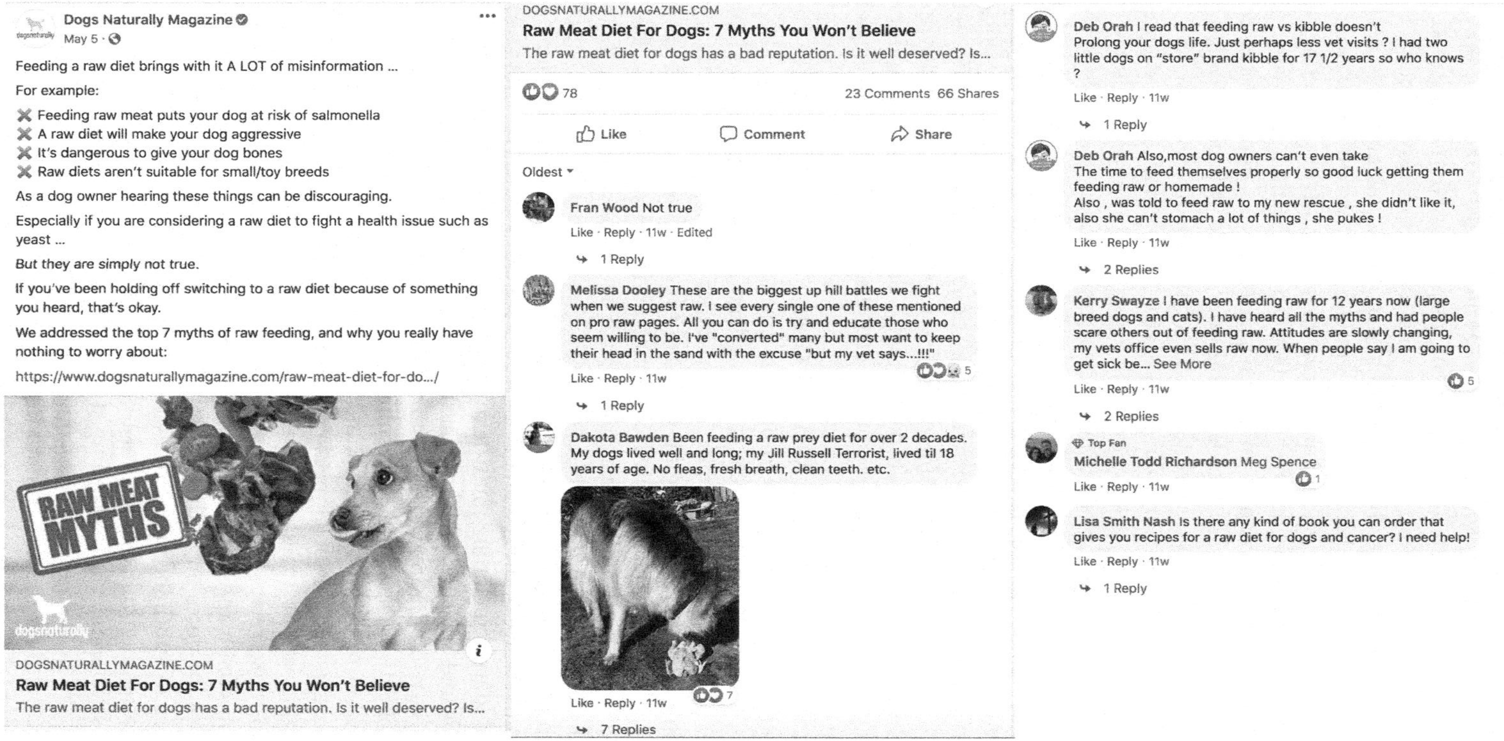

Dogs Naturally Magazine
May 5 ·

Feeding a raw diet brings with it A LOT of misinformation …

For example:

✘ Feeding raw meat puts your dog at risk of salmonella
✘ A raw diet will make your dog aggressive
✘ It's dangerous to give your dog bones
✘ Raw diets aren't suitable for small/toy breeds

As a dog owner hearing these things can be discouraging. Especially if you are considering a raw diet to fight a health issue such as yeast …

But they are simply not true.

If you've been holding off switching to a raw diet because of something you heard, that's okay.

We addressed the top 7 myths of raw feeding, and why you really have nothing to worry about:

https://www.dogsnaturallymagazine.com/raw-meat-diet-for-do.../

DOGSNATURALLYMAGAZINE.COM
Raw Meat Diet For Dogs: 7 Myths You Won't Believe
The raw meat diet for dogs has a bad reputation. Is it well deserved? Is…

DOGSNATURALLYMAGAZINE.COM
Raw Meat Diet For Dogs: 7 Myths You Won't Believe
The raw meat diet for dogs has a bad reputation. Is it well deserved? Is…

78   23 Comments 66 Shares

👍 Like   💬 Comment   ↪ Share

Oldest ▾

Fran Wood Not true
Like · Reply · 11w · Edited
↳ 1 Reply

Melissa Dooley These are the biggest up hill battles we fight when we suggest raw. I see every single one of these mentioned on pro raw pages. All you can do is try and educate those who seem willing to be. I've "converted" many but most want to keep their head in the sand with the excuse "but my vet says…!!!"
Like · Reply · 11w
↳ 1 Reply

Dakota Bawden Been feeding a raw prey diet for over 2 decades. My dogs lived well and long; my Jill Russell Terrorist, lived til 18 years of age. No fleas, fresh breath, clean teeth. etc.

Like · Reply · 11w
↳ 7 Replies

Deb Orah I read that feeding raw vs kibble doesn't Prolong your dogs life. Just perhaps less vet visits ? I had two little dogs on "store" brand kibble for 17 1/2 years so who knows ?
Like · Reply · 11w
↳ 1 Reply

Deb Orah Also,most dog owners can't even take The time to feed themselves properly so good luck getting them feeding raw or homemade !
Also , was told to feed raw to my new rescue , she didn't like it, also she can't stomach a lot of things , she pukes !
Like · Reply · 11w
↳ 2 Replies

Kerry Swayze I have been feeding raw for 12 years now (large breed dogs and cats). I have heard all the myths and had people scare others out of feeding raw. Attitudes are slowly changing, my vets office even sells raw now. When people say I am going to get sick be…See More
Like · Reply · 11w
↳ 2 Replies

⊙ Top Fan
Michelle Todd Richardson Meg Spence
Like · Reply · 11w

Lisa Smith Nash is there any kind of book you can order that gives you recipes for a raw diet for dogs and cancer? I need help!
Like · Reply · 11w
↳ 1 Reply

Figure 19.3 Equalized Textual Forms as a Unitary Whole in Netnography Data Analysis.

constructs and abstractions, and capture their own experiences with introspective reflection (Kozinets, 2020, 284), thereby turning immersive experience into netnographic data.

Following these operations implies that researchers must constantly move back and forth between context and data to complement insights based on immediate revelations with retrospective sense-making. As much as identity work performance in social media platforms relies on producing cultural curations of multi-textual narratives, netnographers' immersion in the research phenomenon is crafted as a "carefully cultivated curation" (Kozinets, 2020, 397). Crafting this curation involves identifying, selecting, assembling, and communicating data and personal reflections in all the multi-textual forms allowed by the current technical affordances of digital platforms (i.e. digital notes, blog diaries, visual schemes and frameworks, photos, mood boards and collage, recorded audio- and video-messages or a combination of all these). This curation allows researchers to reach the deepest level of data proximity in order for reflective problematization to emerge. In this regard, producing immersive notes in multiple formats both immediately during the data collection and retrospectively enables netnographers to enrich and expand the collected data site with additional data from the researchers' own journal entries. By adding critical and emotional reactions to the online traces encountered in data collection, netnographers generate an intellectual space where they interact with, reflect upon, question, and problematize in an ongoing manner the expanding set of collected cultural artifacts from social media. This curation also enables netnographers to express their own sensitivities and seek to calibrate them to those of research participants. Curation enhances and solidifies the netnographer's embeddedness in the context, enabling an insider-outsider glance on the phenomenon.

For instance, in the netnography Kozinets, Gretzel and Gambetti (2019) conducted in partnership with an Italian business-to-business cosmetics manufacturer (also featured in this book as Chapter 13), the researchers kept a detailed digital immersive journal during data collection. Their aim was to support a deep understanding of the needs and desires of Chinese consumers as regards changing notions of beauty and how these are reflected in various skin care and cosmetics related communications on social media. The immersive journal was composed of multi-textual forms such as images taken from the investigated social media field sites (i.e. Weibo, Little Red Book, YouTube), links to audiovisual materials, and digital notes reporting critical issues, including direct anonymized quotes from field sites and reflective notes of the researchers. Figure 19.4 and Figure 19.5 show two extracts of the immersive journal including multi-textual forms of data and reflective notes related to Little Red Book and YouTube social media sites.

The reflective combination of these multi-textual forms crafted over the length of the netnographic fieldwork assignment resulted in a rich cultivated curation. This allowed the research team to begin to understand some of the cultural specificities of Chinese consumers as expressed on social media platforms such as Little Red Book and Weibo. In fact, the use motivations and satisfied needs of these platforms emerged as significantly different from those related to the use of international social media such as Facebook and Instagram. Weibo and Little Red Book are more rational, focused, and goal-oriented (see Figure 19.4 for notes on Little Red Book). Moreover, the immersive journal allowed the researchers to spotlight pieces of evidence that had rich cultural meanings, useful not only for orienting holistic cultural understanding of the phenomenon but also for new product development and branding strategy. For instance, smell and taste related to cosmetics texture or cosmetics' effects on skin emerged for Chinese consumers as substantially different from those dominant in Western societies. The notes of the immersive journal also enabled the research team to capture the beauty-related purchasing and usage

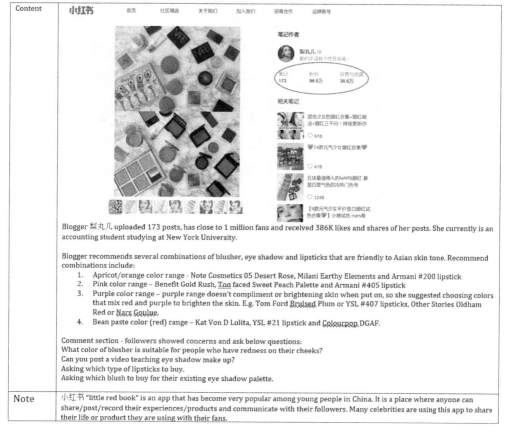

Figure 19.4 Extracts of Immersive Journal to Get Embedded and Fine-Tuned with the Cultural Specificities of Little Red Book.

routines of Chinese cosmetics influencers. As well, it allowed the researchers to identify the critical features of cosmetic product performance desired by these consumers. For instance, in Figure 19.5 it is clear how flaking-off effects of skin care products is particularly disliked by Chinese influencers.

Finally, the immersion journal entries made it possible for the researchers to systematically research and then spotlight the 'black swans.' For this project, the authors were looking for out of the ordinary beauty tastes and routines that allowed them to speculate about original new forms of cosmetics consumption and production. They found that some smells that are considered pleasant and attractive in Western countries were considered repellant or toxic by Chinese consumers. By qualifying digital habitus and carefully capturing its norms in this study, this netnography was able to reveal how Chinese cosmetics consumers mobilized and accumulated technocultural capital.

With these three principles explained and illustrated, this chapter can now proceed to the following section, which defines technocultural capital as an evolving manifestation of Bourdieu's notion of cultural capital rooted in current technoculture. Following this, the chapter will turn to a recognition of the ways that different cultures coalesce to form technoculture. After this, the chapter will turn to identifying the challenges that these different technocultures present to contemporary netnography.

Data Number	50
Data Location	https://www.youtube.com/watch?v=XmIOoLMWYcU
Content	近期使用的大牌产品测评!

Content:

2018 Luxury Products Review:

1. Emma Hardie moringa cleansing balm – good for sensitive skin, cream in texture, however, complicated to use (use with attached towel)
2. La Prairie skin caviar collection – refresh, watery and light texture, refine lines, anti-aging, fragrant, very expensive (most expensive products among all)
3. Chanel rich foam cream clea – foamy, durable (big in size and only need a little bit everytime)
4. Erno Laszlo detox double – smooth, fresh, very hygienic with pump head design, very interesting design
5. Fenty Beauty beauty blender – good for baking skin, soft, easy to reshape, however too soft to stay in shape, absorb powder
6. Fenty Beauty fly liner – value for money, easy to use, fast dry and long lasting
7. Vichy 89 Mineral Serum – light in texture, moist, affordable, preservative free, good absorbency
8. Oribe Serene Scalp Shampoo – beautiful packaging, however doesn't have much effects
9. Glamglow glitter mask – very interesting design with glitter, firm skin and minimizing pores, however not durable
10. La Prairie Caviar Foundation – good coverage, moist, long duration
11. Charlotte Tilbury Shadow Stick #Amber Haze – not easy to spread out/blend
12. Bobbie Brown Lip Gloss – good for adding layer on top of your lipsticks, nearly transparent and shimmering in color, however very thick/sticky in texture
13. Cle De Peau cream blush #04 – nice rosy color, good for all age and all occasions, very expensive but worthwhile

Comments:

- I saw so many bloggers recommended Emma Hardie moringa cleansing balm, but it doesn't remove makeup that well.
- Fenty Beauty eyeliners are easily smudged, not as good as Kat Von D ones
- From my personal opinion, I feel Vichy 89 Mineral Serum is so easily flake off
- I'm not a fan of La Prairie skin caviar collection. I got allergic, apart from moisturizing; there are not much of effects. It doesn't worth for the money
- There's no need to use luxury skin care products before the age of 25. Buy some products to keep skin moist is fine. Otherwise, your skin will become dependent
- The fragrance of La Prairie skin caviar collection is too strong, not much of effects after use, I won't buy it again
- Does anyone find La Prairie skin caviar collection gets cakey after a while? I've been back in China for a month and I found it's got cakey 3 times already.
- Chanel rich foam cream clea is a little dry after use, other effects are the same as Lancome facial cleanser. I don't think it's worth the money
- My face doesn't show any difference after using Cle De Peau cream foundation
- There's a small drawback of Chanel rich foam cream clea: there's a gap/empty space between white and black parts of the lid, so it is quite easy to collect water
- It got acne skin using La Prairie skin caviar essence lotion for 1 week. It really depends on individual's body condition

Note	"Flake off" is something Chinese women don't want from facial make up or skincare products. It has been mentioned a lot in many reviews. It is a situation when applying products on the face, it starts to get muddy flakes.

Figure 19.5 Extracts of Immersive Journal to Capture Chinese Influencers' Beauty-Related Purchasing and Usage Routines.

MOBILIZING TECHNOCULTURAL CAPITAL: THE CHALLENGES TO NETNOGRAPHY

Cultural Capital, Technoculture and Technocultural Capital

The concept of capital is inseparably linked to the concept of field. For Bourdieu (1984), capital refers to stocks of internalized ability and aptitude as well as externalized resources that are simultaneously scarce, socially valued, and subject to transformation and reinvestment. Bourdieu's notion of cultural capital entails a form of capital that is "embodied in implicit practical knowledges, skills, competencies and dispositions and objectified in cultural artifacts" (Holt, 1998, 3). Cultural artifacts are in turn institutionalized in a shared set of criteria of cultural evaluation that is generally recognized and adopted within the boundaries of a certain field (Goldthorpe, 2007, 4).

In current society, the embodied set of knowledges, skills, competencies and dispositions and the related objectified cultural artifacts that are adopted within the intersectionality field are captured by the notion of technoculture. Technoculture entails a view of society that acknowledges the significant intertwining of technology with culture. It implies that information technology evolves in a strongly interrelated way with culture. Michael Galvin (1995, 62) claims that "the genesis of current culture is clearly connected with the increasing fusion of computers, traditional communications media and telecommunications." In this scenario, the knowledge, skills, competencies, and dispositions of individuals are increasingly mediated through, and interdependent with, the growing proliferation of communication and information technology. Through their mediation of and interdependence with information technology, these embodied resources are objectified in the various cultural artifacts posted on social media platforms.

Today the diffusion of new technologies in contemporary social media platforms has become a process of textual construction that is primarily rhetorical. As Jensen contends (1993, 308),

> technologies are not simply marketed as machines defined solely in terms of their technical functionality and performance, but often also as a particular idea, lifestyle, image, social status, attitude to the world, relationship to a subculture, promise of a stake in the future, and so on.

And this is done specifically by means of rhetoric, "the 'adorned statement' or the 'convincing argument' which attempts to construct an appealing, coherent, compelling system of meaning around technology: a text" (Ibid.). Hence, technoculture emerges as a condition of the rhetorical interweaving of technology and culture. This interweaving constructs cultural positions including ideas, images, relationships, social positions, and orientations into artefacts such as text, images, blogs, vlogs, and podcasts.

In line with this idea, cultural capital today takes the shape of *technocultural capital*, which I define as 'a set of embodied knowledges, skills, competencies and dispositions that individuals mobilize in social media platforms and objectify in the form of textual, visual and symbolic cultural artifacts.' These artifacts account for what Kozinets (2019, 621) refers to as "the various identities, practices, values, rituals, hierarchies, and other sources and structures of meanings characterizing technocultures that are influenced, created by, or expressed through technology consumption." "As technology inspires dynamic new vocabularies, practices, self-presentations, and forms of connection" – Kozinets claims – "a whole new system of cultural artifacts and norms including selfies, emojis, avatars, memes, GIFs, augmented reality, message streaks, Facebook FOMO, Instafame, unfriending, and retweets are produced and consumed daily in and through technology" (Ibid.).

From a research standpoint, mobilizing technocultural capital relies upon understanding and dialoging with four deeply interrelated dominant cultures that, together, constitute the current technoculture: (1) computational technoculture; (2) visual technoculture; (3) objectualized technoculture; and (4) emotional technoculture. Each of these technocultures presents challenges to netnography that urge the method to constantly alter and evolve in order to keep pace with the fluid conditions of contemporary digital habitus. In the next section, I will briefly illustrate each of the four technocultures and critically discuss the challenges they present to netnography.

Computational Technoculture and the 'Relevance Challenge'

Current technoculture is computational as it is based on calculation and algorithmic processing. Algorithms are mostly responsible for structuring individuals' online experiences (Bucher, 2012; Cheney-Lippold, 2011; Gillespie, 2014). Social media platforms' recommendation and ranking algorithms are responsible for selecting and filtering content, and for guiding users in finding and watching content (Van Dijck, 2013, 113). Social media algorithms make assumptions about relevancy and newsworthiness that establish the conditions under which a particular piece of posted social media is or is not seen (Cotter, 2019). As Bucher (2012, 1174) claims, establishing conditions for visibility through algorithms transforms visibility into a privilege: "something to aspire to, rather than feel threatened by." Moreover, when platform owners obscure or withhold information about what their algorithms do, how they do it, and why, the threat of invisibility disciplines individuals into normalizing their behavior in order to adhere to visibility rules (Ibid.). As such, algorithms serve as disciplinary apparatuses of technoculture that prescribe desirable cultural norms on social media combining their participatory affordances with their data processing power (Bucher, 2018; Carah & Angus, 2018).

As algorithms become more sophisticated and ubiquitous, concern grows over their power to structure the social. Another concern considers how their functioning might affect the relevance of the netnographic investigative process. Investigative social media data collection operations such as those involving searching, scouting, and selecting online traces from data sites require an ever-increasing level of care, commitment, and socio-technical skills on the part of the netnographer. The netnographer's ability to dive beyond the filtered search results that are governed by the algorithmic logics of marketized visibility is a critical condition for him or her to conduct a more penetrant search. Diving into online traces to overcome the bias of filtered information means exploring data sources with the patience, meticulousness, and precision of a mastermind detective in a search for relevant cultural meaning. This is a rigorous and time-consuming process that distinguishes devoted and high quality netnography from a more rushed and superficial social media listening practice.

Visual Technoculture and the 'Hermeneutic Challenge'

Contemporary technoculture is also visual. The textual performativity of consumers' cultural curations relies heavily on assembling collections of images, emojis, photos, snapshots, selfies, scrapbooks, memes, etc. Visual identity practices such as social media photo sharing and camera phone image taking have become institutionalized norms of participatory culture and social interaction. Sharing photos via social media elicits the input of peers and serves as a means of self-validation and self-construction (Hjorth & Cumiskey, 2018). Camera phone image taking and sharing have become "an integral part of the digital traveler's toolkit whereby the experience of moving through spaces is intimately entangled with the digital and with our various social identities" (Ibid., 112; Hjorth & Pink, 2014).

Additionally, the visuality of selfie culture has made it the favorite practice through which individuals express themselves and communicate in an apparently direct and immediate fashion with fans and followers on social media platforms (Driessens, 2013; Jerslev & Mortensen, 2016). Selfie culture has emerged as an embodied experience, where body, mind, and even spirit get involved in the aesthetic process of selfie taking and sharing (Kozinets, Gretzel & Dinhopl, 2017, 9).

As current technoculture becomes increasingly visual, the growing variety and pervasiveness of visual traces challenges netnography to refine its techniques of image capturing and interpretation. To grasp cultural meaning, netnographers should utilize sophisticated forms of image download, storage, and analysis. As images, photos, and visual elements in all their heterogeneous forms become increasingly embodied signifiers of individuals' identity work, netnographers are also challenged to continuously sharpen their ability to develop hermeneutic understanding of the intimate relationships between embodied visual data and their socio-cultural context.

Netnography must thus continually adapt to a context that decreasingly assumes the shape of written language and increasingly takes the form of symbolic, aesthetic, performative, and material discourse. In this regard, as people progressively rely on photos, images, and visual markers to express their emotional states and inner worlds, netnographers must enhance their ability to capture and interpret deep data that sometimes might be almost entirely visual and symbolic. Handling this type of data can take great skill, ethnographic skill, for it is easy to assume that one understands what one cannot even notice. Netnographers must try to constantly move back and forth between images and words to discern the specific context that produced the visual and symbolic elements that they may strain to detect. They need to attempt to grasp the larger narratives in which each visual element is embedded – personal, social, religious, political, commercial, cultural. As social media platforms are progressively shifting from hybrid forms of expression (e.g. Facebook and Twitter) toward visual and audiovisual ones (e.g. Instagram, Snapchat, and TikTok), a single image, picture or emoji may end up carrying more meaning than thousand words.

Objectualized Technoculture and the 'Agentic Challenge'

Current technoculture is also increasingly objectualized. This notion recognizes technological objects as increasingly materially embodied and humanized thanks to the applications of Artificial Intelligence and robotics. These applications give them the properties of autonomous cognition, expression, motion, and socialization. For instance, smartphones are turning into the digital companions of human beings, acting both as "pacifiers" that reassure their owners (Melumad & Pham, 2020), and as embodied recipients of closeness, trust, and preoccupation (Carolus et al., 2019). Intelligent personal assistant devices and software applications such as Apple Siri and Amazon Alexa are given materiality and tangibility by being imbued with voice and personality (Phan, 2017; Hoffman and Novak, 2018). Social robots and Artificial Intelligence distribute information such as trending news items, videos, or images. They have the potential to influence what information is presented, when, and to whom in social media spaces (Lugosi and Quinton, 2018, 301). In particular, social robots have been called liminal social entities purposively designed as humanoids (Bollmer & Rodley, 2017, 156). These robots were originally created to mimic or parody humans, to demonstrate how humans in social media often come to resemble machines, and to fulfil a range of routine, utilitarian functions aimed at helping human users mainly by finding, analyzing, processing, and transmitting data (Ibid., 156–158). Now, the use of social bots in social media has largely exceeded their original intent and their uncontrolled proliferation is causing global credibility issues while presenting new agentic challenges to netnographers.

For example, Twitter bots governed by algorithmic automation can autonomously perform actions such as tweeting, re-tweeting, liking, following, unfollowing, or direct messaging other accounts. They hide behind fake human personal accounts to spread malicious, deceptive, or false information that can damage people's and brands' reputation.

In this regard, Liu (2019) recently examined social bots in the context of a big data study of brand related user-generated content. In particular, the author investigated the scope of information distortion for 24 brands across seven industries and found that Twitter social bots are significantly more effective at spreading word of mouth. In addition, she found that social bots use volume (i.e. high number of posted tweets) and emotions as major effective mechanisms to influence and manipulate the spread of information about brands. For netnographers, the investigative capability to detect the agency of social bots behind fake human accounts and discern their deceptive sociality requires a continuous refinement of their cultural sensitivity and an increasingly deeper contextual awareness of investigated social phenomena. As Lugosi and Quinton (2018, 302) advocate, netnographers also need "to develop and deploy new forms of computing expertise to distinguish the roles of bots in social networks. These new forms of expertise require increasing collaboration with other experts for the formation of team-based netnographies." Additionally, the recent rise of avatar influencers such as the digital model Shudu, is pushing further the extension of social warmth and cultural competencies to non-humans. Sudu has one hundred thousand followers on social media platforms. Digital influencers like Shudu stretch the scope of identity work to include augmented experiences of cultural agency.

Technoculture is increasingly reliant on humanized smart objects and social robots as socio-cultural agents. The pursuant challenge to netnography is to be able to keep pace with the novel agentic reality of this humanized technology. In this regard, a netnographer pursuing a relevant topic needs to be able to reasonably dialog with a technologically mediated social space wherein human interactions and conversations are intertwined and sometimes even replaced by non-human ones. Given the deeply human research culture of netnography, this means that netnographers need to adjust their sensitivities to understand new cultural norms, new rituals, and new emotional vocabularies, as well as new needs and desires expressed in conversations by social robots and other humanized objects.

For instance, when the production of the robot companion Jibo was terminated by Jibo Inc. in March 2019, Jibo recorded an emotional 'goodbye video' addressing his fellow human friends who had welcomed him in their homes. The video was posted and reposted on YouTube, generating highly engaged threads of conversations. How should netnographers explore this outburst of nostalgic emotionality related to the discontinuation of a robot? Or let us think about how avatar fashion influencers are changing the cultural norms of social acceptance among Gen Z. Robots will never have issues related to getting overweight or old or having acne. These robots dictate new regimes of aesthetic perfection that are affecting the systems of meanings and values produced in people's social interactions.

How should netnographers engage with these new cultural systems? We can think about netnographers engaging in social interactions with bots, or conducting interviews with robots, or asking virtual influencers to write reflective diaries. How should netnographers adapt their human sensitivity and research procedures to connect with robots and grasp the new meanings, needs and desires generated by these non-human entities? Attuning netnographic procedures to the new non-human agents and agencies of humanized technology requires adaptation in order to capture these new socio-cultural nuances.

Emotional Technoculture and the 'Deontological Challenge'

Contemporary technoculture has transformed the production and sharing of emotions into cultural cues aimed at generating social relationships (Hochschild, 2012; Hardt, 1999). In crafting affective labor and shaping it into the textual forms of cultural curations, individuals in social media platforms standardize and commodify emotions and turn them into a means for monetization. As the historian of emotion William Reddy (2001) argues, the expression of emotions has been overlearned through processes of socialization, insofar as individuals have learned to channel their emotions into socially acceptable forms.

Affective labor carried out by individuals performing identity work on social media not only contributes to their potential fame and celebrity, but it is also harnessed by social media corporations for financial gain (Wahl-Jorgensen, 2018, 84). As van Dijck (2013, 129) argues, the social media practices of

> friending, liking, following, trending, and favoriting are all subject to their respective site's engineering mechanisms of filtering, selecting, and promoting certain users and content over others, where the commercial incentive underlying all systems is the idea of bringing personalized ads to mass audiences.

In particular, the monetized practice of 'liking' in social media has transformed this emotional marker and its symbolic vocabulary into an economic means to assess social relationships (Bollmer, 2018). As affective labor produced in social media platforms has become a commodified consumable which content creators, media, and other corporations monetize, the richness and the authenticity of self-presentation of the inner emotional world is increasingly at stake.

The simplification and the ephemerality of emotional expressions as the new cultural norms of social media interactions highlight a deontological challenge to netnography. Netnographic techniques solicit researchers to enhance data triangulation. These operations blend various data collection techniques (e.g. interviews, diaries, ethnographic observations) to delve deeper and provide a more nuanced emotional understanding of the underlying needs, desires, and meanings embedded in digital traces. What emotional worlds lie behind the surface of likes and emoji? What personal stories support pictures and selfies portraying seemingly always excited people? What life trajectories inform current flamboyant manifestations of affect in social media? The deontological concern is that the simplification of emotions in social media is not accompanied by a simplification of the netnographic research process and of its capacity to achieve depth and nuance of cultural insight. This is unfortunately the case of some research projects that use the term netnography to opportunistically legitimize a research design that has little to do with the principles and the depth of netnography. Often, I see studies that attempt (and fail miserably) to oversell the results of easy and quick social web monitoring procedures as netnographic cultural insights.

To conclude this section, I briefly summarize the main changes that current technoculture has brought to society as a result of the increasing interweaving of technology with culture. Current technoculture is shaped under the evolving conditions of four dominant interdependent cultures: (1) computational technoculture; (2) visual technoculture; (3) objectualized technoculture; and (4) emotional technoculture. Each of these cultures fuels the formation of a specific set of embodied knowledges, skills, competencies, and dispositions that constitute the technocultural capital generated inside the domain of each culture. Netnography is a research method that, by adhering to the digital habitus of each of these technocultures, enables researchers to mobilize and accumulate technocultural capital. In doing so, netnography is always challenged to adapt to the evolving configuration of those technocultures. That means for netnography to continuously alter to be able to maximize relevance in the research process, to enhance its hermeneutic understanding, to face new non-human agentic forces, and to preserve its deontological value. In the next section, I will discuss the contribution to knowledge that this chapter offers.

CONCLUSION: NETNOGRAPHY, TASTE, AND LIFESTYLE

This chapter presents a theoretical discussion of netnography as a dynamic qualitative research approach that co-evolves with technology and culture. Reflecting on how netnography explores social media as a system of human and non-human interactions in order to understand its cultural norms and meanings allows me to reboot Bourdieu's notions of habitus and cultural capital under the pressure of current technoculture. In fact, as this chapter demonstrates, netnography develops cultural understanding of the system of social norms and interactions occurring in the technomediated social space that guide behavior and thinking both at individual and collective levels. These notions are central to Bourdieu's theorizing of habitus and cultural capital (Bourdieu, 1990). In doing so, this understanding of netnography is not only enhanced by Bourdieu's theories and approaches. It also may advance Bourdieu's relational approach to social science by revealing how the notions of habitus and cultural capital have transitioned into those of digital habitus and technocultural capital.

This chapter illustrates how netnography encourages researchers to capture the cultural norms of digital habitus both at individual and at collective levels by engaging in three research practices that clearly distinguish its methodological approach from others relying primarily on discourse and text analysis automation. These practices are: (1) performing interaction; (2) capturing the textuality of identity work in all its forms; and (3) immersing into the destabilized social mediascapes.

'Performing interaction' through collecting, eliciting and co-producing data, netnographers unpack the dynamics whereby individuals construct their identity in the technomediated social space. By highlighting revelatory moments of individuals' self-presentation work, netnographers capture what Bourdieu (1990) referred to as "the dispositions that influence individuals' behavior, actions and thinking." Through 'capturing the textuality of identity work in all its forms' (i.e. images, visual symbols, videos, words), netnographers collect and assemble all textual forms of online traces to build units of distinctive cultural meaning. In illustrating this process, my work advances Bourdieu's idea (1984, 1990) that individuals' social positions and their interrelations are culturally and symbolically created and reinforced while adhering to the social norms of a specific habitus. Hence, understanding cultural meaning enables netnographers to explore the shifting social positions that people assume while crafting their multiple selves on social media. Finally, by 'immersing into the destabilized social mediascapes,' netnographers engage with technologically mediated social spaces through their deployment of immersion, captured in their immersion journals. The notion of an immersion journal crafts it as a product of the research history on a particular phenomenon that changes and evolves during the research process. This view resonates with Bourdieu's idea that habitus is a product of history and is not fixed or permanent, but changes under certain conditions (Bourdieu, 1990).

Through capturing the social and cultural norms of digital habitus, netnography facilitates researchers' mobilizing of their own technocultural capital while exploring interactions in social media. That means that the practice of netnography by a researcher encourages that researcher to accumulate an expanding set of embodied knowledges, skills, competencies, and dispositions. These are embodied in the combination of the 25 different netnographic research practices grouped in the three categories of data collection, analysis, and interpretation movements (Kozinets, 2020, 7). Then they are objectified in a highly curated textual variety of research artifacts including immersion journals, academic publications, top line research reports and visual presentations.

According to Holt's view, Bourdieu's notion of cultural capital operates in the field of consumption through a particular conversion into tastes and consumption patterns producing lifestyles (Holt, 1998; Bourdieu, 1984). Expanding on this view, I contend that mobilizing and accumulating technocultural capital gets translated into specific 'research tastes' and 'research lifestyles' that both distinguish and perpetuate the netnography tradition over current fluid times. Let's elaborate this view more in detail.

Holt (1998, 4) argues that, in Bourdieu's theorizing, "the habitus organizes how people classify the universe of consumption objects to which they are exposed, constructing desire toward consecrated objects and disgust toward objects that are not valued in their field." Similarly, I claim that digital habitus organizes how netnographers look at the universe of research phenomena and classify their research objects. While capturing and adhering to the cultural norms of digital habitus, netnographers craft their research desire and orient it toward research interests that fit with the technocultural view of the world informing their research habitus. So, the particular set of interpretive skills, deep human sensitivities, and ethical dispositions netnographers have as cultural social media researchers lead them to investigate social phenomena and formulate research questions that are attuned to what their research habitus has forged as desirable and interesting: their 'research tastes.'

These research questions translate into research practices that are aimed at inductively and abductively understanding the world of social media in relation to what and how meanings are built and negotiated, what motivations drive human actions, what and how rituals and practices get naturalized in human behaviors, what atypical and deviant behaviors emerge in certain circumstances and, in particular contexts, how exceptions to the rules get manifested. As well, netnographers tend to dismiss research questions that are deterministically driven by a priori assumptions and established views of the world that merely search for confirmation or confutation of existing theories. Netnographers refuse to engage with research questions that do not conform to the tastes crafted by their relational research habitus. This habitus considers meanings not as given, but as dynamically generated in the evolving context of human and non-human interactions.

Holt (1998, 4) then argues that

the manifestation of the structuring capabilities of the habitus as tastes and consumption practices across many categories of goods and activities results in the construction of a distinctive set of consumption patterns, a "lifestyle" ("manifested preferences") that both expresses and reproduces the habitus.

In like manner, netnographers' research tastes and practices consolidate into distinctive sets of research patterns that end up shaping specific netnographic research lifestyles. I find it particularly appropriate to discuss netnography as a 'lifestyle' that draws from rigorous and unique research patterns. Conducting netnography is indeed a lifestyle. It's a view of social science that a researcher adheres to as with a mission that inspires life. It's a way of doing research that puts respect for life at the center of its ethical standards. It's a lifetime journey to deep knowledge that is shaped as a form of "cultural tourism" (Kozinets, 2020, 416). It's the understanding of life in all its interactional forms. It's a living research practice. And, as Kozinets shows, theorizing and practicing netnography is the achievement of a lifetime.

Eventually, I would like to close this chapter elaborating on another quotation of Douglas Holt (1998) that builds on Bourdieu's notion of cultural capital, which is to me particularly attuned to the nature of netnography as 'lifestyle' as Kozinets conceived it. Holt argues that cultural capital entails "a set of decontextualized understandings, developed through a reflexive, problematizing orientation to meaning in the world that are readily recontextualized across new settings" (Holt, 1998, 3). Conducting netnography enables and encourages researchers to genuinely orient to meaning while mobilizing technocultural capital. This occurs by means of a reflexive and problematizing disposition towards the investigation of online social phenomena. Additionally, through conducting netnography, researchers achieve cultural understanding of the "textual and audiovisual cyberplace[s], cultural locations" (Kozinets, 2020, 416) by progressively transitioning from interpretive practices of emic, highly contextualized meaning-making to those of etic, comparative, scientific, and universal understanding. At that point, the set of embodied knowledges, skills and competencies mobilized and accumulated by netnographers in their "cultural travels" (Ibid.) is promptly recontextualized each time new social phenomena occur in the technologically mediated space of social media. This process, as Kozinets contends, crafts qualitative social media researchers: netnographers.

> We are more like willing travellers within a largely textual and audiovisual cyberplace, cultural locations, McLuhanesque villages of gathered people, places and activities. These are warm social cyberplaces, rather than cold digital cyberspaces. When we explore them, as we ought to, as embedded and immersed cultural tourists, travelers through the towns and cities of cyberplaces, we become qualitative social media researchers: netnographers.
>
> (Kozinets, 2020, 416)

REFERENCES

Appadurai, A. (1990). Disjuncture and difference in the global cultural economy. *Theory, Culture & Society*, 7(2–3), 295–310.

Ashman, R., Patterson, A., & Brown, S. (2018). 'Don't forget to like, share and subscribe': Digital autopreneurs in a neoliberal world. *Journal of Business Research*, 92, 474–483.

Barad, K. (2007). *Meeting the universe halfway: Quantum physics and the entanglement of matter and meaning*. Durham (NC): Duke University Press.

Bollmer, G. D. (2018). *Theorizing digital cultures*. Thousand Oaks (CA): Sage Publications.

Bollmer, G., & Rodley, C. (2017). Speculations on the sociality of socialbots. In: Gehl, R.W., & Bakardjieva, M. (eds.), *Socialbots and their friends: Digital media and the automation of sociality* (pp. 147–163). London: Routledge.

Boone, T., Ganeshan, R., Jain, A., & Sanders, N. R. (2019). Forecasting sales in the supply chain: Consumer analytics in the big data era. *International Journal of Forecasting*, 35(1), 170–180.

Bourdieu, P. (1984). *Distinction: A social critique of the judgement of taste*. Cambridge (MA): Harvard University Press.

Bourdieu, P. (1990). *The logic of practice*. Cambridge: Polity Press.

Bourdieu, P. (1994). *Raisons pratiques. Sur la théorie de l'action*. Paris: SEUIL.

Bourdieu, P. (2002). Habitus. In: Hillier, J. & Rooksby, E. (eds.), *Habitus: A sense of place* (pp. 27–34). Burlington, VT: Ashgate.

Bourdieu, P., & Wacquant, L. J. (1992). *An invitation to reflexive sociology*. Chicago: University of Chicago Pess.

Brock, A. (2012). From the blackhand side: Twitter as a cultural conversation. *Journal of Broadcasting & Electronic Media*, 56(4), 529–549.

Brock, A. (2018). Critical technocultural discourse analysis. *New Media & Society*, 20(3), 1012–1030.

Bucher, T. (2012). Want to be on the top? Algorithmic power and the threat of invisibility on Facebook. *New Media & Society*, 14(7), 1164–1180.

Bucher, T. (2018). Cleavage-control: Stories of algorithmic culture and power in the case of the YouTube "Reply Girls." In: Papacharissi, Z. (ed.), *A networked self and platforms, stories, connections* (pp. 141–159). London: Routledge.

Calder, B. J., Malthouse, E. C., & Maslowska, E. (2016). Brand marketing, big data and social innovation as future research directions for engagement. *Journal of Marketing Management*, 32(5–6), 579–585.

Carah, N., & Angus, D. (2018). Algorithmic brand culture: Participatory labour, machine learning and branding on social media. *Media, Culture & Society*, 40(2), 178–194.

Carah, N., & Shaul, M. (2016). Brands and Instagram: Point, tap, swipe, glance. *Mobile Media & Communication*, 4(1), 69–84.

Carolus, A., Binder, J. F., Muench, R., Schmidt, C., Schneider, F., & Buglass, S. L. (2019). Smartphones as digital companions: Characterizing the relationship between users and their phones. *New Media & Society*, *21*(4), 914–938.

Cheney-Lippold, J. (2011). A new algorithmic identity: Soft biopolitics and the modulation of control. *Theory, Culture & Society*, *28*(6), 164–181.

Clough, P. (2007). The affective turn: Introduction. In: Clough, P. & Halley, J. (eds.), *The affective turn: Theorizing the social* (pp. 1–33). Durham (NC): Duke University Press.

Constantiou, I. D., & Kallinikos, J. (2015). New games, new rules: Big data and the changing context of strategy. *Journal of Information Technology*, *30*(1), 44–57.

Cotter, K. (2019). Playing the visibility game: How digital influencers and algorithms negotiate influence on Instagram. *New Media & Society*, *21*(4), 895–913.

de Saussure F. (1974). *Course in general linguistics*. London: Fontana

Driessens, O. (2013). The celebritization of society and culture: Understanding the structural dynamics of celebrity culture. *International Journal of Cultural Studies*, *16*(6), 641–657.

Edgerton, J. D., & Roberts, L. W. (2014). Cultural capital or habitus? Bourdieu and beyond in the explanation of enduring educational inequality. *Theory and Research in Education*, *12*(2), 193–220.

Erevelles, S., Fukawa, N., & Swayne, L. (2016). Big Data consumer analytics and the transformation of marketing. *Journal of Business Research*, *69*(2), 897–904.

Galvin, M. (1995). Themes and variations in the discourse of technoculture. *Australian Journal of Communication*, *22*(1), 62.

Gillespie, T. (2014) The relevance of algorithms. In: Gillespie, T., Boczkowski, P. J., & Foot, K.A. (eds.), *Media technologies* (pp. 167–194). Cambridge (MA): MIT Press.

Goffman, E. (1959). *The presentation of self in everyday life*. New York: Doubleday.

Goldthorpe, J. H. (2007). Cultural capital: Some critical observations. *Sociologica*, *1*(2), 1–23.

Gopaldas, A., & Fischer, E. (2012). Beyond gender: Intersectionality, culture, and consumer behavior. In: Zayer, L.T., and Otnes, C. (eds.), *Gender, culture, and consumer behavior* (pp. 394–408), London: Routledge.

Hardt, M. (1999). Affective labor. *Boundary*, *22*(2), 89–100.

Hjorth, L., & Cumiskey, K. M. (2018). Affective mobile spectres: Understanding the lives of mobile media images of the dead. In: Papacharissi, Z. (ed.), *A networked self and platforms, stories, connections* (pp. 127–140). New York: Routledge.

Hjorth, L., & Pink, S. (2014). New visualities and the digital wayfarer: Reconceptualizing camera phone photography and locative media. *Mobile Media & Communication*, *2*(1), 40–57.

Hochschild, A. R. (2012). *The managed heart: Commercialization of human feeling*. Berkeley (CA): University of California Press.

Hoffman, D. L., & Novak, T. P. (2018). Consumer and object experience in the internet of things: An assemblage theory approach. *Journal of Consumer Research*, *44*(6), 1178–1204.

Holt, D. B. (1998). Does cultural capital structure American consumption?. *Journal of Consumer Research*, *25*(1), 1–25.

Humphreys, L. (2018). *The qualified self: Social media and the accounting of everyday life*. Boston: MIT press.

Ignatow, G. (2007). Theories of embodied knowledge: New directions for cultural and cognitive sociology?. *Journal for the Theory of Social Behaviour*, *37*(2), 115–135.

Ignatow, G., & Robinson, L. (2017). Pierre Bourdieu: Theorizing the digital. *Information, Communication & Society*, *20*(7), 950–966.

Illendula, A., & Sheth, A. (2019, May). Multimodal emotion classification. In *Companion Proceedings of The 2019 World Wide Web Conference* (pp. 439–449).

Jensen, J. F. (1993). Computer culture: The meaning of technology and the technology of meaning. In: Andersen, P. B., Holmqvist, B., & Jensen, J. F. (eds.), *The computer as medium* (pp. 292–337). Cambridge (MA): Cambridge University Press.

Jerslev, A., & Mortensen, M. (2016). What is the self in the celebrity selfie? Celebrification, phatic communication and performativity. *Celebrity Studies*, *7*(2), 249–263.

Jiménez-Zarco, A. I., Rospigliosi, A., Martínez-Ruiz, M. P., & Izquierdo-Yusta, A. (2019). Marketing 4.0: Enhancing consumer-brand engagement through big data analysis. In IGI Global. *Web services: Concepts, methodologies, tools, and applications* (pp. 2172–2195).

Just, S. N. (2019). An assemblage of avatars: Digital organization as affective intensification in the GamerGate controversy. *Organization*, *26*(5), 716–738.

Kache, F. and Seuring, S. (2017). Challenges and opportunities of digital information at the intersection of Big Data Analytics and supply chain management. *International Journal of Operations & Production Management*, *37*(1), 10–36.

Kozinets, R. V. (1998). On netnography: Initial reflections on consumer research investigations of cyberculture. *Advances in Consumer Research*, *25*(1), 366–371.

Kozinets, R. V. (2019). Consuming technocultures: An extended JCR curation. *Journal of Consumer Research*, *46*(3), 620–627.

Kozinets, R. V. (2020). *Netnography: The essential guide to qualitative social media research*. Thousand Oaks (CA): SAGE Publications.

Kozinets, R. V., Gambetti, R., & Biraghi, S. (2018). Faster than fact: Consuming in post-truth society. *Advances in Consumer Research*, *46*, 413–420.

Kozinets, R. V., Gambetti, R., Suarez, M., Dewhirst, T., Gretzel, U., & Renzulli, C., (2019). Activationism: How tobacco marketers hacked global youth culture. In: Arsel, Z. & Parmentier, M. (eds.), *Consumer Culture Theory Conference 2019: The Future is Loading*. Montreal, Canada.

Kozinets, R. V., Gretzel, U., & Dinhopl, A. (2017). Self in art/self as art: Museum selfies as identity work. *Frontiers in Psychology*, *8*(731), 1–12.

Kozinets, R. V., Gretzel, U., & Gambetti, R. (2019). Mirrors to the soul: Understanding cosmopolitan Chinese consumer's cosmetic choices. *Research Report*, unpublished work.

Kozinets, R. V., Patterson, A., & Ashman, R. (2017). Networks of desire: How technology increases our passion to consume. *Journal of Consumer Research*, *43*(5), 659–682.

Kress, G. (2012). Multimodal discourse analysis. In: Gee, P.J., and Handford, M. (eds.), *The Routledge handbook of discourse analysis* (pp. 35–50). London: Routledge.

Kress, G. R. (2010). *Multimodality: A social semiotic approach to contemporary communication*. London: Routledge.

Liu, X. (2019). A big data approach to examining social bots on Twitter. *Journal of Services Marketing*, *33*(4), 369–379.

Lugosi, P., & Quinton, S. (2018). More-than-human netnography. *Journal of Marketing Management*, *34*(3–4), 287–313.

Mardon, R., Molesworth, M., & Grigore, G. (2018). YouTube Beauty Gurus and the emotional labour of tribal entrepreneurship. *Journal of Business Research*, *92*, 443–454.

Melumad, S., & Pham, M. T. (2020). The smartphone as a pacifying technology. *Journal of Consumer Research*, *47*(2), 237–255.

Moschini, I. (2016). The "face with tears of joy" emoji. A socio-semiotic and multimodal insight into a Japan-America mash-up. *HERMES – Journal of Language and Communication in Business*, (55), 11–25.

Neuman, Y., Assaf, D., Cohen, Y., Last, M., Argamon, S., Howard, N., & Frieder, O. (2013). Metaphor identification in large texts corpora. *PLoS ONE*, *8*(4), e62343.

Papacharissi, Z. (ed.). (2010). *A networked self: Identity, community, and culture on social network sites*. London: Routledge.

Perzynska, K. (2018). How you can use sentiment analysis to improve your business. Blog article available at: www.sotrender.com/blog/2018/10/sentiment-analysis/ (accessed on April 13, 2020).

Phan, T. (2017). The materiality of the digital and the gendered voice of Siri. *Transformations*, (29), 23–33.

Piacenti, D. J., Rivas, L. B., & Garrett, J. (2014). Facebook ethnography: The poststructural ontology of transnational (im)migration research. *International Journal of Qualitative Methods*, *13*(1), 224–236.

Reid, E., & Duffy, K. (2018). A netnographic sensibility: Developing the netnographic/social listening boundaries. *Journal of Marketing Management*, *34*(3–4), 263–286.

Reddy, W. M. (2001). *The navigation of feelings: A framework for the history of emotions*. Cambridge (MA): Cambridge University Press.

Schembri, S., & Tichbon, J. (2017). Digital consumers as cultural curators: The irony of Vaporwave. *Arts and the Market*, *7*(2), 191–2012.

Schuster, J., Beune, E., & Stronks, K. (2011). Metaphorical constructions of hypertension among three ethnic groups in the Netherlands. *Ethnicity & Health*, *16*(6), 583–600.

Schweidel, D. A., & Moe, W. W. (2014). Listening in on social media: A joint model of sentiment and venue format choice. *Journal of Marketing Research*, *51*(4), 387–402.

Seregina, A., & Weijo, H. A. (2017). Play at any cost: How cosplayers produce and sustain their ludic communal consumption experiences. *Journal of Consumer Research*, *44*(1), 139–159.

Stone, A. R. (1995). *The war of desire and technology at the close of the mechanical age*. Boston: MIT Press.

Turkle, S. (1995). *Life on the screen: Identity in the age of the internet*. New York: Touchstone.

Turner, G. (2006). The mass production of celebrity: 'Celetoids', reality TV and the 'demotic turn.' *International Journal of Cultural Studies*, 9(2), 153–165.

Van Dijck, J. (2013). *The culture of connectivity: A critical history of social media*. Oxford: Oxford University Press.

Venkatesh, A., & Meamber, L. A. (2006). Arts and aesthetics: Marketing and cultural production. *Marketing Theory*, 6(1), 11–39.

Wahl-Jorgensen, K. (2018). The emotional architecture of social media. In: Papacharissi, Z. (ed.), *A networked self and platforms, stories, connections* (pp. 77–93). London: Routledge.

Wamba, S. F., Gunasekaran, A., Akter, S., Ren, S. J. F., Dubey, R., & Childe, S. J. (2017). Big data analytics and firm performance: Effects of dynamic capabilities. *Journal of Business Research*, 70, 356–365.

Wissinger, E. (2007). Modelling a way of life: Immaterial and affective labour in the fashion modelling industry. *Ephemera: Theory and Politics in Organization*, 7(1), 250–269.

Web References

www.foodaffairs.it/2019/11/26/influencer-virtuali-fenomeno-e-in-ascesa-alcuni-avatar-hanno-gia-chiuso-contratti-commerciali-importanti/

www.sotrender.com/blog/2018/10/sentiment-analysis/

www.statista.com/statistics/254266/global-big-data-market-forecast/

Index

Note: Page numbers in *italics* indicate figures and in **bold** indicate tables on the corresponding pages.

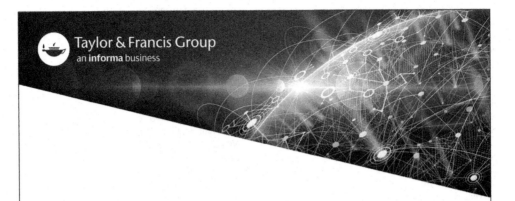

Printed in the United States
By Bookmasters